best hikes with

WESTERN
WASHINGTON
& THE CASCADES

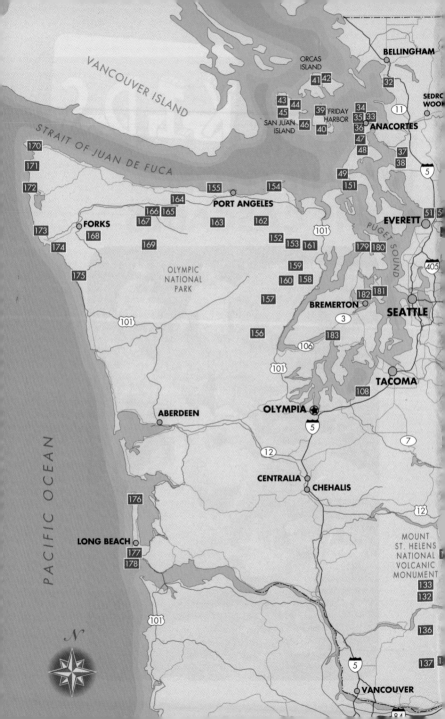

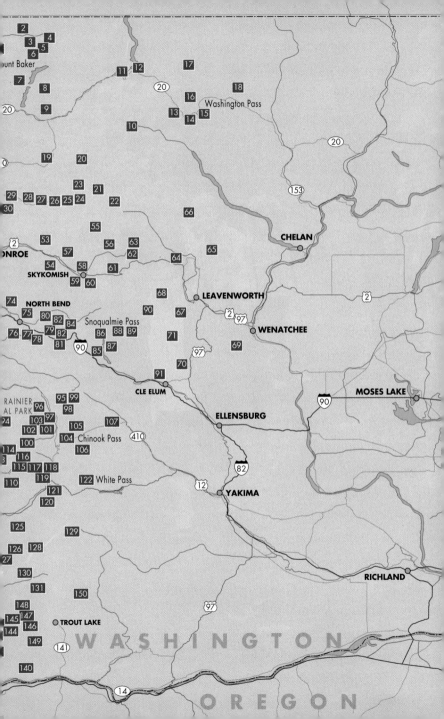

best hikes with KIDS

WESTERN WASHINGTON & THE CASCADES

**Joan Burton with
photos by Ira Spring**

THE MOUNTAINEERS BOOKS

THE MOUNTAINEERS BOOKS
*is the nonprofit publishing arm of The Mountaineers Club, an
organization founded in 1906 and dedicated to the exploration,
preservation, and enjoyment of outdoor and wilderness areas.*

1001 SW Klickitat Way, Suite 201, Seattle, WA 98134

© 2006 The Mountaineers
All rights reserved
First edition: first printing 2006, second printing 2006, third printing 2007

Manufactured in Canada

Project editor: Laura Drury
Editor: Christine Clifton-Thornton
Cover, Book design and Layout: Mayumi Thompson
Mapmaker: Moore Creative Designs
Illustrator: Judy Shimono
Cover and page 1 photographs: © Veer
Frontispiece photograph: *Suspension bridges make hiking fun.*
All photos by Ira Spring and family with "Kirkendall/Spring
Photographers" contributions unless otherwise noted

Library of Congress Cataloging-in-Publication Data
Burton, Joan, 1935-
  Best hikes with kids in western Washington & the Cascades / Joan
Burton; photos by Ira Spring.
      p. cm.
  Rev. ed. of: Best hikes with children in western Washington. 2nd ed.
1998-1999.
  Includes bibliographical references and index.
  ISBN 0-89886-566-2 (pbk.)
  1. Hiking--Washington (State), Western--Guidebooks. 2.
Mountaineering--Cascade Range--Guidebooks. 3. Family
recreation--Northwest, Pacific--Guidebooks. 4.
Children--Travel--Northwest, Pacific--Guidebooks. 5. Washington
(State), Western--Guidebooks. 6. Cascade Range--Guidebooks. 7.
Northwest, Pacific--Guidebooks. I. Spring, Ira. II. Burton, Joan, 1935-
Best hikes with children in western Washington. III. Title.
  GV199.42.W2B87 2006
  917.97--dc22
                                    2005037113

♻ Printed on recycled paper
ISBN 10: 0-89886-566-2
ISBN 13: 978-0-89886-566-0

CONTENTS

OLYMPIC PENINSULA

LEGEND

———	paved road or highway	～～	waterfall
——	secondary paved road	※ ※ ※	marsh
▬▬▬▬	improved road	🝆	glacier
═══	unimproved road	▲	mountain summit
------	primitive road	🕱 or ⌂	lookout (tower or on ground)
•••••••••	trail described	▰	guard station
·············	other trail	♠	ranger station
···········➤	trail continues	■	building
90	interstate highway	] [	bridge
2	US highway	) (	pass
530	state highway	♠	tree or forest
92	county road	❦	flowers
39	forest primary road	▲	campground
689	forest secondary road	⌂	campsite
7902	trail number	⪥	picnic area
S	hike start point	✕	mine
	body of water	🚗	parking
～～	river or stream	📷	viewpoint

ACKNOWLEDGMENTS

With profound gratitude I dedicate this edition to the late Ira Spring. Without his encouragement and loyal support, this book would not have been published.

I also want to thank Gary Rose for his patient support and help in seeking out new trails. In addition, I am grateful to Christine Clifton-Thornton for her splendid and sensitive editing; to Mayumi Thompson for her fine work with a variety of photographs; to Laura Drury for her capable handling of the manuscript; and to John and Vicky Spring for their helpful contributions to driving directions, maps, and a majority of the scenic photographs.

PREFACE

I wrote this book for you because I want your children to experience the love of Western Washington wild places that I felt when I was a child. My parents helped to instill that feeling in me because they, too, loved wilderness. For that I thank them. When I was a girl, there were no hiking guidebooks. People went exploring on trails with maps that weren't very accurate. Finding trailheads was often like going on a treasure hunt. There were no Gore-Tex, polyester, polar fleece, or sunscreen. There were no hiking boots. We got by with wool sweaters, parkas, and men's work boots. Children wore saddle oxfords and jeans. We could buy army surplus wool olive drab pants, and canvas parkas that looked like huge, stiff, khaki anoraks. For boots, we went to the Penney's or Sears work boot departments and tried on boys' boots until we found ones that fit. Then we took them to a shoe repair place and had lugs pounded into the soles. If we were going hiking on snow and might be sunburned, we wore zinc oxide, also called clown white, on our faces. When we got home and scrubbed it off, our faces looked as though we had developed skin infections.

When I was very young, we went camping at Snoqualmie Pass on the bus. We had to take the bus because there was gasoline rationing due to the war, and families had only a limited number of coupons to buy gas. Mom, my sister, my brother, and I rode the bus to the summit with the tent and sleeping bags, and then we carried them to a campsite. After work, Dad came up to the Denny Creek Campground on a later bus. We had no camp stove, so we cooked over a fire, as I recall. Food burns easily over a fire unless you're used to cooking that way, and we tried not to be critical of scorched beans for dinner. There were no showers or hot running water. I remember getting up in the night to use the outhouse. There was a full moon, so my sister and I walked through the campground by its light. To keep ourselves from being scared, we sang at the top of our lungs, "Mairzy doats and dozy doats and liddle lamzy divey."

When we were eight and nine, my father took my sister and me hiking to Melakwa Lake, our first real hike. That's still a long, steep trail, about 4½ miles one way, with about 2300 feet of elevation gain. Today, I wouldn't put it in this book because it's too difficult, but we didn't know that at the time. So we started up.

When we passed the Denny Creek Water Slide, it didn't occur to us to stop and play in the water the way many children do now, and when we passed the Keekwulee Waterfall, we were amazed because we'd never seen anything like that beautiful cascade before. When the trail took us through the giant rock slide, I was afraid the large boulders would start rolling around us, so I tiptoed stealthily through them.

But we felt elated when we reached Melakwa Lake. It was small and deep and dark blue, and since it was the first alpine lake I'd ever seen, it was, of course, the most beautiful one. Dad said he was proud of us and that we were strong and fast. Of course, we believed him. Tired as we were when we got down, we definitely wanted to go hiking again.

Today, you who have so much more gear and so many more camping conveniences can still help your children to feel that same sense of awe and wonder I felt when I saw my first alpine lake.

PARKING FEES AT WASHINGTON STATE PARKS

As this book goes to print, the Washington State government is repealing the $5 day day-use parking fee from its 120 state parks, effective April 9, 2006. Please disregard parking fee information that may be included in the descriptions of hikes located in state parks.

INTRODUCTION

Skunk cabbage in bloom

Hiking routes in Western Washington—unlike those in Eastern Washington, the desert southwest, or even the Sierras—are likely to be green and lush. Even on clear summer days most trails will start in trees. Above tree line you will look down on green velvet folds of tree-covered hills. You will also get used to seeing patches of logged-off "clear-cuts," much like shaved skin or moth-eaten blankets. Children shouldn't be dismayed at the unsightliness; tell them that no matter how steep the slope, the trees always grow back.

Moisture is another continuing factor. Mud will accompany many parts of the trails you choose, originating from rainfall, melting snow, spray from waterfalls, or changing streambeds. Most kids love mud if it isn't deep, but be prepared with adequate footwear. Lightweight tennis shoes may be fine on a paved trail or on gravel, but they will be soaked in no time in typical Western Washington mud. Find boots or shoes for your kids heavy enough to withstand some of it, and relax about their getting mud on pant legs and the seats of the car. Today's high-tech fabrics also make hiking in wetter weather an enjoyable option. Layering fleece, rain gear, and other weather-appropriate clothing will help keep children—and therefore parents—warm, dry, and happy.

BEST HIKES TO WILDFLOWERS

Spider Meadow, Hike 66
Esmeralda Basin, Hike 71
Ira Spring Trail, Hike 80
Spray Park, Hike 93
Sheep Lake, Hike 105

Alta Vista and Panorama Point, Hike 114
Snowgrass Flats, Hike 129
Bird Creek Meadows, Hike 150
Hurricane Hill, Hike 163

Western Washington is home to five glacier-covered volcanoes. Many hikes feature overlooks that offer views of the effects of glaciers and volcanoes. The work they have done on the landscape is spectacular, and the region's beauty will spoil you for hiking in other places. But you might as well understand them and tell your kids so they can understand them, too.

The volcanoes—Mount Baker, Glacier Peak, Mount Rainier, Mount Adams, and Mount St. Helens—erupt dramatically from time to time. They are not likely to do this without some warning, but when they do, they transform themselves and much of the surrounding landscape. One of our most recent major eruptions came from Mount St. Helens. She blew out her north side in a huge cloud of ash, which settled in new places and changed the shapes of Spirit Lake and the Toutle River. The heat from the eruption melted some of her glaciers, and that hot water mixed with ash and mud came roaring down the mountainside with the speed of a freight train and then solidified into new earth.

Western Washington glaciers are another kind of transforming feature. They are living, moving rivers of ice that gouge out pathways down their mountainsides. Along their edges, they pile up long ridges of loose gravel and boulders called moraines. The glaciers you and your kids can see today are small examples of the huge continental ice sheets that carved out Puget Sound, the Strait of Juan de Fuca, Hood Canal, and much of the Cascades. They reached as far south as Olympia. The last continental glacier only retreated north about 12,000 years ago, so its tracks are easy to see, if you know how to look for them.

Other distinguishing features of Western Washington are our many mountain lakes and waterfalls, also the result of all that glacial carving and the volcanic uplifts. Kids love reaching lakes and waterfalls; many of these are short hikes with wading and swimming potential, although water temperatures are

Ebey's Landing

uniformly cold. Meadows filled with flowers often accompany hikes to lakes. Animals and birds drink from them, so your kids can watch for them, too.

Beach hikes—along Puget Sound, the San Juans, the Strait of Juan de Fuca, and the ocean—are a delight. Western Washington has so much shoreline that families can afford to be particular about seeing additional attractions, such as lighthouses, ocean surf, traveling whales, and migrating snow geese. Unlike the beaches of Southern California and Florida, Western Washington beaches are wild and usually windy. Instead of soft sand, the shore is often made up of gravel, medium-sized rocks, or rocky outcrops. Don't expect to be able to stretch out to suntan or fall asleep. Prevailing breezes, usually from the west, won't allow much of that. Neither should you expect lifeguards or hot dog and cool drink stands. Plan to carry in your own food and drink, because these are wild beaches that belong to the public. But in how many other places in the continental Unite States can you still find Japanese fishing ball floats? Or see migrating pods of gray whales and orcas? Or watch great blue herons feed their young in nests on the tops of trees?

There are so many wonders in Western Washington, a whole lifetime will not be enough.

BEST HIKES FOR BUILDING SAND CASTLES

Bowman Bay/Rosario Head Trail, Hike 36
Spencer Spit, Hike 39
Cattle Point Lighthouse, Hike 46
Ebey's Landing, Hike 49
Point Wilson, Hike 151

Dungeness Spit, Hike 154
Sand Point, Hike 172
Leadbetter Point State Park, Hike 176
Point No Point, Hike 179
Foulweather Bluff Preserve, Hike 180

HIKING WITH KIDS

Since my first book came out, I have heard from parents that some hikes turned out to be more challenging, and harder work, than they expected. Were my children super athletes? Did they never whine, or was I immune to whining, tears, and long uphill grinds? How could I have made those hikes sound so easy and rewarding?

Of course, hindsight does filter out sweat, tears, and long switchbacks. But I have to repeat my message: My kids hiked because they had fun. They didn't have fun at every step, but they did love the taste of adventure hiking brought them. I believe they even enjoyed testing themselves. Certainly they enjoyed competing with one another on trails. So my answer is still yes—hiking with my kids was fun, and hiking with your own can be fun and rewarding for both you and your children.

Young hikers explore the fascinating diversity on the forest floor.

BEST HIKES TO WATERFALLS

Boulder River Waterfall, Hike 19	Comet Falls and Van Trump Park,
Wallace Falls State Park, Hike 53	Hike 113
Bridal Veil Falls, Hike 54	Falls Creek Falls, Hike 141
Snoqualmie Falls, Hike 74	Marymere Falls, Hike 165

My four-year-old granddaughter likes to climb logs and boulders and throw stones in the water. No surprise there, you say. But the time she takes to do those things is not time spent on the trail. I have to remember my own preaching and try to be patient with her when we go hiking together. Maybe you already know about patience, but as a grandmother I had to learn it all over again. Of course, watching her smile at her achievements makes it all worthwhile. And, eventually, we always reach our destination.

Read on for some of the strategies that worked with my children when they were young, susceptible, and believed everything I told them.

1. Appoint a "First Leader." I rotated this official designation among my three children. Somehow, being tagged "First Leader" imparted status—and extra energy, at least for a while. Unspoken competition between brothers and sisters can be a powerful motivating force (which is why we did not encourage walking sticks). It's a good idea to agree in advance on a point at which the official title rotates again.

2. Plan frequent "energy stops." As in, "When we get to that creek ahead, we'll have an energy stop, where we'll have some . . . . "

3. Provide energy food. Trail mix, candy, fruit, or a favorite family treat. Never called candy, and always rationed out in tiny increments to prolong its effectiveness. Popeye's spinach comes to mind.

4. Take a friend along. Aches, pains, and complaints are often forgotten when there is a companion the child's own age along on the hike. The child will not want to look slow or tired in front of the friend, and a little friendly rivalry, not unlike sibling rivalry, won't hurt.

5. Praise, praise, praise. Only a parent knows how thick to spread this, but positive reinforcement may have the most enduring result of all. Over fifty years since that hike to Melakwa Lake, I still remember what a fuss my father made about how strong and fast we were. His praise was probably vast exaggeration, but consider the effect it had.

6. Have patience. This means taking time, if necessary, to inspect every creek, throw sticks and stones over bridges, and look up for birds and down at animal tracks. Plan the hike from the perspective of small legs. If parents want to get home (or into a campsite) before dark, they must plan ahead for a pace to fit the child's ability and attention span. Try not to look at your watch any more than necessary, or the child will suspect you are not having as much fun as he or she is.

Bonfires may be permitted on beach below high tide line.

Hiking with little children requires planning, patience, psychology, strategy, and, at some points, outright bribery. Is it worth it? Of course it is! You, the parents, can introduce them to the outdoors, have some "family time," and hike to places you've wanted to see anyway. With luck your children may grow up to love the mountains, rivers, lakes, and beaches, and be willing to carry their own packs.

CAMPING WITH KIDS

Some parents like to introduce kids to the outdoors with car camps and day hikes, gradually building up to backpacking adventures. Others who are new parents but experienced backpackers only need to adapt their usual backpacking gear and tactics to their own children.

Although the emphasis is on hiking, this book also offers opportunities for both kinds of camping:

Snowy owl

trail-side camping, when you're out on an overnight backpacking trip; and car camping, for when you'd like to explore day hikes that are a little farther from your front door. Western Washington ranges from deep forest, foothills, and mountains to saltwater and ocean shoreline within its length of 250 miles and width of 200 miles. Even when relying on ferries to the Olympic Peninsula and San Juan Islands, you can usually travel to most trailheads in less than three hours. It's always practical to become familiar with the trails closest to home, but to get the most use from this book, you and your kids may want to explore other parts of the region as well. Car camping can give you easy access to enough trails to keep you active for an entire vacation. For those who are interested in finding campgrounds near the trails, you'll find a handy list at the back of this book (see "Appendix A: Commercial Campgrounds Near the Hikes").

Backpack camping and car camping require different mind-sets, different preparations, and different gear. Although you will need reservations on holidays for such popular destinations as Moran State Park, in general, car camping with kids can be more spontaneous. You can fill up the car with gear without thinking of its weight, buy food en route to camp, and come home if the weather turns bad. If you are planning a backpack with kids, you will need to plan more carefully. Food, stove, sleeping bags, tent, and weather-appropriate clothing need to be weighed, packaged, and chosen with care. Bailing out if the weather changes takes longer, and kids need to have appropriate parkas and boots for any weather. If you're new to camping, you may wish to pick up one of the numerous books available on the topic for further information.

BEST HIKES ON BARRIER-FREE TRAILS

Rainy Lake, Hike 14
Washington Park, Hike 34
Deception Pass State Park, Hike 47
Troublesome Creek, Hike 55
Iron Goat Trail, Hike 61
Snoqualmie Falls, Hike 74
Little Kachess Lakeshore, Hike 85

Coal Mines Trail, Hike 91
Alta Vista and Panorama Point, Hike 114
Murphy Grade Trail, Hike 137
Beacon Rock State Park, Hike 139
Theler Wetlands Trails, Hike 183

PARENTAL ATTITUDES

Children take their cues from grown-ups about how safe and non-threatening the woods and mountains are. If you are comfortable hiking in diverse places and weather conditions, your children usually will feel secure and comfortable, too. That is not to say you might not have some perfectly horrid experiences. My youngest cut a tooth in the middle of the night once and cried incessantly while we hiked out, reached the car, and drove almost a hundred miles home.

My daughter Carol says she remembers riding piggyback, or in a forerunner of today's child carrier, and putting her hands over my eyes because it was fun when I would stop and say I couldn't see. She also remembers untreated boots and soaking clothes that got wet and cold in the rain and on the wet brush alongside the path when she was First Leader.

On the other hand, we did have some triumphs. As a family recreational activity, hiking became an important way to give my children a sense of their ability to succeed at difficult but satisfying undertakings. A day hike that gave my two younger children, at twelve and thirteen, a real sense of achievement was the trail to Camp Muir. I do not recommend this hike for little children. It is steep, arduous, long, and, in fog, treacherous. But on a beautiful, windy day in late July, we started up from Paradise with boots, day packs, and wind gear. The kids knew their father and I had each climbed Mount Rainier, and that this was the way to the climbers' high camp.

Opposite page: Looking at a banana slug

Five hours went by—all spent switch backing up steep snow, the guide hut always receding, like a mirage, before us. The children were weary and discouraged at how far and how steep the hike was turning out to be. We developed an unspoken unity of purpose. We were going to make Camp Muir—together. Dick, my son, would go ahead for a while and then wait for us. Carol, who was small but wiry, would lag behind, discouraged, and then surge ahead. We talked about what the summit climb is like, and the kids said later that those conversations and the collective family pride in achievement meant much to them. They knew that sometime, somehow, we were going to make it.

When we finally climbed over the Muir rocks to the coffin-shaped nests there, the wind was fierce. We hunkered down in a nest to escape the wind and ate our lunch, rejoicing. Our own attitudes helped them to meet an important test successfully. What better gifts can parents give than self-sufficiency and self-confidence?

GOOD OUTDOOR MANNERS

Hiking families have an obligation to teach children good outdoor manners. The hiker's motto should be, "Leave trails and campsites as clean as—or cleaner than—you found them." Parents can set an example by cleaning up other people's messy camps and by carrying out or burning leftover trash. Do not leave old plastic tarps behind for the next camping family. They blow around, are quickly ripped and tattered, and add to the litter. In fact, anything you can carry in, you can carry out. Think about how your family feels at seeing old tin cans, bottles, and plastic containers in places they have hiked miles to see.

Tell children they must not drop candy or gum wrappers, orange peels, or peanut or eggshells. These things take a long time to break down, and petrified orange peels are not an archaeological find we want to leave to posterity. Also, don't bury garbage; it doesn't stay covered for long.

Carry out cans, aluminum foil, and disposable diapers. One way to handle such materials in parents' packs is to include several large, zip-able plastic bags for garbage, wet clothing, and the things children find along the way that they want to bring home.

Teach your children to dispose of toilet paper properly. Burying it with their stools used to be acceptable, but little creatures dig up the paper and strew it about. I've seen campsites so littered with toilet paper that the prospect of camping there was disgusting. If campfires are allowed at your site, you can burn toilet paper; otherwise, put it in plastic bags and pack it out. Parents should check their children's toilet area after use to be sure they have the technique down and the area is usable by the next visitors.

Dogs are permitted on national forest trails but are absolutely not allowed in national parks. Since my first book came out, I have seen many more families with large, unleashed dogs on trails. Although children may love day hiking with their pet, its presence in a backpacking campsite may impact birds and small animals and annoy other campers who came partly to get away from domestic animals.

ENCOUNTERING WILDLIFE

Wildlife encounters on the trail are usually exciting to kids and can become treasured memories. Common mammals seen on mountain trails in Western Washington are deer, marmots, chipmunks, ground squirrels, and raccoons. Less common are elk, fox, marten, lynx, and cougar, none of which want you to see them and will try to remain hidden. Bears are hazards seldom encountered when hiking in the Northwest with kids, but anything is possible. Usually bears do not want anything to do with families and will turn away from human encounters unless they are mothers who think they are forced to defend cubs. Obviously you won't want to put a mother bear into that position. If you do encounter a bear or cougar, tell your children not to turn their backs on the animal. Make enough noise to make your presence known and move slowly in the opposite direction.

A newborn fawn is a wonderful sight, but leave quickly so that its mother can return.

Common birds seen on land and near water are gulls, crows, hawks, blue herons, and ravens. Less common birds in the mountains are juncos, winter wrens, flickers, kingfishers, and pileated woodpeckers. Near saltwater in early spring kids can look for snow geese and tundra swans. Consider yourself lucky if you see flocks of them.

It can be even more exciting to see wildlife in their natural habitat when your kids can identify them on their own. There are numerous field guides to animals and birds of Western Washington; for a few of my favorites, please see Appendix C: Other Helpful Books.

Clarks nutcracker, also called a camp robber

BEST HIKES TO SEE WILDLIFE AND BIRDS

Skagit Wildlife Area, Hike 37—birds
Big Ditch, Hike 38—birds
Lime Kiln State Park, Hike 45—whales
Cattle Point Lighthouse, Hike 46—whales
Jetty Island, Hike 51—birds

Glacier Basin, Hike 100—marmots
Nisqually National Wildlife Refuge, Hike 108—birds
Snowgrass Flats, Hike 129—marmots and goats
Dungeness Spit, Hike 154—birds
Hoh River Rain Forest, Hike 169—elk

WHAT TO TAKE

If you are planning a day hike with kids, the equipment you bring along need not be as complicated as that needed for a backpack trip. The important point is that the kids feel comfortable with their boots and pack.

Boots

Most of the athletic shoes that children now wear can be used for hiking on short, gentle trails. The features of leather boots that make them better for kids on steep, rocky trails are their ankle support and their lug soles. Athletic shoes often have smooth soles that can make them skid when kids are coming down a smooth, slick, or wet surface. I recently watched a large group of children from a day camp descend the Rattlesnake Ledge trail. Several fell or slipped because their shoes did not grip the steep dirt slopes. When you are considering footwear, comfort and safety are, of course, your first priorities. Pick out hiking shoes that have an aggressive tread to be sure your kids will have enough traction when they hike.

I bought one pair of good boots for the first child, passed them down the line, and traded outgrown hand-me-downs with other families. Some outdoor equipment stores will take back usable children's boots for their rental trade and offer a price based on their value, which can be applied to the next pair.

When buying boots (for children or adults), keep in mind that boots that don't fit properly can make their owner utterly miserable (so can wet tennis shoes). It is therefore important to make sure your child's boots fit properly. They should be snug enough to prevent chafing but not so tight that they pinch toes. After buying your child a pair of boots, have him or her wear them inside the house for several days before using them outdoors. This will not only help to break in the boots but will often reveal poorly fitting ones while it's still possible to return them. Usually, an ill-fitting pair that has not been worn outside can be returned for full value. Even well-fitting boots, however, need to be broken in before they are suitable for an extended hike. Otherwise, blisters are virtually certain. For that reason, children forced to hike far in stiff new boots may never willingly hike anywhere again.

Packs

Most children carry book bags to school. Dora the Explorer calls hers a backpack, so your kids will

Hiking with Grandma

use the same name. These serve admirably as hiking day packs as well, but child-size overnight packs also are available at most outdoor stores. Parents can calculate how soon they will be outgrown and how much use they will get. Sometimes, packs are a source of rivalry among little children who are likely to gauge another child's load by size alone. Unless a child has his or her own pack, good parental strategy is to fill an adult day pack with the child's extra clothing, take a tuck in the straps, and allow him or her to appear to be carrying an enormous load. This is a sure-fire morale booster for a kid. Other children on the trail are not likely to heft one another's packs, so no one but the parents will know how much it holds.

The Ten Essentials

Over the years, The Mountaineers has compiled a list of ten items that should be taken on every hike. These Ten Essentials not only make your trip more comfortable but also equip you to cope with emergencies caused by bad weather, injury, or other unforeseen circumstances.

THE TEN ESSENTIALS: A SYSTEMS APPROACH

1. Navigation (map and compass)
2. Sun protection (sunglasses and sunscreen)
3. Insulation (extra clothing)
4. Illumination (headlamp or flashlight)
5. First-aid supplies
6. Fire (firestarter and matches/lighter)
7. Repair kit and tools (including knife)
8. Nutrition (extra food)
9. Hydration (extra water)
10. Emergency shelter

Children require a few extra essentials. The items mentioned below are ones I have found useful:

1. Child-safe protection from bugs and sun. Mosquitoes, no-see-ums, gnats, deerflies, and sunburn can make anyone miserable. Obviously, you will need protection from insects and sun. But chemical products designed for adult skin—particularly sun creams with high screen factors—may be too harsh for children. Take the time to check and test untried products before you leave home. Don't assume they will be safe if there is even a possibility of an allergic reaction—2 miles away from the car and 50 miles from home is no place to find out.

2. Extra bug protection. Be sure each child has a long-sleeved shirt to wear when bugs attack. There may even be times when a cap, gloves, and long pants will be needed. Repellent helps some but is overrated. Give the kids (and yourselves) personal "habitats"—a 6-foot length of no-see-um netting for each camper, light enough to wad up in a

Small creatures are fun to study.

    pocket and large enough to cover the head and be tucked under the child at dinner time.

3. Allergy and sting medication. If your child is allergic to bee or wasp stings, be sure to carry the appropriate medications prescribed or recommended by your physician.

4. Extra first-aid kit supplies. Your first-aid kit should contain any special medicines or supplies your child may need, such as extra moleskin to prevent blisters on tender feet, extra toilet paper, and some baking soda to plaster on nettle or other stings. A product called Second Skin can cover and help heal a blister already causing pain.

5. Swimming gear. Do not encourage children to go into lakes in jeans, because wet jeans can become extremely cold and uncomfortable later. Carry shorts or bathing suits for wading and swimming. Also, hidden hazards may lie on lake bottoms. Carry an extra pair of tennis shoes or rubber sandals for the child to wade in, to protect against sharp rocks and sticks buried in muddy lake bottoms.

BEST HIKES FOR LAKE SWIMMING

Cutthroat Lake, Hike 16
Kelcema Lake, Hike 25
Pete Lake, Hike 88
Cooper Lake and River Walk, Hike 89
Greenwater Lakes, Hike 95

Packwood Lake, Hike 120
Takhlakh Lake and Takh Takh Meadow, Hike 133
Thomas Lake, Hike 142
Lower Lena Lake, Hike 157

Food

Food is a matter of family preference, of course. My family enjoyed meals whose ingredients came from the grocery store rather than from sporting goods shops. Freeze-dried foods are not only more expensive but also less tasty than familiar home favorites. Don't experiment with unknown, gourmet foods on a camping trip with children. Comfort foods are one-pot meals—such as stew, chili, and chicken and noodles—that children know from home. Day-hike foods should be combinations of nuts, fruit, candies, raisins, cheese, and crackers that are easy to carry without being crushed in the pack and that impart energy.

Water

Drinking water on a hike is cause for concern and preparation. Do not trust that streams and lakes will supply you with pure water. Most mountain water is safe but much is not, and there's no way to tell. If the trail is popular and the lake is crowded, be suspicious. Carry a canteen or plastic bottle of water or flavored drinks for the trail. (If you carry in cans of juice or soda pop, be sure to carry out empties.) Cooking water must be boiled at least twenty minutes to be safe. Or use a water-filtering device.

SAFETY

Backcountry travel, even on day hikes, entails unavoidable risks that every hiker assumes and must be aware of and respect. You can minimize your risks by being knowledgeable, prepared, and alert. There isn't space in this book for a general treatise on wilderness safety, but there are a number of good books and courses on the subject, and you should take advantage of them to increase your knowledge. Just as important, you should always be aware of your own limitations and the limitations of those in your party, as well as the conditions existing when and where you are traveling. If conditions are dangerous or if you are not prepared to deal with them safely, change your plans! It is better to have wasted a few days than to be the subject of a wilderness rescue.

Follow the leader. (Photo by Veer)

These warnings are not intended to keep you out of the wilderness. Most people enjoy safe trips through the backcountry every year. However, one element of the beauty, freedom, and excitement of the wilderness is the presence of risks that do not confront us at home. When you travel in the backcountry, you assume those risks. They can be met safely but only if you exercise your own independent good judgment and common sense.

Hypothermia

Most of the mountain lakes described here are very cold, and weather conditions in the mountains can change abruptly. Parents should be aware of the hazards of hypothermia and carry extra clothing and perhaps a thermos of cocoa or hot soup. Because of their relatively small body size, little children are vulnerable to hypothermia sooner than are adults exposed to the same conditions. In fact, a parent may not even recognize the symptoms in children. Children with first-stage hypothermia can be listless, whiny, and unwilling to cooperate, long before physical signs, like shivering, start to appear. Since these symptoms can also occur on hikes when children are only tired, bored, or hungry, it is important to rule out hypothermia before assuming some other cause. Early morning, late afternoon and evening, and periods of cool, overcast weather are times to be particularly alert to your child's behavior and to take immediate steps to re-warm him or her if appropriate.

BEST HIKES IN WINTER

Boulder River Waterfall, Hike 19
Old Sauk River, Hike 20
Whistle Lake, Hike 33
Washington Park, Hike 34
Lime Kiln State Park, Hike 45
Trail of Two Forests, Hike 132
Ape Cave, Hike 133
Murphy Grade Trail, Hike 137
Dungeness Spit, Hike 154

Cape Flattery, Hike 170
Sand Point, Hike 172
Third Beach, Hike 174
Leadbetter Point SP, Hike 176
Benson Beach, Hike 177
Lighthouse Traverse, Hike 178
Point No Point, Hike 179
Grand Forest Park, Hike 181
Gazzam Lake Park, Hike 182

Crime

Theft, both in camps and from parked cars at trailheads, has become a major problem. So many hikers' cars have been vandalized that wise hikers arrange to be dropped off and picked up from trailheads. If you must leave a car parked at a trailhead for several days, don't tempt thieves by leaving expensive clothing and gear in plain view.

Carefully studying the ferns (Photo by Tara Irvin)

HOW TO USE THIS BOOK

Most of the hikes described in this guidebook are in the Cascade Range or the Olympic Mountains. Some are found in nearby foothills and lowlands. The hikes are numbered consecutively but generally are grouped by the major highways from which they are accessible. This arrangement makes it easy for readers to find the hikes they want. See the table of contents for a complete list of hikes.

Each hike description includes important things to know before you head out in a section called **Before You Go;** a summary of hike information, in **About the Hike;** driving directions, in **Getting There;** symbols for features of special interest; and the description itself, in **On the Trail,** which gives detailed information about the trail. Note that road mileage is expressed in decimals rounded to the nearest tenth of a mile to correspond to odometer readings. Trail mileage is expressed in fractions, because decimals imply a greater degree of accuracy than is possible or practical on trails. Even so, all mileages are as accurate as possible.

Before You Go

This section offers important information you'll want to note before you head for the trail. **Current conditions** lists the phone numbers of the appropriate ranger districts that you can call for current trail information such as closures, late-season snow, and the like. The **Maps** section notes those maps you'll want to bring with you (available at most outdoor equipment stores; see also "Maps," later in this chapter). And you will also find information on whether any special permits or other fees are required (see also "Wilderness Regulations, Permits, and Fees," later in this chapter).

About the Hike

This section includes hike statistics to help you choose the hikes that are best suited to you and your family. Hikes are categorized as either day hikes or backpacks. The great majority of hikes can be completed in one day, but camping opportunities are plentiful and have been noted for families who are more adventurous or experienced. Some trips are primarily overnight excursions, but beginning sections can make good day hikes.

Round-trip mileage is given for each hike, and the elevation gain noted is the total number of feet you will climb on the trail. Taken together,

Where do these steps lead? (© Radu Razvan / dreamstime.com)

these figures should give you an idea of the difficulty of any given trail. Hikes are rated as **easy, moderate,** or **difficult.** These ratings are only approximations. I tried to factor in distances, elevation gains, and trail conditions, but even those are not altogether objective criteria. I thought of giving minimum age levels for trails but found that to be even more subjective: A trail that one five-year-old is capable of hiking may be too difficult for another. Many hikes that are rated moderate or difficult contain shorter, easier sections that make excellent day hikes in their own right. So if you want a shorter outing, don't restrict your search only to those hikes I have rated as easy. Instead, scan the more difficult trips for what I call "turnarounds," which are marked by a special symbol (see "Key to Symbols", later in this chapter). Turnarounds are satisfying destinations that make fine picnic spots and feature scenic views or other natural attractions. You can change direction at a turnaround and feel well satisfied with your hike.

I have also indicated the months during which each trail is free of snow. This can vary from year to year. Early or late in the season, when there may be some doubt about snow conditions, call the local ranger station in the area where you want to hike for current information.

BEST HIKES FOR FISHING

Cutthroad Lake, Hike 16
Barclay Lake, Hike 58
Lake Dorothy, Hike 59
Mirror Lake, Hike 87
Pete Lake, Hike 88

Cooper Lake and River Walk, Hike 89
Hyas Lakes, Hike 90
Packwood Lake, Hike 120
Takhlakh Lake and Takh Takh Meadow, Hike 133

Getting There

Driving directions generally begin from the nearest landmark, such as a town or major highway. Distances to be driven are rounded off to the nearest decimal. At the end of the driving directions you'll find the starting-point elevation. This is provided to suggest the kind of environment you will be hiking in, what clothing you and your kids need, and how likely it is that snow will have melted or fallen recently. A higher beginning elevation—especially coupled with a greater elevation gain—is a good indication that a call to the ranger district noted in the "Before You Go" section is a good idea.

Maps

The maps in this book are for orientation only. Always bring the current maps that cover your area and a compass with you on your hike—and

"Grandpa, come see the huge fish!" (Photo by Laura Drury)

know how to use them. Topographic maps show terrain and altitude by means of contour lines and provide a fairly accurate way of gauging trail steepness and general terrain features. Green Trails maps are one of two types of topographic maps widely used by local hikers. The second type is published by the United States Geologic Survey (USGS). Although widely available, many USGS maps are often out-of-date, and they may not give recent road or trail numbers. Green Trails maps are listed first because they are updated more often and show all existing trails in green, features that are particularly important for beginning hikers.

An appropriate U.S. Forest Service or National Park Service map is also listed for each hike. These maps generally do not show contours, but they do give the names and numbers of all access roads, which no other types of map do. This information is particularly important for hikers venturing into an area for the first time.

The numbering of national forest roads has become rather complicated. Major forest roads are identified by two- or four-digit numbers, but those designating minor roads may have seven digits. In such numbers, the first three digits indicate the main road, and the remainder identify a particular spur leading off the main one. Be sure the map you carry is as up-to-date as possible.

Wilderness Regulations, Permits, and Fees

With the increasingly heavy use of Washington's backcountry, many parks, wilderness areas, and national forests have instituted permit requirements or user fees that affect both day hikers and backpackers. Whether you need a permit depends on where you are going and how long you will stay. State parks, national forests, and Fish and Wildlife Reserves require posting a current paid permit on your vehicle. As of

Kids working together

now, overnight backcountry trips in Mount Rainier, North Cascades, and Olympic National Parks require a permit, while day trips do not. Many of Washington's federally designated wilderness areas require permits for both day use and overnight stays. Permit requirements for national parks and wilderness areas, as well as other fees such as those assessed for parking at state parks, are listed in the "Before You Go" sections that precede the hikes.

Permits can be obtained at ranger stations and national park information centers as well as at many trailheads and some sporting goods stores. Fees generally are nominal.

Another regulation to be aware of concerns party size. In designated wilderness areas and national parks, the maximum number of visitors in any one group is twelve.

In some wildernesses, no campfires are allowed, and camping along lakeshores must be at least 200 feet from the shoreline.

Keep in mind that permit requirements and other regulations can and do change, and that information on the permit status of national forest areas has not been included. It is always best to call the pertinent ranger district office or information center (listed in "Before You Go") to determine the situation at the time you wish to hike.

Key to Symbols

 Day hikes. These are hikes that can be completed in a single day. While most trips allow camping, few require it.

 Backpack trips. These are hikes whose length or difficulty makes camping out either necessary or recommended for most families.

 Easy trails. These are relatively short, smooth, gentle trails suitable for small children or first-time hikers.

 Moderate trails. Most of these feature more than 500 feet of elevation gain. The trails may be rough and uneven. Hikers should wear lug-soled boots and be sure to carry the Ten Essentials (see "What to Bring," earlier in this chapter).

 Difficult trails. These are often rough and involve considerable elevation gain or distance. They are suitable for older or experienced children. Lug-soled boots and the Ten Essentials are standard equipment.

    Hikable season(s). The best times of year to hike each trail are indicated by the following symbols: flower—spring; sun—summer; leaf—fall; snowflake—winter.

Turnarounds. These are places, mostly along moderate or difficult trails, where families can cut their hikes short yet still have satisfying outings. Turnarounds usually offer picnic opportunities, views, or special natural attractions.

 Cautions. These mark potential hazards—cliffs, stream crossings, and the like—where close supervision of children is strongly recommended.

BEST HIKES TO MEADOWS

Excelsior Mountain, Hike 2
Spray Park, Hike 93
Noble Knob, Hike 99
Naches Peak Loop, Hike 104
Twin Sisters Lakes, Hike 106
Alta Vista and Panorama Point,
   Hike 114

Snowgrass Flats, Hike 129
Indian Heaven Wilderness
   Vacation, Hike 145
Bird Creek Meadows, Hike 150
Hurricane Hill, Hike 163

For More Information

For those who are new to the Pacific Northwest and to hiking its trails, there are several local environmental organizations that support missions of exploring and enjoying the mountains, forests, and waterways of the Northwest that you might wish to contact. These groups work to preserve the natural environment, by example and by the encouragement of protective legislation; provide educational opportunities in fulfillment of these purposes; and encourage a spirit of good fellowship among all lovers of outdoor life. The oldest of these Northwest environmental organizations is The Mountaineers, founded in 1906. Parents can call for information about specific activities being offered.

The Mountaineers: (206) 284-6310; *www.mountaineers.org;* 300 Third Avenue West, Seattle, WA, 98119

The Nature Conservancy: (206) 343-4344; *www.nature.org;* 217 Pine Street, Seattle, WA 98101

The Sierra Club: *www.sierraclub.org;* regional office: (206) 378-0114; 180 Nickerson Street, Seattle, WA 98109 or Cascade chapter: (206) 523-2147

The Wilderness Society: (206) 624-6430; *www.wilderness.org;* 1424 Fourth Street, Seattle, WA 98101

Washington Trails Association: (206) 625-1367; *www.wta.org;* 2019 Third Avenue, Suite 100, Seattle, WA 98121

Ferns and mass growing on a tree rather than the ground

A NOTE ABOUT SAFETY

Safety is an important concern in all outdoor activities. No guidebook can alert you to every hazard or anticipate the limitations of every reader. Therefore, the descriptions of roads, trails, routes, and natural features in this book are not representations that a particular place or excursion will be safe for your party. When you follow any of the routes described in this book, you assume responsibility for your own safety. Under normal conditions, such excursions require the usual attention to traffic, road and trail conditions, weather, terrain, the capabilities of your party, and other factors. Keeping informed on current conditions and exercising common sense are the keys to a safe, enjoyable outing.

—*The Mountaineers Books*

MOUNT BAKER HIGHWAY: STATE ROUTE 542

 ount Baker hikes offer views of two majestic glaciated peaks and prompt children to ask questions about volcanoes and glaciers. One interpretive sign suggests that Mount Baker is a "dragon with a fire in its belly." Children can imagine that if the dragon awakes, he may spit fire. The glaciers that have formed on the side of Mount Baker while it sleeps (and on Mount Shuksan, which is not a volcano) are slow-moving rivers of ice. They crack when they move over large boulders and ridges, and then turn into frozen waterfalls when they pour themselves over cliffs. Children can look for crevasses and ice falls on the two white mountains from trails to Artist Ridge, Heliotrope Ridge, and Table Mountain.

1 HELIOTROPE RIDGE

BEFORE YOU GO
Maps Green Trails No. 13 Mount Baker; USGS Groat Mountain, Mt. Baker
Current conditions Glacier Public Service Center (360) 599-2714
Northwest Forest Pass required

ABOUT THE HIKE
Day hike or backpack
Difficult for children
August–September
5½ miles
2300 feet elevation gain

GETTING THERE
- In Bellingham, leave I-5 at exit 255.
- Go east on Mount Baker Highway 542 for 33 miles to Glacier.
- At 1 mile beyond Glacier, turn right on Glacier Creek Road No. 39.
- Go 8 miles to the trailhead parking lot, elevation 3700 feet.

ON THE TRAIL
This hike provides a child with a chance to glimpse alpine wonders—to see a glacier headwall and its savage crevasses and to hear the groaning and cracking sounds of an icefall on a shoulder of Mount Baker. Many summit climbers use this route, so children may admire them at close range as well. While experienced hikers travel this route from early July, because three creek crossings are very difficult during the

Coleman Glacier

high-water periods of snowmelt, it is best to wait until late summer to take children.

The rough, well-used trail gains 1000 feet in 2 switchbacking miles. At 1¾ miles, cross the first of the three difficult streams. At 2 miles, pass the site of the old Kulshan Cabin and break out of timber into open meadows and all-summer snowfields at the beginning of Heliotrope Ridge. At ¾ mile more is a young moraine overlooking Coleman Glacier, elevation 6000 feet.

The aggressive Coleman Glacier frequently obliges visitors by putting on some sort of show. And even if it doesn't stage a noisy avalanche, icefall, or spectacular panorama of broken crevasses, you can depend on hearing the marmots and pikas whistling messages to their families. Look for marmot burrows, where they retreat for safety and where they hibernate, usually from September to April. Pikas like rock slides

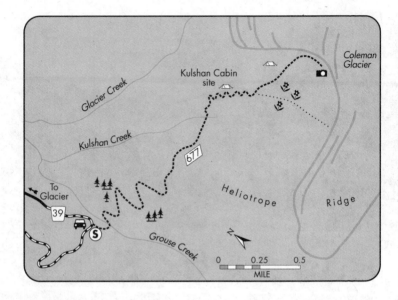

rather than burrows. These small members of the rabbit family spend the winter in rock slides, nibbling on the hay they gathered and cured the previous summer. Scan rock slides for "cony haystacks" of succulent meadow plants left to cure in the sun.

The ridge has several possible car campsites if you want to stay.

 EXCELSIOR MOUNTAIN

BEFORE YOU GO
Maps Green Trails No. 13 Mount Baker; USGS Bearpaw Mountain
Current conditions Glacier Public Service Center (360) 599-2714
Northwest Forest Pass required

ABOUT THE HIKE
Day hike or backpack
Moderate for children
Mid-July–September
7 miles
1200 feet elevation gain

GETTING THERE
■ In Bellingham, leave I-5 at exit 255.
■ Go east on Mount Baker Highway 542 for 33 miles to Glacier.

- At 2 miles beyond Glacier, turn left on Canyon Creek Road No. 31.
- Drive 15 miles to the parking lot and trail No. 625, elevation 4200 feet.

ON THE TRAIL

My children called this the Sound of Music Mountain because its alpine meadows and spectacular views of Mount Baker, Mount Shuksan, and peaks across the border into Canada reminded them of the movie scenery. The mountain is actually named for a long-ago mine called the Great Excelsior. The trail is neither steep nor gentle, gaining about 500 feet a mile. It can be very muddy when the snow is melting or after several days of rain.

Hike through lush woodland for 1 mile to a junction with the Canyon Ridge trail. Keep right and continue past the two small, marshy, but picturesque Dam-

Excelsior Mountain and Mount Baker

fino Lakes (so named because when two early travelers came here, one asked, "What lakes are these?" and the other said, "Damfino!").

At 2½ miles from the road, enter superb green meadows and cross a stream where the last drops quit flowing by mid-August. To the right

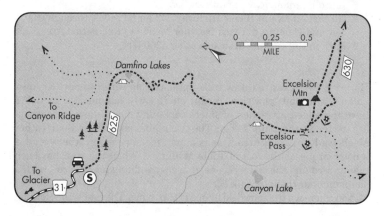

are campsites without views. At 3 miles, reach Excelsior Pass, elevation 5400 feet, and the first view of Mount Baker across the deep Nooksack valley. It is a wonderful place to have lunch, but the best is a bit farther. Either follow the trail contouring around the mountain or take the steep, boot-beaten shortcut another ½ mile to the peak itself, 5699-foot Excelsior Mountain.

Be careful not to stumble—the views are so breathtaking one may forget about feet. Mount Baker, Mount Shuksan, and the Canadian Border Peaks loom large enough that children may ask if they can stay and climb them tomorrow. In settled weather, you can sleep on the summit where the fire-lookout cabin used to be. Camping here is unforgettable, we found: Imagine moonlight on two glaciated mountains and settlement lights on the shores of Puget Sound.

BAGLEY LAKES

BEFORE YOU GO
Maps Green Trails No. 14 Mt. Shuksan; USGS Shuksan Arm; USFS Mt. Baker–Snoqualmie
Current conditions Glacier Public Service Center (360) 599-2714
Northwest Forest Pass required

ABOUT THE HIKE
Day hike
Easy to moderate for children
Late July through September
2 miles
250 feet elevation gain

GETTING THERE
- In Bellingham, leave I-5 at exit 255.
- Go east on Mount Baker Highway 542 for 54 miles, through Glacier and Deming, to reach Heather Meadows Recreation Area.
- Park in the parking area, elevation 4300 feet.

ON THE TRAIL
Here are two lakes to throw rocks into, ice-cold water to put toes into, and a year-round snow slope to play on. In early summer Bagley Lakes have the added attraction of skiers careening down snow slopes, hoping to stop at the water's edge. The two alpine lakes lie in the Heather Meadows Recreation Area. One is a man-made reservoir; the second is a deep cirque at the foot of Table Mountain. When the trail has been maintained and the snow is gone, it is easy walking for children, with a small dam for them to walk across.

You can reach the snowfield by one of two routes. The first is the Herman

Saddle–Bagley Lakes Trail, opposite a ski lift, which passes both lakes. The other is the nature trail beginning at the Austin Pass Information Center. These two trails could be united to form a 2½-mile loop.

For the Herman Saddle–Bagley Lakes Trail, go right into the huge parking lot behind the service buildings near Mount Baker Lodge and find the trail on the left side of the lot.

The trail descends sharply 60 feet, crosses a dam, and, with some ups and downs, traverses past lower Bagley Lake to the upper Bagley Lake. Hike to the snowfield at the head of the lake. Or stop at a small beach just short of the cliff. Expect wet sections: Melting snowbanks keep the trail wet all summer.

To reach upper Bagley Lake and its snowfield via the nature trail, drive from the ski lift 1 short mile uphill to the Austin Pass Information Center. Southwest of the information center, find the wide nature trail descending toward Table Mountain through meadows covered with heather and blueberries. (We picked a bucketful in early September.) At the nature trail's lowest point, a trail descends to the head of the lake, the snowfield, and a shallow beach for wading. This section is always

Lower Bagley Lake and Table Mountain

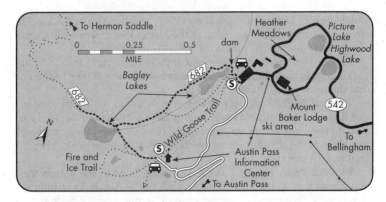

wet due to melting snow. You can connect to the various loops on the steep 1-mile connector trail, the Wild Goose Trail, which saves backtracking. Elevation loss is about 250 feet, which must be regained on your way out.

4 ARTIST RIDGE

BEFORE YOU GO
Maps Green Trails No. 14 Mt. Shuksan; USGS Shuksan Arm
Current conditions Glacier Public Service Center (360) 599-2714
Northwest Forest Pass required

ABOUT THE HIKE
Day hike
Easy for children
Late July through September
1-mile loop
200 feet elevation gain and loss

GETTING THERE
- In Bellingham, leave I-5 at exit 255.
- Go east on Mount Baker Highway 542 for 54 miles, through Glacier and Deming, to reach Heather Meadows Recreation Area.
- Find the road behind the ski lift building; go another 2.5 miles to the road end and trailhead, on the south side of the parking lot near the rest room, elevation 5100 feet.

ON THE TRAIL
A short, gentle, paved loop leads to kid-size, heather-framed tarns (small lakes sculpted in bedrock by a passing glacier) and summer

Walking through heather fields

snowbanks, dramatic views of Mount Baker and Mount Shuksan, and lessons in volcano behavior. Signs along the way give explanatory geological facts, in terms kids can understand, about the formation of Mount Shuksan and Mount Baker. The trail ends a few feet from the top of Artist Point. For those with very young children, this makes a picturesque, short alternative.

Begin alongside summer snowbanks. The first interpretive signs explain Mount Baker's hidden volcanic core in child-appealing language: "The dragon with a fire in its belly." Like all dormant volcanoes in the Northwest, Mount Baker could erupt again at any time. Its most recent activity was in 1976, when it began to emit clouds of steam and ash, giving the Forest Service enough of a scare that they closed Baker Lake's campgrounds for a time. At the top, climbers still can smell sulfur in the hot volcanic breath of the dragon, waiting and thinking about breathing his fire again.

Signs also explain the formation of Mount Shuksan, the yellow band of rocks on Shuksan Arm, and the fragile alpine environment. Look in

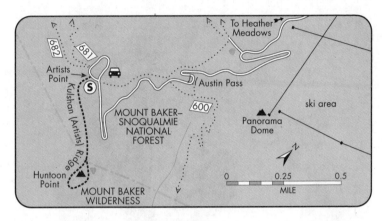

the opposite direction at Mount Shuksan's enormous hanging glaciers, which are hundreds of feet thick. Like waterfalls of ice, they flow over rock, break, and crash with avalanche thunder below.

The Artist Ridge Trail mounts small knolls crested with heather. In August kids can look for ripe blueberries and huckleberries. Ponds and tarns of snowmelt water warmed by the summer sun make wonderful wading pools. What more can children ask for? The last and largest pool is the prettiest one for capturing the breathtaking views in its reflection. Get here early on a clear day for an undisturbed image. At the end of the ridge the trail loops back to the parking lot.

 TABLE MOUNTAIN

BEFORE YOU GO
Maps Green Trails No. 14 Mt. Shuksan; USGS Shuksan Arm; USFS Mt. Baker–Snoqualmie
Current conditions Mount Baker Ranger District (360) 856-5700
Northwest Forest Pass required

ABOUT THE HIKE
Day hike
Moderate for children
Late July through October
Summit 1½ miles; traverse closed
600 feet elevation gain

GETTING THERE
- In Bellingham, leave I-5 at exit 255.
- Go east on Mount Baker Highway 542 for 54 miles, through Glacier and Deming, to reach Heather Meadows Recreation Area.

■ Find the road behind the ski lift building; go another 2.5 miles to the road end and trailhead, on the west side of the parking lot, elevation 5100 feet.

ON THE TRAIL

An exciting, steep, and very short exposed trail leads to a broad summit plateau between Mount Baker and Mount Shuksan. We carried one of our babies in a backpack to the top when she was less than a year old, and I met a father leading a four-year-old who had also been carried

A child adds a rock to the cairn on Table Mountain.

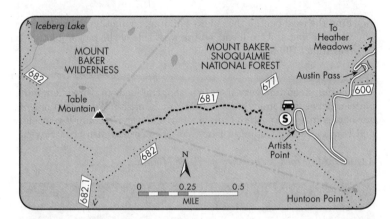

there in a pack when he was younger but was now walking it for the first time. I overheard a small girl on her way up the cliffs ask, "Mother, how are we ever going to get down?" The trail may not scare all children, but it does frighten some parents, who find it alarmingly exposed. Parental guidance is needed. Although hundreds of families climb Table Mountain every year, if you are not comfortable on the trail, don't take your children. There are other trails. But rest assured, the blasted rock inclines are wide and gentle. Arriving at the summit cairns (piles of rocks) rewards children with a sense of achievement and satisfaction. Sometimes this trail does not thaw out until mid-August, and some years not at all. Do not attempt it until the snow is gone from the cliffs.

The Table Mountain Trail has been rebuilt several times. For the first ½ mile the trail climbs easily around and over knolls, passing a small tarn and distorted ancient alpine trees that will frame views of Mount Shuksan and Mount Baker for your camera. Children may want to stop to check for tadpoles in the snowmelt pond before starting up.

In the last ¼ mile the trail turns steep and switchbacks up slabs of the near-vertical cliff. Hold on to your children here. A misstep would be serious. Some of the rock steps are very big for short-legged hikers. If the trail seems scary now, you should have seen it before it was widened. The sense of accomplishment and bravery children feel as they make their way up the little mountain is wonderful to see. The trail levels abruptly near the top; a few feet more brings children to the cairns at the top.

Look first at magnificent Mount Shuksan, named by the Skagit Indians (the name means "rocky and precipitous"), then back to Mount Baker, named Koma Kulshan, or "white, steep mountain," by the Nooksack Indians. Look down to Bagley Lakes (Hike 3) far below. Table Mountain is part of the volcanic formation left by one of Baker's earlier eruptions. The summit is a mile long, truly a tabletop, with edges that seem to drop off to eternity.

CHAIN LAKES

BEFORE YOU GO
Maps Green Trails No. 14
Mount Shuksan; USGS
Shuksan Arm
Current conditions Glacier
Public Service Center (360)
599-2714
**Northwest Forest Pass
required**

ABOUT THE HIKE
Day hike or backpack
Easy to moderate for children
Late July–October
3½-plus miles
400 feet elevation loss and gain

GETTING THERE

- In Bellingham, leave I-5 at exit 255.
- Go east on Mount Baker Highway 542 for 54 miles, through Glacier and Deming, to reach Heather Meadows Recreation Area.
- Find the road behind the ski lift building; go another 2.5 miles to the road end and trailhead, to the left of the Table Mountain trailhead on the Mount Baker side of the parking lot, elevation 5100 feet.

ON THE TRAIL

This group of four alpine lakes has enough scenic campsites with views to accommodate many families. If you wish, you can move camp from lake to lake along the chain and enjoy different views and different settings each

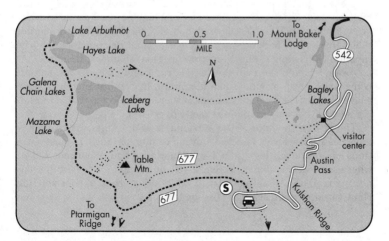

Mazama Lake, smallest of the four Chain Lakes

day. Expect blueberries in August and September and fish in Hayes and Arbuthnot Lakes anytime.

The trail drops a few feet, then contours around the side of Table Mountain, with views of parkland meadows below and Mount Baker above. Columnar andesite formations of ancient lava flows alternate along the trail with horizontal layers of 10,000-year-old ash and pumice; those from different eruptions exhibit different colors. Tell the kids the layers are like squeezed fillings in sandwiches. They may not be impressed when you tell them much of this ash was blown out "only" 10,000 years ago, but their interest may perk up when they learn Mount Baker is thought to be capable of exploding again at any time, just like Mount St. Helens.

Around 1 mile the trail divides. Go right and climb to the highest point on the way around Table Mountain, the trail descends a steep snowfield that lasts to late summer. If there is a safe runout below, sliding may be in order, but tennis shoes will get wet.

The first of the lakes, little Mazama, is at 1¾ miles. In another ¼ mile, beautiful Iceberg Lake calls to you to stop for lunch, at least. Continue on and down less than 1 mile to Hayes and Arbuthnot Lakes, where some of the shores are black volcanic sand. A steep 1-mile connecting trail, the Wild Goose Trail, will take you back to your starting point without backtracking or having to walk the road.

STATE ROUTE 20 WEST OF WASHINGTON PASS

The beauty of the North Cascades is the result of glacially carved lakes and long valleys. Tell children that Baker and Ross Lakes are reservoirs formed from old river valleys by dams, but other smaller lakes, such as Anderson Lake, Watson Lake, Blue Lake, and Cutthroat Lake, were scoured out by glaciers, and not too long ago. This beautiful cross-state passage is only open for part of the year and is sometimes compared to passages through the Alps. Stop in Newhalem at the interpretive center to view a three-dimensional map of North Cascades National Park and Ross Lake. The North Cascades Institute Environmental Center on Diablo Lake offers more information about the area. You can contact them before you go to check out their programs: (360) 856-5700 ext. 209 or *NCI@ncascades.org.*

 SCOTT PAUL TRAIL

BEFORE YOU GO
Maps Green Trails No. 45 Hamilton
Current conditions Mount Baker Ranger District (360) 856-5700
Northwest Forest Pass required

ABOUT THE HIKE
Day hike
Difficult for children
Mid-July–October
7½-mile loop
1400 feet elevation gain

GETTING THERE
- Leave I-5 at exit 232/Highway 20 and go east 23 miles to milepost 82.
- Turn left on Baker Lake Road/Road No. 11 and go 12.5 miles.
- Just past the Rocky Creek bridge, turn left on Road No. 12 and go 3.5 miles to a junction.
- Turn right on Sulphur Creek Road No. 13 and follow it for 5.3 miles to the Schriebers Meadow trailhead, elevation 3300 feet.

ON THE TRAIL
This amazing trail offers children the chance to see glaciers close-up and learn about their effects on the landscape. They can cross glacial streams on two swaying suspension bridges, peer up at the glacier's snout, and then climb the moraines it left behind. The sound of boulders

being slammed against the floor of the stream and the groans of moving ice are unforgettable, high-alpine sound effects. I heard one child say the bridge was "so bouncy you don't have to jump on it!" Scott Paul was a trails foreman for the Mount Baker Ranger District who, before his death in 1993, helped to make sure this trail would be built. Note that the bridges on this trail are seasonal. They are removed in late September and are not put back in place until late June, and the creeks should not be forded. Be sure to call the district office to check that the bridges are in place before heading out.

Begin at the trailhead for Park Butte and Railroad Grade, but in 100 feet turn right onto the signed Scott Paul Trail. Your loop will bring you back via the Railroad Grade Trail. Climb steeply in old-growth forest for 2 miles. A short section crosses a well-named Rocky Creek on a seasonal suspension bridge. At the first viewpoint you'll

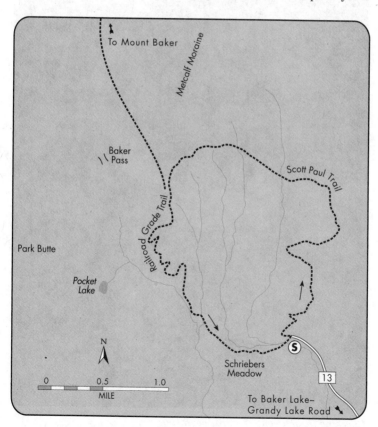

Checking the map with the trailhead sign

find supreme views of Mount Baker and Mount Shuksan. If your children are small this would be enough for a turnaround point, but you'd miss the meadow flowers and ripe blueberries in season, and the up-close glacier experience.

At 5 miles cross a glacial moraine. Tell children the glacier pushes its rubble down the mountain like a tractor and leaves it in long gravel ridges along its path. When they get to the deep gorge below Easton Glacier, children won't believe their eyes. Pause with them and look up at it. This is an active glacier, grinding boulders and turning them into rubble. Stop and listen to it chew.

Drop steeply to the next seasonal suspension bridge over the creek. Cross and climb steeply up the moraine on the other side to connect with the Railroad Grade Trail. Continue for the 2½ miles down to the trailhead. Another possibility for especially strong child hikers is to take the wonderful Park Butte Lookout Trail, an additional 2½-mile out-and-back side trip from a marked fork in the Scott Paul Trail.

ANDERSON AND WATSON LAKES

BEFORE YOU GO
Maps Green Trails No. 46 Lake Shannon; USFS Mount Baker–Snoqualmie
Current conditions Mount Baker Ranger District (360) 856-5700
Northwest Forest Pass required; Wilderness Permit required if going to Watson Lake

ABOUT THE HIKE
Day hike or backpack
Difficult for children
July–October
6 miles
800 feet elevation gain

GETTING THERE
- Leave I-5 at exit 232/Highway 20 and go east 23 miles to milepost 82.
- Turn left on Baker Lake Road/Road No. 11 and go 14 miles.
- Turn right on the Baker Dam–Baker Campground road. In 1 mile, drive over the Upper Baker Dam.
- After crossing the dam, go left on gravel Road No. 1107 and drive 8 miles.
- At a junction, go left on Road No. 1107-002 and drive 1.5 miles to the trailhead, on the right, elevation 4200 feet.

ON THE TRAIL

These five very popular alpine lakes are surrounded by acres of meadows, cliffs, and gorgeous scenery, and offer families diverse opportunities to camp, fish, wade, and explore. The views of Mount Baker, Mount Watson, and Anderson Butte can tempt hikers to go on and on, although trails are rough, sometimes very steep, and filled with roots and rocks. Note that in the event of a security threat, the dam road may be closed; be sure to call ahead.

The first mile gently climbs through very large old-growth Douglas-firs. At 1 mile pass the side trail to Anderson Butte, site of a former fire lookout. The main trail loses 100 feet and then climbs through meadows to the high point at 4900 feet before dropping steeply to a junction at about 2 miles from the trailhead.

Here the trail splits. The left fork climbs 150 feet over a ridge, enters the Noisy-Diobsud Wilderness, and drops steeply to more meadows and the shore of glacier-carved Upper Watson Lake, at 4500 feet. Lower Watson Lake, the larger of the two, is a short ½ mile farther. Campsites here have views of the lake and of the glaciers on Bacon Peak.

The right fork is a rough, up-and-down ½ mile to Lower Anderson Lake, at 4500 feet; you'll find campsites on both sides and a view of Mount Baker from the meadows. The lake is small enough, like the baby bear's chair, to be "just right" for small children.

Upper Watson Lake

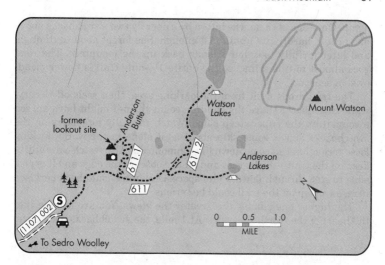

9 SAUK MOUNTAIN

BEFORE YOU GO
Maps Green Trails No. 46
Lake Shannon; USGS Sauk
Mountain
Current conditions Mount
Baker Ranger District (360)
856-5700

ABOUT THE HIKE
Day hike
Moderate to difficult for children
Mid-July–October
**Lookout trail: 2 miles; ridge
top: 2²/₃ miles; Sauk Lake:
3 miles**
1650 feet elevation gain

GETTING THERE

- Leave I-5 at exit 230/Highway 20 and drive 36 miles east to milepost 96, at the west boundary of Rockport State Park.
- Turn left onto Road No. 1030 and go 8 miles up an increasingly steep grade to the road end and parking area, elevation 4300 feet.

ON THE TRAIL

Exposed switchbacks ascend a dizzyingly steep alpine meadow to panoramic views of Whitehorse Mountain, Mount Baker, and Mount Shuksan, and the merging of the serpentine Sauk, Skagit, and Cascade Rivers. This is not a trail for toddlers, but my children loved it when they were six, seven, and eight, and we returned to it again and again. Once one of them was bitten by a deer fly two switchbacks above me; I could hardly run uphill fast enough. She forgot about it, though, and later joyfully took her friends back up the mountain. The road goes almost to timberline, so the entire 1⅓-mile trail is flower meadows, in season.

The trail drops a bit from the parking area, then reels off twenty-eight switchbacks (have the children count them—I might have missed a couple) up the super-steep slope. Watch carefully for hikers on the switchbacks above; some skip about as if alone in the world, kicking loose rocks that can come down like cannonballs. Also watch carefully to keep on the trail—thick grass and foliage obscure the edge and it is possible to step through flowers into space. Children should be supervised here, as a step off the trail could be serious.

The higher one climbs, the greater the views. You are looking into the heart of the North Cascades. At 1 mile, the switchbacks end on the

Flower fields on Sauk Mountain

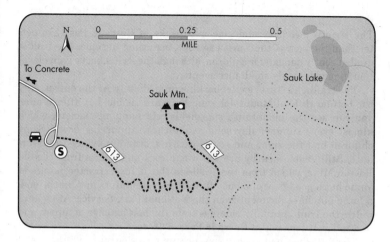

crest of the summit ridge and an intersection. The old lookout site to the
left is reached by a ½-mile climb along the sidehill. Or, you can stay
to the right at the intersection for a 1½-mile walk to Sauk Lake.
Even on a foggy day there are flowery rewards; on a clear day, expect
magnificence.

10 CASCADE PASS

BEFORE YOU GO
Maps Green Trails No. 80
Cascade Pass; USGS Cascade
Pass
Current conditions
Marblemount Ranger District
(360) 873-4500

ABOUT THE HIKE
Day hike
Moderate to difficult for
children
Mid-July–October
7 miles
1800 feet elevation gain

GETTING THERE
- Leave I-5 at exit 230/High-
  way 20 and drive east to
  Marblemount.
- In Marblemount, instead of turning left with the main highway,
  continue straight, taking Cascade River Road across the Skagit
  River.
- Drive about 25 miles to a large parking lot at the road end, eleva-
  tion 3600 feet.

The superb meadows and glaciered peaks of Cascade Pass are better than the best of the European Alps, according to some. The trail is graded gently enough for children, although the switchbacks gain elevation in maddeningly small increments.

The trailhead starts switchbacking immediately. At the outset, only the bottom cliffs of Mount Johannesburg are visible, but after a mile, you can see the mountain's snowfields and hanging glaciers, which almost every summer day send avalanches thundering down. Some children find the sight and sound exciting; others may need reassurance. Still visible nearby are the waste rock and debris from the old Boston Mine, which from the 1890s to the 1970s extracted no ore of value but a good deal of money from stock speculators and, in the end, a large purchase payment from the National Park Service. At about 3 miles, the trail gradually emerges from the last patches of forest, and at 4 miles, it tops out at Cascade Pass, 5392 feet.

The pass has had such heavy use that erosion has left the metal benchmark 2 feet above the ground surface! Camping is forbidden, to allow fragile meadows to recover from overuse. You can rest on logs and stare east down Stehekin valley or turn around to face Inspiration Glacier on Eldorado Peak. "Through-hikers" travel this trail from Stehekin down to the trailhead to avoid the trip down Lake Chelan and crossing the Cascades.

Flowers climb the slopes in every direction. Clumps of subalpine fir and mountain hemlock beside the scree slopes or next to snow and rock outcrops are the only trees at this altitude, but below are deep green forests rolling out like magic carpets. A park ranger is frequently stationed at the pass and will identify Eldorado, Forbidden, and

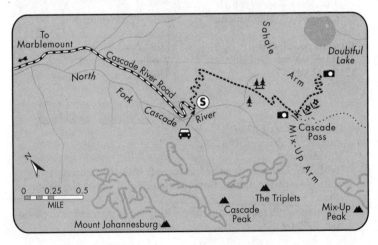

Enjoying the view on Cascade Pass

other peaks. Well-worn trails, excellent for older children, lead up in two directions: south to Mix-Up Arm and north up toward Sahale Arm, from which the trail dips abruptly to the deep cirque of Doubtful Lake, beautiful as late as October in some years.

At the pass, in season, are myriad flower species and gasp-provoking views. Or you can come in late fall to admire the color of the vine maple and huckleberry leaves and the dusting of powdered-sugar snow on the summits.

THUNDER KNOB

BEFORE YOU GO
Maps Green Trails No. 48
Diablo Dam; USGS Diablo
Dam; North Cascades National Recreation Area map
Current conditions
Marblemount Ranger District
(360) 873-4500

ABOUT THE HIKE
Day hike
Easy for children
Year round
3½ miles
625 feet elevation gain

GETTING THERE

- Leave I-5 at exit 230/Highway 20 and go east to Newhalem.
- Check your odometer and continue another 10 miles to Colonial Creek Campground and milepost 130. Park in the trailhead parking area on the left side of the highway, elevation 1200 feet.
- *If coming from the east on Highway 20,* drive across the Thunder Arm Bridge to find the trailhead on the right, directly after the bridge.

ON THE TRAIL

This short, well-constructed new trail goes to breathtaking viewpoints. The grade is so gentle that, if it were paved, it could be a barrier-free trail. Children can look down on Thunder Arm with its unearthly turquoise water

Diablo Lake from Thunder Knob

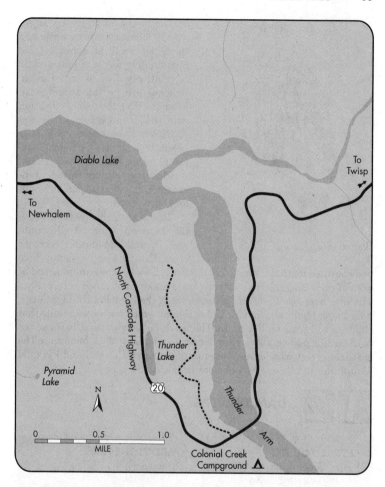

and across to enormous glaciated peaks and spires, from three sitting areas at the summit of Thunder Knob. They will dream of paddling a canoe on the still waters or climbing these surrounding mountains someday.

The campground is divided by the highway. Begin by walking into the north side of Colonial Creek Campground. The road is frequently gated. Following the trail signs, stay right where the road divides, and walk pavement past campsites one through ten. Beyond the tenth campsite the road was ripped up and covered by gravel and boulders when Colonial Creek flooded in 2003. The trail crosses two of the deepest flood channels on large logs before entering the forest and crossing the original channel on a well-constructed bridge.

Barred owl

The sound of traffic on Highway 20 follows you for a while and then dies away at about 1 mile. Surrounding forest of pine and fir is relatively free of underbrush. Benches are provided frequently. After the first 250 feet of elevation gain, the gleaming turquoise jewel of Diablo Lake begins to appear below through tree trunks. Year-round birds include the pileated woodpecker, varied thrush, red-breasted nuthatch, Steller's jay, and barred owl.

To the east, the enormous saddle between Colonial Mountain and Pyramid Mountain becomes clear. Pass a small swampy lake and continue on to the summit of the Knob. Two benches are provided at each of three magnificent viewpoints and make great lunch or rest stops. The first one, looking south, gives views of the Seattle City Light dock, Sourdough Mountain, and McMillan Spires, which has two summits that children will say look like tusks. The north-facing viewpoint looks across to the traffic pullout above Thunder Arm and mighty Jack Mountain. The east-facing viewpoint gives close-ups of glaciated Colonial and Pyramid Mountains and the majesty of distant Cascade Pass peaks.

 DAM TRAVERSE

BEFORE YOU GO
Maps Green Trails No. 48 Diablo Dam; USGS Diablo Dam; North Cascades National Park handout
Current conditions Marblemount Ranger District (360) 873-4500

ABOUT THE HIKE
Day hike
Difficult for children
June to November
Ross Dam: 3½ miles; Lake Diablo: 11½ miles
Ross Dam: 700 feet elevation loss; Lake Diablo: 500 feet elevation gain

GETTING THERE
■ Leave I-5 at exit 230/Highway 20 and drive east past Newhalem, crossing the Skagit River at the upper end of Gorge

Lake. Continue another 7 miles to the Diablo Dam turnoff.

- *With two cars:* Turn left, drive across the dam, and go to the end of the road, leaving one car at the interpretive center parking lot.
- Back on the highway, continue another 4 miles to the Ross Lake trailhead, on the left side of the highway, elevation 2200 feet.

ON THE TRAIL

Adventure-loving families will love the excitement of crossing two dams of the Skagit River: 389-foot-high Diablo Dam to drive across, and 540-foot-high Ross Dam to walk across. The reward for the short, steep descent between them is a close-up look at a major hydroelectric project for Seattle City Light in the heart of the North Cascades. With the aid of two cars, you can continue by trail to the level of the beautiful turquoise-green waters of Diablo Lake.

Find the trail in the upper half of the parking area just beside the highway. The trail drops steeply, crossing Happy Creek and switchbacking within sight of a series of small waterfalls. Children will enjoy descending parallel to the falling water.

At approximately 1 mile and after a loss of 400 feet, reach a service road. Go right, and marvel at mammoth Ross Dam. Keep a good hold on children when walking across Ross Dam. As you look up fjordlike Ross Lake, imagine yourself in Norway. Then turn and gaze down the massive concave face of the dam. Keep a close eye on children, who may be tempted to climb the pipes alongside the railing as you cross.

This controversial structure has an interesting history. J. D. Ross, first head of Seattle City Light, proposed and executed a series of dams on the Skagit at a time when there was no environmental movement to protest the plan. Today the dams probably would not have been built. Throughout the 1960s and 1970s the threat of raising Ross Dam above its current level angered both Canadians, who did not want the lake to extend any farther into Canada, and the awakening American

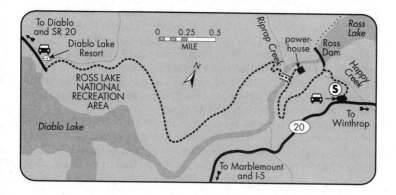

Looking down on Ross Dam

environmental movement, which opposed the loss of more wilderness river valleys. The issue was finally settled in 1984, and Ross Dam will never be raised. Enough is enough.

"Why is the water above the dam a different color than the water below?" my children asked. "Easy," answered their father. "They've taken all the electricity out of it." Actually, the water below Diablo Dam is not clearer, but Diablo Lake appears different because some of its water comes from glaciers that contain scoured Skagit gneiss and granite rock, which colors the water an unearthly turquoise green. For an explanation of glacial scouring and a sample of Skagit gneiss, stop at the Diablo Lake overlook, halfway between Diablo Lake and the Ross Dam pullout, where you'll find interpretive signs.

To continue the traverse, retrace your steps back to the junction with the service road and go straight ahead, following the road as it switchbacks for ¾ mile, dropping another 300 feet to the powerhouse with its mysterious humming sound, elevation 1310 feet. Children will ask what it is doing to remove the electricity from the water. If you are lucky, a guided boat tour may be there just as you arrive, which will help answer their questions.

Cross the Skagit River on a suspension bridge, and look back up at the towering dam, then climb by trail, switchbacking up the opposite side to gain 500 feet in ¾ mile. For the next mile traverse down along the steep canyon wall—another place to hold on to children—with dramatic views down to Diablo Lake and across to the glaciers on glorious Colonial Peak that help to color Diablo Lake. The trail turns away from the river, and the remaining 2 miles to the lower trailhead are in forest.

 LAKE ANN

BEFORE YOU GO
Maps Green Trails No. 49 Mount Logan, No. 50 Washington Pass; USFS Okanogan
Current conditions Methow Valley Ranger District (509) 996-4003
Northwest Forest Pass required

ABOUT THE HIKE
Day hike or backpack
Easy for children
Mid-July–September
3½ miles
700 feet elevation gain

GETTING THERE

■ Leave I-5 at exit 230/Highway 20 and drive east to Rainy Pass, at milepost 158.

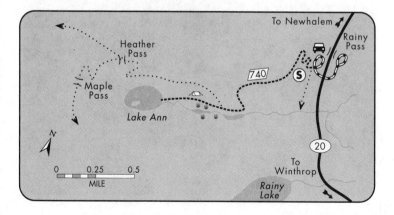

■ Park at the south-side rest area, elevation 4800 feet. Find the trail marked "Lakes Trails"; 10 feet along it is the one marked "Lake Ann–Maple Pass."

ON THE TRAIL

This short walk takes you from the highway to the high country, complete with alpine scenery. In early summer the lake might even hold a few floating icebergs!

The hiker-only trail starts on a gentle grade through a rock slide for a scant mile. At 1¼ miles is a junction; go left, on the lower trail. The way narrows with roots, rocks, and marshy areas that may impede small feet but allow their owners to inspect frogs at close range. At 1½ miles, the trail comes to Lake Ann, elevation 5475 feet.

Small children can wade in the outlet stream, the ponds, and the marsh below the lake. Even if the lake has icebergs, the possibilities for stick- and stone-throwing are infinite, and there's ample room to play.

Trail to Lake Anne

Camping is not allowed on the lakeshore, but the sites ¼-mile back are good. For older kids, an excellent but steep 7-mile loop trail can take you up to Maple Pass and back to Lake Ann.

 RAINY LAKE

BEFORE YOU GO
Maps Green Trails No. 50 Washington Pass; USFS Wenatchee and Okanogan
Current conditions Methow Valley Ranger District (509) 996-4003
Northwest Forest Pass required

ABOUT THE HIKE
Day hike
Easy for children
Late July to October
2 miles
70 feet elevation gain

GETTING THERE

- Leave I-5 at exit 230/Highway 20 and drive east toward Winthrop.
- At Rainy Pass, milepost 158, turn west into the rest area and find the Rainy Lake trailhead on the highway's south side, elevation 4800 feet.

ON THE TRAIL

Although it does not go downhill in both directions, this trail is the next-best thing. It is the finest example I know of a wheelchair-accessible alpine lake. It offers a fine way for wheelchair-bound sightseers, or parents with babies in strollers, to see an alpine cirque lake rimmed by rocky cliffs

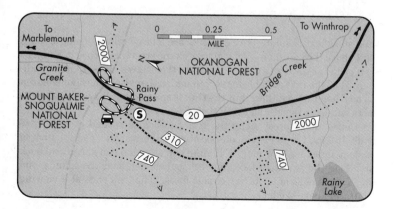

End of Rainy Lake Trail

and snowfields. Children can expect to see a large waterfall on the south cliff above the lakeshore, and a glacier on the crest high above it. Families can picnic at the trail's end and imagine themselves miles from the highway. The lake isn't suitable for swimming, so there isn't much for children to do when they get there, but the trail is so easy that they will enjoy the hike and have something to tell their friends about.

Dense, dark forest along the trail muffles the sound of cars by ½ mile. In fact, I found Audubon Society members at this point, listening in deep forest for bird songs. Children can skip and run ahead and back safely on the paved surface, but feel the wonder, hear the sounds, and smell the smells of a North Cascade forest. The trail ends at a viewing platform above the lake.

BLUE LAKE

BEFORE YOU GO
Maps Green Trails No.
50 Washington Pass; USFS
Wenatchee and Okanogan
Current conditions Methow
Valley Ranger District (509)
996-4003
**Northwest Forest Pass
required**

ABOUT THE HIKE
Day hike or backpack
Moderate for children
Mid-July–October
4 miles
1050 feet elevation gain

GETTING THERE

- Leave I-5 at exit 230/Highway 20 and drive east to 1 mile west of Washington Pass, at milepost 161.
- The signed Blue Lake trailhead, No. 314, is on the south side of the road, elevation 5200 feet.

ON THE TRAIL

Many lakes have been named Blue, but to date this is the only one reached by a designated National Recreation Trail, a formal recognition of its outstanding beauty that does not, unfortunately, preserve it from logging or motorcycles. There is an abandoned old miner's cabin at the lake and campsites are plentiful near the shoreline.

Before leaving the car, gaze up at Liberty Bell Mountain. Its bell

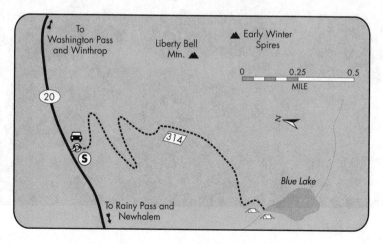

shape seems to change as the trail ascends, and it becomes more like a turreted castle. Climbers headed to Early Winter Spires share this trail before turning left for their high camp in meadows below the cliffs.

Trail No. 314 is in good shape and modestly steep. At first, highway sounds follow hikers, but at ½ mile they fade out as the path switchbacks from forest to flower-covered avalanche slope. The mix of trees shifts to subalpine firs and larches, and heather begins to appear. At 2 miles, cross the outlet stream; a few feet farther, at 6254 feet, beautiful Blue Lake appears. Depending on the season it may be snow-covered or contain icebergs.

The lake is set in a deep cirque below rugged cliffs. For most of the summer, the water is kept ice-cold by snow fingers beside a rock slide at the far end. Good campsites lie on both sides of the outlet stream. The old miner's cabin should not be relied upon for shelter.

Blue Lake

STATE ROUTE 20 EAST OF WASHINGTON PASS

 CUTTHROAT LAKE

BEFORE YOU GO
Maps Green Trails No. 50 Washington Pass; USFS Wenatchee and Okanogan
Current conditions Methow Valley Ranger District (509) 996-4003
Northwest Forest Pass required

ABOUT THE HIKE
Day hike or backpack
Easy for children
July to October
4 miles
400 feet elevation gain

GETTING THERE
- Leave I-5 at exit 230/Highway 20 and drive east to 4.6 miles east of Washington Pass.
- Near the Cutthroat Creek Bridge and milepost 166, turn uphill on Cutthroat Creek Road No. 400 and go 1 mile to the trailhead parking lot, elevation 4580 feet.

ON THE TRAIL
A shallow mountain lake beneath the towering cliffs of Cutthroat Peak is only 2 miles and one gentle shower-bath waterfall from the highway. Boulders, grass, and reeds ring the lake. Families can camp ¼ mile from the shoreline, where there is a creek to play in and clumps of trees to hide in. The trail's builders cut a wide swath through the trees for the benefit of horse riders, leaving very little shade on a hot day, so it's best to make this hike early or late in the day.

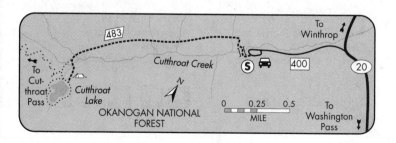

Packing up the tent

Find the trail at the west end of the parking area. Cross the bridge to the north side of Cutthroat Creek, and begin to climb gradually through pines and firs. At 1 mile look back up at impressive Silver Star Mountain. Just before the lake, cross the creek again, then come to the first camping area and a very rough trail that circles the lake. Cutthroat fishermen who want a higher vantage for casting may choose the boulders at the north end of the lake. Older children like to jump into the water from them, which the fishermen may not appreciate.

I saw my first pine marten in trees near the lake here, looking like a large weasel. He darted across the trail in front of me so fast I could not see him clearly, and then climbed a tree close by and growled angrily above my head at my invasion of his property. If you and your children are curious about what lies above, another 2 miles of trail climbing will bring you up Cutthroat Pass, with views down on the lake and occasional sightings of mountain goats.

17 BENSON PASS

BEFORE YOU GO
Maps Green Trails No. 18 Pasayten, No. 50 Washington Pass; USFS Wenatchee and Okanogan
Current conditions Methow Valley Ranger District (509) 996-4003
Northwest Forest Pass required

ABOUT THE HIKE
Day hike or backpack
Easy for children
July through October
4 miles
200 feet elevation loss

GETTING THERE

- Driving North Cascades Highway 20 in the Methow valley, between Early Winters and Winthrop, take Lost River Road north, signed "Mazama."
- In Mazama, turn left on Mazama Road and go 9 miles. The road becomes Road No. 5400 and turns steep and narrow, crossing the one-car-wide Dead Horse Pass; drive with caution.
- About 20 miles from Mazama reach Harts Pass. Turn right on Slate Peak Road No. (5400)600 and drive to the first switchback, at 1.5 miles, signed for the Pacific Crest Trail and Windy Pass. Park at the small pulloff; elevation is 6800 feet.

ON THE TRAIL

A minimum effort yields some of the most gorgeous views and flower-covered meadows in the state. The hike on the Pacific Crest Trail from Harts Pass is gentle enough for a four-year-old yet awe-inspiring for hikers of all ages. But be prepared for a shock. Across the valley, bulldozer tracks zigzag through beautiful alpine meadows, the work of a modern prospector operating under laws passed 140 years ago and not yet amended to fit the twenty-first century.

The trail starts with a short climb into a meadow and then levels out to join the Pacific Crest Trail as it contours under the summit of Slate Peak and its old lookout tower. Look out to Silver Star, the Mount Gardner massif, Azurite Peak, and Colonial Peak in the distance. Watch or hold children to make sure they don't stumble—the slope on the left, the view side, drops thousands of feet to Slate Creek. The flowers here are the envy of gardeners for their diversity and constant bloom throughout the summer season. In August, expect bluebells, shrubby cinquefoil, stonecrop, lupine, and Indian paintbrush.

At 1¾ miles, the trail contours above Benson Basin and, at 2 miles, reaches Benson Pass, elevation 6700 feet, with views down the West Fork of the Pasayten River. There are two small campsites here, with water several hundred feet back along the trail. For better camping,

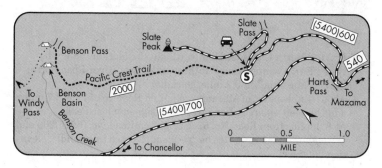

Pacific Crest Trail, near Benson Pass

drop 250 feet into Benson Basin. Practice leave-no-trace camping here, using a stove instead of a fire—the small subalpine fir and larches at 6500 feet took a long time to grow. Windy Pass is 2 miles farther, offering different panoramas and more beauty-spot gardens—but then, so does the entire route to the Canadian Border. The kids will dream of the time they can hike there.

GOAT PEAK

BEFORE YOU GO
Maps Green Trails No. 51 Mazama; USGS McLeod Mountain
Current conditions Methow Ranger District (509) 996-4003
Northwest Forest Pass required

ABOUT THE HIKE
Day hike
Difficult for children
July–October
2 miles
1400 feet elevation gain

GETTING THERE

- Driving North Cascades Highway 20 in the Methow valley, between Early Winters and Winthrop, take Lost River Road north, signed "Mazama." In 0.2 mile, go right.
- About 4 miles east of Mazama, go left on Road No. 52 for 3.7 miles and then left again on Road No. 5225, signed "Goat Peak."
- At 8.3 miles from Road No. 52, go right on Road No. (5225)200 and drive another 2.5 miles to the trailhead, located in a saddle, elevation 5600 feet.

ON THE TRAIL

A lookout building still occupied by a volunteer in fire season is excitement enough to make this steep and rocky trail seem less steep and rocky. From the North Cascades Highway near Early Winters, you can point it out to the children—a tiny tower perched atop the Goat Wall at the highest point on the northern horizon. Once up there, they can peer down to the highway where the cars look like brightly colored ants running along a black ribbon.

The lookout was originally reached—and supplied—by a much longer trail, but a logging road has shortened the walk, and a helicopter does the supplying. The mountain goats for which the peak was named, once so abundant, were slaughtered in the 1920s. However, as hunting regulations have become more sensible, goats are reoccupying parts of their old range. Methow valley folks say they have, now and then, spied goats on Goat Wall, the side of Goat Peak facing the highway.

Goat Peak trail No. 457 begins in subalpine fir and lodgepole pine,

Lookout on Goat Peak, Silver Star Mountain in background

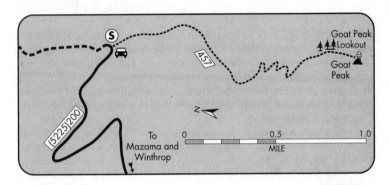

traversing a rocky ridge top, and then ascends rocky meadows. In about ½ mile, it tilts upward and steeply switchbacks to a 6800-foot shoulder with good views. It's another half mile of easy ups and downs along the ridge top, culminating in a final steep climb to the summit and lookout tower at 7000 feet.

The ridge vistas are magnificent, spreading east to farms of the Methow valley and southwest to Silver Star, Mount Gardner, and Varden Creek, hidden by the jumble of mountains around the Golden Horn. Children will enjoy talking with the lookout's fire warden about how to spot fires.

MOUNTAIN LOOP HIGHWAY
STATE ROUTE 530

Mountain Loop hikes generally are short and easy. Trails to such lakes as Boardman, Heather, Twenty-Two, Independence, and Kelcema are popular and offer other attractions as well, such as waterfalls, ripe berries, water activities, and views of surrounding central Cascade peaks. The two Robe Canyon hikes follow parts of an old nineteenth-century railroad right-of-way above the churning South Fork of the Stillaguamish. The Old Sauk River trail follows that river's white water along its banks. Stops in Granite Falls and Darrington as entry or exit points offer children chances to stretch and enjoy ice cream.

Part of the Mountain Loop Highway, between Bedal Creek and the Monte Cristo Lakes, was closed due to a washout. At the time of this printing the anticipated reopening of the full loop road is expected to be in the summer of 2008. Driving directions take you to the hikes in this section via the nearest access roads that bypass this closure. Please contact the Darrington Ranger District at (360) 436-1155, or *www.fs.fed.us/r6/mbs*, for updates.

BOULDER RIVER WATERFALL

BEFORE YOU GO
Maps Green Trails No. 77
Oso, No. 109 Granite Falls;
USGS Meadow Mountain
Current conditions
Darrington Ranger District
(360) 436-1155
Wilderness Permit required

ABOUT THE HIKE
Day hike or backpack
Easy for children
Year round
2½ miles
250 feet elevation gain

GETTING THERE
- Leave I-5 at exit 208 and drive east on Highway 530 through Arlington.
- Go 19.5 miles from I-5 to French Creek Road/Road No. 2010, at milepost 41. Turn right.
- Drive 3.8 miles to the road end and trailhead, elevation 950 feet.

ON THE TRAIL
A gentle trail, smooth and level enough for small children, takes families comfortably through old-growth forest beside a glacier-fed river in the Boulder River Wilderness. A magnificent destination is the spectacular lace-curtain waterfall at 1¼ miles. A bit beyond, an open area by the river makes a pleasant camp or lunch stop. A particular reason for preserving this valley as wilderness is that it contains one of the few remaining low-elevation old-growth forests. Foresters estimate the age of some of the trees at 750 years. All along the path look for awesome

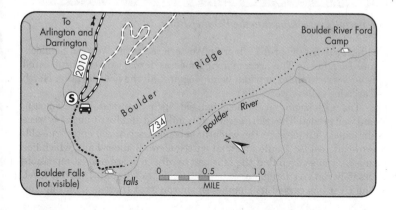

Waterfalls cascading into the Boulder River

old-growth Sitka spruce, silver fir, Western red cedar, Western hemlock, and Douglas-fir. The accompanying mosses, ferns, berries, shrubs, and flowers are samples of what, before logging, all the low-elevation North Cascades valleys were like.

The walk begins on the bed of an old logging railroad—wide, smooth, and well graded. The trail narrows at ½ mile and ambles through big trees shrouded with moss. At the wilderness boundary you will enter true old-growth forest. At 1 mile, the trail passes above Boulder Falls, which lies in a canyon so deep that the falls can hardly be heard and is impossible to safely view. A short distance beyond, a side trail drops to the river level. The river has carved its channel so sharply that there is no floodplain, leaving the trail nowhere to go except on a narrow shelf between cliffs. At 1¼ miles, find the first of two waterfalls tumbling off cliffs on the far side of the gorge into the river. By midsummer, the tumble is a quiet trickle, but thanks to the low elevation, hikers can come in early spring and even winter, when higher trails are plugged up with snow, to see the wall-curtain waterfall at its peak.

Red cedar

Children enjoy hopping about in the spray and mist. This makes a fine lunch stop or turnaround. The trail continues another 3 miles to Boulder River Ford Camp where the trail abruptly ends.

  OLD SAUK RIVER

BEFORE YOU GO
Map Green Trails No. 111
Sloan Peak
Current conditions
Darrington Ranger District
(360) 436-1155
Northwest Forest Pass required

ABOUT THE HIKE
Day hike
Easy for children
Year round
6 miles
No elevation gain

GETTING THERE

- Leave I-5 at exit 208, heading east on Highway 530 through Arlington to Darrington.
- At the stop sign in Darrington turn right (south) on Darrington Clear Creek Road, which becomes Road No. 20 (Mountain Loop Highway).
- At 3.3 miles from the stop sign in Darrington, look for the trail sign and parking area on the left, elevation 600 feet.

ON THE TRAIL

A lowland, level walk along the Sauk River bed is a Hansel and Gretel wonderland, easy enough for small children or disabled walkers, yet luminously lovely year round. The deep forested trail skirts white-water vistas and then meanders around side streams, pools, and seep ponds where in the heat of summer children can safely play. The Sauk

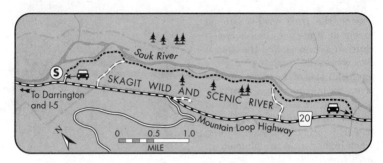

is one of Washington's most scenic rivers, yet this trail along its banks is often overlooked as a family hike. The forest is a magical study in shades of green.

This trail was heavily damaged in the floods of Fall 2003 and extensively rebuilt by volunteers from Washington Trail Association in 2004. Much of this trail has been rerouted but still allows for a great lowland hike in all seasons. Children and adults alike will witness the power of the river, which during the flooding found new courses to flow. The milky-greenish color of the water is due to glacier melt and is colored by hundreds of years of silt ground under the pressure of the ice flowing down Glacier Peak, miles above.

Begin walking through old Douglas-fir, Western hemlock, Western red cedar, red alder, vine maple, and bigleaf maple trees toward the riverbank. Tell children the area was logged in the early part of the twentieth century. A few remnant giant firs remain, and occasional cedar stumps with notches cut from their bases tell the story. It's not ancient forest, but the characteristics of a climax fir and hemlock forest are beginning to emerge. Tell children that a climax forest is one in which most of the trees have reached maturity. Mosses, probably cattail moss and goose-necked moss, encrust and festoon tree limbs and the forest floor as well in a thick carpet. In winter when tree trunks are bare, the light through the trees is filtered through the greenness. Leaning, slender, velvet-covered trunks of alder and vine maple frame views of the river, changing the outlook at every step. The new fronds of sword fern, deer fern, and lady fern emerge from the moss in late April, along with tiny white forest flowers—foamflower, youth-on-age, and vanilla-leaf.

Children can look for salmonberry bushes, with their spring scarlet flowers and summer salmon-colored fruit; and thimbleberry bushes, with white flowers and soft red berries in midsummer. On hot summer days, children can look for those overgrown bumblebees, the hummingbirds, as they fly or stand vibrating on air, inches away from red blossoms.

Bracket fungus, or "conks"—wedge-shaped growths with a hard, dark, upper side and a soft, cream-colored underside—extend out horizontally from the trunks of dying Douglas-firs. Beautiful and varicolored lichens spread over the white bark of the alders. Some leathery green lichens, such as freckle pelt and lungwort, lie loose on the forest floor. Tell children they are considered delicious salad by deer and elk. A particularly spooky, pale-green lichen called common witch's hair hangs from the branches of trees like a tangled mass of wispy, pale, gray-green hair.

The level trail winds through the forest to provide up-close and personal views of the river. The only sound is the rush of the water plummeting over semisubmerged rocks, splashing, rushing, and cascading. Outspreading elderly bigleaf maples shade the trail from the sun's brunt until late afternoon. This trail gains very little elevation in the miles it follows the Sauk River, and the tread is smooth and well maintained.

The Sauk is one of the tributaries of the Skagit, which is a federally designated Wild and Scenic River. The Sauk has changed its course many times over the years and has recently eaten away its banks, so the trail has been rebuilt again by volunteers from the Washington Trails

Fern-edged Sauk River Trail

Association to accommodate this temperamental river. Children will enjoy speculating about how high it gets during flood time and how it deposits its load of logs and stumps. After the walk along the bank, children will enjoy the drive back along the lower river.

In early spring, children can look for gelatinous masses of frog eggs in puddles and backwater pools. If they look closely enough, they can see tiny tadpoles moving in their sacs.

 NORTH FORK SAUK FALLS

BEFORE YOU GO
Maps Green Trails Sloan Peak 111, USGS Sloan Peak
Current conditions Darrington Ranger District (360) 436-1155
Northwest Forest Pass required

ABOUT THE HIKE
Day hike
Easy for children
Year round
½ mile
150 feet elevation loss

GETTING THERE
- Leave I-5 at exit 208 heading east on Highway 530 through Arlington to Darrington.
- At the stop sign in Darrington, turn right (south) on Darrington Clear Creek Road, which becomes Road No. 20 (Mountain Loop Highway).
- Drive 17 miles to milepost 13 and turn left onto Sloan Creek Road No. 49. Go about 1 mile and look for the trail sign and parking area on the right, elevation 1600 feet.

Note: At the time of this printing part of the Mountain Loop Highway, between Bedal Creek and the Monte Cristo Lakes, was closed due to a washout. The anticipated reopening of the full loop road is expected to be in summer of 2008. This trail can only be accessed from the Darrington side of the Mountain Loop Highway, as the driving directions indicate. Please contact the Darrington Ranger District or *www.fs.fed .us/r6/mbs* for updates.

Opposite page: Feeling the spray of the falls

ON THE TRAIL

Drop down a short trail on gentle switchbacks to a powerful and exciting waterfall, particularly torrential during spring run-off. Children will be eager to see it for themselves after they hear its roar. What they will behold is the falls making a sharp right turn to enter a rocky canyon. White water leaps up and children will giggle at the feel of spray on their faces. Hold hands and do not venture onto the narrow ledge at the bottom of the trail. Viewing is fine from the stopping point above it, at least during periods of high run-off.

The quarter-mile woodland trail has rails and steps to make the descent safe and easier. The river descends into a rocky canyon, and though the falls are not high, perhaps only 45 feet, their ferocity, particularly in the spring, makes them wonderful to see. Combine the walk to the falls with any of the other North Fork Sauk River hikes.

 ENGLES GROVE TRAIL NO. 642

BEFORE YOU GO
Maps Green Trails No. 111 Sloan Peak; USGS Sloan Peak
Current conditions Darrington Ranger District (360) 436-1155
Northwest Forest Pass required

ABOUT THE HIKE
Day hike
Easy for children
April to November
½ **mile**
No elevation gain

GETTING THERE

- Leave I-5 at exit 208 and head east on Highway 530 through Arlington to Darrington.
- At the stop sign in Darrington, turn right (south) on Darrington Clear Creek Road, which becomes Road No. 20 (Mountain Loop Highway).
- At 17 miles from the stop sign in Darrington, turn left at milepost 13 onto Sloan Creek Road No. 49.
- In about 3.4 miles look for the trail sign and parking area on the right, elevation 1600 feet.

Note: At the time of this printing part of the Mountain Loop Highway, between Bedal Creek and the Monte Cristo Lakes, was closed due to a washout. The anticipated reopening of the full loop road is expected to be in summer of 2008. This trail can only be accessed from the Darrington side of the Mountain Loop Highway, as the driving directions indicate. Please contact the Darrington Ranger District or *www.fs.fed.us/r6/mbs* for updates.

Harold Engles' cedar tree (Photo by Gary Rose)

ON THE TRAIL

Who was Harold Engles and why is this grove of giant trees named for him? From the road you can't even see them. Is it worthwhile stopping? Yes, it certainly is. Harold Engles, a Darrington Forest Service supervisor for almost forty years and an environmentalist before the word came into popular usage, saved a corridor of these cedar giants from the voracious logging of his time by simply moving logging boundaries to protect the trees. The grove of trees on the riverbank may easily be 1000 years old. A whole classroom full of children might not be able to put their arms around the base of the largest one.

Tell children Harold lived to be ninety-six years old. He explored and made first ascents of many of the mountains they can see. He decided a lookout on the summit of nearby Three Fingers would be useful, but since there was no place on the summit to build one, he ordered that the top 20 feet of the mountain be blasted off to make a building site. Such a decision would be unthinkable today, but to make room for the building's footings, it was done. That lookout is still standing and experienced hikers climb ladders now to reach it.

Walk through the stumps of the cut cedars to reach the huge, living patriarchs. Many old cedars have lost their tops to windstorms and lightning, but the bases of their trunks are enormous. The largest cedar displays a photo of Engles standing next to its trunk in the snow.

 INDEPENDENCE LAKE

BEFORE YOU GO
Map Green Trails No. 110 Silverton
Current conditions
Darrington Ranger District (360) 436-1155; Verlot Public Service Center (360) 691-7791
Northwest Forest Pass required

ABOUT THE HIKE
Day hike or backpack
Moderate for children
July–October
1½ miles
200 feet elevation gain in, 100 feet out

GETTING THERE
- Leave I-5 at exit 194 and go east on US 2.
- In 2.2 miles exit US 2 onto State Highway 204 toward Lake Stevens.
- In 2.6 miles, at the second stoplight, go left onto Highway 9 northbound.
- In 1.7 miles go right onto Highway 92, and drive 8.2 miles to Granite Falls.
- At the second stop sign in Granite Falls, turn left onto Mountain Loop Highway.
- Enter Verlot 11 miles from Granite Falls and find the Verlot USFS Public Information Service Center.
- At 15 miles past the service center, turn left (north) onto Coal Lake Road No. 4060 and continue 4.8 miles to the trailhead and

limited parking at the end of the road, elevation 3600 feet.

Note: At the time of this printing part of the Mountain Loop Highway, between Bedal Creek and the Monte Cristo Lakes, was closed due to a washout. The anticipated reopening of the full loop road is expected to be in summer of 2008. This trail can only be accessed from the Verlot side of the Mountain Loop Highway, as the driving directions indicate. Please contact the Darrington Ranger District, the Verlot Public Service Center, or *www.fs.fed.us/r6/mbs* for updates.

ON THE TRAIL

Close enough to the road for families with small children, small enough to retain warmth from the summer sun, and large enough for numerous campsites, Independence Lake was named for a nearby nineteenth-century mining claim. One August, my delighted children swam all afternoon, disappointed only that we had not brought camping gear so we could stay overnight.

Trail No. 712 may be hard to find as the brush at the beginning of the trail sometimes is overgrown. Look for the trail on the upper hillside of the parking lot. After zigzagging a few hundred yards, it enters old-growth forest, descends ¼ mile, and then climbs gradually for the remaining ½ mile. Roots and rocks in the trail may trip up very young children, but the distance is so short that toddlers can be carried. Watch for wild lily-of-the-valley and salmonberries.

The trail climbs again, gradually, to reach the lake, a very deep one set beneath rock cliffs 1000 feet tall. Independence Lake, elevation 3700 feet, is popular with fishermen. My children thought the northwest end was sunnier and best for swimming. If your children want more hiking options, you can follow a good trail that takes off from the

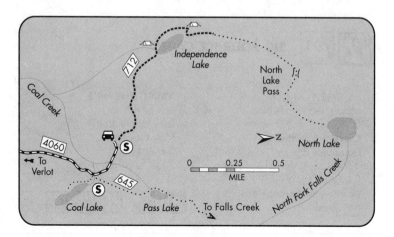

Campsite at Independence Lake

lake to reach North Lake Pass in 1⅓ miles and North Lake in another 1¾ miles.

There are at least six campsites for those who would like to overnight here.

 BIG FOUR ICE CAVES

BEFORE YOU GO
Map Green Trails No. 110 Silverton
Current conditions
Darrington Ranger District (360) 436-1155; Verlot Public Service Center (360) 691-7791
Northwest Forest Pass required

ABOUT THE HIKE
Day hike
Easy for children
May–November
2 miles
200 feet elevation gain

GETTING THERE

- Leave I-5 at exit 194 and go east on US 2.
- In 2.2 miles exit US 2 onto State Highway 204 toward Lake Stevens.
- In 2.6 miles, at the second stoplight, go left onto Highway 9 northbound.
- In 1.7 miles go right onto Highway 92, and drive 8.2 miles to Granite Falls.
- At the second stop sign in Granite Falls, turn left onto Mountain Loop Highway.
- Enter Verlot 11 miles past Granite Falls, and find the Verlot USFS Public Information Service Center.
- At 14.5 miles beyond the service center, turn right (south) to the trailhead, elevation 1700 feet.

Note: At the time of this printing part of the Mountain Loop Highway, between Bedal Creek and the Monte Cristo Lakes, was closed due to a washout. The anticipated reopening of the full loop road is expected to be in summer of 2008. This trail can only be accessed from the Verlot side of the Mountain Loop Highway, as the driving directions indicate. Please contact the Darrington Ranger District, the Verlot Public Service Center, or *www.fs.fed.us/r6/mbs* for updates.

ON THE TRAIL

The nearly level trail, smooth and well maintained, crosses a series of bridges and marsh-spanning plank walkways to arrive at ice caves lying at the base of the 4000-foot north face of Big Four Mountain. Hike to a stopping point beneath the wide cirque headwall, dappled with snow patches and waterfalls. The ice caves are formed when the undersides of avalanche snowbanks melt from the action of water and wind. They vary in size and shape from year to year and do not open until midsummer. In light snowfall years the snow caves may completely melt out by August, so be sure to call ahead. Note that the caves are extremely dangerous and are never safe to enter—ceilings have been known to collapse and tourists have been killed.

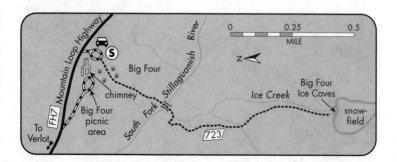

Find the plank trail crossing the marsh (it used to be a golf course!) and swamp. Older kids will have fun stamping along the planks and bridges. Hold tight to the hands of pre-schoolers here. The marsh is punctuated with bright-yellow skunk cabbage, marsh marigolds, and such birds as kingfishers, nuthatches, and hairy woodpeckers. The gnawed branches and trees are signs that beavers are at work. Naturalists love this trail because some plants and trees are those usually found at much higher subalpine elevations.

Cross the South Fork of the Stillaguamish at ½ mile and Ice Creek immediately afterward. Two benches offer welcome seats for parents packing babies. A gentle uphill walk through forest leads to the big picture of Big Four Mountain. The caves can be seen at the foot of a snowfield fan. If you examine the great cliff, you can spot the avalanche chutes down which snow avalanches in winter and water falls year

Plank walkway en route to the ice caves

round. If it's a hot day, cool off near the refrigerated caves and enjoy their unusual shapes and pale blue tones. If you come in early spring you may see and hear the avalanches sweep down.

 KELCEMA LAKE

BEFORE YOU GO
Maps Green Trails No. 110 Silverton; USFS Mount Baker–Snoqualmie
Current conditions
Darrington Ranger District (360) 436-1155; Verlot Public Service Center (360) 691-7791
Wilderness Permit and Northwest Forest Pass required

ABOUT THE HIKE
Day hike or backpack
Easy for children
June–October
1¼ miles
80 feet elevation gain

GETTING THERE
- Leave I-5 at exit 194 and go east on US 2.
- In 2.2 miles exit US 2 onto State Highway 204 toward Lake Stevens.
- In 2.6 miles, at the second stoplight, go left onto Highway 9 northbound.

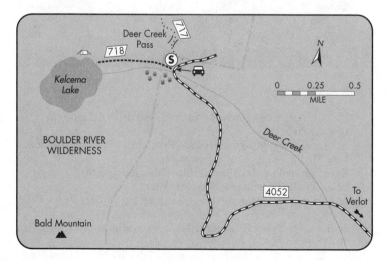

Camp at Kelcema Lake

- In 1.7 miles go right onto Highway 92, and drive 8.2 miles to Granite Falls.
- At the second stop sign in Granite Falls, turn left onto Mountain Loop Highway.
- Enter Verlot 11 miles after Granite Falls, and find the Verlot USFS Public Information Service Center.
- At 12.5 miles past the service center, turn left on Deer Creek Road No. 4052.
- Follow Deer Creek Road 4.2 miles to the trailhead, elevation 3075 feet.

Note: At the time of this printing part of the Mountain Loop Highway, between Bedal Creek and the Monte Cristo Lakes, was closed due to a washout. The anticipated reopening of the full loop road is expected to be in summer of 2008. This trail can only be accessed from the Verlot side of the Mountain Loop Highway, as the driving directions indicate. Please contact the Darrington Ranger District, the Verlot Public Service Center, or *www.fs.fed.us/r6/mbs* for updates.

ON THE TRAIL

This hike takes you through subalpine forest to a large cirque lake. Small children can happily throw stones and sticks in the water for hours or jump in for other water games. This site was once a Boy Scout camp, attained only by a trail that started way down in the valley bottom and climbed all the way in virgin forest.

Trail No. 718 starts in a small marshy meadow. In June, you can see bog orchids, marsh marigolds, grass-of-Parnassus, and chocolate bells here. The trail enters Boulder River Wilderness and penetrates an old forest, cresting a small knoll that overlooks the lake outfall. Part of the trail is over glacier-carved bedrock, exposed by trail builders for the width of the trail. In ½ mile is the lake, elevation 3142 feet. Some 1600 feet above looms Bald Mountain (a different Bald Mountain than the one seen from Boardman Lake, Hike 27).

Large campsites lie amid rock buttresses. The water, dark and deep, appears to have fish. Picture Boy Scouts swimming in its cold waters when they camped here. On the north side of the lake are large, old, and splendid Alaska cedars, many more campsites, and a backcountry toilet.

 MALLARDY RIDGE/WALT BAILEY TRAIL

BEFORE YOU GO
Maps Green Trails No. 110 Silverton; USGS Mallardy Ridge
Current conditions
Darrington Ranger District
(360) 436-1155
Northwest Forest Pass required

ABOUT THE HIKE
Day hike or backpack
Difficult for children
July–October
8 miles
1800 feet elevation gain

GETTING THERE

- Leave I-5 at exit 194 and go east on US 2.
- In 2.2 miles exit US 2 onto State Highway 204 toward Lake Stevens.
- In 2.6 miles, at the second stoplight, go left onto Highway 9 northbound.

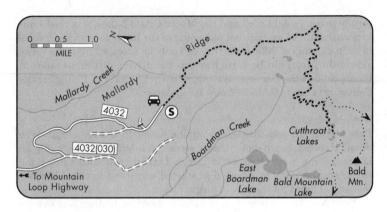

- In 1.7 miles go right onto Highway 92, and drive 8.2 miles to Granite Falls.
- At the second stop sign in Granite Falls, turn left onto Mountain Loop Highway.
- Enter Verlot 11 miles after Granite Falls, and find the Verlot USFS Public Information Service Center.
- At 7 miles beyond the service center, find Mallardy Road No. 4030 on the right; the turnoff is just before Red Bridge.
- Follow Mallardy Road for 1 mile to turn right at Road No. 4032. Drive 5.7 miles to the trailhead at the road end, elevation 3085 feet.

Note: At the time of this printing part of the Mountain Loop Highway, between Bedal Creek and the Monte Cristo Lakes, was closed due to a washout. The anticipated reopening of the full loop road is expected to be in summer of 2008. This trail can only be accessed from the Verlot side of the Mountain Loop Highway, as the driving directions indicate. Please contact the Darrington Ranger District, the Verlot Public Service Center, or *www.fs.fed.us/r6/mbs* for updates.

ON THE TRAIL

These five exquisite alpine lakes are remote enough to be relatively uncrowded. Families who wish to camp can spend several days admiring the lakes' contours or wandering and exploring. Most of the trail was built by Walt Bailey and his friends from Volunteers for Outdoor Washington, who learned their techniques during the Civilian Conservation Corps era. This was a period in the 1930s when the federal government paid workers to build trails, roads, and bridges. The trail has steep switchbacks and narrow tread. It is recommended for children anyway because it provides fairly direct access to these beautiful lakes.

The narrow trail starts out in an overgrown clear-cut and enters old-growth forest in a short distance. The way climbs steadily southeast, steeply at times, contouring on the valley wall above Boardman Creek. At about 1 mile, the path drops slightly and crosses a small creek into meadows. This could make a satisfactory turnaround point for day hikers. Then the trail starts up again and continues, often in marshy areas, to a 3680-foot high point with small glades of heather and blueberries, before dropping 200 feet to a lovely meadow at about 1¾ miles. This would make another good turnaround point for young hikers. The way continues to drop another 200 feet to pass beneath and alongside a high cliff, crosses a rock slide, and then starts up.

With many berry- and heather-covered ups and downs, the trail climbs to the first Cutthroat Lake at 4200 feet, about 4 miles from the road.

Cutthroat Lake

Follow the trail to the largest lake, which features a rocky island and coves and inlets to tempt swimmers and campers. The trail leads to other lakelets, some with metal fire rings and campsites. The terrain is heather-covered hummocks, big subalpine trees, large white granodiorite boulders, and grassy meadows. For a special treat, hike it in the fall when red autumn colors stain the meadows and boulders. Children will want to stay here and play in these beautiful alpine ponds that are just their size.

BOARDMAN LAKE AND LAKE EVAN TRAIL

BEFORE YOU GO
Map Green Trails No. 110 Silverton
Current conditions Darrington Ranger District (360) 436-1155
Northwest Forest Pass required

ABOUT THE HIKE
Day hike or backpack
Easy for children
Mid-June–October
1¾ miles
200 feet elevation gain

GETTING THERE
- Leave I-5 at exit 194 and go east on US 2.
- In 2.2 miles exit US 2 onto State Highway 204 toward Lake Stevens.
- In 2.6 miles, at the second stoplight, go left onto Highway 9 northbound.
- In 1.7 miles go right onto Highway 92, and drive 8.2 miles to Granite Falls.

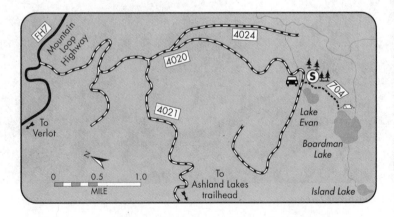

Well-maintained trail to Boardman Lake

- At the second stop sign in Granite Falls, turn left onto Mountain Loop Highway.
- Enter Verlot 11 miles after Granite Falls, and find the Verlot USFS Public Information Service Center.
- At 4.5 miles past the service center, turn right (south) on Schweitzer Creek Road No. 4020. Find the trailhead on the left in 5 miles, elevation 2800 feet. Parking is limited.

Note: At the time of this printing part of the Mountain Loop Highway, between Bedal Creek and the Monte Cristo Lakes, was closed due to a washout. The anticipated reopening of the full loop road is expected to be in summer of 2008. This trail can only be accessed from the Verlot side of the Mountain Loop Highway, as the driving directions indicate. Please contact the Darrington Ranger District, the Verlot Public Service Center, or *www.fs.fed.us/r6/mbs* for updates.

ON THE TRAIL

Two large forest lakes lie within 1 mile of the parking area. The first, Lake Evan, is just off the road—convenient for parents of pre-schoolers who seek a wooded picnic spot. The second, Boardman Lake, with only 200 feet of trail elevation in 1 mile, is deeper, cleaner, and larger, and offers trout fishing and views of Bald Mountain. Children will enjoy wading and splashing from the shore, whether the stay is for a day or overnight.

Trail No. 704 is smooth and well maintained. The path travels through gardenlike old-growth forest whose immense cedars are often topless. These patriarchs are many centuries in the growing and centuries in the dying, bit by bit, as the trees die from the top down. Lake Evan has one marshy campsite and a backcountry toilet.

Climb a small ridge above the outlet creek to look down on Boardman Lake, elevation 2981 feet. It offers five sites plus a group camp, each equipped with benches and fire pits. I have even enjoyed this short hike in midwinter snow, when no one else was around. In midsummer, children can feast on the delicious ripe huckleberries that flourish along the shore.

 LAKE TWENTY-TWO

BEFORE YOU GO
Maps Green Trails No. 109 Granite Falls; USGS Verlot, Mallardy Ridge
Current conditions Darrington Ranger District (360) 436-1155
Northwest Forest Pass required

ABOUT THE HIKE
Day hike
Moderate for children
Mid-June through October
5½ miles
1300 feet elevation gain

GETTING THERE
- Leave I-5 at exit 194 and go east on US 2.
- In 2.2 miles exit US 2 onto State Highway 204 toward Lake Stevens.
- In 2.6 miles, at the second stoplight, go left onto Highway 9 northbound.
- In 1.7 miles go right onto Highway 92, and drive 8.2 miles to Granite Falls.
- At the second stop sign in Granite Falls, turn left onto Mountain Loop Highway.
- Enter Verlot 11 miles beyond Granite Falls; continue past the Verlot USFS Public Information Service Center 2 miles to find the

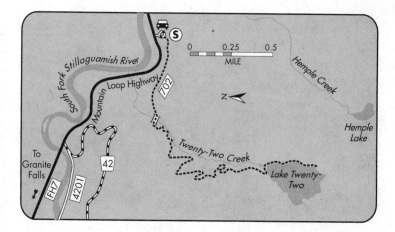

trailhead on the right, elevation 1100 feet. Parking is limited to the established parking lot; parking is *not* allowed on the highway.

Note: At the time of this printing part of the Mountain Loop Highway, between Bedal Creek and the Monte Cristo Lakes, was closed due to a washout. The anticipated reopening of the full loop road is expected to be in summer of 2008. This trail can only be accessed from the Verlot side of the Mountain Loop Highway, as the driving directions indicate. Please contact the Darrington Ranger District, the Verlot Public Service Center, or *www.fs.fed.us/r6/mbs* for updates.

ON THE TRAIL

The most popular trail in the Stillaguamish valley climbs through ancient cedar trees, past picture-perfect waterfalls, and up an old rock slide overgrown with bright vine maple to a cliff-bordered subalpine lake. The lake's elevation is low enough that you can take children here quite early in summer or in late October. This trail has been re-worked to smooth out formerly rough rock- and root-covered areas. A massive new bridge crosses the creek, and a trail with new boardwalks circling the lake gives access to the backside of the lake.

The wide trail immediately plunges into deep shade, contouring the hillside to Twenty-Two Creek and crossing it on a "Billy Goat Gruff" bridge in ⅓ mile. Small children love looking down from the bridge to the white tumult of waterfalls below.

Beyond the bridge, the trail begins a series of switchbacks, climbing steadily through old-growth forest, crossing a talus slope bright with vine maple in autumn, and passing several exciting waterfalls. At 2¾ miles find the outlet of Lake Twenty-Two, elevation 2400 feet.

One year, we found it still snowed in on the Fourth of July, but that

was an unusual year. Usually the only permanent snowfield is at the lake's far end. This trail is so popular that you are unlikely to find solitude on any day of the week. No camping is permitted.

 HEATHER LAKE

BEFORE YOU GO
Map Green Trails No. 109
Granite Falls
Current conditions
Darrington Ranger District
(360) 436-1155
**Northwest Forest Pass
required**

ABOUT THE HIKE
Day hike or backpack
Moderate for children
Mid-June through October
4 miles
800 feet elevation gain

GETTING THERE
- Leave I-5 at exit 194 and go east on US 2.
- In 2.2 miles exit US 2 on State Highway 204 toward Lake Stevens.
- In 2.6 miles, at the second stoplight, go left onto Highway 9 northbound.
- In 1.7 miles go right onto Highway 92, and drive 8.2 miles to Granite Falls.
- At the second stop sign in Granite Falls turn left onto Mountain Loop Highway.
- Enter Verlot 11 miles beyond Granite Falls and continue past the Verlot USFS Public Information Service Center 1 mile.

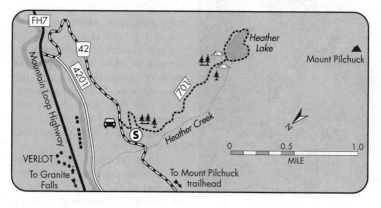

Opposite page: Bridge over Twenty-Two Creek

■ Just over the Pilchuck River bridge turn right (south) on Pilchuck Road No. 42 and continue 1.5 miles to the trailhead, on the left, elevation 1600 feet.

Note: At the time of this printing part of the Mountain Loop Highway, between Bedal Creek and the Monte Cristo Lakes, was closed due to a washout. The anticipated reopening of the full loop road is expected to be in summer of 2008. This trail can only be accessed from the Verlot side of the Mountain Loop Highway, as the driving directions indicate. Please contact the Darrington Ranger District, the Verlot Public Service Center, or *www.fs.fed.us/r6/mbs* for updates.

ON THE TRAIL

The steep and rocky trail ascends through magnificent old-growth cedar and hemlock to a lake in a cirque at the foot of Mount Pilchuck. The trail begins on a 1940s logging road, comfortably wide but surfaced with sharp rock. Children will find footing difficult in places, and toddlers may need to be carried. The last ½ mile winds through old first-growth trees. The lake is large enough for children to wade and splash in.

Trail No. 701 begins across the road from the parking area. Start up in second-growth forest and discover that at 1 mile the beauty begins. The trail passes old Western red and Alaska yellow cedars and follows Heather Creek upward. A waterfall is a good place for a rest stop; large, flat rocks are even provided by Mother Nature.

Woodsy trail to Heather Lake

The sounds of Heather Creek call hikers up to its source. In the next mile, six more switchbacks culminate in a puncheon bridge, where the trail levels out. Begin a slight descent through open forest to a meadow basin, under the walls of Mount Pilchuck, and the lake, elevation 2400 feet. A boardwalk trail now goes all the way around the lake. Children will love circling it and seeing the coves and inlets up close.

Campsites are few, and the Forest Service permits none within 100 feet of the shore in order to let some of the mud start growing flowers again. Swimming on the south shore of the lake is a sure-fire delight for children. The lake is so popular that all camps are filled early on weekends, so a better plan is to come on a weekday.

 ROBE CANYON

BEFORE YOU GO
Map Green Trails No. 109
Granite Falls
Current conditions
Snohomish County Parks (425)
388-3411

ABOUT THE HIKE
Day hike
Moderate for children
March to November
3½ miles
200 feet elevation loss

GETTING THERE

- Leave I-5 at exit 194 and go east on US 2.
- In 2.2 miles exit US 2 on State Highway 204 toward Lake Stevens.
- In 2.6 miles, at the second stoplight, go left onto Highway 9 northbound.
- In 1.7 miles go right onto Highway 92, and drive 8.2 miles to Granite Falls.
- At the second stop sign in Granite Falls turn left onto Mountain Loop Highway.
- At 7.5 miles beyond Granite Falls, watch for the trailhead at a brick sign on the right that reads "Old Robe Trail"; the turnoff to Road No. 41 is on the left, elevation is 1050 feet.

Note: At the time of this printing part of the Mountain Loop Highway, between Bedal Creek and the Monte Cristo Lakes, was closed due to a washout. The anticipated reopening of the full loop road is expected to be in summer of 2008. This trail can only be accessed from the Verlot side of the Mountain Loop Highway, as the driving directions indicate. Please contact the Darrington Ranger District, the Verlot Public Service Center, or *www.fs.fed.us/r6/mbs* for updates.

ON THE TRAIL

This short trail, framed by moss-covered trees leaning over a spectacular river gorge, will appeal to all lovers of beauty, history, and adventure, and will fill any child with delight and wonder. It follows the railroad bed of the ore train that ran from Monte Cristo to Everett over a hundred years ago. The railroad grade is part of the new Robe Canyon Historic Park. Washouts and slides have changed the surface, but occasional reminders of the train route remain. Private land lies

South Fork Stillaguamish River in the Robe Valley

on either side of the trail in some locations; be sure to stay on the trail. Although the trail is relatively easy, in a few places above the river, slides have narrowed the railroad bed to only inches. Children should be watched carefully.

In the first half mile, the trail switchbacks down through a clear-cut. Boy Scout Troop No. 41 of Lake Stevens has added a picnic table at a viewpoint where you may pause. Follow the trail toward the South Fork of the Stillaguamish River. The river grows louder as you approach. In April expect to find skunk cabbage, yellow violets, and tule reeds in swampy places. Reach the river at ¾ mile, where you will find bigleaf maples with their elbows wrapped in moss, and an enormous, spreading, old-growth Sitka spruce.

Because it is a former railroad grade, the trail is mostly level, but it does have several creeks to cross, a rock slide to scramble over, and that narrow section where a slip could be serious. The river gorge has wonderful white-water rapids and narrow channels enclosed by basalt cliffs.

When the mining railroad was being planned by the Rockefeller-Colby-Hoyt interests in 1892, a local engineer named M. Q. Barlow surveyed a route alongside the mountains but some distance above the river, saying that this route would avoid the effects of winter and spring washouts common in the Northwest. "Nonsense," said the New York financiers. "We have the best engineers in the world. This river is a mere trout stream compared to some they have surveyed, and straight down the river gorge is where this railroad will be built." Construction was completed in 1893 at a cost of millions of dollars.

In the winter of 1896 and again in 1897, floods reached the roofs of the tunnels, sweeping away all the timbers and ties. The railroad was rebuilt, and it reopened in 1900, but successive winter avalanches damaged the tracks, and from 1903 to 1907, no ore was shipped. From 1913 to 1920, some ore was shipped from Monte Cristo to Everett refineries, but by that time the Rockefeller financing had pulled out. Let's hope Barlow had a chance to say, "I told you so."

At 1 mile, duck the spray of a small waterfall on the right and look for a remnant of an old concrete and stone railroad grade. Occasional terracing and timber reinforcements show up from here on as the river descends into a canyonlike gorge. The first embedded railway ties

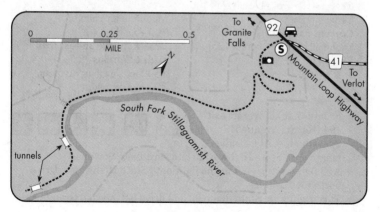

appear about ¼ mile from the entrance to the gorge. Look to your left down a drop of 25 feet to the raging Stillaguamish, and to your right up a cliff wall.

At 1¼ miles you can see the dramatic entrance of Tunnel No. 6—a huge black hole blasted through the basalt, 300 feet long and nearly 30 feet high. Please note that no tunnel is considered completely safe. Enter its jaws at 1¾ miles. Children will be excited at the prospect of walking through it and listening to the sound of leaching water dripping, and parents can be assured that the passage is open. You can use a flashlight to be sure of footing and to inspect the blasted ceiling and parts of old railroad ties, but you usually do not need one since there is light from the other end. This is a good turnaround point.

Changing seasons and water levels vary the difficulty and hazards of this hike. During summer low-water periods, children can scramble in some places to the river's edge. During high-water periods, after fall rains or spring snowmelt, the river boils and thunders down the gorge, with occasional boulders tumbling along with it. During midwinter you may find ice caps on rocks in the river and icicles hanging from the canyon walls, and if the trail is icy, footing can be dangerous.

Beyond this tunnel, the gorge narrows and the river becomes wilder and noisier. In another ¼ mile find the shorter tunnel, No. 5, which is only 100 feet long. Stop at the edge of the gorge for lunch and a view of the white-water rapids of the turbulent South Fork rushing by. Beyond the tunnel, the passage is dangerous for children.

 LIME KILN TRAIL

BEFORE YOU GO
Map Green Trails No. 109 Granite Falls
Current conditions Snohomish County Parks (425) 388-3411

ABOUT THE HIKE
Day hike
Moderate for children
Year round
Lime kiln: 5½ miles; trail end: 6½ miles
160 feet elevation gain out, 300 feet on return

GETTING THERE
■ From I-5, take Everett exit 194 (Hewitt Avenue/US 2) eastbound. At 2.1 miles merge onto State Highway 204, toward Lake Stevens.
■ At 2.6 miles, turn left at the light onto State Highway 9. Drive north for 1.7 miles.
■ Turn right onto State Route 92 and drive 8.2 miles to Granite Falls.

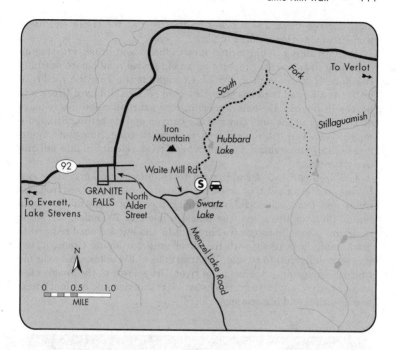

- Proceed through three controlled intersections, and at the North Alder Street stop sign turn right. Drive 0.2 mile to the street end.
- Turn left onto Menzel Lake Road and drive 1.2 miles to Waite Mill Road.
- Go 0.5 mile to the school bus turnaround, where the road branches. Take the left branch and follow it to the road end and trailhead, elevation 700 feet.

ON THE TRAIL

This lesser-known end of Robe Canyon once contained the historic Everett and Monte Cristo Railway line that carried silver and gold. The railroad was built in 1892 and continued to run intermittently, when not closed by floods and slides, until the mines closed in 1920. The lower part continued to be used as a logging railroad until 1934. Today the old railroad grade makes a beautiful walk above and alongside the churning South Fork of the Stillaguamish River. Set aside as part of the new Robe Canyon Historic Park, the safe, nearly level ledge walk is suitable for small children because there is so little elevation gain and loss, and the ledge is wide.

The small stone limekiln destination is only part of the appeal of this trail. The river canyon itself is eerie, with rapids and leaning chartreuse moss-covered trees. The beaches by the river at the trail's end are a wonderful place for children to play.

Begin walking in old second-growth forest and brush, crossing an easement over private property on an old gravel road before reaching the Robe Historic Park at 1 mile. Go right at the T on the road/trail until the old road becomes trail. The trail crosses Hubbard Creek and passes Hubbard Lake before reaching the railroad right-of-way ledge at 1¾ mile and the first views of the canyon and its boiling Stillaguamish River. The ledge walk part is about ¾ mile. Snowmelt determines the water volume, so expect peak river velocity in late fall and early spring.

Children can look for old metal relics: bits of crockery, rusty saw blades, and even old boot soles left behind by mine workers from decades ago. Don't allow children to pick them up; other hikers would like to discover them, too. The limekiln itself, at 2¾ miles, is a stone structure where limestone was brought in and burned until reduced to marketable lime. Along with the silver ore from Monte Cristo, it, too, was sent to Everett to be sold. The trail ends at 3¼ miles, where the old railroad bridge once spanned the river. Drop down to the river's edge and a beach of sand and gravel, listen to its thunder, and eat lunch next to a beautiful and historic spot.

Trailhead sign for Robe Historic Park

I-5: BELLINGHAM SOUTH TO STANWOOD

oastal walks from Bellingham to Stanwood provide children with year-round opportunities to see waterfowl on Puget Sound bays and to walk along dikes, marshes, and wetland. In early spring expect to see snow geese and tundra swans. Fragrance and Whistle Lakes are lowland forested lakes, much like higher mountain lakes but open to families during all seasons. Washington Park, Fidalgo Island, and Sugarloaf Mountain, near Anacortes, offer children chances to look down on whales, barges, ferries, and recreational craft on Puget Sound waters.

 FRAGRANCE LAKE

BEFORE YOU GO
Map Larrabee State Park brochure
Current conditions
Washington State Parks/ Larabee State Park (360) 902-8842

ABOUT THE HIKE
Day hike
Moderate for children
Year round
4 miles
900 feet elevation gain

GETTING THERE

- From Mount Vernon, drive I-5 north to exit 231 and go west and north 15 miles on Chuckanut Drive/Highway 11 to Larrabee State Park.
- To the north, across from the two entrance roads, is a parking place for four or five cars, a trail sign, and the trailhead, elevation 130 feet.

ON THE TRAIL

This beautiful 2-mile trail through low-elevation, old-growth cedars and firs leads upward to a serene woodland lake. The trail, recommended for older children, has a view of boats in Wildcat Cove. Downed nurse logs supporting young hemlocks are a common sight, but children will laugh at the sight of a nurse rock at about 1 mile, with tree roots wrapping the oblong rock like cord around a package. Fragrance Lake is crescent-shaped, has trout and skipping water bugs, and can be circled on a level shoreline trail. Ask your children how they think this lake got its name.

Following the signs, walk the Interurban Trail north for about 500 feet, then go right, plunging into the dense forest on the Fragrance Lake Trail. The trail heads upward, gaining elevation in steep switchbacks. Fire apparently swept up the hillside fairly recently, because the bases of a number of massive firs are blackened. The trail is in fine condition and even provides a bench at one point where families can pause to listen to birds. We watched a nuthatch rhythmically bobbing up and down, and inspected pileated woodpecker holes as rectangular as window frames. In about a mile, make a short side trip left to face the view over Samish Bay. Children can gaze out to Fidalgo, Cypress, Orcas, Samish, and Lummi Islands, then look straight down on the boats and rafts bobbing in Wildcat Cove beneath them. Return to the sometimes-muddy trail, drop down to cross a small creek on a bridge, and continue left and upward.

Intercept the shorter trail ¼ mile before the lake. Mountain bikers have discovered the lake-circling trail, and a number of them join hikers on the trail here. Be prepared for the possibility that one may come upon you suddenly. Not all riders are cautious, and the brush may hide short kids from them until the last second.

Tall salmonberry bushes, alders, and maples screen the first view of the lake. Not to worry, as the shoreline is clearly accessible a bit farther along. A Tinker toy-shaped maple with right-angled bends in its trunk bears investigation by families with small children. At 1030 feet

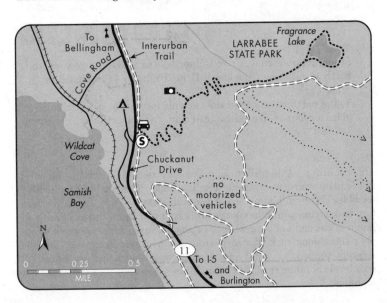

Fragrance Lake

elevation, the lake surface is smooth and on a clear day reflects Chuckanut Mountain. The morning we were here, a pair of American widgeons skidded to a landing across the water.

  WHISTLE LAKE

BEFORE YOU GO
Map Available at Anacortes Visitors Information Center, or you can place an order: Anacortes Community Forest Lands, P.O. Box 547, Anacortes, WA 98221; or (360) 293-1918
Current conditions
Anacortes Visitor Information Center (360) 293-3832

ABOUT THE HIKE
Day hike
Easy for children
Year round
6½ miles
No elevation gain

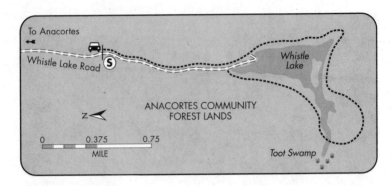

GETTING THERE

- From I-5 take exit 230 and follow Highway 20 west toward Anacortes; stay right where it divides. Follow the highway spur to its end on Commercial Avenue in Anacortes.
- Instead of following the main route into the city, turn left and go 0.3 mile to Commercial Avenue's end. Go right to St. Mary's Drive, left again for one block, and then turn right on Hillcrest.
- Drive past a cemetery and turn right again onto Whistle Lake Road. Follow signs to Whistle Lake, marked "ACFL" for Anacortes Community Forest Lands, and a parking lot, elevation 430 feet.

ON THE TRAIL

This gorgeous former city watershed has become the Anacortes Community Forest Lands. Because it has been protected for decades, Whistle Lake and its network of forest trails have a quiet woodland beauty. Children will think that the lake, seen from several overlooks, is like a wilderness fjord, with its rocky cliffs, steep island, and forested shoreline. The wonder is that, because of the low elevation, this area can be enjoyed at any time of year. With life vests, younger children can safely play on the steep shore or swim in the deep lake. The day we were here a platoon of happy children were all swimming and splashing, wearing life vests.

Although it has been logged, the 2200-acre park still contains some old-growth firs, a flourishing grove of madronas, and many mature cedars and hemlocks. The 25 miles of numbered trails and old roadbeds are designated for different kinds of use: Some are for hiking only, and others are open to bicycles, motorcycles, and horses.

Walk the gated road about ¾ mile to the lake. Numbered trails offer alternative routes around the lake. To stay close to the water except for the high cliff area, and to circumnavigate the lake, stay on trails 20, 205, and 204. Follow the up-and-down 2½-mile trail that circles the lake. It has fascinating views of the island, Toot Swamp, and private picnic spots, but it offers poor swimming for very young children. No campfires are allowed.

Although the spider web of trails is complex, rewards in the Anacortes Community Forest Lands are great. We heard a varied thrush one March day, saw several excellent examples of standing old firs riddled with woodpecker-drilled holes, glimpsed the red flash of a pileated woodpecker's head, and felt the warmth of sunlight filtering through old forest canopy.

Whistle Lake, a great place to swim

WASHINGTON PARK

BEFORE YOU GO
Map Available at Anacortes Visitors Information Center, or you can place an order: Anacortes Community Forest Lands, P.O. Box 547, Anacortes, WA 98221; or (360) 293-1918
Current conditions Anacortes Park Department/ Washington Park Office (360) 293-1927

ABOUT THE HIKE
Day hike
Easy for children
Year round
4²⁄₃ mile loop
No elevation gain

GETTING THERE

- From I-5 take exit 230 and drive west on Highway 20 through Anacortes.
- Follow signs to the San Juan ferry terminal, then continue straight past to the turnoff for Washington Park, heading west.
- At milepost 55-S, still on Highway 20, turn west onto Sunset Avenue.
- Drive 0.8 mile to the Loop Road parking area, elevation sea level.

ON THE TRAIL

Anacortes saved the 200 acres of land for this park decades ago, and what a treasure it is. Children will love being able to walk around Green Point, look out toward Rosario Strait and the San Juans, watch for orcas and porpoises, and then circle back toward the Anacortes waterfront alongside Burrows Channel. The beauty of mossy rock outcrops over water views contrasts with the woodland trail and lush evergreen forest. Have the kids watch for ferries, barges, bald eagles, harbor seals, hawks, and unusual wild flowers usually seen east of the Cascades.

Begin on the Fidalgo Loop trail, below the paved road, to reach Green Point at ¼ mile. Green Point is a grassy bank with benches, tables, and good views of such birds as black oystercatchers with their bright red legs, double-crested cormorants, and

Porpoise

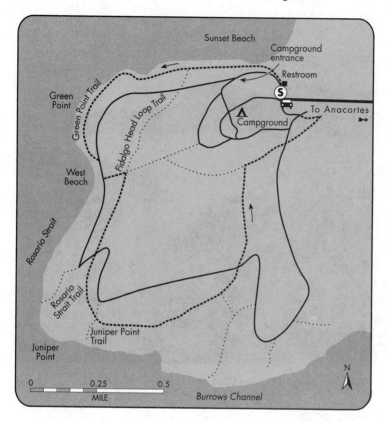

hooded mergansers. Kids will enjoy its beach access at low tide. Join the paved road briefly until you can intercept the Fidalgo Loop Trail again. At Juniper Point, and again at Burrows Bay, there are short, dead-end trails leading out to viewpoints with startling drop-offs. Hold onto hands if you go.

Because of the high, dry exposure on the rock outcrops, some of the flowers you may see are yellow bell, Jeffrey's shootingstars, chocolate lily, calypso orchids, scarlet gilia, blue camas, white (death) camas, fawn lily, yellow monkeyflower, and sea blush. All of them usually grow east of the Cascades. Ask the kids why they think they are growing here.

Madronas and old junipers lean out over the water to frame stunning views. After the Channel View trail lookout point, the Fidalgo Loop trail turns inland again, crossing the paved road through forest and leading you back to the parking lot.

Sweeping view of Burrows Channel

 SUGARLOAF MOUNTAIN

BEFORE YOU GO
Map Available at Anacortes
Visitors Information Center,
or you can place an order:
Anacortes Community Forest
Lands, P.O. Box 547,
Anacortes, WA 98221 or
(360) 293-1918
Current conditions
Anacortes Visitor Information
Center (360) 293-3832

ABOUT THE HIKE
Day hike
Moderate for children
Year round
½ mile
200 feet elevation gain

GETTING THERE

- From I-5 at exit 230, drive west toward Anacortes on Highway 20.
- In 11.1 miles Highway 20 splits. At the traffic light turn left toward Deception Pass/Whidbey Island/Oak Harbor.
- In just less than 2 miles turn right onto Campbell Lake Road.
- Drive 1.5 miles past Lake Campbell (on your left) to a Y and a small general store.
- At the Y turn right onto Heart Lake Road, and in less than 1.5 miles turn right onto Mount Erie Road/Auld Drive.
- Drive 0.7 mile to the trailhead and a small parking area on the left, elevation 750 feet.

ON THE TRAIL

Kids can climb a small mountain and see a magnificent panorama of the San Juan Islands, the Olympic Mountains, Lake Erie, Whidbey Island, and the Strait of Juan de Fuca as their reward for this short summit hike. The views are almost as good as those from Mount Erie, which you

Lake Erie from Sugarloaf Mountain

can drive to, but your children will not be crowded by motorbikes and the mobs who drive to the summit on a clear day. The Sugarloaf Mountain trail is just one of a network of trails in the area that can be followed using the Anacortes Parks Department map and local trail signboards, offering the potential of an enjoyable, all-day adventure for families. For Sugarloaf Mountain, take a lunch and a map, and plan to watch ship traffic in the strait and the sailboats on Lake Erie. Soak in the beauty of the drowned mountain range that has become the San Juans.

Head upward on a narrow trail that passes by rock outcrops covered with moss and lichen and goes through woodland areas. Many alternative trails thread across the mountain, some switchbacking, others leading directly upward. Any will get you to the top, so choose the one whose grade best suits your children. Kids may find the network of possible routes confusing and want to know which is the "real trail"? They are all real. Close to the summit, a dying tree dropped an arching limb just over the trail. Stepping under it, children may feel as if they are walking into a picture frame. In ⅓ mile, expect to find the first view westward, toward Lake Erie and the strait.

A moss-covered rounded rock outcrop, which would be termed a "bald" in the Great Smokies, is Sugarloaf's summit. With a map, help children identify Skagit, Kiket, and Hope Islands to the southeast, Mount Erie to the south, and the eastern shores of Whidbey Island. At any time of the year the views are glorious.

 BOWMAN BAY/ROSARIO HEAD TRAIL

BEFORE YOU GO
Maps Available at Deception Pass State Park headquarters; USGS Deception Pass
Current conditions Washington State Parks (360) 902-8844
State park annual or day-use pass required

ABOUT THE HIKE
Day hike
Easy for children
Year round
2½-miles
Minimal elevation gain

GETTING THERE
- From I-5 at exit 230, drive west toward Anacortes on Highway 20.
- In 11.1 miles Highway 20 splits. At the traffic light turn left toward Deception Pass/Whidbey Island/Oak Harbor.
- In 7.8 miles see Pass Lake on your right. At the south end by the boat launch turn right onto Rosario Road.

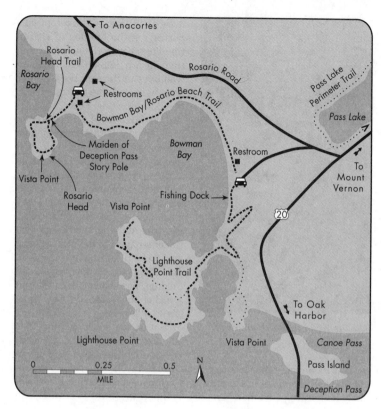

- Immediately on your left is the entrance to Bowman Bay/Rosario State Park. Take the well-signed road down to the parking area, elevation sea level.

ON THE TRAIL

Another gorgeous scenic loop hike around rocky points and through an old forest on Fidalgo Head will delight children. Some of it is on low, sandy beach, but rocky areas also offer them pools to explore at low tide. Year-round views are of Deception Pass, Rosario Strait, the Strait of Juan de Fuca, the Olympics, birds, seals, and all kinds of recreational and commercial fishing boats struggling against or with the Deception Pass current. Caution should be taken by families with small children because some trails have steep drop-offs and none have railings.

Begin on the Rosario Head trail or the Bowman Bay trail, depending on where you park. As you emerge from forest after ¼ mile onto the low beach, listen for the cries of gulls, pass a picnic area, and fishing

The fun of a beach (Photo by Laura Drury)

dock, then look at the totem pole portraying the Maiden of Deception Pass. Kids will enjoy learning that she is a Samish Tribe maiden who lives in the sea. Look for her kelp hair and the clamshells in her clothing.

Continue on the Lighthouse Point Trail around vista points through forest of leaning madronas, salal, and second-growth cedars. Little inlets and bays empty at low tide and fill at high tide. If children could not hear the roar of trucks on the bridges, they might believe they were on a wilderness trail. At the lighthouse, look for a ladder strapped to the rocks leading upward for those who can manage it. This climb is not a safe venture for children, nor should they ever run ahead on the trails with steep drop-offs on cliffs below.

But at sea level, look for little islands of rock lying exposed at low tide. On the return trip, if water is low enough, take time to explore the beautiful tide pools containing starfish, anemones, sculpins, and echinoderms. Marine birds will likely be hunting for lunch here, too. Children will want to stay as long as the tide allows.

Anemone

SKAGIT WILDLIFE AREA

BEFORE YOU GO
Maps Skagit County map;
Skagit Wildlife Area map;
USGS Conway
Current conditions
Washington Department of
Fish and Wildlife Regional
Office (425) 775-1311; Skagit
office (360) 445-4441
**State game access permit
required; available at
sporting goods stores
where fishing licenses
are sold**

ABOUT THE HIKE
Day hike
Easy for children
Most of the year
2-mile loop
No elevation gain

GETTING THERE
- From I-5 at exit 221, go west on State Highway 534 E and drive 0.1 mile to the town of Conway.
- Turn right onto Fir Island Road and find the first of two entrances at 1.7 miles; turn left (south) on Wylie Road and drive 1 mile. The second entrance is at 2.3 miles; turn left onto a dirt road, signed "Hayton/Fir Island Access Road." The trail is at sea level.

Snow geese

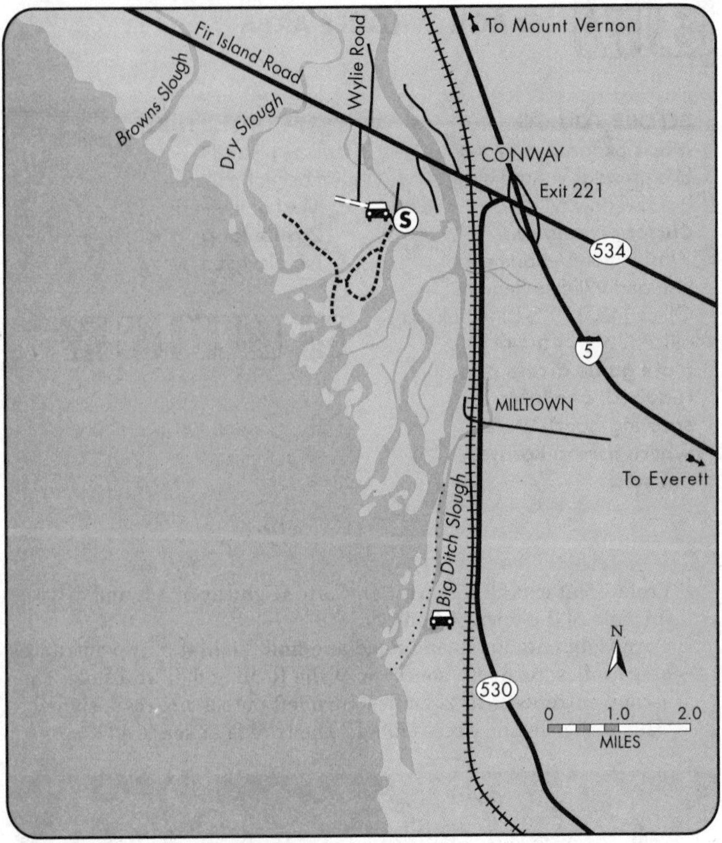

ON THE TRAIL

Here is a tideland marsh children will love at anytime but especially in the winter when migrating snow geese and protected trumpeter and tundra swans settle around them on the dikes and fields. The whirring sound of the big white birds as they call, land, and feed in the fields is unlike any other. Up to 200,000 swans can be seen here at a time in the winter and as many as 100,000 ducks in the fall. The Skagit delta provides a 400-acre wetland recreation area with walks along the dikes out to the saltwater; this land is recognized as an important resting area for migrating birds. Some of these dikes may be reduced in the future in the name of salmon restoration. Do not venture out during hunting season, which is from October through January.

The 2-mile loop out on the dikes toward the sound is on the raised trail; a covered picnic area offers refuge in the rain. Views of the North Cascades and stunning close-ups of Mount Baker hover above the marshy bays, fields, and mud-flats. Nearly 200 species of birds have been sighted here. A barred owl was resting on a branch behind the headquarter building when we were here, and we watched flocks of tundra swans flying above us in close formation. The wetland habitat supports blue and green pelicans, cranes, curlews, woodpeckers, wood ducks, harbor seals, river otters, beaver, black-tailed deer and coyotes. Be alert to changing tides.

  BIG DITCH

BEFORE YOU GO

Maps Skagit County map; Skagit Wildlife Area map; USGS Conway

Current conditions Washington Department of Fish and Wildlife Regional Office (425) 775-1311; Skagit office (360) 445-4441

State game access permit required; available at sporting goods stores where fishing licenses are sold

ABOUT THE HIKE

Day hike
Easy for children
Most of the year
½ mile and up
No elevation gain

GETTING THERE

■ From I-5 take exit 212 (Stanwood/Camano Island) and drive west 5 miles on Highway 532.

■ Turn right on Pioneer Highway SR 530 and follow it for 2.6 miles to reach a road labeled "Old Pacific Highway."

■ Cross the road and then some railroad tracks but continue west on a gravel road labeled "Big Ditch Access." Drive 0.1 mile to reach the parking lot of the Big Ditch portion of the Skagit Wildlife Refuge, at sea level.

ON THE TRAIL

Don't be put off by the name. A walk along a dike near the southeast shore of Skagit Bay and inside the Skagit Wildlife Recreation Area provides families with wide views of birds and saltwater marshes. Except during hunting season (October through January), this is a wondrous

Great Blue Heron sentinel

place to see eagles, ducks, trumpeter and tundra swans, snow geese, dunlins, red-winged blackbirds, kestrels, and peregrine falcons. Children will have a hard time understanding why some of the time the birds are provided refuge here, and some of the time they are hunted. Once I saw a snowy owl perched here on nearby driftwood, doing his own hunting.

Go through a turnstile in a gate and hike across the top of the dike, built half a century ago to drain local farmers' fields. Point out to children that the one-way valve protects the fields from tidal water backing up into the fields. You can walk left (west) for ¼ mile to the slough's southernmost point where it empties into Puget Sound, or right (north) for a mile or more along the dike. If you walk north you will pass privately owned duck-hunting cabins, but you will still be on public land. On a good day Mount Baker and the Twin Sisters may float above on the northern horizon. In February the fields may be white with snow geese and trumpeter swans and you will hear the sounds of their murmuring.

Opposite page: Enjoying the view (Photo by Joan Burton)

hese San Juan Island hikes are a special collection of trails on the three islands, offering glimpses of migrating whales and flotillas of fishing boats. Historic points on San Juan Island trails make reference to the Pig War between the British and the Americans, which children will enjoy. Hikes to Spencer Spit and Watmough Bay, on Lopez Island, help children imagine what life as a homesteader here must have been like. Orcas Island hikes, such as the Mountain Lake and Twin Lakes trails, are unique because they give kids the feeling of being high on a mountain on an island. Be sure to see the airplanelike views from the summit of Mount Constitution and to swim in Cascade Lake in Moran State Park while you are on Orcas.

LOPEZ ISLAND

 SPENCER SPIT STATE PARK

BEFORE YOU GO
Map Washington State Parks map
Current conditions Washington State Parks (360) 902-8844; Washington State Ferry schedule (800) 84-FERRY
State park annual or day-use pass required; reservations for camping required; permit required for gathering shellfish

ABOUT THE HIKE
Day hike or backpack
Easy for children
Year round
½ mile
No elevation gain

GETTING THERE
- Leave I-5 at exit 230. Go west onto Highway 20 for 15.6 miles into Anacortes.
- Continue on the Highway 20 Spur, then go left on 12th Street at the stoplight.
- Arrive at the San Juan Ferry Terminal in 3 miles. Take a ferry to Lopez Island.
- Leave the ferry and travel south on Ferry Road 1.1 miles to a left turn onto Port Stanley Road.
- In 2.5 miles turn left onto Baker View Road.

Driftwood fort on Spencer Spit

■ In another 0.5 mile, at the first corner, drive straight into the park entrance and follow signs to beach-access parking, elevation 50 feet.

ON THE TRAIL

A child-fascinating sand spit encloses a saltwater lagoon in a state park on Lopez Island. Homesteaded at the beginning of the century, the spit houses a replica of the original settler's cabin at its tip, inviting children to come and play. Two mirages may disappoint them, however: No, the spit does not reach Frost Island (there is a deep, swift channel separating them), and no, they cannot play in the lagoon and marsh. These are fragile areas reserved for birds and marine life. But abundant other activities present themselves to kids, and they will not want to leave Spencer Spit. Be certain to check the ferry schedule before you go, and remember that on sunny summer weekends, the wait for the ferry can be long. Reservations for camping on the island should be made well in advance for the best chance of getting a spot.

Drop to the beach on a 100-yard-long wooded trail. Although the spit is shaped like a hollow triangle, because of outflow creeks, only one leg of the triangle can be walked to the spit's end. A half-mile-long built-up trail makes easy walking for small kids, but so does the gently sloping, south-facing beach. Digging for cockles, mussels, butter clams, horse clams, and geoducks is excellent during low tides. Water heated by the sun as it returns over tide flats is warm enough for children to swim in.

Within the spit, in the marshy lagoon, kids can look for gulls, ducks, great blue herons, geese, and many sandpipers—large and small.

The old log cabin is a magnetic feature, drawing children in to explore and speculate about what it was like to live there. Did homesteaders live mainly on clams and fish? What was it like here during winter storms? Families can take shelter from the wind and munch on sandwiches brought from home. Fires should be built only in the circular fire pits provided in the picnic area.

A mandatory walk to the farthest point of the spit provides more questions. Will the spit keep on growing? Will it ever reach Frost Island across the narrow stretch of water? Why not?

Walk-in campsites along the shoreline (reservations required) make it possible for families to camp and enjoy the beauty of the San Juans, lighted ferryboats coming and going, and glorious views of Mount Baker, best seen at sunset and sunrise.

 WATMOUGH BAY

BEFORE YOU GO
Maps Lopez Island map; USGS Richardson
Current conditions San Juan Land Bank (360) 378-4402; Bureau of Land Management (509) 665-2100; Washington State Ferry schedule (800) 84-FERRY

ABOUT THE HIKE
Day hike
Easy for children
Year round
1 mile
No elevation gain

GETTING THERE
- Leave I-5 at exit 230. Go west onto Highway 20 for 15.6 miles into Anacortes.
- Continue on the Highway 20 Spur, then go left on 12th Street at the stoplight.
- Arrive at the San Juan Ferry Terminal in 3 miles. Take a ferry to Lopez Island.
- From the ferry landing on Lopez Island, drive 2.1 miles on Ferry Road, then jog left and then right again onto Center Road.
- Follow it south 5.6 miles to the Mud Bay Road intersection, and turn left onto it.
- Turn left at Huggins Road onto Watmough Head Road and continue for 0.8 mile to the road end and signed trailhead, elevation sea level.

ON THE TRAIL

An intimate, secluded cove on the southeast corner of Lopez Island offers views of Rosario Strait due east to radio towers on Mount Erie, and a gentle sand and gravel beach for swimmers. On either side of the bay are the steep rock cliffs of Watmough Head on the left and Chadwick Head on the right. The short forest trail is old second-growth woodland, maintained jointly by the Bureau of Land Management and the San Juan County Land Bank. Children will enjoy the seclusion and beauty of this beach. Swimming is good when water is warmed after it returns over sand heated by the sun. Be certain to check the ferry schedule before you go, and remember that on sunny summer weekends, the wait

Watmough Bay (Photo by Jessi Christiansen)

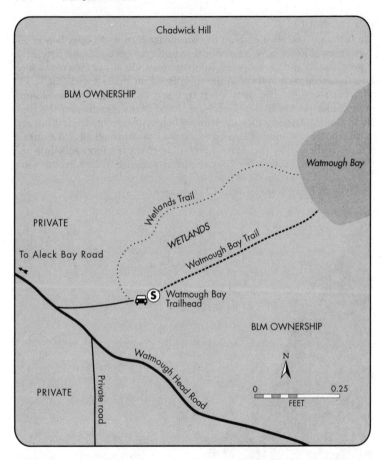

for the ferry can be long. Reservations for camping on the island should be made well in advance for the best chance of getting a spot.

Native American tribes came to the San Juan Islands from the mainland and Canada to bury their dead on wooden platforms in sacred burial places under cliffs such as these. Indians picked berries and burned island grasslands to improve hunting 10,000 to 15,000 years ago. The earliest Europeans here were Spanish and Portuguese explorers. Watmough Head's pioneer homesteaders were the Chadwick family, who built a home looking down on the bay here in 1873.

Walk ½ mile through forest on a straight, level trail. Pass a cattail-filled swamp on the left and come out through driftwood to the gentle, square-shaped bay. No camping is allowed, but take a picnic lunch and plan to stay awhile at this charming, pristine beach.

ORCAS ISLAND

 MOUNTAIN LAKE AND TWIN LAKES

BEFORE YOU GO
Maps Washington State Parks map; Moran State Park handout
Current conditions Moran State Park (360) 902-8844; Washington State Ferry schedule (800) 84-FERRY
State park annual or day-use pass required

ABOUT THE HIKE
Day hike or backpack
Moderate for children
March to November
4- to 6¼-mile loop
400 feet elevation gain

GETTING THERE

- Leave I-5 at exit 230. Go west on Highway 20 for 15.6 miles into Anacortes.
- Continue on the Highway 20 Spur, then go left on 12th Street at the stoplight.
- Arrive at the San Juan Ferry Terminal in 3 miles. Take a ferry to Orcas Island.
- After exiting the ferry, turn left and follow signs to Moran State Park, reached in 14 miles, about 5 miles past the town of East Sound.
- Once in the park, turn left onto Mount Constitution Road.
- At 2 miles turn right into Mountain Lake Landing and park near the landing dock and trailhead, elevation 1100 feet.

ON THE TRAIL

What child could resist walking through forest on this wide, easy trail, sometimes at lake level, sometimes 100 feet above it? Waves lap and slurp alongside. Fish jump and jump again. In April, May, and June, ospreys swoop and cry to hikers, almost as if taunting them. Take a lunch and find a sandy beach at the halfway point where

Osprey

the kids can splash and swim. For some, the 4-mile route around Mountain Lake will be enough; for others, the additional 2¼ miles round trip off the Mountain Lake route to Twin Lakes is an added adventure. The Twin Lakes destination includes a single family-size campsite, making this a possible backpack trip. Be certain to check the ferry schedule before you go, and remember that on sunny summer weekends, the wait for the ferry can be long. Reservations for camping on the island should be made well in advance for the best chance of getting a spot.

Begin hiking counterclockwise, following the shore to Cascade Creek, the lake's outlet creek, and a tiered concrete dam, built to supply water to the community of Olga. Drop below the dam, passing a side trail to Cascade Creek, and briefly follow a construction road. Pass a trail for Mount Pickett, and then bear left on the lake trail, skirting its shore. Old snags standing in the water attract woodpeckers and other birds. Children can listen for their rat-a-tat, and the haunting sounds of ospreys' calls. The trail zigzags away from the lake through forest, then begins a gradual climb to high, mossy rock bluffs with the best views of Mount Constitution on a clear day. Kids will enjoy switchbacking steeply down through mossy rocks to the lake level again. They may wonder about the rocky islands stretched along the length of the lake. Have these islets been explored? Could they walk out on a tiny peninsula and swim to the closest one?

In shallow coves at the north end of the lake, kids can wade and swim in the cool water. In 2⅛ miles from the trailhead, find a branching trail leading to Twin Lakes. These two little lakes on a ridge below Mount Constitution will appeal to children who will find them just their size. Swimming and wading in both of them is cold but possible in their shallow coves. A good campsite on the southeast shore of the smaller lake would make a private camp for one family. Continue hiking on the Bonnie Sliger Trail from the parking area beside the campground on Mountain Lake. The trails here were originally built in the 1930s,

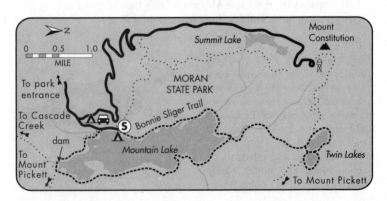

View of Mountain and Twin Lakes

but this one was improved and named for a young Youth Conservation Corps supervisor who died from a fall at nearby Doe Bay in 1977. The two lakes are small but appeal to children because of their mountain-on-an-island setting. Only a small ridge separates them. When the kids reach the outfall creek, they can see and hear it tumbling below.

Returning to the Mountain Lake loop, keep left through an open glade of alders and maples and round the lake's end. Shady groves exist alongside inlets and bays on the west side of Mountain Lake, sheltering a few areas shallow enough for kids to swim in. The east side has at least two 100-foot climbs, plus numerous ups and downs. The west side has one high point. Continue to the trail's starting point and a walk-in camping area on a little peninsula. Trail-side camping is not allowed.

OBSTRUCTION PASS

BEFORE YOU GO
Map San Juan County road map
Current conditions Moran State Park (360) 902-8844; Washington State Ferry schedule (800) 84-FERRY
State park annual or day-use pass required

ABOUT THE HIKE
Day hike or backpack
Easy for children
Year round
1 mile
100 feet elevation loss

GETTING THERE

- Leave I-5 at exit 230. Go west on Highway 20 for 15.6 miles into Anacortes.
- Continue on the Highway 20 Spur, then go left on 12th Street at the stoplight.
- Arrive at the San Juan Ferry Terminal in 3 miles. Take a ferry to Orcas Island.
- Turn left after exiting the ferry and follow signs to Moran State Park, reached in 14 miles, about 5 miles past the town of East Sound.
- In the park, pass Cascade Lake and continue 3 more miles.
- Turn left onto Doe Bay Road. In 0.5 mile turn right at the Y in the road, and follow signs to Obstruction Pass Park. Find the trailhead at the parking lot, elevation sea level.

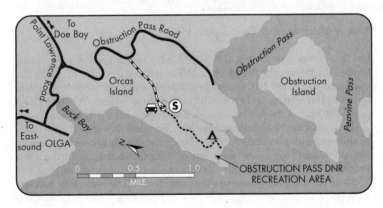

End of Obstruction Pass Trail

ON THE TRAIL

A secluded Orcas Island beach offers children good beachcombing, with small coves on the west side that are safe for wading and swimming. Reach this state park and campsite by a short forest walk to a pebble beach. Kids can watch for kayakers, who like to put in on this beach. Although this is a short hike, plan to spend a good part of the day seeing the many sights at this lesser-known park. Be certain to check the ferry schedule before you go, and remember that on sunny summer weekends, the wait for the ferry can be long. Reservations for camping on the island should be made well in advance for the best chance of getting a spot.

Begin hiking on a level trail through mixed alder and fir forest with windfall from the great Siberian Express storm of 1989 and two north-easterlies of 1990, mostly cleared now. Lush ferns and salal enrich the trail above East Sound, but steep banks and drop-offs near the end of the trail mean children should not run ahead or be unaccompanied. Short side trails lead to cliffs above the water that offer views up East Sound to Olga and Rosario Resort. At ½ mile the trail reaches a walk-in campground, circles the camp area, then drops 15 feet to the crescent-shaped beach and views of the west side of Orcas and Lopez Islands, with ferries approaching and leaving Upright Head on Lopez.

At high tide children will enjoy playing and looking for agates and other treasures on the steep beach made up of multicolored pebbles. At low tide they can explore tide pools on either side of the bay. Kayakers wearing hooded wet suits frequently arrive or depart, providing enter-tainment for curious children, and yachts sometimes sail in to tie up to one of the mooring buoys just offshore. Other views from this beach are of Obstruction and Blakely Islands; if you look to the east, you will see Frost Island, off Spencer Spit (Hike 39).

SAN JUAN ISLAND

 ENGLISH CAMP AND BELL POINT

BEFORE YOU GO
Maps San Juan Island National Historical Park brochure; USGS Roche Harbor
Current conditions English and American Camp Information (360) 378-2902; Washington State Ferry schedule (800) 84-FERRY

ABOUT THE HIKE
Day hike
Easy for children
Year round
1-mile loop
No elevation gain

GETTING THERE
- Leave I-5 at exit 230. Go west on Highway 20 for 15.6 miles into Anacortes.
- Continue on the Highway 20 Spur, then go left on 12th Street at the stoplight.
- Arrive at the San Juan Ferry Terminal in 3 miles. Take a ferry to Friday Harbor on San Juan Island.
- Departing the ferry, follow Spring Street up through town, and then follow signs to Roche Harbor, on Roche Harbor Road
- At 9.5 miles from the ferry dock, the road takes a sharp turn at Westcott Bay. Turn left and follow West Valley Road 1.5 miles to the signed entrance to English Camp and the parking lot, elevation 100 feet.

ON THE TRAIL
This level forest and waterfront trail will entice children along the shoreline of San Juan Island's Garrison Bay and around Bell Point to a low bank picnic area with a view of Westcott Bay. Tell them to watch for eagles and osprey when the tide is low. The birds pick up exposed clams for their dinners, then swoop upward and drop them on the rocks below to crack them open. For information on digging your own shellfish on Bell Point

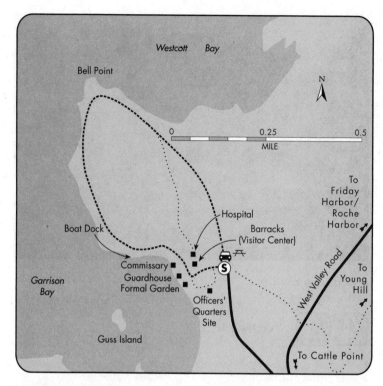

shores, check with rangers for permits, locations, and limits. If the tide is out, you can also reach Bell Cove along the beach. Little wild blackberries in season are another temptation. Be certain to check the ferry schedule before you go, and remember that on sunny summer weekends, the wait for the ferry can be long. Reservations for camping on the island should be made well in advance for the best chance of getting a spot.

The garden and restored buildings of English Camp are remnants of the 150-year-old Pig War, when both the Americans and British claimed San Juan Island and maintained garrisons of soldiers for twelve years before the boundary was settled. Kids will enjoy the video explaining how both nations almost went to war over an American's shooting of a British pig.

After seeing the restored blockhouse, formal flower garden, and hospital, find the trailhead in the forest to the north of the parade ground. Follow the water-level path around the point and enjoy views of San Juan Island harbors and beaches framed through leaning madrona tree trunks. Wild turkeys are common on San Juan Island and one may surprise you and your children with its cackles and gobbles.

British garden built at the time of the Pig War

 YOUNG HILL

BEFORE YOU GO
Maps San Juan Island map; English Camp handout; USGS Roche Harbor
Current conditions English Camp information (360) 378-2902; Washington State Ferry schedule (800) 84-FERRY

ABOUT THE HIKE
Day hike
Moderate for children
Year round
2½ miles
650 feet elevation gain

GETTING THERE

- Leave I-5 at exit 230. Go west on Highway 20 for 15.6 miles into Anacortes.
- Continue on the Highway 20 Spur, then go left on 12th Street at the stoplight.
- Arrive at the San Juan Ferry Terminal in 3 miles. Take a ferry to Friday Harbor on San Juan Island.
- Departing the ferry, follow Spring Street up through town and then follow signs to "Roche Harbor" on Roche Harbor Road.

■ At 9.5 miles from the ferry dock the road takes a sharp turn at Westcott Bay. Turn left and follow West Valley Road to the signed entrance to English Camp in 1.5 miles. The trailhead is at the top side of the parking lot, elevation 100 feet.

ON THE TRAIL

A short, steep trail runs east from San Juan Island's English Camp through second-growth forest and up Young Hill to afford the kids a spectacular view of bays and coves of its northwest end. The effort to reach it is well worthwhile. Along the way, look for a nineteenth-century cemetery for the seven British soldiers who died of natural causes during the Pig War. A hundred feet from the top, find an interpretive display that names the sights you see below. Be certain to check the ferry schedule before you go, and remember that on sunny summer weekends, the wait for the ferry can be long. Reservations for camping on the island should be made well in advance for the best chance of getting a spot.

Begin walking below the West Valley Road, cross it, and continue climbing on a former service road past the short side trail to the cemetery. Plan to stop for it on the way down. Turn left at the fork and climb steadily along the north shoulder of the mountain to the rock outcrop platform just below the summit.

Views are like those from a plane. Kids can gaze out over Garrison Bay to Haro Strait and Vancouver Island. Closer bays look like small lakes. Climb another hundred feet to the highest point on San Juan Island; look east to Mount Baker and Mount Erie on Fidalgo Island, and south to the Olympic Mountains. There is an interpretive sign here that details the view before you. Watch children feel the satisfaction of reaching a remarkable view where the British marines had an observation post 150 years ago.

Trail leading up Young Hill

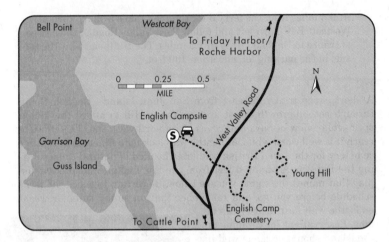

The old cemetery in a grass clearing has a white picket fence around the ornate Victorian gravestones. Children will want to read about how the servicemen died and to speculate about what it was like to live and die here, stationed so far from home.

4 5 LIME KILN STATE PARK

BEFORE YOU GO
Maps San Juan National Historical Park brochure; USGS Roche Harbor
Current conditions Washington State Parks (360) 902-8844; Washington State Ferry schedule (800) 84-FERRY
State park annual or day-use pass required

ABOUT THE HIKE
Day hike
Easy for children
Year round
1½ miles
Minimal elevation gain

GETTING THERE

- Leave I-5 at exit 230. Go west on Highway 20 for 15.6 miles into Anacortes.
- Continue on the Highway 20 Spur, then go left on 12th Street at the stoplight.
- Arrive at the San Juan Ferry Terminal in 3 miles. Take a ferry to Friday Harbor on San Juan Island.

- Departing the ferry, follow Spring Street up through town, past the shopping center by the airport. The road becomes San Juan Valley Road.
- About 1.5 miles from the dock, turn left (south) onto Douglas Road, which eventually becomes Bailer Hill Road and then West Side Road.
- Lime Kiln State Park is about 9 miles from the ferry dock, on the left. The trail is at sea level.

ON THE TRAIL

Here in a state park on San Juan Island are opportunities to view passing whales and a 1919 lighthouse, along with a reconstructed beachside furnace where limestone used to be cooked down, then shipped all over the world. Be certain to check the ferry schedule before you go, and

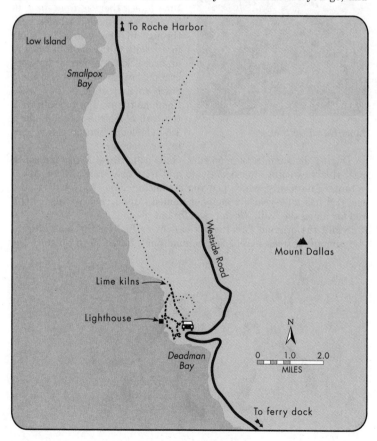

Lime Kiln Lighthouse

remember that on sunny summer weekends, the wait for the ferry can be long. State Parks suggests using the bus system to reach the park rather than driving a car in heavy summer traffic onto the ferry. Reservations for camping on the island should be made well in advance for the best chance of getting a spot.

Children will love standing on the rock beside the lighthouse watching for the dorsal fins and spouts of passing orcas. The best time to see them is from June to September, although whales pass throughout the year. The short forest walk to the old kiln leads to an overlook of the former lime operation, but the kids can also climb down to inspect it if they wish. Combine the trail to the kiln with the trail along the shoreline for a 1½-mile loop. Sunset views here are spectacular.

During the summer salmon run, whale pods travel north and south past this viewpoint almost daily, to and from the Fraser River. Ask a volunteer naturalist which pod you are seeing. Some have babies, and one pod has a 90-year-old member named Cappuccino. We also saw a red fox along the trail, which posed for our photos.

Sadly, the original forest was clear-cut as fuel for the lime kiln, so the remaining trees, except for the madronas, have grown up since the

Fox

kiln's operating days. Lime was formed from ancient seashells buried in a trench millions of years ago. San Juan's supply of lime was so abundant that processing it became the island's major industry for 90 years, until the middle of the twentieth century. Miners dug out the raw limestone and then sent it down the cliffs in little train cars to the wood-fired kiln, which had to be heated up to 2000 degrees to cook the limestone. Twenty tons of limestone would be transformed into 9 tons of lime in a day. What would it have been like to do the work? Tell the kids that the white streaks they can see along the cliffs are remnants of the lime-making process. Excavations and remains of old buildings can still be seen here beyond the border of the park. The lighthouse has been in continuous operation since 1919 and is listed in the National Register of Historic Places.

 CATTLE POINT LIGHTHOUSE

BEFORE YOU GO
Maps San Juan National Historical Park brochure; USGS False Bay
Current conditions San Juan County Parks (360) 378-8420; Washington State Ferry schedule (800) 84-FERRY

ABOUT THE HIKE
Day hike
Easy for children
Year round
¼-mile loop, plus numerous nearby trails
100 feet elevation gain from lighthouse to beach

GETTING THERE

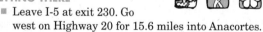

- Leave I-5 at exit 230. Go west on Highway 20 for 15.6 miles into Anacortes.
- Continue on the Highway 20 Spur, then go left on 12th Street at the stoplight.
- Arrive at the San Juan Ferry Terminal in 3 miles. Take a ferry to Friday Harbor on San Juan Island.
- Departing the ferry, follow Spring Street through town and up the hill past the fire station. Turn left onto Argyle Road, which becomes Cattle Point Road.
- At 6 miles from the ferry terminal, enter American Camp. Proceed through the park until the road turns sharply north at Cattle Point, elevation sea level.

ON THE TRAIL

A glacier-scraped rock point and a lighthouse at San Juan Island's Cattle Point Lighthouse Recreation Site separate a Department of Natural Resources interpretive center and picnic area. Children can walk the gravel

Lighthouse and seascape beyond

beach out to the rock point and then climb up the sand dune hill to the old lighthouse to complete the loop. Whale watching is superb during the summer months, as evidenced by a constant flotilla of whale-watching boats. The sweeping view is of the Strait of Juan de Fuca, Haro Strait, Lopez Island, Port Townsend, Port Angeles, and the Olympic Mountains. There are numerous trails at American Camp to explore, making this an ideal spot for a weekend of fun. Be certain to check the ferry schedule before you go, and remember that on sunny summer weekends, the wait for the ferry can be long. Reservations for camping on the island should be made well in advance for the best chance of getting a spot.

Because of the Fraser River salmon runs in the channel and strait, your chances of seeing seals and whales here are excellent during June and July and more sporadic in August and September. A concrete building, once a Coast Guard radio station, has become a picnic shelter with a fireplace for stormy days.

Begin by scanning the water for marine animals and birds. Oyster-catchers, gulls, and cormorants are common on the rocky islands in Cattle Pass. On the rocks below the lighthouse, children can see evidences of the ancient glacier in the deep grooves carved in a north-to-south direction. Watching the spectacular currents can be mesmerizing. Climb steeply to reach the lighthouse. The sand dunes 80 feet above the rocks and around the lighthouse are a great discovery for kids. They can jump and slide until they are tired. A trail through beach plants leads back to the parking area.

After the hike, drive back ½ mile to South Beach for more long, low, sandy beaches with picnic areas, beach logs to sit on, and waves from the wakes of freighters.

Opposite page: Hiking on Whidbey Island (Photo by Tara Irvin)

WHIDBEY ISLAND AND EVERETT **AREA**

The Whidbey Island and Everett area hikes include such lovely trails as Goose Rock, at Deception Pass, and halfway down the island, Ebey's Landing, a low beach walk with a high bank above it offering viewpoints down the strait. Spencer Island, east of Everett, can give families a birding walk and a view of aging tugboats moored along Ebey Slough, and Jetty Island, in Everett's harbor, is a low sand island dredged up out of the river mouth, accessible by walk-on ferry during summer months. Osprey and cormorants are easy to see from Jetty Island, where they have nested on old pilings.

WHIDBEY ISLAND

DECEPTION PASS STATE PARK

BEFORE YOU GO
Map USGS Deception Pass
Current conditions
Washington State Parks (360) 902-8844; Washington State Ferry schedule (800) 84-FERRY
State park annual or day-use pass required

ABOUT THE HIKE
Day hike
Easy for children
Year round
First loop: 1 mile; second loop: 2 miles
200 feet elevation gain

GETTING THERE
- Leave I-5 at exit 230. Go west on Highway 20 toward Anacortes.
- In 11.1 miles Highway 20 splits at a traffic light; go left (south) toward Deception Pass/Whidbey Island/Oak Harbor.
- In 8 miles cross over Deception Pass. In 1 mile from the bridge turn right into the park. Follow the main park road past the camping areas to the day-use parking next to Cranberry Lake, at sea level.

ON THE TRAIL
Deception Pass is an ideal place to take children for a day, a weekend, or a week, offering a lot of sand to shovel, scoop, and play in; a mammoth bridge to gaze up at; eagles to spot; boats to watch; and numerous forest trails to explore.

Of the many trails to explore, the two described here are my favorites

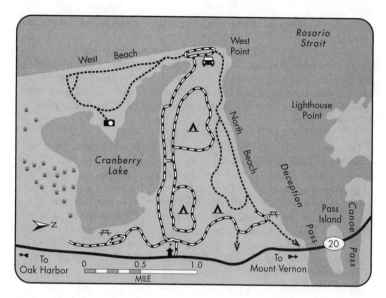

with children. If your children are like mine, they will first want to head for the sand dunes. On the Cranberry Lake side of the parking lot, find the paved trail behind the rest rooms. The trail passes a series of dunes covered with sedge, beach morning glory, and beach pea. A sign marked "Foredunes" describes those closest to the shoreline. Stay on the trail. The vegetation and dunes are too fragile even for little feet.

In ¼ mile, reach the park boundary. For sand play, turn right and go to the beach. For a 1-mile loop hike, go left past more sand dunes, signed "Precipitation Dunes." Climb a wooden platform for an overlook of marshes and tea-colored Cranberry Lake. Yes, wild cranberries grow here—some at the edge of the lake. Another bog plant, Labrador tea, also thrives in this acid soil. (You can recognize it by its small, leathery, yellow-green leaves.) Rub a leaf and hold it next to your face to smell its pungent aroma.

The 2-mile second loop hike begins at the other end of the parking lot and takes the trail over the rocky headland of West Point and then drops to the first beach of North Bay. Expect to see large old Douglas-firs framing views of the water, which will probably be filled with sailboats, fishing vessels, and tugboats pulling logs, all waiting for the tide to turn and run in their direction.

From the first bay, bear left into woods past a car campground and go about ¼ mile to the next beach. At low tide, the beach can be walked. Look up at the bridge and note how small the people standing on it seem. This beautiful bridge was built during the Depression to provide a way for Whidbey Island farmers to get their crops to market without relying on a ferry.

Look still higher for eagles soaring (we saw four one March day) above the water. You can also see scaups, coots, scoters, and all kinds of ducks. Continue ¼ mile to the third beach. At the headland above the third beach, turn right and follow the curving road up past park headquarters and then downhill past Cranberry Lake to the parking lot.

Long ago during a time of hunger, says an old Indian legend, the mice had been searching for where the humans had hidden their food. One night the mice overheard the humans say that they kept their stores of grain tucked away inside Douglas-fir cones. The mice ran to the tops of the trees and climbed inside the cones. The cones clamped shut on the mice, leaving only their tails and hind legs exposed. If your children look closely, they can find tiny legs and tails on the outside of each cone they pick up today. Look also for fresh piles of cones left by squirrels that cut out the seeds or nuts nature has tucked away inside them.

Deception Pass Bridge

GOOSE ROCK

BEFORE YOU GO
Map Deception Pass State Park brochure
Current conditions Washington State Parks (360) 902-8844
State park annual or day-use pass required

ABOUT THE HIKE
Day hike
Moderate for children
Year round
1¼-mile loop
475 feet elevation gain if you climb, minimal if you don't

GETTING THERE
- Leave I-5 at exit 230. Go west on Highway 20 toward Anacortes.
- In 11.1 miles Highway 20 splits at a traffic light; go left (south) toward Deception Pass/Whidbey Island/Oak Harbor.
- In 8 miles cross over the Deception Pass bridges. Park in the small lot south of the second bridge. The trailhead is to the east, across the busy road, but a stairway under the bridge on the west side brings you safely under it to the beginning of the Perimeter Trail loop, elevation 50 feet.

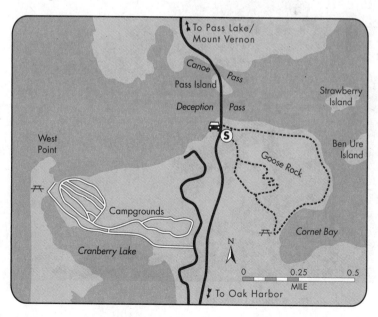

ON THE TRAIL

A large monolithic rock on the south side of Deception Pass offers children views of the pass, Cornet Bay, and, from its summit, out over the straits and Skagit Flats. You and your children can circle Goose Rock on a mostly level perimeter trail or go up to its rocky top, where your outlook over north Whidbey Island and Puget Sound is like that from a small plane.

On the trail, begin by walking east along Deception Pass, gazing across at Pass Island and its rocky cliffs. Tell children if they look closely they can find an old quarry halfway up one cliff, dug by prisoners early

View from trail around Goose Rock

in the century. Prisoners lived below it on the shore from 1909 until 1923, struggling to mine limestone. Escape across the pass by swimming through its currents was impossible. Ask children what they think their lives would have been like as mining prisoners living there.

The trail follows around the perimeter of the rock. Old fir trees have been saved, providing shade and habitat. The trail gradually drops to the water's edge, leading past leaning madronas and moored boats. On the west side

Pied Billed Grebe

in Coronet Bay look for a marina, occasional seals, blue herons, loons, grebes, scoters, mergansers, harlequin ducks, cormorants, and bald eagles. A gate and path for the Coronet Bay Youth Camp leads left.

The trail offers the choice of a steep ascent or the rest of the circumnavigation of the rock. When you come to a fork, take the right one, uphill, if you would like the summit view. This rock is in the rain shadow, so some trees and shrubs are like those from the dry side of the Cascades. If you go up, you will see moss gardens with wildflowers typical of mountain elevations, such as Indian paintbrush, chocolate lilies, camas, and yellow fritillaries. Sweeping views from the summit south are down Whidbey past Oak Harbor and west out to the Strait of Juan de Fuca. Drop to the road to return to the car.

49 EBEY'S LANDING

BEFORE YOU GO
Map None
Current conditions Nature Conservancy (206) 343-4344

ABOUT THE HIKE
Day hike
Easy for children
Year round
3½-mile loop
200 feet elevation loss

GETTING THERE

- Leave I-5 at exit 230. Go west on Highway 20 toward Anacortes.

- In 11.1 miles Highway 20 splits at a traffic light; turn left (south) toward Deception Pass/Whidbey Island/Oak Harbor.

▪ Arrive in Coupeville in about 25 miles. Just before the pedestrian overpass, turn left at Terry Road, which becomes Ebey Landing Road. Follow Ebey Landing Road as it switchbacks down to the water and find parking in the lot at the end, elevation sea level.

ON THE TRAIL

In our family, the beach of the Ebey's Landing National Historic Preserve is the most beloved of the state's inland sea hikes. The Nature Conservancy purchased this land and made it into a Nature Conservancy Preserve. My children loved Ebey's Landing for its beauty, its history, and its endless opportunities for play. The trail on the bluff above the beach has some steep portions that are a struggle for pre-schoolers. But once on top, my kids would gaze, entranced, down to the long tidal lagoon; west to Port Townsend, the Olympics, and the strait; and south to Mount Rainier. If taking a ferry to Whidbey Island, be certain to check the schedule before you go, and remember that on sunny summer weekends, the wait for the ferry can be long. Reservations for camping on the island should be made well in advance for the best chance of getting a spot.

Ebey's Landing Inn, listed on the National Historic Register, stands back in a field behind a locked gate. It is the old house with the distinctive moss-covered roof and two tall chimneys. Colonel Isaac Ebey settled here in 1850 and was beheaded by Haida Indians as retaliation for the killing of a chief in 1857. The inn, built in 1860, continued to operate until the 1920s. Its plans are still held in the Library of Congress, but the inn is not open to the public.

Those with very young children should walk the beach north 1 mile to Perego's Lagoon and devote the day to waves and driftwood. Families with older children can do a loop, starting either with beach or bluff. We always preferred to begin with the bluff.

To do so, walk north from the parking lot and shortly ascend the low

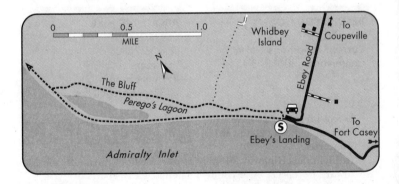

Running on the beach

bank to a path paralleling the cultivated field. The bank tilts up steeply to become bluff, passing the front edge of a forest of Douglas-fir, Sitka spruce, and pines contorted by prevailing winds. Trees lean pictur-esquely, framing Mount Rainier and the Olympics. The glorious views over table-flat Ebey's Prairie, the most continuously farmed land in the state, include the strait and the ocean horizon far beyond. Once atop the bluff, the level path is bordered by wild roses, broom, paintbrush, and wind-groomed salal. Prevailing winds on the bluff are so severe that the trees assume grotesque shapes. At about 1½ miles, descend a very steep trail to the north end of Perego's Lagoon below, where children can skip rocks and play in the driftwood, watching for loons and seals in the waves.

Walk south to your car along a shore offering superb beachcomb-ing. Some years the lagoon has fresh water; in others the banks are breached and the lagoon is tidal. When this happens, the return trip is on a narrow path along the bluff side of the lagoon.

EVERETT AREA

 SPENCER ISLAND

BEFORE YOU GO
Maps Snohomish County park map; USGS Everett
Current conditions Snohomish County Parks and Recreation Information (425) 355-6600

ABOUT THE HIKE
Day hike
Easy for children
Year round
3 to 5 miles
No elevation gain

GETTING THERE

- From I-5 northbound at Everett, take exit 195. At the base of the off ramp turn left onto East Marine View Drive.
- After winding along the bluff above the Snohomish River, take the first right off SR 529 (North Smith Island Access).
- Where the road divides, stay left, following signs to Langus Riverfront Park. The road follows the river's edge, passes through Dagmar's Marina, and divides at the edge of I-5. Stay right to find

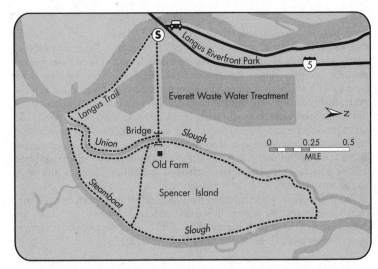

Children playing on board walk on Spencer Island

the first of several parking areas. Park and walk 1 mile east along the paved Langus Trail to the Spencer Island Bridge, elevation sea level.

ON THE TRAIL

A small island east of Everett and bordered in the Snohomish River estuary by Union Slough and Steamboat Slough is divided into both a county park and a state game area, allowing bird hunting during the winter season. Children will enjoy the county park portion, which features birds and wildlife, thriving in an ecosystem made up of fresh water from the river and saltwater from Port Gardner Bay. Children will also enjoy the chance to walk along the levees and dikes and to see waterfowl and shorebirds at any time of year. During hunting season (October–January) stay away from the north portion of the island. How do the birds know where they are safe? The kids may well ask.

The bridge you must cross, brought from another location, was called a jackknife drawbridge. Ask children to guess why. When the island was being used for farming in the 1930s, a dike was built to control the impact of tidal water. An old barn here once belonged to John Spencer, the original farmer for whom the island was named. It is said to have been rolled on logs from across the island into this position.

You can walk along the shore from the north end of the park to the bridge and back. Or walk around part of the perimeter of the south portion of the island. The bridge across the Steamboat Slough on the southeast end of the island is washed out, so you cannot complete this as a loop hike and must return the way you came. The trail surface, a kind of sawdust called hog fuel, is eroding and may need to be replaced. Cross the wetland for close-up views of ponds and drowned vegetation.

The sounds of the freeway lessen and you can view the graveyard of old houseboats and tugboats in various states of age and disrepair, permanently tied up along the banks of the slough. What stories these old boats could tell! Birdwatchers see many kinds of shorebirds and migrating species on Spencer Island. Year-round birds, such as eagles, great horned owls, kingfishers, hawks, gulls, and even pileated woodpeckers, can surprise children anytime. To the north you may see Mount Baker and to the south on a clear day Mount Rainier.

 JETTY ISLAND

BEFORE YOU GO
Maps USGS Everett; Everett city map or Snohomish County map
Current conditions Everett Parks and Recreation Dept. (425) 257-8304; schedule for walk-on ferry (360) 257-8304

ABOUT THE HIKE
Day hike
Easy for children
Ferry access Fourth of July to Labor Day; accessible by kayak or canoe year-round
½ mile to 2 miles
No elevation gain

GETTING THERE

■ Driving southbound on I-5, take exit 194 and head west on Hewitt; northbound, take exit 193 and head west on Pacific. Both streets connect to West Marine View Drive.

■ Turn north onto West Marine View Drive and proceed past the Navy's Everett home port. In another mile turn left at the sign for the public boat launch.

■ To catch the free foot ferry to the south end of Jetty Island, park in the well-signed parking lot, elevation sea level.

ON THE TRAIL

A magical small island dredged up more than a century ago from Everett's harbor and framed by piles of jetty rock lies in Port Gardner Bay across from the mouth of the Snohomish River. It is accessible by foot ferry in summer months only. Children can ride across in five minutes to a wild beach with birds and driftwood and sand to play in. The ferry runs about every half-hour from 10:30 AM to 5:30 PM from Wednesday to Saturday and 11:00 AM to 5:30 PM on Sunday. There is no boat on Monday and Tuesday. Or you can paddle a kayak or canoe to the island year round. The ferry lands on the south end, so to be alone, paddle to the north end instead.

The harbor and Snohomish River channel were dredged as a breakwater and to keep marine worms from drilling into visiting ships. Explain to the kids that the worms cannot live in freshwater and the creation of the island kept most of the saltwater out of the harbor. Piled-up sand from the dredging became a 2-mile-long undeveloped island, now loved for its wilderness feeling, warm-water beach, and abundant birds. Children can find their way along a path bordered by dune grass, pickleweed, and beach peas. Only a few trees have taken root, and the driftwood is abundant.

From the island, the views east are to the mouth of the Snohomish River, past old pilings inhabited by nesting cormorants and ospreys

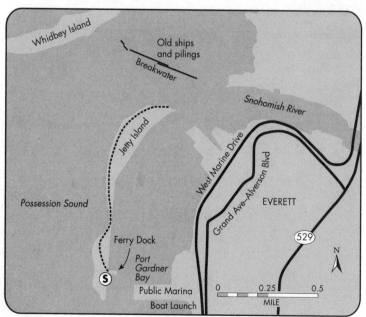

Eagle on its perch

and along the Everett waterfront. Look west to Possession Sound and Whidbey Island and the strait beyond. There is a half-mile interpretive trail and much more to see on your own. Sea birds such as sandpipers, dunlin and sanderling, ducks, and geese nest on the island in the grasses that shelter them. Nesting pairs of Caspian terns, various gulls, kildeer, and sandpipers may turn up.

Urge children to observe them carefully but to leave wildlife untouched. When the tide turns, the shallow water on the west side is warm enough to wade and play in. Although you are just a short distance from Everett, the only sounds you will hear are the calls of osprey and gulls and distant motors.

tevens Pass trails range in elevation from the low woodland trail to Lord Hill, out of Monroe, up to the summit of Stevens Pass and beyond. Heybrook Lookout is a short hike to a restored forest lookout near the town of Index, with dramatic outlooks over the Skykomish River and to Mount Index. Evergreen Mountain, with another restored lookout, is near the proposed Wild Sky Wilderness. More trails continue to the summit of the pass, including the scenic Iron Goat Trail, following the old Great Northern Railroad route. At the summit, the hikes include a favorite trail to Lake Janus. The trails to the east include Heather and Hidden Lakes, lying above Lake Wenatchee; Eightmile Lake and Icicle Gorge, out of Leavenworth; and alpine Clara and Marion Lakes, near Mission Ridge above Wenatchee. Two longer hikes, Spider Meadow and Mad River, offer children eastern flowery meadow trails.

US 2 WEST OF STEVENS PASS

 LORD HILL REGIONAL PARK

BEFORE YOU GO
Maps Lord Hill Regional Park map; USGS Maltby
Current conditions
Snohomish County Parks and Recreation Information (425) 388-6600

ABOUT THE HIKE
Day hike
Moderate for children
Year round
6 to 10 miles
300 feet elevation gain; 500 feet loss to Snohomish River

GETTING THERE

- Leave I-5 at exit 194 and head east toward Snohomish on US 2.
- In 8.5 miles take the second Snohomish exit (88th Street).
- Turn right onto 2nd Avenue.
- Turn left onto Lincoln Avenue South, which becomes the old Snohomish–Monroe Highway.
- Turn right onto 127th Avenue SE; go south approximately 2.25 miles.
- Turn left onto 150th Street SE and drive to the park entrance on the left, elevation 100 feet.

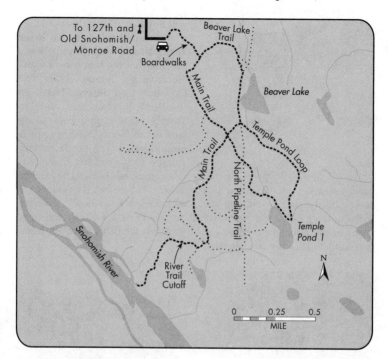

Northwest of Snohomish, a large wooded ridge more than 600 feet high has been made into a county park, used year-round. It features marshy beaver ponds, loop trails with delightful outlooks over the Snohomish valley and south to Mount Rainier, and a descent trail to the banks of the Snohomish River. Children can enjoy these trails any time, if mud isn't a problem, and what child doesn't enjoy getting muddy?

Mitchell Lord, for whom the park was named, owned the land and homestead until 1884. Have the kids look for his former home at the intersection of 127th Avenue SE and the old Snohomish–Monroe Highway. Today, second-growth timber covers the hills logged in the 1930s and surrounds a number of the park's wetland ponds and springs. A map available at the trailhead suggests such destinations as Devil's Butte Lookout, the park's highpoint at 580 feet; Temple Ponds 1 and 2; Beaver Lake; English Pond; and Bald Hill Pond.

From the parking lot walk through old maples, cedars, hemlocks, and alders, over four boardwalks crossing muddy spots, to a junction at ¼ mile. Run-off and springs have combined to produce several large ponds where beavers have left their imprint in the regional park. In the fall the trail is covered with gold leaves, which children

Beaver

will enjoy scuffling through.

You can choose between River Trail, Beaver Lake, and North Pipeline, but the best beaver viewing is in the Temple Ponds. The loop trip past Beaver Lake, up the North Pipeline trail, down to Temple Pond 1, and back along part of the North Pipeline trail is recommended. The ponds contain stumps and snags left from long-ago logging, but beavers have since built a series of grass-covered dams. Children can search for evidence of their activity, such as chewed sticks with bark removed, and a beaver lodge in the small pond just north of Temple Pond 1. Or they can walk down to the Snohomish River's edge to watch for fish and small boats careening past in the swift current.

Old beaver pond on Lord Hill

WALLACE FALLS STATE PARK

BEFORE YOU GO
Maps Green Trails No. 142
Index; USGS Gold Bar
Current conditions
Washington State Parks (360)
902-8844
**State park annual or
day-use pass required**

ABOUT THE HIKE
Day hike
Moderate for children
April–November
5 miles
880 feet elevation gain

GETTING THERE
- Take US 2 (Stevens Pass Highway) east 12 miles from Monroe to Gold Bar.
- Once in Gold Bar, follow the brown park signs 2 miles northeast to the park headquarters and trailhead, elevation 300 feet.

ON THE TRAIL
Wallace Falls is a spectacular cataract that is visible from as far as the Stevens Pass Highway, miles away. In recent years, it has become easily accessible. (Parking is limited at this site; plan to arrive early for the best availability.) The trail is short and sometimes steep, and can be muddy in spring and fall. However, the low elevation means it is open for walking when the highlands are snowed in. Hazards are minimal except at the trail's end, overlooking the falls, where spray makes every surface slippery and requires that every child's hand be held tight. One Mother's Day, I took two toddlers, a baby, and two grandmothers to Wallace Falls. The kids had a grand time (and were carried much of the way), but the grandmothers never forgave me!

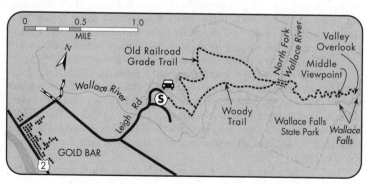

Checking out Wallace Falls

The trail starts on a service road under powerlines, enters woods, and in a long ¼ mile forks. At the junction you can choose between a former railroad grade on a gentle incline or a steeper 1-mile trail near Wallace River at the top of which the two trails rejoin. From there you can cross the North Fork of the Wallace River and climb ¼ mile to a shelter with the first overlook of the falls, elevation 650 feet. This is a good turnaround, resting point, or picnic destination if children are young. The riverbank offers joys that may be sufficiently satisfying.

But if the roaring of the falls cannot be resisted, climb steeply onward in old forest, to a better viewpoint at 1120 feet. At 2½ miles you will reach the top of the falls you saw from the highway below. For even closer views of the thundering cataract, continue ½ mile to the Middle Viewpoint, an ideal place to appreciate the deafening sound of the huge volume of water. Save all commentary for later. The falls dominate any conversation.

Much of the inspiration for the rebuilding and maintenance of this trail came from Greg Ball, former Washington Trails Association Director. He loved this trail and helped others see how important it is to maintain this very popular route.

Finally, ½ mile above the North Fork bridge, the trail ends at Valley Overlook, elevation 1500 feet, a beautiful and triumphant overlook.

 BRIDAL VEIL FALLS

BEFORE YOU GO
Maps Green Trails No. 142 Index; USGS Index
Current conditions Skykomish Ranger District (360) 677-2414
Northwest Forest Pass required

ABOUT THE HIKE
Day hike or backpack
Moderate for children
May to October
4 miles
1000 feet elevation gain

GETTING THERE

- Drive US 2 (Stevens Pass Highway) 20 miles east from Monroe.
- At milepost 35, just before crossing the bridge over the Skykomish River, turn right at a sign marked "Mt. Index Road."
- Drive 0.3 mile and bear right. Continue 600 feet to the parking area on the left, elevation 600 feet.

ON THE TRAIL

A beautiful waterfall flows out of Lake Serene above and cascades below the rugged east wall of Mount Index at the end of a safe trail, No. 1068, up the east side of Bridal Veil Creek. Bridal Veil Falls is reached by way

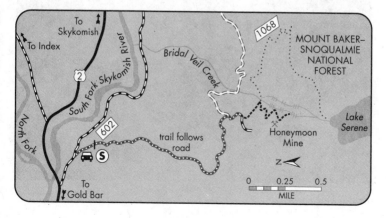

of a side trail off the main trail to Lake Serene (a 7-mile round-trip hike for those with more ambitious children); don't be alarmed that all the signs direct you to Lake Serene—while not one directs you to the falls. On arrival at your destination, take time to enjoy a stunning view of Bridal Veil Falls, and climb flights of steps paralleling the falls. Children will be fascinated as they look up a 100-foot rock face to see the streams of water that make up the bridal veil pouring directly beside them. An old nearby mine, the Honeymoon Mine, brought nineteenth-century travelers to the Lake Serene area.

The trail begins as an abandoned logging road for 1½ miles, narrows

Bridal Veil Falls

briefly to trail dimensions, and then wanders through a washed-out section of about ¼ mile, which will be challenging for small children.

Within 1000 feet is a junction. The left fork continues to Lake Serene. Take the right one and listen for the approaching sounds of Bridal Veil Falls in the distance. A sign marks the detour to the falls as only ½ mile. However, the trail contains several hundred feet of inclined constructed stairs, well worth your effort for the spectacular vista attained at the waterfall. Children will love standing in the

Bewick's wren

wind, spray, and mist of the falls, which cascade in several ribbons of water across the cliffs.

Children will feel they are in a rain forest. Ask them to look at the lush forest around them, with enormous old cedar stumps and full-grown hemlocks emerging from them. If you can hear them above the sound of the water, listen for the intricate trilling of Swainson's thrush and the Bewick's wren. From beside the waterfall look out to views of the Monte Cristo peaks and down to the Skykomish River and the granite cliffs along Index's Town Wall.

 TROUBLESOME CREEK

BEFORE YOU GO
Maps Green Trails No. 143 Monte Cristo; USGS Monte Cristo; USFS Mt. Baker–Snoqualmie
Current conditions Skykomish Ranger District (360) 677-2414
Northwest Forest Pass required

ABOUT THE HIKE
Day hike
Easy for children
March to November
½-mile loop
25 feet elevation gain

GETTING THERE
▪ From I-5, drive east on US 2 toward Stevens Pass. Turn left at the Index turnoff onto County Road No. 63, and travel 1 mile to a bridge.

- Rather than going into Index, turn right, staying on County Road No. 63 for 10.3 miles to Troublesome Creek Campground.
- Drive through the campground to the lower level to find the trailhead, elevation 1258 feet.

ON THE TRAIL

This marvelous short, old-growth loop trail crosses Troublesome Creek twice within ½ mile. Although it is labeled a nature trail, there are no interpretive signs. However, you will find plenty of benches at beauty-spot viewpoints where parents of small children can pause, rest, and talk about the cycle of renewal in old-growth forest. There is such a magical feel to this place that your children will almost expect to see Hansel and Gretel tiptoeing through the forest ahead of them.

Start your hike on either side of the creek; the loop is good either way. It is described here going counterclockwise. Begin by passing the lower footbridge and starting upstream on the right side. You will travel past old cedars and firs, some of which have been dying back for centuries; they are so enormous, it would require eight to ten children to circle their girth. Ask your children to guess how old the trees might be. Look for young and middle-aged trees interspersed with the ancient ones. The first miners to come to the Skykomish River valley used this creek to get to gold, silver, and copper claims high above. At the farthest point upstream, the constructed trail ends next to a 500-year-old fir tree and a bench. Just around the other side of the fir is a large, flat rock beside the creek, suitable for a picnic spread. Stop to rest and enjoy the tumbling creek and its unusual colors, caused by dissolved minerals in the water.

Turn and start downstream again, crossing the creek on the upper footbridge. Old, unmaintained side trails (perhaps remnants of miners' trails) depart from the main trail in several places, calling to children to come explore, but some of the old trails dead-end near the water and may not be safe. Hiking alongside this creek is never troublesome,

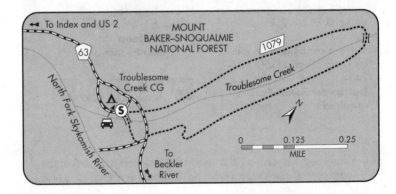

Bridge across Troublesome Creek

despite the name. The stream has a spellbinding beauty, particularly when its rapids break over water-scoured bedrock. Along the bank in summer low-water times are small, rocky beaches where children might safely play. Mossy skeletons of old trees frame outlooks over white-water rapids. Pass under a rock bridge, cross over the first footbridge, and return to your car, feeling a bit as if you are returning from Alice's Wonderland up through the rabbit hole.

EVERGREEN MOUNTAIN

BEFORE YOU GO
Maps Green Trails: No. 143 Monte Cristo; USGS Evergreen Mountain
Current conditions Skykomish Ranger District (360) 677-2414
Northwest Forest Pass required

ABOUT THE HIKE
Day hike
Difficult for children
August to October
3 miles
1300 feet elevation gain

GETTING THERE
- Drive US 2 (Stevens Pass Highway) 33 miles east of Monroe to Sky-komish. At 0.5 mile east of Skykomish, before the highway crosses the river again, turn left (north) onto Beckler River Road No. 65.

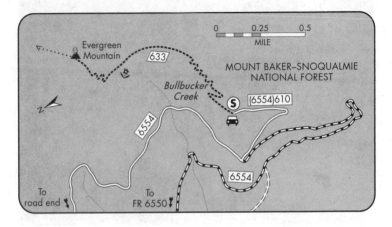

- Drive 8 miles, passing several junctions, including the lower junction of Road No. 6550. Stay left on Road No. 65 and continue approximately 5 miles north to Jack Pass.
- At Jack Pass, turn right onto the upper portion of Road No. 6550 and drive about 1 mile to Road No. 6554 and a gate. *Note:* The gate on this road is closed from November until whenever the road is snow free; call ahead to be sure the road is open.
- Turn right onto Road No. (6554)610 and drive 6.5 miles to the trailhead, elevation 4160 feet.

ON THE TRAIL

Here is a gorgeous mountain meadow hike near the proposed Wild Sky Wilderness. Short enough for children, with beautiful panoramic views in every direction, the trail is steep and has no let-ups. The former lookout and enemy aircraft-spotting station found here has been declared a National Historic Monument and has recently been restored. You can rent the lookout for a night and plan to spend sunset and sunrise enjoying the views here with your family. (Please respect the privacy of any renters at the lookout during your hike.) Check with the Skykomish Ranger District for rates and availability. Luscious blueberries ripen along the trail in August and September. Carry water, as there is none on the trail and none at the lookout.

At the trailhead, marvel at views in every direction. Look north to the spectacular Monte Cristo peaks and the fang of Sloan, and south to the Dutch Miller Gap peaks. Listen for the sounds of bees in the alpine flowers, and for bird songs. Tell children that Evergreen Mountain burned out of control for most of the summer of 1967, and no one expected it ever to be green again. Yet today, looking up through snags and stumps, the remnants of that fire, you will find green meadows with abundant flowers and thirty-year-old alpine and noble firs. The mountain is renewing itself.

Start uphill steeply through the clear-cut of fire-damaged timber from the old burn. The meadow flowers are amazingly diverse and continuously in bloom. We saw masses of blazing golden arnica, glacier lilies, penstemon, lupine, columbine, tiger lilies, and paintbrush amid clumps of little trees. At ¼ mile reach a stand of old trees that escaped the flames and provides shade today. The steepness of the trail eases a bit before coming out of the trees onto a little saddle (elevation 5300 feet). If your family does not wish to reach the lookout, this makes a good turnaround point.

Traveling up from the saddle in midsummer is a treat for any family because of the exceptional show of wildflowers. Continue another ⅓ mile up the steep east side of the mountain to the closed lookout, built in 1935. Sit down and bring out the lemonade. Kids will like knowing this fire lookout was used during the war as an aircraft-spotting station. Bring a good Forest Service map to help you identify the many peaks, rivers, and valleys from the 360-degree span. The satisfaction of having climbed to the top of a mountain on a clear day is one a child will cherish forever.

Fire lookout on Evergreen Mountain

HEYBROOK LOOKOUT

BEFORE YOU GO
Maps Green Trails No. 142
Index; USGS Index
Current conditions
Skykomish Ranger District
(360) 677-2414
**Northwest Forest Pass
required**

ABOUT THE HIKE
Day hike
Moderate for children
Year round
2 miles
900 feet elevation gain

GETTING THERE
■ Drive US 2 (Stevens Pass Highway) to 23 miles east of Monroe.
■ At 2 miles east of Index, near milepost 37, look for a large pulloff
area on the left (north) side of the road, elevation 800 feet.

ON THE TRAIL
Here is a restored fire lookout close to the proposed Wild Sky Wilderness
and low enough for year-round hikes on a trail short enough for young
children. Because the slope faces south, this hike can be done in winter
months when most trails are filled with snow. The wooded path switchbacks up through second-growth forest to a restored lookout building
perched on top of a wooden tower. Children will enjoy mounting the steps
to the top, and viewing the sharp north, middle, and main peaks of Mount
Index; Mount Baring; Mount Persis; and the Skykomish River valley

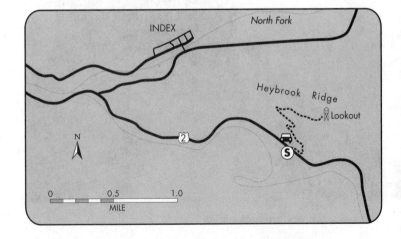

lying before them, just as old-time fire lookouts did. Dramatic Bridal Veil Falls pours from Lake Serene across the valley below Mount Index (see Hike 54). The lookout was rebuilt by the Forest Service and has been saved as a National Historic Monument. It will be available for rental in 2007. It is maintained by the Everett Mountaineers. Work crews access it by a service road, once the only lookout access.

The short, steep, Forest Service trail No. 1070 has rocky outcrops, and ancient stumps that bear the telltale wedge cuts of long-ago loggers. Second-growth trees have grown since clear-cuts in the 1920s. Children enjoy peering up at mossy snags, stepping over little creeks, and gazing out at widening views of the river below and rugged peaks across the way. In the

Restored lookout tower

fall, big leaf maples turn bright gold, and on a foggy day they appear as bright as headlamps lighting the way as fog swirls over the river. Huge boulders and rocky cliffs lie on either side of the trail. Massive Mounts Index and Baring seem close enough to touch. Children can climb the stairs of the lookout to a locked hatch and the walk-around deck. Vandals have made this protection of the building necessary and the Everett Mountaineers are determined to maintain it in good condition.

 BARCLAY LAKE

BEFORE YOU GO
Maps Green Trails No. 143 Monte Cristo; USGS Baring
Current conditions
Skykomish Ranger District (360) 677-2414
Northwest Forest Pass required

ABOUT THE HIKE
Day hike or backpack
Easy for children
June–October
4 miles
220 feet elevation gain

GETTING THERE

- Drive US 2 (Stevens Pass Highway) 29 miles east of Monroe to the town of Baring.
- Turn left (north) onto Barclay Creek Road No. 6024. The road is directly across from Der Baring Store and is signed "635th Place Northeast."
- Cross a railroad track and continue for 4 miles to the road end at the trailhead, elevation 2200 feet.

Barclay Lake is great on a sunny afternoon.

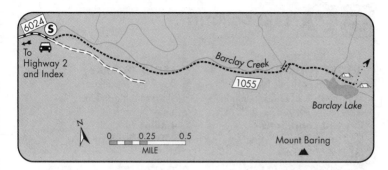

ON THE TRAIL

This shallow, low-elevation (2442 feet) forest lake lies beneath the massive and spectacular north face of Mount Baring. Children will enjoy the chance to wade, splash, and paddle in this quiet lake, and parents will appreciate the fact that campsites are close enough to the road for them to make extra trips to the car if necessary. The trail is smooth and gradual, through old-growth forest.

Barclay Lake trail No. 1055 drops from the left side of the road to Barclay Creek and proceeds upstream on an easy, well-maintained trail featuring boardwalks and log ends. Cross the creek on a bridge. This bridge was replaced in part by funds from the Spring Family Trails Trust, which is supported by sales of this and other books. Watch for a house-size boulder beside the trail; the moss-covered overhang forms a magical cave. I told my children that elves and dwarves used to live here before America was discovered. It's a short distance from here to the lake.

Campsites extend along the entire north shore of the lake. The Forest Service discourages use of those within 50 feet of the lakeshore; if you decide to stay, try to cooperate. Boulders rolling down to dam the creek may have formed Barclay Lake. The lake level drops late in the year when it drains underground.

Gazing up in open-mouthed awe at Mount Baring is enough entertainment for a lot of folks. How did such a piece of landscape ever come to be? That's a long and complicated story, involving mountain building, plate tectonics, and so on. But the steepness is relatively recent and simple in origin. Of course, it's a hard job convincing kids a glacier did this. ("Well, where is it then?" they ask. The answer to this is, "Gone back to Canada for more ice.")

There is a sandy beach for waders and swimmers and fishing for everyone. Expect weekends to be crowded.

LAKE DOROTHY

BEFORE YOU GO
Maps Green Trails No. 175 Skykomish; USGS Snoqualmie Lake
Current conditions Skykomish Ranger District (360) 677-2414
Wilderness Permit and Northwest Forest Pass required

ABOUT THE HIKE
Day hike or backpack
Moderate for children
June–October
4 miles
858 feet elevation gain

GETTING THERE
- Drive US 2 (Stevens Pass Highway) 30 miles east of Monroe.
- Just west of the highway tunnel on US 2, turn right (south) onto the Old Cascade Highway, signed to Money Creek Campground.
- Drive the Old Cascade Highway for 1 mile and then turn right (south) onto Miller River Road No. 6410.
- Drive 9.5 miles to the road's end at the trailhead, elevation 2250 feet.

ON THE TRAIL
This short, very popular, and much-used trail along the rushing Miller River leads quickly to one of the largest forest lakes in the Alpine Lakes Wilderness. Opportunities for water activities are abundant. The track has been rebuilt and is pleasant walking for children. However, the last ½ mile is steep, climbing to the source of the Miller, lovely Lake Dorothy.

Volunteers from the Washington Trails Association have repaired this trail, which was damaged by flooding. It starts in big old cedars and firs. Boggy spots are lighted in spring by torch-like skunk cabbage. The

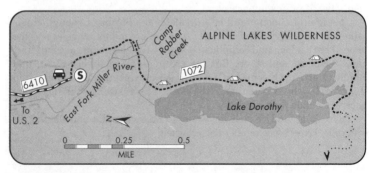

Camp Robber Creek bridge on Lake Dorothy Trail

trail crosses Camp Robber Creek on a bridge that is in its own right a sufficient destination and a possible turnaround. Children can spend a lunch hour stomping back and forth on the bridge to see if their stomps can compete with the waterfall's roar. They may not bring on a camp robber, but if they do not recognize John Muir's favorite bird, the water ouzel, tell them to watch for a gray bird skittering along the surface of the water, pausing now and then to perch on a rock, dip-dip-dipping at the knees.

Actually, after Camp Robber Creek, the final bit of trail to the lake and its outlet logjam, at 3058 feet, are almost an anticlimax. The trail continues along the lakeshore to the head, with choice campsites for families arriving early on weekends or midweek. Do not expect to be alone. Rocky cliffs rise high on the opposite shore of this large woodland lake in the mountains.

TONGA RIDGE

BEFORE YOU GO
Maps Green Trails No. 176
Stevens Pass; No. 175 Sky-
komish; USGS Skykomish
Current conditions
Skykomish Ranger District
(360) 677-2414
**Wilderness Permit and
Northwest Forest Pass
required**

ABOUT THE HIKE
Day hike or backpack
Moderate for children
July–October
6 miles
500 feet elevation gain

At this time the extent of the 2006 flood
damage is unknown. Call ahead to the
managing agency for the current conditions before heading out.

GETTING THERE

- Drive US 2 (Stevens Pass Highway) 35 miles east of Monroe.
- At 1.7 miles east of Skykomish, turn right (south) onto Foss River Road No. 68.
- Drive 3.5 miles to a junction with Road No. 6830 and turn left.
- Drive 6 miles to Spur Road No. 310 and turn right onto the spur.
- Drive 1 mile to the trailhead and limited parking at the end of the road, elevation 4300 feet.

ON THE TRAIL

A trail gradual enough to stroll with small children climbs easily into meadowlands, with views of Glacier Peak and the Central Cascades. In fall, there are huckleberries to pick; on early summer mornings, children

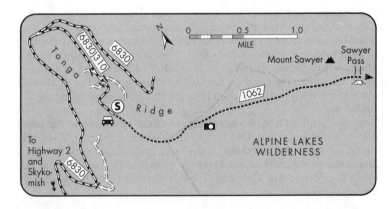

can watch for deer. Be sure to bring enough water, especially if you plan to camp, as there is no water available on the trail.

The road ends virtually at timberline, amid spectacular views of Index, Persis, Baring, and Glacier Peak. Why leave the car at all? Because the meadows beckon.

Begin on an old fire trail ascending modestly through a forest of mixed conifers. In 1 mile, the trail breaks out of the forest into broad meadows. The view south to the craggy peaks along the Cascade Crest is superb. The trail now follows the crest through meadows of huckleberry and heather.

Trail on Tonga Ridge (Photo by Bob Burton)

The views cannot improve—they just change from one gorgeous vista to another. At 3 miles, you'll find sometimes watered and sometimes dry campsites at Sawyer Pass, 4800 feet. Enjoy this hike in late September for spectacular fall colors and blueberries, but be sure before you go that hunting season has not yet started.

  IRON GOAT TRAIL

BEFORE YOU GO
Maps On reader boards at trailheads; brochure available from the Forest Service; on the Internet at *www.irongoat.org*; Green Trails map No. 176 Stevens Pass; USGS Scenic
Current conditions
Skykomish Ranger District (360) 677-2414
Northwest Forest Pass required

ABOUT THE HIKE
Day hike
Easy for children
May to November
Upper trail: 13½ miles;
lower trail: 2 miles
800 feet elevation gain and loss

GETTING THERE

■ *Martin Creek Trailhead:* Drive US 2 (Stevens Pass Highway) to 6 miles east of the town of Skykomish. At milepost 55, turn left (north) onto the Old Cascade Highway/Road No. 67.

- ■ Drive 2.3 miles to a junction with Road No. 6710. Turn left (north) and drive 1.4 miles to the parking lot/trailhead, elevation 2400 feet.
- ■ *Wellington Trailhead:* Drive US 2 (Stevens Pass Highway) to 15 miles east of Skykomish. At milepost 64, turn left (north) onto the Old Stevens Pass Highway. (Because of limited sight distance, if you are coming from the west, proceed to Stevens Pass and turn around at the crest of the hill where visibility is optimum. Then return westbound to the turn at milepost 64.)
- ■ Drive 2.8 miles on Old Stevens Pass Highway to a junction with Road No. 050. Turn right to the parking lot and trailhead, elevation 3100 feet.

ON THE TRAIL

A child can walk part of the old Great Northern Railroad right-of-way and peek into a dark and spooky blocked tunnel. A century ago the last spike of this railway was driven, to enable the Great Northern to cross the Cascades at Stevens Pass. Reminisce about the excitement of the

Snow shed on the historic Iron Goat Trail

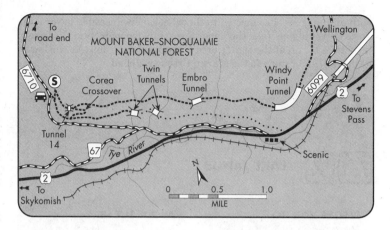

old steam engines thundering uphill, belching great puffs of smoke and steam in the cold mountain air.

Abandoned in 1929, after the big tunnel was built, the old grade was almost lost, but thanks to thousands of volunteer hours and donated materials by the Volunteers of Washington, the railroad grade is now a trail into history. Eventually the trail will reach near the summit of Stevens Pass. It now reaches the site of the tragic 1910 Wellington avalanche that swept away standing train cars and most of its passengers. Look for relics. Bits of ancient cable, tie bolts, and even a coal scuttle lies rusting along the way.

James J. Hill, known as the Empire Builder, chose the Rocky Mountain goat as his railroad's emblem, hence the name Iron Goat Trail. Mountain goats are still occasionally seen in the Stevens Pass area, so watch for them on the rocky avalanche slope across the valley. Children will be fascinated by the long-ago tale of the stranded passenger cars, held in place by avalanches on the tracks in front and behind them. A handful of passengers walked down steep slopes to safety, but the majority waited in train cars that were eventually rolled down the slope by a monster avalanche, where ninety-six passengers died. Stop at Scenic in 2007 to view the Interpretive Site with a kiosk, historic caboose, and access to the railroad grade of the Iron Goat Trail.

Begin among old alders along a shelf overlooking the Skykomish River valley and US 2. At ¼ mile children have the choice of climbing a short 100 feet to the upper trail or continuing on the easy barrier-free trail to the outlook and century-old snow shed and double tunnel.

The trail goes from Martin Creek past Windy Point to Wellington, the site of the avalanche disaster. Pass the Windy Point Tunnel. Children can step into the mouth of the tunnel but should not go beyond the barricades. At 3¼ miles come to a cleared viewpoint overlooking the valley and into the peaks of the Stevens Pass area. The trail is Z-shaped, with an upper level connected to the wheelchair-accessible lower level. To go to Wellington, take the upper-level trail. On your return for a loop hike, take a trail at the sign "Corea Crossover," drop down to the lower-level trail, and return to the Martin Creek trailhead.

US 2 EAST OF STEVENS PASS

 LAKE JANUS

BEFORE YOU GO
Maps Green Trails No. 144 Benchmark Mountain; USFS Okanogan and Wenatchee
Current conditions Lake Wenatchee Ranger District (509) 763-3103
Northwest Forest Pass required

ABOUT THE HIKE
Day hike or backpack
Moderate for children
Mid-July–October
7 miles
650 feet elevation gain in, 700 feet out

GETTING THERE
- From US 2 at 4.25 miles east of Stevens Pass, turn left (north) onto Smith Brook Road/Road No. 6700. Use caution at this intersection.
- In 2.8 miles, look for the trailhead and limited parking on the left (north) side of the road, elevation 4200 feet.

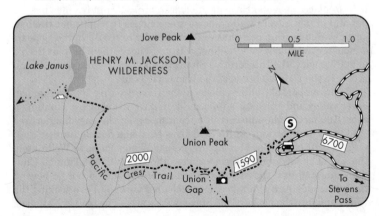

Fun on the lake shore (Photo by Ellen Burton)

ON THE TRAIL

The Roman god Janus had two faces so he could see in two directions at once. A traveler on this trail through the Henry M. Jackson Wilderness can look toward both eastern and western Washington while walking a part of the ridge that separates them—the Cascade Crest. Lake Janus, a beauty, is set among alpine meadows at the base of 6007-foot Jove Peak. Adults will enjoy the scenery along the way; children can play in the lake. The trail has some steep portions but is smooth and well- maintained. Note that there is a 700-foot descent; it must be climbed on the return.

Trail No. 1590 switchbacks steeply up to intersect the Pacific Crest

Trail at Union Gap, elevation 4680 feet. Views east are toward forests of larch, shimmering aspen, and pines along Nason Creek. The views to the west are dark with Douglas-fir, hemlock, and cedar. Follow the trail to the left for about a level mile, then climb about 400 feet before descending to the lakeshore.

Or at Union Gap, go right, following the Pacific Crest Trail northward, losing 650 feet to pass under cliffs of Union Peak. From this low point, the trail climbs again to the shores of Lake Janus, elevation 4146 feet, 3½ miles from the road.

Camping here is good but crowded by Pacific Crest Trail traffic. The water is clear, deep, and cold; children will find it better for skipping stones than for bathing. If you decide to stay, bring a stove—fuel wood is scarce and fires are prohibited. Children will enjoy seeing through-hikers backpacking on this trail on their way to Canada or Mexico.

 HEATHER LAKE

BEFORE YOU GO
Maps Green Trails No. 144 Benchmark Mountain; USFS Okanogan and Wenatchee
Current conditions Lake Wenatchee Ranger District (509) 763-3103
Wilderness Permit and Northwest Forest Pass required

ABOUT THE HIKE
Day hike or backpack
Difficult for children
July–October
6½ miles
1300 feet elevation gain

GETTING THERE

■ There are two ways to the Heather Lake trailhead. From Stevens Pass, drive 4.5 miles east on US 2, turn left on Smith Brook Road No. 6700, and go over Rainy Pass. Continue 12.8 miles on gravel Road No. 6700, then turn left on Road No. 6701 and drive to its end at the Heather Lake trailhead.

■ Or, from the north end of Lake Wenatchee, go left on Little Wenatchee River Road No. 65 and then turn left on Road No. 6700 (also known as Smith Brook Road).

■ Cross the Little Wenatchee River and continue on Road No. 6700 for 0.5 mile (call ahead to check on road closure due to late snow-melt). Turn right (north) on Road No. 6701 and drive 4.7 miles.

■ Turn left on Road No. 6701 and go another 2.3 miles to the road end and trailhead, elevation 2600 feet.

ON THE TRAIL

The trail is steep; the lake is big and beautiful. The hot summer day when I was here, children were having a fine time swimming and playing on the rocks around the shore.

The trail begins in old-growth unprotected Wenatchee National Forest. At 1 mile, it crosses Lake Creek and enters the Henry M. Jackson Wilderness. At 1½ miles, a series of murderously steep switchbacks climbs 900 feet in a very long mile that will seem like ten. (I went by two boys trying to lug an inflated raft up this trail. I wonder if they made it—the last I saw of them they were complaining from underneath it in muffled voices that there was no place to set it down.) The grade finally eases and continues another ¾ mile to sparkling Heather Lake, elevation 3953 feet, in a glacier-scooped cirque basin beneath Grizzly Peak. Many good campsites are scattered about among berry bushes and driftwood. Each comes with a view.

Logjam makes a good dock at Heather Lake.

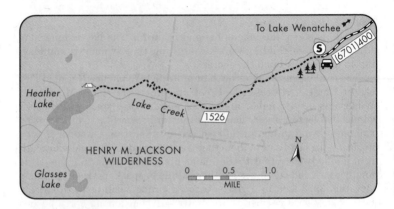

 **HIDDEN LAKE**

BEFORE YOU GO
Maps Green Trails No. 145
Wenatchee Lake; USFS
Okanogan and Wenatchee
Current conditions Lake
Wenatchee Ranger District
(509) 763-3103
**Northwest Forest Pass
required**

ABOUT THE HIKE
Day hike or backpack
Easy for children
May–November
1 mile
300 feet elevation gain

GETTING THERE

- From US 2 between Stevens Pass and Leavenworth, turn north on Highway 207 toward Lake Wenatchee.
- At 4 miles, turn left to Lake Wenatchee State Park. In a short distance (before the park boundary), turn left again on South Shore Road No. 6607.
- Just before Glacier View Campground, at 5 miles, turn left on a spur to the trailhead, elevation 2000 feet.

ON THE TRAIL

Hidden Lake lies unseen scarcely a half mile above huge Lake Wenatchee. Many families will prefer Hidden Lake, away from the crowds at Lake Wenatchee State Park, for its ponderosa-pine setting and that special feeling only a mountain lake located away from a road can provide. One

Taking a break at Hidden Lake

sunny afternoon, I watched many parents with toddlers and babies dabbling at the water's edge.

A new reroute of trail No. 1510 takes you through forests on gradual switchbacks upward. Lost on the way is the racket of powerboats on Lake Wenatchee and the sight of large trailers and campers.

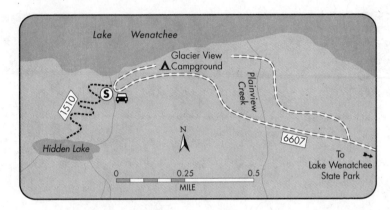

Hidden Lake, elevation 2500 feet, is long and narrow and wraps itself around the base of Nason Ridge. Boulders surround the shore on three sides. A large one makes a particularly fine swimming launch. Families, fishermen, and bathers floating in rafts for the joy of floating have a wonderful time in its cool waters.

MAD RIVER VACATION

BEFORE YOU GO
Maps Green Trails No.
146 Plain; USGS Chikamin
Creek; USFS Okanogan and
Wenatchee
Current conditions Entiat
Ranger District (509) 784-1511
**Northwest Forest Pass
required**

ABOUT THE HIKE
Backpack
Moderate for children
Mid-July–October
**Campsites: 5, 7, and 12
miles; loop trip: 12 miles**
1250 feet elevation gain

GETTING THERE
- From US 2 between Stevens Pass and Leavenworth, turn north on Highway 207 toward Lake Wenatchee State Park.
- Pass the park and, at 4 miles from US 2, just past the Wenatchee River Bridge, go straight ahead on Chiwawa Loop Road.
- Cross the Chiwawa River and at 4.2 miles, turn a sharp left on Road 6100.
- In another 1.6 miles, at Deep Creek Campground, go right on Road No. 6101, signed Maverick Saddle.

■ An even rougher road, probably best walked, leads 0.3 mile to the trailhead, signed "Mad River Trail 1409," elevation 4250 feet.

ON THE TRAIL

Here is a glorious place to take children for three days or a week. You'll find streams to wade in, a lake to swim in, loop trips, and viewpoints—all on a plateau where the subalpine forest is richly filled with flowery alpine meadows.

Hikers seldom use the area because it is open to motorcyclists. But they should. At midweek, wheels are scarce. Then families can have miles of wild area to themselves. Even on weekends, machine riders go home by nightfall. Hikers can always hike without any motorcycle interference before July 4. There are countless campsites to choose from. Pick the one that suits your pleasure and your speed.

The first mile of trail has few steep ups and downs. A sturdy bridge spans Mad River, which is not much of a river here near the headwaters but rather a splendid creek. At 2½ miles find the first of many attractive streamside campsites; here you can adjust your ambitions to the capabilities of your children. At 4 miles, cross the river on a driftwood log and at 4½ miles, recross on boulders. At 5 miles enter the first of the meadows, and at 6 miles reach unmanned Blue Creek Camp Guard Station, an old log cabin, built in the 1920s—an ideal place for a base camp, elevation 6100 feet.

Old guard station near Mad River

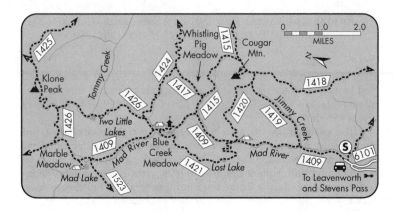

Day trips abound. Hike 2 more miles to beautiful, blue Mad Lake on a fairly level trail through meadows and subalpine forest; swimming is good on a small beach at the inlet. Hike to Two Little Lakes at 2½ miles; or loop through Whistling Pig Meadow, named for its colony of marmots. A more strenuous hike is to the top of Cougar Mountain for panoramic views of forest and mountains. The map will suggest other loops.

Be aware that half of the motorcycle drivers on these trails are courteous and will slow down when passing you; the other half, mainly unsupervised youngsters, whiz by at full speed, using hikers as part of an obstacle course.

66 SPIDER MEADOW

BEFORE YOU GO
Maps Green Trails No. 113 Holden; USFS Okanogan and Wenatchee
Current conditions Lake Wenatchee Ranger District (509) 763-3103
Wilderness Permit and Northwest Forest Pass required

ABOUT THE HIKE
Day hike or backpack
Difficult for children
July–October
10 miles
2000 feet elevation gain

Opposite page: Walking through Spider Meadow

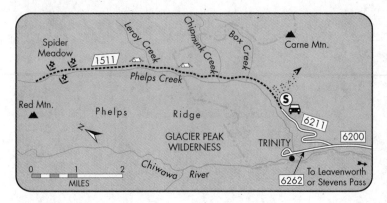

GETTING THERE

- From Stevens Pass, drive US 2 east 17 miles and turn north on the Lake Wenatchee Road. Pass Wenatchee State Park and cross the Wenatchee River.
- Turn right at the final junction, go 1.5 miles, and then turn left on Chiwawa River Road No. 6200, signed "Trinity." Drive 22 miles.
- Turn right on Road No. 6211, signed "Phelps Creek," and go 2.5 miles to a gate and the trailhead, elevation 3500 feet.

ON THE TRAIL

Beneath a spectacular headwall of cliffs and waterfalls sprawls a marvelous wide meadow valley, the reward for a 5-mile walk into Glacier Peak Wilderness. Elevation gain is gradual enough that the kids will not have any one steep area to climb in a short distance. Camp amid flower fields, beside a cold meandering stream. Children will find that the deer here are almost tame.

The hike begins on an old miners' road, passing the Carne Mountain trail at ¼ mile, Box Creek at 1 mile, and Chipmunk Creek at 1¾ miles, a good turnaround close to Phelps Creek. At 2⅔ miles, where the road becomes trail, enter Glacier Peak Wilderness. At 3½ miles, cross Leroy Creek and pass the Leroy Creek trail.

All of the creeks are delightful resting places—and campsites, if necessary. From Leroy Creek, it's an easy 1½ miles through spruce, noble fir, and alpine flowers, or berries in season, to Spider Meadow, elevation 5500 feet.

The parkland extends more than a mile north and south, bordered up-valley by the cliffs of Dumbbell and Red Mountains. Campsites edge the meadow; walk to the upper end for more secluded campsites at the base of a talus slope and to see the ruins of an old miner's cabin. Above lies 7100-foot Spider Gap with a small glacier lying in it. In early morning or evening, children may see the curious deer approach camp and play, chasing each other through the meadow flowers.

EIGHTMILE LAKE

BEFORE YOU GO
Maps Green Trails No. 177 Chiwaukam Mountains; USGS Cashmere Mountain; USFS Okanogan and Wenatchee
Current conditions Leavenworth Ranger District (509) 548-6977
Wilderness Permit and Northwest Forest Pass required

ABOUT THE HIKE
Day hike or backpack
Difficult for children
May–November
6½ miles
1360 feet elevation gain

GETTING THERE

- From US 2 at the west end of Leavenworth, turn right (south) on Icicle Road and drive 8.5 miles.
- Turn left on Eightmile Creek Road No. 7601 and drive 3 miles to Eightmile Creek trail No. 1552, elevation 2900 feet.

ON THE TRAIL

The Icicle River valley burned in the summer of 1994. At least one-third of the trees along this trail—ponderosa pine, hemlocks, and cedars—were transformed into charred sentinels and silver forest. New life is generating, however, as it always has. Children will enjoy seeing the vestiges of old stumps surrounded by green growth and hearing the story of searing crown fires roaring up Eightmile Creek. The lake is still a lovely glacier-carved irrigation reservoir with a dam at one end. Poignantly, signs requesting that no campfires be built near the

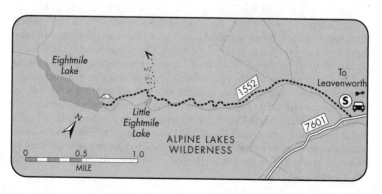

Glacier-carved Eightmile Lake

shoreline are posted on burned trees along the shoreline.

Begin with a steep ½-mile ascent through partially burned trees, wild roses, and fireweed. The next ½ mile on an old logging roadbed will be easier before you turn into a grove of scorched and scarred old-growth trees alongside the white water of Eightmile Creek in the Alpine Lakes Wilderness. This would make a good resting place or turnaround point.

At 2½ miles, start upward again. Look closely for places along the needle-carpeted trail where the stumps burned so hot into the ground that the roots left holes shaped like octopus tentacles; new growth may have covered over these interesting holes. Climbing steadily, at 3 miles the trail comes to a small lake that fluctuates according to water needs below. Continue up another ½ mile through a massive red rock slide. The reward for your 3¼ miles is Eightmile Lake, elevation 4461 feet.

This lake and Little Eightmile were dammed to supply water for irrigation and for the Icicle Creek fish hatchery. Look for the vintage 1930s hand-built stone dam and its ruined, rusty petcock. Swimming here, amid glacier-carved rocks and driftwood logs, can be refreshing—that is to say, cold—but after the hot trail, good . . . very good. Campsites are on the shoreline to the right.

ICICLE GORGE

BEFORE YOU GO
Maps Green Trails No. 171
Chiwaukum Mountains
Current conditions
Leavenworth Ranger District
(509) 548-6977
**Northwest Forest Pass
required**

ABOUT THE HIKE
Day hike
Easy for children
Late May–October
4-mile loop
100 feet elevation gain and loss

GETTING THERE

- At a gas station on US 2 at the west end of Leavenworth, turn south onto Icicle Road.
- Drive 16.5 miles to Chatter Creek Campground. Icicle Road becomes Road No. 7600.
- About 0.75 mile past Chatter Creek Campground, turn left into a large parking lot and find the well-marked trailhead, elevation 2800 feet.

ON THE TRAIL

This is a delightful walk along the banks of Icicle Creek, which alternates between a rippling creek and an angry torrent within a narrow rock canyon. Along with views for parents are opportunities for kids to get their feet wet. Forest fires left this woodland area untouched, so families can cool off in the shade of old trees on a hot day along the banks of the creek.

We met many families with small children on this trail. At one point

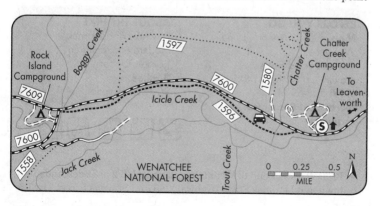

Chatter Creek trail bridge over Icicle Creek

on a hot August day we saw folks sitting on folding camp chairs in the middle of the Icicle River with their children playing in the water beside them. Whether they were hikers was hard to tell, but they were cooling off in an unusual way.

Icicle Gorge Trail No. 1596 leads you sometimes next to the creek, sometimes out of sight of the creek but never out of its sound. Look for several spurs to bluffs, where you can show the children the foaming white water below. The trail, with ups and downs, travels along both sides of the creek. Cross the creek on a wooden footbridge at Rock Island Campground at the top end of the loop.

 CLARA AND MARION LAKES

BEFORE YOU GO
Map USFS Okanogan and Wenatchee
Current conditions
Leavenworth Ranger District
(509) 548-6977
Northwest Forest Pass required

ABOUT THE HIKE
Day hike or backpack
Moderate for children
July to October
3 miles
900 feet elevation gain

GETTING THERE

- From the west end of Wenatchee, stay on US 2 as it descends into town and becomes State Highway 285 and Stevens Street. In 1.5

miles Stevens Street becomes Squilchuck Road. Turn left on Mission Street.

■ In 6.5 miles bear right onto Wenatchee Mountain Road, which becomes Mission Ridge Road as it winds up the hill toward the ski area.

■ Find the trailhead for Squilchuck Trail No. 1200 in the large Mission Ridge parking lot on the far right side, elevation 4600 feet.

ON THE TRAIL

Small, shallow Clara Lake is surrounded by fir and larch trees, with meadows and a rock slide at the end of a very steep trail. Because the lake bottom is sand, children can safely play in water warmed by summer sun. On a hot day even parents will want a refreshing wade. Try this hike in late September or early October, when the larch trees have turned golden.

Children attempting this hike should be strong and accustomed to steep trails, as this one is a huffer-puffer, climbing 900 feet in 1 mile through lava scree. The good part is the trail is short. The bad part is that it is also open to motorbikes and horses.

The trail starts steeply and stays steep, passing through a forest of fir and ponderosa pine. A confusing mixture of shortcuts and old trails might make you wonder if you are on the right trail. Snowmobiles also use this path in the winter. The trail alternates between forest and the rubble of an old lava flow, zigzagging upward. Once in forest no motorbikes are allowed. At ⅓ mile look for an intersection; go left about 200 feet on an abandoned road, then right on the trail again. Cross a creek at ¾ mile. Just before 1 mile the climb eases off; at 1¼ miles look for a junction signed "Liberty—Beehive." This trail leads to a swampy pond. Go left, and in ¼ mile, after passing a marsh, arrive at little Clara Lake, gleaming in the sunlight. This lake has a sister around the corner. Lake Marion has a more fluctuating water level. Both lakes are fed by cold underground springs, so though children will want to wade, they won't stay in long.

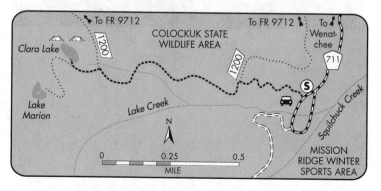

Meadow flowers surround the shoreline, and there are two nice camp-sites, one on the right side of the lake and one on the left side, next to a hollow tree that looks like a guardhouse in front of a queen's palace. All it needs is a soldier in a red coat. While here, we came across a snowshoe rabbit in summer coloring, carrying a baby bunny in her mouth.

Clara Lake

he Snoqualmie Pass/I-90 corridor trails start on the east side at Blewett Pass with an old lookout, Red Top, and the north fork Teanaway with Esmeralda Basin. Other east-side I-90 trails families love are Rachel Lake, Pete and Hyas Lakes, and the historic Coal Mines Trail, between Cle Elum and Roslyn. Be sure to stop in that town to see the place where the television series *Northern Exposure* was filmed. Hikes near North Bend include such spectacular destinations as Snoqualmie Falls, Little Si, Rattlesnake Lake and Ledge, Otter Falls, Twin Falls, and Talapus Lake. Even small children can make the short hike to the plunge pool of Franklin Falls out of the Denny Creek area and slide on the Denny Creek Water Slide. The most popular hike in the state, the trail to Snow Lake, has its trailhead near the Alpental ski area.

BLEWETT PASS HIGHWAY 97

 RED TOP LOOKOUT

BEFORE YOU GO
Maps Green Trails No. 209 Mt. Stuart, No. 210 Liberty; USGS Mt. Stuart
Current conditions Cle Elum Ranger District (509) 852-1100
Northwest Forest Pass required

ABOUT THE HIKE
Day hike
Easy for children
June–October
2 miles
360 feet elevation gain

GETTING THERE
■ Leave I-90 at exit 85, east of Cle Elum. Take Highway 970/90 north for 18 miles.
■ Just beyond Mineral Springs Campground, turn left (west) off Highway 97 and then go north on Road No. 9738.
■ In 2.6 miles turn left onto Road No. 9702. Drive 4.5 miles more to the trailhead of trail No. 1364, elevation 5000 feet.

ON THE TRAIL
Children will enjoy the short hike to this high lookout perched on a cliff, but they will gasp at its sweeping views. Still used during fire season, the building is locked at most other times. No matter. The flower-lined

Red Top Lookout perched on a mountaintop

path leads through very old trees and rock outcrops to views of the
Mount Stuart area similar to those of the Swiss Alps. Mount Rainier and
Mount Adams float above the skyline. The kids can dream of someday
becoming mountain climbers.

Look up to the skyline and help kids find the tiny lookout building
perched there like a toy box on stilts. Start walking along an old road,
which enters ancient forest briefly. When the path emerges into steep
rock outcrops, the desert and alpine flower show starts. Depending on
the season you may see lupine, wild mustard, forget-me-not, paintbrush,
and balsamroot. In less than 1 mile the trail traverses cliffs, winds
around the pinnacle on which the lookout sits on stilts, and brings you
to the foot of its ladder. Be careful of loose rock along this section, and
be sure to carry water. From the trail we saw soaring ravens, and a pine
siskin went by below us.

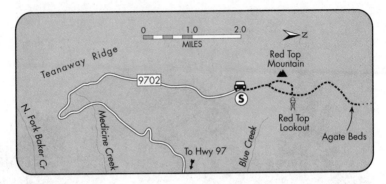

This area is known for its agates and thunder eggs. In fact, they are called Red Top thunder eggs and have been dug out of the ground here for decades. A thunder egg looks like an ordinary rock, but inside, it contains crystals that can be made into jewelry. Tell children that the crystals were once liquid trapped inside, and as the liquid dried slowly, it turned into crystals. You can walk from the same trailhead for another mile to find the agate bed excavation sites, in the form of dug-up ground. The rockhounds who do the digging camp at the road's end in order to spend time searching the rocks below the lookout for undiscovered treasures.

 ESMERALDA BASIN

BEFORE YOU GO
Maps Green Trails No. 209 Mt. Stuart; USFS Okanogan and Wenatchee
Current conditions Cle Elum Ranger District (509) 852-1100
Northwest Forest Pass required

ABOUT THE HIKE
Day hike or backpack
Moderate for children
June to October
6 miles
1200 feet elevation gain

GETTING THERE

■ Leave I-90 at exit 85, east of Cle Elum. On the eastern outskirts of town, bear left onto US Highway 970, which becomes Highway 97, toward Wenatchee.
■ In 5 miles, turn sharply onto Teanaway River Road. Drive 13.5 miles to a junction at 29 Pines Campground.

▪ Stay right, pass Beverly Camp, and at 23 miles reach the end of the road and the trailhead of trail No. 1394, elevation 4243 feet.

ON THE TRAIL

One of the wonderful aspects of the Teanaway River valley (Indian for "Place of Fish and Berries") is the promise of sunshine. Although the weather may be cool and wet in Seattle, the Teanaway valley, in the rain shadow of the Cascades, usually has dependable sunshine.

An old miners' access road to long-ago gold mines now switchbacks through flower-filled meadows to high viewpoints. Children will be intrigued by the sight of rock climbers with their curious gear, leaving from the same trailhead to climb Ingalls Peak. The trail is wide and gains elevation gradually between rugged ridges, past flower gardens renowned among botanists for their rare and unusual species.

Begin steeply on an old mining road built in 1910 between Esmeralda Peak, on the left, and Teanaway Peak, on the right, alongside rushing Esmeralda Creek. If a child can be lured up the first ¼ mile of this climb, the rest will be relatively easy. Switchback above the creek past several possible campsites (if you are on a first backpack with a baby, a camp along the river here would be a good choice), then gain elevation more gradually until ½ mile, where the trail splits to the right for Ingalls Way.

Red columbine, a common flower in the Cascades

Since the trail is an old road, it is wide enough for families to walk hold-ing hands at the beginning. Continue past a swampy meadow filled in late June and early July with white bog orchids, hot-pink shooting stars, and little red "elephant's heads." (Kids should look for the tiny elephants' uplifted trunks.)

Rockeries filled with showy flowers improve in color and diversity with every step. The trail is steep and rough in places and has numer-ous creeks in early summer, where young children will need help. An un-marked fork at 1¼ miles has logs barring one way. Go right and gauge the elevation you've gained by the cliffs and snow patches on the opposite wall. Look for lavender mats of creeping phlox, pink Indian paintbrush, scarlet gilia, and cream-colored pussy toes. (Have the kids look for the kittens' tiny paw pads.) Some rockeries have clumps of delicate *Lewisia columbiana,* with a tiny pink stripe on each petal.

At 2 miles reach Esmeralda Basin, the site of an old gold-mining camp. Stop to look, munch, and enjoy. Pull out your map to identify the peaks and ridges around you. If your family has sufficient energy, continue 1 mile more on easy switchbacks up to Fortune Creek Pass for the satis-faction of reaching the high point and wonderful views of the Cle Elum drainage, Mount Hinman, Mount Daniels, and Cathedral Peak. In early fall the basin may be filled with golden larches, each surrounded by pools of fallen gold needles.

The distinctive pink-red cliffs of the Teanaway valley are as fascinating to children today as they were to their grandfathers. If the kids' eyes are sharp, they may see tailings from miners' tunnels along the base of the cliffs. Explain that the miners took gold, silver, copper, and chrome ore from these mountains but not in sufficient quantities to pay them a living wage. Instead, they took the samples to speculators who bought stock in the mines.

I-90 WEST OF SNOQUALMIE PASS

 RED TOWN AND COAL CREEK LOOP TRAIL

BEFORE YOU GO
Maps Green Trails No. 203S
Cougar Mountain; Cougar
Mountain Wildland map
available at trailhead; USGS
Mercer Island, Issaquah
Current conditions King
County Parks and Recreation
Dept. (206) 296-4232

ABOUT THE HIKE
Day hike
Easy for children
Year round
3 miles
Minimal elevation gain

GETTING THERE

■ East of Factoria, leave I-90 at exit 13 and drive south on Lakemont
Boulevard Southeast for 3.1 miles.

■ Look for the signed, gravel entrance to the Red Town trailhead on
the left, and the Cougar Mountain Wildland Park entrance, elevation, 640 feet.

ON THE TRAIL

A historic coal mining area, close to Renton, offers children glimpses
of century-old mining artifacts in the midst of second-growth forest. A
replica coal car filled with coal sits in front of a blocked mine shaft, the
Ford Slope Mine, and its vent. The mine shaft dropped 3500 feet to 200
feet below sea level. Nearby look for a display of Asahel Curtis photos of
miners and their 1870s vintage railroad and mill.

This industry was vital to the growth of early Seattle, and its remnant relics are part of the local heritage. Red Town is the name of the
mining community that worked these coal mines until 1926. Tell your
kids that children played merry-go-round on the railroad turntable
when no one was looking. The town's baseball team once played ball on
the restored meadow the trail passes. A network of trails makes a loop
walk possible for kids.

From the parking area you can loop either clockwise or counterclockwise. By turning right, or counterclockwise, you can avoid a short climb
at the beginning. Walk around a service gate and up a gravel road to an
intersection with China Crest Trail W-5. Turn left at the Rainbow Town

Huckleberry

Trail W-3, dropping to the informational kiosk and coal car. The kids will want to go into the mouth of the sealed mine shaft but should be warned that for safety reasons they cannot. Look up instead to find a large H on a tree trunk, where the steam hoist for the coal cars once worked. You can walk along Coal Creek on a short loop, W-4, that takes you past the remnants of the old sawmill and dam for the millpond and then leads you back to the Rainbow Town Trail again.

Go uphill, past the vent from another mining shaft and its collapsed entrance. Continue until you intersect with Red Town Trail W-2, a county road. Pass a metal trough once used to water horses and then, on the right, find the restored meadow and Wildside Trail W-1. Native plants such as wild currant, lupine, columbine, kinnikinnick, vine maple, yarrow, false Solomon's-seal, and red huckleberry have been planted on the former baseball field. Walk through on the loop path to see what is in bloom.

Step up on the bridge and over Coal Creek to continue on Wildside Trail, passing the steam hoist trail again. One last trail option, the Bagley Seam Trail W-10, leads past an exposed layer of coal, much like that which was first found here in 1863. Join the Red Town Trail W-2 again to bring you back to the parking lot.

Mining displays along Red Town Trail

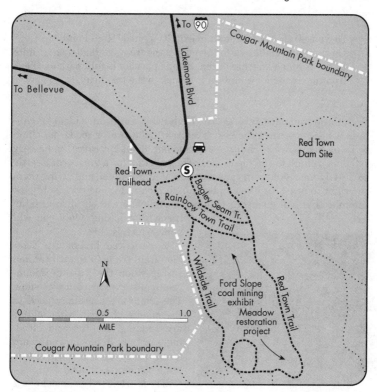

7 3 HIGH POINT

BEFORE YOU GO
Maps Green Trails No. 204S
Tiger Mountain; USGS Fall
City; check trailhead reader
board
Current conditions King
County Parks and Recreation
Dept. (206) 296-4232

ABOUT THE HIKE
Day hike
Moderate to difficult for children
Year round
Talus Rocks: 2½ miles;
West Tiger Vista: 5 miles
600 feet and 1800 feet
elevation gain

GETTING THERE

- Drive I-90 east of Issaquah to exit 20, signed "High Point."
- Go right and right again, then drive the frontage road a short mile to the trailhead parking area. If the upper lot is full, park on the frontage road below and walk it back to the trailheads.

ON THE TRAIL

With three trail opportunities, the High Point trailhead is ideal for children. Choose between the easy Tradition Lake trail, a moderate climb to Talus Rocks where children can find out about bat caves, and a very strenuous climb to the top of West Tiger Vista 3 for a view over Seattle to the Olympic Mountains and south to Mount Rainier, and giving them the right to boast they've climbed a real mountain. The trick is to pick the hike that will give your children a challenge without discouraging them from hiking. Only you will know which is best.

Experienced hikers use Tiger Mountain trails in the winter and spring when the Cascade Mountain trails are buried under snow. The trails are especially good in the middle of April, when alders are budding, trillium and bleeding heart are in bloom, and sword ferns unfurl their fronds, resembling elephants' trunks.

The loop trip to Tradition Lake is level and rewarding for those with small children. Even those pushing a stroller could manage this trail. Benches along the way and good interpretive signs help. Look for plaques with embossed prints of the tracks of deer, dog, cougar, and raccoon. At the lake the children can scan the water for ducks and water lilies.

For Talus Rocks, follow the West Tiger Vista 3 Trail about 500 feet and go right on Bus Trail (a very old, rusty tour bus explains the name and may make your kids laugh) a short 1000 feet. Then go left on Nook Trail for a long mile. The way starts out easy but gets

Interpretive sign along the trail

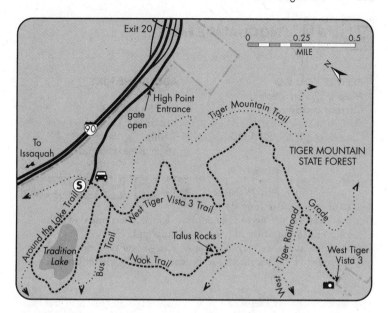

progressively steeper. At about 1½ miles, reach the large moss-covered boulders. A circular trail squeezes through a narrow passage and passes a deep hole, the overhangs, and the fenced-off Bat Cave. Tell the kids that bats are nocturnal, so they are seldom seen, but they contribute to our well-being by consuming vast numbers of harmful and pesky flying insects, including mosquitoes, every night.

West Tiger Vista 3 Trail is a very steep trail for children, climbing 800 feet a mile, but if your children are up to it, reaching a summit will reward them. From the parking area, follow the West Tiger Vista 3 Trail, passing Bus Trail on the right, Tiger Mountain Trail on the left, and, in about ¾ mile, Connector Trail on the right (not recommended for children). At 2 miles, cross the West Tiger Railroad Grade, where the trees become shorter and windswept. At 2½ miles, arrive at the bald summit, rewarding views, and a well-deserved rest.

Bat

SNOQUALMIE FALLS

BEFORE YOU GO
Map USGS Snoqualmie
Current conditions
Snoqualmie Chamber of
Commerce (425) 888-4440

ABOUT THE HIKE
Day hike
Easy for children
Year round
1 mile
Minimal elevation gain

GETTING THERE

- Leave I-90 at exit 25 (State Route 18, Snoqualmie Parkway) and go left, across Snoqualmie Ridge. Continue down the long hill to the railroad tracks and stoplight.
- Turn left at the well-signed intersection, go over the bridge, and drive 0.3 mile to the parking area at Snoqualmie Falls Visitor Center.

ON THE TRAIL

This short hike to the base of a 268-foot waterfall, so beautiful the Indians considered it a sacred place, is easy at any time of year. Puget Sound Energy has harnessed the waterfall's force and provided the combination of road and trail, but the rocky riverbed beach, sandbars, bedrock benches, caves, and pools have been appropriated by kids and families. Snoqualmie Falls is 100 feet higher than Niagara Falls.

Begin by walking around the power station gate and down the paved South East Fish Hatchery Road to the station house. Beside it, the bank serves as a launching point for kayaks, canoes, and rafts. Children will want to gaze at the interesting craft bobbing and balancing in the eddying current in front of them. Pass the trail from the visitor's center and take the second trail, behind the power station. Part of this trail is completely enclosed with fencing, like a cage. Kids can listen to the hum, and look through powerhouse windows to the turbines generating power from the waterfall for 16,000 homes. On the other side of the cage, you can follow the trail either down to the rocky riverbed or on a fenced boardwalk to a dead-end viewpoint of the falls.

To continue beyond the viewpoint, walk back toward the powerhouse and find a short path to the river. Once on the riverbed, proceed through boulders toward the waterfall as close as you wish. In midsummer when water levels are low, children stop to wade in pools at the river's edge. Families find niches and boulders along the bank for picnicking in the mist and spray. At the base of the majestic falls, people stop and stare

Opposite page: Snoqualmie Falls on the Snoqualmie River

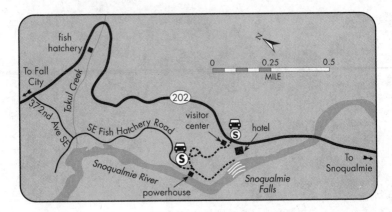

wordlessly upward at the plunging, free-falling curtain of water. The sight is so compelling it is hard to turn away.

Hikers can often be seen walking down from the platform to the river bed and even wandering close to the falls. However, the river's water volume can change without notice because it is a dam-controlled river. Getting close to the falls is dangerous as well. Please keep children from going any farther than the viewing platform.

 LITTLE SI

BEFORE YOU GO
Maps Green Trails No. 206S Mt. Si; USGS North Bend, Mt. Si
Current conditions Snoqualmie Chamber of Commerce (425) 888-4440; Snoqualmie Ranger District (425) 888-1421

ABOUT THE HIKE
Day hike
Moderate for children
Year round
5 miles
1500 feet elevation gain

GETTING THERE
- Leave I-90 at exit 31 and follow signs into North Bend.
- At a stoplight in town, turn right (east) onto Southeast North Bend Way. Drive 1.5 miles.
- Turn left (north) onto SE Mount Si Road, also signed "432nd Street," and drive 0.5 mile over a bridge to the new DNR parking lot on the left, elevation 500 feet.

ON THE TRAIL

Too many beginners with children take them on the Mount Si Trail, which proves to be so difficult that the kids may never want to hike again. Overlooked is kid-size Little Si, which is also difficult but more realistic, offering children the challenge and satisfaction of climbing to a rocky summit with a view.

The trail starts up steeply, entering trees at ¼ mile. The trail has been rebuilt and joins an older one with signed junctions, which indicate trails leading left for rock-climbing routes and right for hiking trails. Your route will lead west, between Big and Little Si; wind around Little Si; and bring you up its west ridge.

The two Si's are examples of different kinds of rock. Mount Si is old, slowly cooled magma from deep beneath the surface of the earth, called gabbro. Little Si is volcanic rock that cooled more quickly, from beneath an oceanic lava flow, with telltale crystalline outcrops. Enormous old boulders have tumbled down the cliff separating the two peaks; the resulting rock slide is now covered by moss and shaded by firs and hemlocks.

The trail starts steeply up again on the west side of the mountain, over roots and rocky ledges. Some ledges come equipped with trees and branches just the right size for handholds, but the steps can be long for short legs.

At the summit a dry microclimate has encouraged pine and manzanitas to grow. As you rest, explain plate tectonics to your kids with visual aids. Tell them that the plate beneath the ocean shoves against the plate of the continent zone, and as a result rocks are crunched, folded, and "smooshed." At the same time the oceanic plate dives under the continental one. Only after centuries of uplifting and erosion can we see the results.

You may want to compare the chunks of different kinds of rock mixed together to the nuts, fruits, and batter in a fruitcake. The rocks have

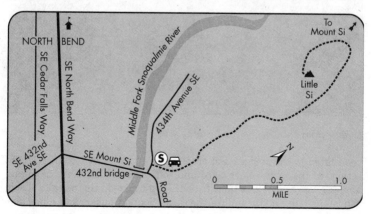

Hikers enjoy the view on the Little Si trail.

been lifted to the surface and eroded away, so we can see the tectonic action. In the mixture are hard and soft pieces—hard blobs as big as Mount Si, or as small as their fist—the fruit mixed into the cake of soft sandstone. After all the uplifts, the Puget Sound Glacier came along and scraped the rocks, leaving long scratches. Only the little haystack on the summit of Mount Si protruded above the glacier and was not affected.

At Little Si's summit children can look out over the Middle Snoqualmie River and valley, then back to massive Mount Si in the other direction. Tell them that when they get a little older, that summit can be their objective.

RATTLESNAKE LAKE AND LEDGE

BEFORE YOU GO
Maps Green Trails No. 205S Rattlesnake, 206 Bandera; USGS North Bend; Cedar River Watershed map
Current conditions Mountains to Sound Greenway (206) 382-5565; Snoqualmie Ranger District (425) 888-1421

ABOUT THE HIKE
Day hike
Moderate for children
Year round
Up ledge: 4 miles; around lake: 2 miles
1174 feet elevation gain

GETTING THERE

- From I-90 east of North Bend, take exit 32 onto 436th Street.
- Go right (south) on 436th Avenue SE, which becomes Cedar Falls Road, and drive 2.7 miles to reach the park.
- Just before entering the park's gate, turn either direction into the Rattlesnake Ledge trailhead parking lot. To reach the trailhead, walk on the graveled road that bends around the north side of Rattlesnake Lake, elevation 920 feet.

ON THE TRAIL

A wide trail runs around scenic Rattlesnake Lake past a picnic area on the west side to the south end. On a hot day instead of climbing to the ledge, the kids may prefer to stay here for wading and swimming, or that may instead be a reward you can offer them after they return. Another reward after the hike is the Cedar River Watershed Visitors Center, where an early town called Cedar Falls once stood and which contains natural history and artistic exhibits children will love. In the Rain Drum Courtyard you can listen to drums being played by amplified raindrops.

Rattlesnake Ledge has been beloved for decades as the easternmost peak of the Issaquah Alps, and for its great 270-degree outlook over Mount Si, Mount Washington, Chester Morse and Rattlesnake Lakes, and the Middle Fork Snoqualmie valley. The improved ledge trail is the result of thousands of hours of work by volunteer crews, which worked to lengthen it and make the grade more gradual. Children love taking their dogs along. They may guess why it's called Rattlesnake Ledge. Tell them early settlers thought the whispering sound of grasses blowing in the wind sounded like rattles, but there are no snakes here.

At one time the area at the base of the ledge was called Rattlesnake Prairie. Indians dug camas bulbs growing here for their winter food. The city of Seattle appropriated Chester Morse Lake for a water intake in the 1880s and closed the watershed in 1911, but the land is still managed by the city. In 1912, the town of Monckton stood where the lake now lies; in 1915, that town was flooded when a dam failed.

Begin upward on the trail in old second-growth forest on gradual switchbacks. Children will see occasional giant boulders, left by the

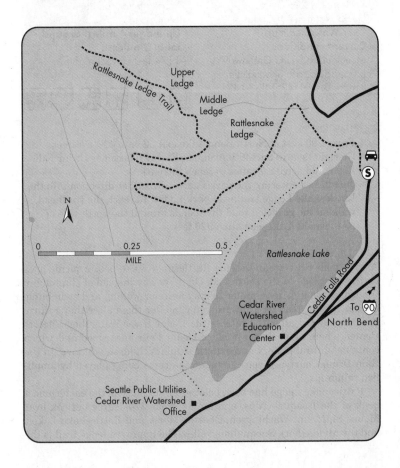

Admiring the view from Rattlesnake Ledge

glacier, that are studded and encrusted with ferns and moss, along with old cedar stumps left over from logging days. At about 1 mile the kids can expect the first view straight down to Rattlesnake Lake. At 2 miles the trail divides. Go right for the final short, steep climb to the rock ledges and sweeping views of the Middle Fork Snoqualmie valley. Hang onto the hands of children here because the drop is severe. Sit down, get out the map and lunch and enjoy the spectacle of Mount Si, Mount Washington, Chester Morse Lake, Rattlesnake Lake, and the Middle Fork Snoqualmie valley around and beneath you.

 OTTER FALLS

BEFORE YOU GO
Maps Green Trails No. 174 Mount Si; USFS Mt. Baker–Snoqualmie
Current conditions
Snoqualmie Ranger District (425) 888-1421
Northwest Forest Pass required

ABOUT THE HIKE
Day hike
Moderate for children
March–November
7 miles
650 feet elevation gain

GETTING THERE
- Drive I-90 past North Bend to exit 34 and Truck Town. Turn north and pass the commercial stations in 1 mile to reach Middle Fork Snoqualmie Road.

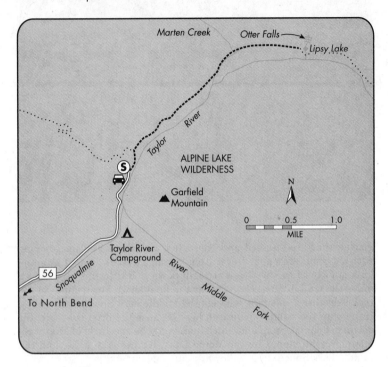

- Turn right and drive 10 miles on Road 56 to the Taylor River Bridge and the end of the road, elevation 1225 feet.

ON THE TRAIL

A former road, now a trail, follows alongside the Taylor River to a waterfall, giving children views of creeks and tributaries as they enter into the river. Otter Falls is the destination and climax of the hike. Children will be awestruck by the old-growth cedar forest leading up to the falls and by its plunge pool. Don't count on seeing an otter, though. Explain to them that river otters are rarely available for viewing on schedule. The falls, however, are dependably there and will provide a whole series of little cataracts, pools, water slides, foam, and spray.

Begin walking across the bridge and continue past Quartz Creek Road alongside the Taylor River. The massive mountain looming overhead is Garfield, no relation to the comic cat but named for a president. After 3 miles through second-growth forest of alder and maple, arrive at Marten Creek with its new bridge over a splashing tributary waterfall.

Continue another 1¼ mile to a small side trail on the left leading up through old-growth forest. It may not be well marked. Massive cedar trees here have trunks that might require eight or ten children to circle. Continue on and drop down to the plunge pool of Otter Falls. The cataract falling into it from above is not vertical but slips down at an unusual diagonal slant. Find a place on the shoreline where you can gaze and enjoy its beauty. When I was there, a family with kids was paddling in inner tubes around the plunge pool.

Otter Falls and its plunge pool

TWIN FALLS STATE PARK

BEFORE YOU GO
Maps Green Trails No. 206
Bandera, No. 206S Mount Si
Current conditions
Washington State Parks (360)
902-8844
**State park annual or
day-use pass required**

ABOUT THE HIKE
Day hike
Easy for children
April to November
1½ miles
300 feet elevation gain and loss

GETTING THERE

■ Just east of North Bend, leave I-90 at exit 34 (Edgewick Road) and turn right on 468th Avenue SE. Drive 0.6 mile.

■ Turn left on SE 159th and find a parking lot in another 0.6 mile at the road's end, elevation 600 feet.

ON THE TRAIL

This Washington State Parks trail was rebuilt in late 1989 as compensation for a new hydroelectric project, the Weeks Falls Power Plant, farther up the river. The walk through magnificent old-growth forest leads to views of two South Fork Snoqualmie River waterfalls. Children will love everything about this hike: the moss-covered nurse logs, the enormous cedar and fir trees, the panoramic view at waterfall level from a viewing platform, and the bridge crossing over and between two waterfalls. The wonder of falling water forming into spray—dropping, dropping, and then becoming river again—holds timeless fascination for children of all ages.

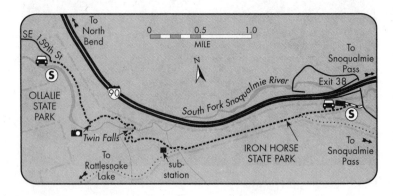

Hikers enjoying enormous old-growth trees along Twin Falls trail

Beginning at the lower end of the trail, walk a graveled and graded surface past moss-covered second-growth alder and maple. As you follow the river, larger and older evergreens provide canopy. In a short mile the trail switchbacks 300 feet up a rocky moraine for a first view of the fan-shaped 90-foot lower falls at a three-way trail fork. For the best view, go right 20 feet. This makes a fine turnaround point, or you can stop at the river's edge for a picnic. To continue on, choose the middle trail, leading down to the river. Once there, turn right, off the trail, beside a truly enormous old fir, perhaps 700 years old, and pause on the river's edge: Directly over everything hovers 1300-foot Mount Washington, clear-cut on this side.

From the river, the trail climbs again. The kids will love the side trip down a flight of 103 steps to a viewing platform opposite the falls. Families stand transfixed at the spectacular sight of the sculpted cliff covered by falling white water. Children can imagine they are suspended over the river and look down at caves behind the falls that have been eroded by the water's force. The caves are frequently filled with branches and logs, held in place by the waterfall.

Back on the trail, continue up a fern-covered ridge, at times within sound of the freeway, past enormous moss-covered gray blocks of basalt that look like Inca ruins. Reach the bridge over the top of the falls 1¾ miles from the lower parking lot. The bridge is substantial enough for the most timid; from here, stop to gaze at the powerful two-stage upper falls. Jagged gray boulders lined with maidenhair ferns channel the water first right, then left. For other impressive views, cross the bridge and walk ¼ mile to another enormous old tree, where a family can munch on sandwiches and ponder the force of water.

 TALAPUS LAKE

BEFORE YOU GO
Maps Green Trails No. 206 Bandera; USGS Bandera
Current conditions
Snoqualmie Ranger District (360) 888-1421
Wilderness Permit and Northwest Forest Pass required

ABOUT THE HIKE
Day hike or backpack
Moderate for children
July–October
5 miles
1120 feet elevation gain

GETTING THERE
- Leave I-90 at exit 45 (signed "USFS 9030"). At the stop sign turn north.
- Turn left on Road 9030 and drive 0.75 mile.
- Turn right at the junction, following Road No. 9030 uphill to the trailhead at the end of the road, elevation 2600 feet.

ON THE TRAIL
Easy access, a short trail, camping, fishing, and proximity to Olallie and many other lakes are the reasons Talapus is one of the most popular lakes in the greater Snoqualmie Pass area.

Trail No. 1039 begins in a former clear-cut with deciduous undergrowth over an old roadbed. The trail climbs gradually in long switchbacks, narrowing as it enters second growth. At 1 mile you come close to a stream with large rocks for resting on. Some can serve as picnic tables if this is your lunch stop.

At 1¾ miles, the trail levels and enters the Alpine Lakes Wilderness, where you will see enormous old-growth cedars. Watch for wild lily-of-the-valley and the tiny pink bells of twinflower lining the trail.

The trail follows the lake's outlet stream, zigzagging toward and away from it. Some of the zags also make good resting places. Just before the lake is a fork, with the right trail offering more campsites but the left with some good ones as well. At 2 miles expect the first view of the lake, set in a deeply wooded basin, elevation 3680 feet. There are at least fifteen campsites for the 4000 or more visitors a year this lake receives. The day I was there, sixteen Cub Scouts were having their fishing lines threaded by their grandfathers. Somebody asked who was going to catch the first fish. All sixteen shouted, "I am!"

Talapus Lake

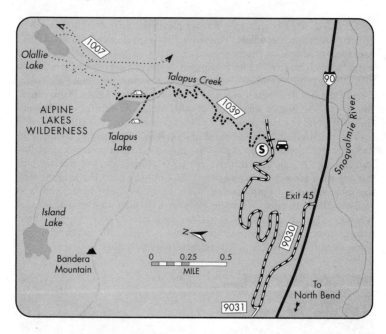

If your young hikers still have energy to burn, they can continue another ¾ mile to Olallie Lake, 3600 feet. Its beautiful lakeside camps are bigger and have more water-level access than those at Talapus Lake.

80 IRA SPRING TRAIL

BEFORE YOU GO
Map Green Trails No. 206 Bandera
Current conditions Snoqualmie Ranger District (360) 888-1421
Northwest Forest Pass required; Wilderness Permit required for Mason Lake

ABOUT THE HIKE
Day hike
Difficult for children
June–October
6 miles
2100 feet elevation gain

GETTING THERE
■ Drive I-90 east to exit 45. Cross under the freeway and turn left on Road No. 9031.

■ Drive 0.5 mile to a junction and continue straight on Road No. 9031 for 3 miles to the trailhead of Trail No. 1039, elevation 2280 feet.

ON THE TRAIL

Photographer and trails advocate Ira Spring campaigned for the building of this trail for thirty years, and I am sure he would have loved to have walked the finished trail, which was completed shortly after he passed away. Today you can see for yourself that it was worth the wait and is worthy of his name. The trail takes hikers high above the Snoqualmie valley, with views west on a clear day to Seattle, east toward the pass, and south to a part of the Iron Horse Trail. Children will love the challenge of the steep trail and the reward of Mason Lake, waiting on the other side of Bandera Ridge. They may even want to climb Mount Defiance above the lake.

Fill out a trail permit if you plan to go to Mason Lake in the Alpine Lakes Wilderness and begin upward on an old fire crew road framed by maples and alders. At ½ mile pass the Little Mason Creek waterfall cascading above and below the trail. The tree canopy continues until the first startling glimpse straight down the hillside to the highway.

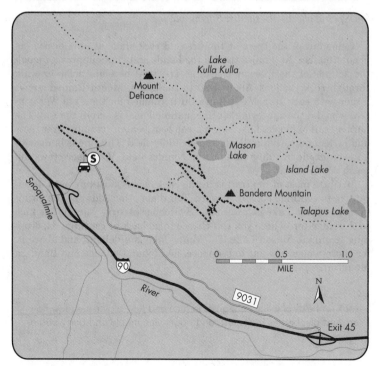

Pat Spring checks out the Ira Spring plaque.

Come out of the trees at the first old rock slide, at an elevation of about 700 feet. At 2 miles the old road ends and views improve, though the sounds of the freeway continue. The trail becomes a flower walk through rock gardens. Above I-90 to the south, Mount Rainier grows larger with each step. McClellan's Butte (named for the Civil War general who did the surveying for Snoqualmie Pass) is across the way. The former trail to Mason Lake was a steep boot-beaten scramble over roots and rocks and with a difficult huge boulder field. This one is built with an even grade, winding around the boulder field. Volunteer crews did much of the work.

Because most of the trail is in the open, some kids may need an incentive to continue steeply upward. Tell them other kids say the swimming in Mason Lake is "awesome." Switchbacks carry you and the kids to the ridge top, where you can choose to go back or continue on, dropping ½ mile to Mason Lake. The alpine lake is a delight, and above it, for those who still want to see more, lie Mount Defiance and Bandera Mountain.

Look for fields of white bear-grass in June and July, alpine meadow flowers and blueberries in August, and bright vine maple and berry bushes in September.

LAKE ANNETTE

BEFORE YOU GO
Maps Green Trails No. 207
Snoqualmie Pass; USFS Mount
Baker–Snoqualmie
Current conditions
Snoqualmie Ranger District
(360) 888-1421
**Northwest Forest Pass
required**

ABOUT THE HIKE
Day hike or backpack
Difficult for children
June–October
7½ miles
1700 feet elevation gain

GETTING THERE

- From I-90 east of North Bend, take exit 47 (Asahel Curtis/Denny Creek).
- At the first stop sign turn right, and at the second stop sign turn left.
- In 0.5 mile, park in the large parking area, elevation 1900 feet. The trail begins on the east side of the parking area.

ON THE TRAIL

Begin by inspecting the interpretive kiosk in the parking lot telling about the Ashahel Curtis Nature Trail. A long, steep, woodland trail ascends the val-

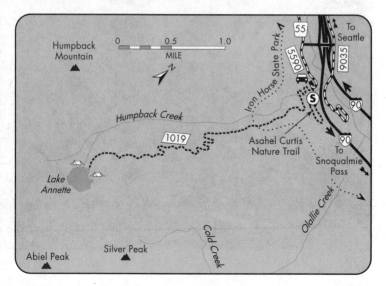

ley beneath Silver Peak to a cirque lake fed by waterfalls. Kids enjoy splashing around in the creeks crossed on the way and playing in the lake-outlet stream. This lake is so popular that you should not expect to be alone.

In the first ¼ mile the trail crosses Humpback Creek. The new bridge was installed in 2004 with a grant from the Spring Family Trails Trust. For the first ¾ mile the trail ascends old clear-cuts to the abandoned Milwaukee Railroad grade, which is now part of Iron Horse State Park. A split-log bench is a nice place to rest before starting up a series of steep switchbacks on the western slope of Silver Peak. The trail follows Humpback Creek through stands of large, very old cedar. At one point, the trail is a log 50 feet long and 3 feet wide, with shallow steps cut into it. The last mile is more gradual, crossing rock slides ornamented in spring by clumps of trillium, glacier lily, and Canadian dogwood.

At 3¾ miles come to the lake, elevation 3600 feet. Trout fishing is said to be very good. The north shore is designated "day use only." Campsites are on the shoreline beyond the outlet. There is also camping on the ridge on the south side. If you camp, have the kids look up the thousands of feet of rock slides to the tops of Silver, Abiel, and Tinkham Peaks.

Lake Annette

DENNY CREEK WATER SLIDE

BEFORE YOU GO
Maps Green Trails No. 207
Snoqualmie Pass; USGS
Snoqualmie Pass
Current conditions
Snoqualmie Ranger District
(360) 888-1421
**Wilderness Permit and
Northwest Forest Pass
required**

ABOUT THE HIKE
Day hike
Easy for children
May–November
2½ miles
500 feet elevation gain

GETTING THERE

- Leave I-90 east of North Bend at exit 47. Turn north at the exit ramp, go over the interstate, and turn right at the T in the road.
- In 0.25 mile turn left on Denny Creek Road No. 58. Drive 2.5 miles.
- Just beyond the Denny Creek Campground, turn left on the paved road. Continue 0.25 mile to the end of the road and trailhead, elevation 2500 feet. Parking is limited; do not block the private driveways along the road.

ON THE TRAIL

On a hot day, this natural water slide can send children out of their minds with glee. One mother with three kids under seven told me they had played there for three hours—until the sun went down and they finally began to feel the cold.

Trail No. 1014 begins in impressive old forest. At ¼ mile, it crosses a log bridge children will like. Shortly they will be astonished to walk

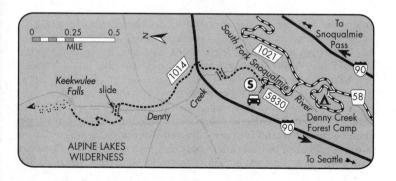

A natural water slide at Denny Creek

under the freeway, to hear cars and trucks rumbling and roaring directly over their heads, and to peek up through the bridge grates at big black tires rolling by at high speeds. At 1 mile the trail enters the Alpine Lakes Wilderness, and freeway sounds fade away in the distance. A gradual climb along Denny Creek leads to a section of bedrock, elevation 2800 feet, where the water spreads out into the water slide.

Water volume may be dangerously torrential in the spring, but in later months it dwindles to a gentle and safe flow. At the same time, temperatures rise and kids are attracted like dragonflies. The slide is a wide expanse of bedrock where the creek first narrows to a footstep's width and then widens to slip down the rocky slab. Walk upstream 300 feet to a cascade for children to run under—another exhilarating experience. In the winter the slippery rocks are encrusted with ice and, though beautiful, are not to be trusted for children to walk on.

 FRANKLIN FALLS

BEFORE YOU GO
Maps Green Trails No. 207 Snoqualmie Pass; USFS Mount Baker–Snoqualmie
Current conditions Snoqualmie Ranger District (360) 888-1421
Northwest Forest Pass required

ABOUT THE HIKE
Day hike
Easy for children
July–October
2 miles
100 feet elevation gain

GETTING THERE
- Leave I-90 east of North Bend at exit 47. Turn north at the exit ramp, go over the interstate, and turn right at the T in the road.
- In 0.25 mile turn left on Denny Creek Road No. 58. Drive 2.5 miles.
- Just beyond the Denny Creek Campground, turn left on the paved road.
- Look for parking before the bridge and the trailhead on east side of road, elevation 2500 feet.

ON THE TRAIL
This is a paradise for kids! Standing beside the 70-foot falls on a warm day, children scream with joy at the cold spray in their faces. The gravel bar and the creek into which the water falls usually are crowded with

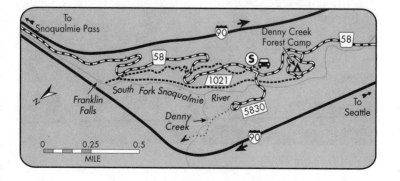

children wading, splashing, playing on the rocks, and "fishing"—as if the fish would endure such company! Traffic is loud on the Denny Creek section of freeway directly above them, but the kids are oblivious.

On the right side of the junction, marked with a wagon wheel, is the historic Snoqualmie Pass Wagon Road, once crossed by pioneers, which climbs in 1 mile to Franklin Falls. On the left side, on Road No. 5830, is the Franklin Falls trail, also 1 mile in length, starting near the concrete bridge. The reconstruction of this trail was paid for by a grant from the Spring Family Trail Trust; Washington Trails Association volunteers regularly work on this trail, too.

The sometimes-muddy ¼-mile trail joins the wagon road and regular trail and then drops to the falls, the final few feet blasted out of solid rock. There is no guardrail, so children will need supervision and young children will need help. The last 200 yards are surfaced with sharp rocks and could be difficult for pre-schoolers to walk through, so parents should plan to carry them here.

Fun at Franklin Falls

Families blink their eyes in disbelief as they see the falls, creek, large gravel bar, and rock walls for the first time. When I was here on a hot summer day, people were picnicking on blankets, watching their children happily engrossed in all manner of water activities.

 SNOW LAKE

BEFORE YOU GO
Maps Green Trails No. 207 Snoqualmie Pass; USGS Snoqualmie Pass
Current conditions Snoqualmie Ranger District (360) 888-1421
Wilderness Permit and Northwest Forest Pass required

ABOUT THE HIKE
Day hike or backpack
Moderate for children
July–October
8 miles
1300 feet elevation gain in, 400 feet out

GETTING THERE

- Leave I-90 at exit 52 at Snoqualmie Pass. Turn north and take the second right, onto Alpental Road.
- Drive 1.5 miles and park in the large gravel lot to the left. The trailhead is on the right, elevation 3100 feet.

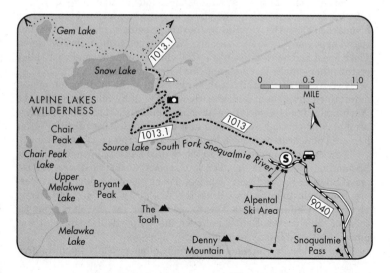

Barefoot at Snow Lake

ON THE TRAIL

Snow Lake is one of the most popular hikes in the Snoqualmie Pass area. The trail, though, is long and steep for children and has endured erosion from the constant stream of thousands of hikers. My own kids rebelled at backpacking it when they were eight, nine, and ten, and we bivouacked along the way. But the next day, seeing the lake, they wished they'd kept going and camped there. We returned to do so several times. The rugged and beautiful setting—tall cliffs on one side and vast valley on the other—make it memorable for hikers of all ages.

Trail No. 1013, starting on the uphill side of the parking lot, is well maintained throughout and recently was rebuilt by volunteers from the Washington Trails Association. At about 2 miles, short switchbacks have been blasted through rock slides and up through belts of cliffs. Water bars and puncheon have been built to control water erosion and mud.

The views begin here, down to the Source Lake valley and up to the Snoqualmie Pass mountains. The track opens out into heather and flowers at Snow Lake Saddle, at 4400 feet. Peaks along the ridge to the west are, from right to left, Chair Peak, the Tooth, Bryant Peak, and Denny Mountain. (Children will be able to see in their shapes the reasons for some of their names. Denny, however, has no particular shape; it was named for David Denny, one of Seattle's pioneers.)

From the saddle, the sometimes muddy, slippery trail (watch children carefully) drops 400 feet to the shores of the lake, elevation 4016 feet, about 4 miles from the parking lot.

The lake is large enough to accommodate a lot of hikers, fishermen, photographers, and picnickers, and it usually does so; over 10,000 hikers a year choose it as their destination. To get away from some of the crowds and out of the day-use area to the camping area, try the northeast shoreline beyond the outlet, or go in 1 more mile to tiny Gem Lake. The views one way are down to the vast gulf of the Middle Fork Snoqualmie and the other way across the lake to snowfields extending down to the shore.

I-90 EAST OF SNOQUALMIE PASS

 LITTLE KACHESS LAKESHORE

BEFORE YOU GO
Maps Green Trails No. 208 Kachess Lake; USGS Kachess Lake; free handout
Current conditions Cle Elum Ranger District (509) 852-1100
Parking fee

ABOUT THE HIKE
Day hike
Easy for children
May to October
½ mile to 2 miles
No elevation gain

GETTING THERE

- Drive I-90 east of Snoqualmie Pass to exit 62.
- Turn north and follow Road No. 49 for 5.5 miles to the Kachess Campground entrance station at the end of the paved road, elevation 2254 feet.

ON THE TRAIL

Kachess Campground has some great hikes for young children, with big trees, lakeshore walks, and beaches to throw rocks from.

Big Tree Nature Trail. At the first intersection, cross the road. Just to the right find the unsigned ¼-mile Big Tree Nature Trail through a temple of ancient trees, with a magnificent old tree called Methuselah, an inspiration for children, parents, and grandparents.

Lakeshore Trail No. 1312. For small children, the ½-mile Lakeshore Trail will be the star attraction. After entering the campground, turn left to the picnic area. Walk along on the one-way Box Canyon

Campground Loop Road and find the Lakeshore trailhead just short of campsite 172. The trail skirts the high-water mark. Kachess Lake is a reservoir, and water laps the trail in early summer. By late summer the lake level may be 60 feet down. Be sure to follow the lakeshore as it detours around a former campsite loop, now set aside as a wildlife reserve. The trail ends between campsites 72 and 74 on the Lodge Creek Campsite Loop. However, there is no parking here.

Box Canyon Barrier-free Trail. From the campground entrance, turn left at the first intersection and drive past the campground loops, picnic area, boat launch, and a circular parking area to the trailhead parking area, elevation 2000 feet. Here is a trail for parents with children in strollers or wheelchairs. The highlight of this enchanting barrier-free trail is the bridge crossing of Box Creek, built in the 1980s by volunteers for the Student Conservation Association. The trail ends in a short ½ mile at a lake-viewing platform.

Little Kachess Lakeshore. Trail No. 1312 continues on but cannot be recommended for young children. The tread in places is rough and at one place follows a narrow ledge across a 100-foot vertical cliff just spitting distance from the water, a place where teenagers would love to give gray hairs to their parents. Older children will enjoy the views of kayakers on

Little Kachess Lakeshore from the trail

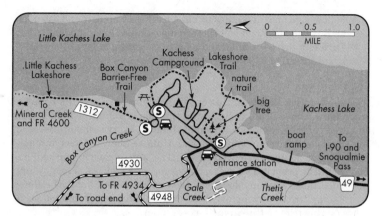

the lake, and the huge old trees that were bent by snowpack when the trees were young, which now have crooks in their trunks.

At about 2 miles look for a small, rocky island used by kayakers for camping, which could be a miniature Treasure Island. The trail doesn't go near the water, but the vistas are sweeping and the niches in the cliffs hold a colorful display of flowers in early summer. Among the rocks look for different varieties and shades of penstemon, scarlet gilia, calypso orchids, coral-bells, Indian paintbrush, and larkspur. When water levels are down you can walk out to the island; this is a muddy walk when water levels first drop but dry later on. The trail ends 4½ miles from campsite 172, at the Cooper Creek road and the Mineral Creek trailhead.

 RACHEL LAKE

BEFORE YOU GO
Maps Green Trails No. 207 Snoqualmie Pass; USGS Chikamin Peak
Current conditions Cle Elum Ranger District (509) 852-1100
Wilderness Permit and Northwest Forest Pass required

ABOUT THE HIKE
Day hike or backpack
Difficult for children
July–October
8 miles
1900 feet elevation gain

GETTING THERE

■ Drive I-90 to east of Snoqualmie Pass and take the Lake Kachess exit 62.

- Follow signs north 5 miles to Lake Kachess Campground, turn left on Box Canyon Road No. 4930, and go 4 miles to a junction.
- Turn left, drive 0.2 mile, and park in the crowded lot at the trailhead, elevation 2800 feet.

ON THE TRAIL

The outstanding beauty of this exquisite alpine lake and the bonus of more lakes above it, all carved from the side of Rampart Ridge, draw hundreds of hikers, many with small children, every summer weekend. Yet this is one of the toughest-to-walk trails in the Cascades and definitely is not for inexperienced hikers. The way is clearly marked, but you should be prepared for rocks, roots, mud, and crawl-over logs. Adults and older kids frequently do Rachel Lake as a day hike, but it's better as a three-day trip. Carry a stove, because campfires are prohibited at all lakes on this trail in the Alpine Lakes Wilderness.

Rachel Lake trail No. 1313 leaves the upper side of the parking lot in a forest filled with huckleberries. The tread is rough and narrow, contouring the side of a hill toward Box Canyon Creek. At ½ mile, the trail improves somewhat, and enters the Alpine Lakes Wilderness. You'll find campsites at 1 mile. Follow the trail along the creek for the next 2 miles, always within sight and sound of it. At 2½ miles, the trail crosses several streams and switchbacks uphill beside a waterfall, a good place to rest and cool hands and faces in anticipation of the next 1½ miles, which climb 1300 feet. At about 3 miles, the trail passes beside a waterfall—another good resting point, with a free shower thrown in. (Some children go wild, soaking heads, feet, or even entire bodies in the falls.) From here, the trail is at its worst, climbing over rocks, boulders, and roots and up streambeds until, at 4 miles, the grade abruptly levels out at deep blue Rachel Lake, elevation 4700 feet. The sound of the outlet stream will tip you off that you are approaching it.

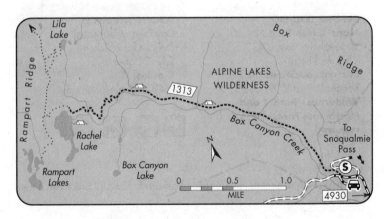

View of Rachel Lake

Numerous campsites are scattered on both sides of the outlet stream.

If your children (and you) survive the trail to Rachel Lake, the middle day of a three-day trip can be the best. From the lake outlet, climb the boot-beaten trail to the right, ascending 600 feet up the very steep mountainside to the broad saddle between Rampart Ridge and Alta Mountain. Take the trail left for an up-and-down ½ mile to Rampart Lakes, a magnificent chain of tarns set in glacier-scoured bedrock bowls. Children can wade, swim, and throw rocks; parents can sketch or photograph these picture-perfect settings.

87 MIRROR LAKE

BEFORE YOU GO
Maps Green Trails No. 207 Snoqualmie Pass; USGS Lost Lake
Current conditions Cle Elum Ranger District (509) 852-1100
Northwest Forest Pass required

ABOUT THE HIKE
Day hike or backpack
Easy for children
June–October
2 miles
600 feet elevation gain

GETTING THERE

- Drive I-90 to the Stampede Pass exit 62, east of Snoqualmie Pass.
- Turn south on Road No. 54, pass Crystal Springs Campground, cross the Yakima River bridge, and, at 1.2 miles, go right on Road No. 5480.

- In 6.2 miles reach a five-way junction.
- Take the second road to the right, pass Lost Lake, and continue another 2.2 miles to the trailhead, elevation 3600 feet.

ON THE TRAIL

This large, clear blue mountain lake lies at the foot of Tinkham Peak. Fishermen, backpacking families, and climbers all can find something to enjoy. I saw one fisherman with a 19-inch rainbow trout on his line and a smile on his face. This is a "hikers only" trail, rough in places,

Hikers near Mirror Lake on the Pacific Crest Trail

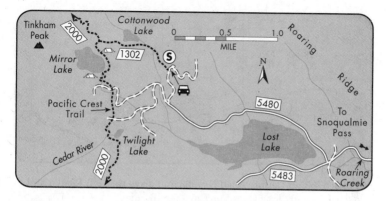

muddy in others, with several small streams to cross. Fortunately, the trail is very short, so little legs should be able to manage.

Trail No. 1302 begins in a clear-cut but in 200 yards enters old-growth forest and at ½ mile reaches shallow, reed-filled Cottonwood Lake, beneath the open slopes of Roaring Ridge. Camping and wading are possible here.

Continue another ½ mile, passing large boulders, to Mirror Lake, elevation 4200 feet. Clear and deep, with eleven campsites on both its north and south ends (and a few in the middle), Mirror Lake reflects whatever a hiker wants to see in it. Gaze upward 1000 feet to the crags of Tinkham Peak, or, as one child urged me, visit the waterfall below the lake's outfall stream. "You wouldn't want to miss seeing it," she said.

PETE LAKE

BEFORE YOU GO
Maps Green Trails No.
208 Lake Kachess; USFS
Wenatchee
Current conditions Cle Elum
Ranger District (509) 852-1100
**Wilderness Permit and
Northwest Forest Pass
required**

ABOUT THE HIKE
Day hike or backpack
Moderate for children
July–October
10 miles
200 feet elevation gain

GETTING THERE

■ Drive I-90 east of Snoqualmie Pass and take exit 80, signed "Salmon la Sac–Roslyn." Cross over the freeway and drive 3 miles.

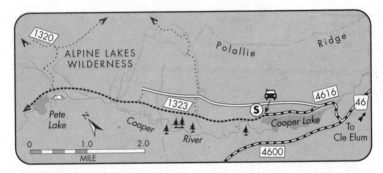

- Turn left on County Road No. 903 and drive through Roslyn and Ronald and along Cle Elum Lake for 16 miles.
- Turn left on Cooper Lake Road No. 46, go 4.7 miles, and turn right on Road No. 4616.
- Cross the Cooper River on a cement bridge, pass a campground and boat launch, and at 1.8 miles from Road No. 46 find the trailhead, elevation 2800 feet.

ON THE TRAIL

Large, woodland Pete Lake makes a popular family campsite at the end of a gentle trail through old-growth forest. Children will joyfully throw sticks and stones in three or four creeks along the way. At the lake, they can also wade and swim, because the water, while not warm, is also not ice cold. Because there is no special turnaround point, this hike is best for an overnight trip.

Cooper River trail No. 1323 joins a lakeshore path and winds through virgin timber and undergrowth. At about 4 miles come to a giant rock slide and the last little climb before reaching the lake, elevation 2980 feet. These campsites are much used and very popular. In early summer the streams entering the lake may be high and will require children to hop logs and boulders to cross them. Many kids love the challenge. Others may want to be carried.

To the west of the lake are exciting views of Overcoat and Bears

Old log cabin on the shore of Pete Lake

Breast Mountains. I have pictures of my three children beneath the peaks, sitting on a log and eating their breakfast porridge like the three bears.

 COOPER LAKE AND RIVER WALK

BEFORE YOU GO
Map Green Trails No. 208 Kachess Lake
Current conditions Cle Elum Ranger District (509) 852-1100
Northwest Forest Pass required

ABOUT THE HIKE
Day hike
Easy to moderate for children
June–October
8 miles
400 feet elevation gain

GETTING THERE

- *Cooper Lake trailhead:* Drive I-90 east of Snoqualmie Pass to exit 80, signed "Salmon la Sac–Roslyn." Cross over the freeway and drive 3 miles.
- Turn left on County Road No. 903 and drive through Roslyn and Ronald and along Cle Elum Lake for 16 miles.
- Turn left on Cooper Lake Road No. 46. Go 4.7 miles and turn right on Road No. 4616.
- Cross the Cooper River on a cement bridge and find the trailhead on the right (northeast) side of the road, elevation 2800 feet.
- *Salmon La Sac trailhead:* Keep heading north on County Road No. 903 until you pass the historic Salmon la Sac Guard Station.
- In about 0.25 mile from the station take a left and cross the Cle Elum River on a high bridge. Spur Road No. 111 winds about 0.5 mile past cabins and campgrounds and ends at the trailhead.

ON THE TRAIL

This trail follows the north bank of the river and is a lovely walk that you can begin from either end. A road also leads to Cooper Lake, but it is south of the river, out of sight. Ride if you will, but you and the children will miss out on some good things. A longer sylvan walk along the Cooper River leads families through old-growth forestland, some of which was owned by a timber company but has been saved by a land exchange. Clear-cuts are visible across the river on steep hillsides. The trail leads to lovely Cooper Lake, lying alongside the Alpine Lakes Wilderness. Children were wading and floating on inner tubes when we were here.

From the Cooper Lake trailhead, begin by heading downstream. The trail enters a mature forest, but you can glimpse some clear-cuts higher on the hills. The trail here is easy, and within ¼ mile you will pass some ancient Douglas-fir and cedar trees, surrounded by smaller, younger trees. This is classic old-growth forest. Soon the trail drops to the river, which is a good lunch spot or turnaround point for families with small children. About a mile down the trail, you may notice some small stumps. These were the last trees cut, but to avoid building roads, the timber company lifted these logs out by helicopters.

Back at the trailhead, you can drive (or walk) ¼ mile farther to reach Cooper Lake. On a hot July day, teenagers were swinging on a rope over a deep pool and then dropping into the cold water, calling out the temperature to envious spectators on the bank. Forest flowers include lupine, pipsissewa, wild roses, vanilla-leaf (which when dried smells sweet), tiger lily, and twining twinflowers. The old-growth forest of fir, hemlock, and silver fir offers cool shade on a hot day, and the sound of rapids and rushing water is never distant.

Follow the Cooper River to Cooper Lake

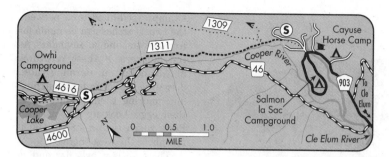

The longer walk starts near the Salmon la Sac campground. The trail climbs above the river with views to noisy cascades. In about 3 miles reach the old-growth grove and then the upper trailhead. Cross the road and find the trail that parallels the road to the campground and picnic area by the lake.

90 HYAS LAKES

BEFORE YOU GO
Maps Green Trails No. 176 Stevens Pass; USFS Wenatchee
Current conditions Cle Elum Ranger District (509) 852-1100
Wilderness Permit and Northwest Forest Pass required

ABOUT THE HIKE
Day hike or backpack
Easy for children
June–November
Hyas Lake: 3 miles; Upper Hyas Lake: 5 miles
50 feet elevation gain

GETTING THERE
- Drive I-90 to exit 80, east of Snoqualmie Pass, signed "Salmon la Sac–Roslyn." Cross over the freeway and drive 3 miles.
- Turn left on County Road No. 903. Wind through the old mining town of Roslyn and pass Cle Elum Lake.
- At 17 miles from Roslyn, just beyond the Salmon la Sac Guard Station, go right on Road No. 4330.
- Drive 15 more miles to its end and Hyas Lakes trail No. 1376, elevation 3400 feet.

ON THE TRAIL
Two large forested lakes—very popular and with campsites almost beyond counting—wait at the end of a gradual trail through fine old forest. From camps near the shores of either Hyas or Upper Hyas Lakes, or from the

Hyas Lake

swampy reed-filled area between the two, searches can be made for frogs, newts, and salamanders. As the numbers of these creatures are dwindling at alarming rates, discourage children from catching and injuring them or disturbing their eggs. Look up to Cathedral Rock, which rises a striking 6000 feet above the west shores.

The trail is nearly flat and so wide that hikers can walk abreast. Three or four creeks can be difficult to cross in the high waters of early summer, but later they make good spots to rest or play. An easy 1½-mile trek leads to the larger of the two Hyas Lakes. Another easy mile takes you to Upper Hyas Lake, elevation 3450 feet.

Campsites are scattered along both lakes. The first lakeshore camp has the best swimming beach, but you must arrive very early (preferably by Friday evening) to have a chance to get it. Note that the sandy beach ends in an abrupt drop-off, so keep a careful eye on

non-swimmers. Some camps at Upper Hyas Lake are large enough for several congenial families to camp together. Downed logs and the exposed roots of enormous old trees provide play places for children and their real or imaginary friends.

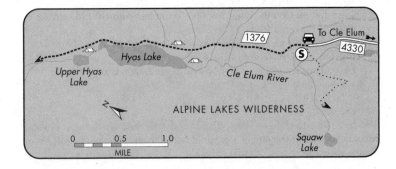

COAL MINES TRAIL

BEFORE YOU GO
Maps Green Trails No. 241
Cle Elum; USGS Cle Elum; USFS
Wenatchee and Okanogan;
tour guide available at Cle Elum
Chamber of Commerce
Current conditions Cle Elum
Chamber of Commerce (509)
674-5958

ABOUT THE HIKE
Day hike
Easy for children
April–November
6 miles
No elevation gain

GETTING THERE

- Take I-90 east to exit 84 at Cle Elum. Take a slight right turn onto First Street West, passing a Safeway store on your right.
- At the bottom of the hill on the main street into Cle Elum, turn left onto Stafford Street and drive for one block to the trailhead, on Second Street West. Parking is along the right side of the street.
- Find the trailhead across the street, at the intersection of Second Street West and Stafford Street, elevation 1905 feet.

ON THE TRAIL

A level, former railroad grade turned into trail that runs from Cle Elum to Roslyn offers children an easy walk through mining history. Relics of the lives of coal miners from the early part of the twentieth century line the wide, gravel path, and heaps of old coal slag call out to be climbed. Apparently bikers also climb them, so be alert to user conflicts. But children will gasp at the hazards miners lived with and the stories of historic disastrous fires and explosions told in the handout tour guide. In the fall, the trail color is gold, gold, gold, as far as the eyes can see. Cottonwoods and maples line the path and their leaves will light your way.

Begin by walking past the old No. 7 mine and learning about a fire that burned in its dump for many years. Continue past remainders of various ethnic settlements (many miners came from Eastern Europe) and find the No. 5 mine, where ten miners died in an explosion. Old concrete piers suggest that coal was loaded from mining coal cars into railroad boxcars here. Near Roslyn you will come to the No. 1 mine, where forty-five miners died in a fire caused by burning miners' lamps. At the town of Roslyn find benches and tables in the city park for a picnic.

Or continue on to nearby Ronald to see more heaps of coal slag and a café called Old Number Three, after another nearby mine. Both towns are living examples of history and contain charming Victorian homes

and churches. The Roslyn Café used in the television show *Northern Exposure* is still open, and the kids might enjoy seeing its trademark sign. The tour guide may be available at the trailhead and can also be found at the Cle Elum Visitor Center.

Hikers on Coal Mines Trail

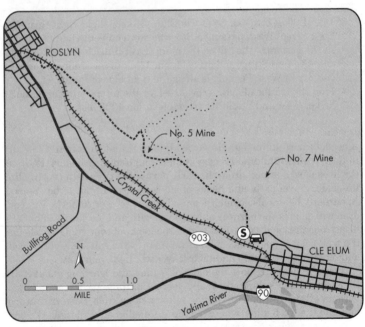

Opposite page: Mount Rainier (Photo by Nancy L. Higgins)

MOUNT RAINIER

ount Rainier National Park has access points from the north, at the Carbon and Mowich entrances, with wonderful trails to Eunice Lake and Tolmie Peak Lookout, Spray Park, and other trails just outside the park's northern entrances. From State Highway 410 kids will enjoy the hikes to Greenwater Lakes; to Clear West Peak, a former lookout; and from Cayuse Pass to another lookout, Noble Knob. Entering the park at the White River entrance gives children access to alpine meadow trails to Dege Peak, Burroughs Mountain, and Mount Fremont, still another lookout. From Chinook Pass families can walk the incredibly beautiful Naches Peak Loop or climb to Sheep Lake. Boulder Cave, with its resident bats is another option to the east. The park's southwest entrance leads the way to the exquisite high-alpine meadows of Comet Falls and Alta Vista, a day of wading at Faraway Rock, summer snow at Snow Lake, and immense ancient trees in the Grove of the Patriarchs. Be sure to stop at Paradise for an ice cream cone and to get acquainted with the resident bird camp robbers and chipmunks. More trails outside the park to the south with breathtaking outlooks include High Rock, Lake Christine, and Glacier View.

MOUNT RAINIER NATIONAL PARK: HIGHWAY 165 CARBON RIVER AND MOWICH LAKE ENTRANCES

EUNICE LAKE AND TOLMIE PEAK LOOKOUT

BEFORE YOU GO
Maps Green Trails No. 269 Mount Rainier West; USGS Mowich Lake; Mount Rainier National Park Backcountry Trip Planner
Current conditions Mount Rainier National Park (360) 569-2211
National park annual or day-use pass required; backcountry permit required for camping

ABOUT THE HIKE
Day hike
Easy for children
Mid-July–October
4 miles
500 feet elevation gain in, 200 feet out

At this time the extent of the 2006 flood damage is unknown. Call ahead to the managing agency for the current conditions before heading out.

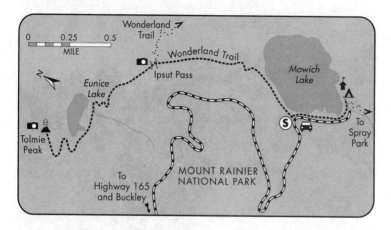

GETTING THERE

- From Buckley, follow Highways 162 and 165 through Wilkeson and Carbonado, past the high, narrow bridge over the Carbon River, to the fork beyond.
- Keep right at the fork and follow the road to its end in 17 miles at Mowich Lake and a small parking lot, elevation 4929 feet.

ON THE TRAIL

One of the loveliest alpine lakes in Mount Rainier National Park is reached by a short hike from Mowich Lake. But above Eunice Lake is the real treat: a steep, short trail climbs to the spectacular view found at the Tolmie Peak Lookout, which is staffed by a volunteer in the summer months. Children are perfectly enchanted by Eunice Lake as well. One hot day I heard a mother ask, "Who wants to climb to the summit?" Four children playing on the shore replied in unison, "Not me!"

Actually, two trails depart from the parking lot. The trail to Spray Park (Hike 93) heads downhill from the walk-in campsite on the south side of Mowich Lake near the outlet stream. The trail to Eunice Lake—a short segment of the Wonderland Trail—begins on the opposite side of the parking lot. It rounds the lakeshore through old-growth noble and silver firs and Alaska cedars and then parallels the nearby road to the pass just mentioned. At 1½ miles is a junction. The Wonderland Trail goes right, over Ipsut Pass. Your way goes left on the Eunice Lake trail, but take the time to walk the Wonderland Trail a few feet to look out over the sweeping green velvet Carbon River valley.

The trail to Eunice Lake drops 100 feet to skirt a cliff and then climbs ½ mile to berry-filled meadows and the lakeshore, 5354 feet. Mount Rainier is suddenly and vastly apparent.

If children can bear to leave the water play, the 1-mile hike up to

Eunice Lake and Mount Rainier

the Tolmie Peak Lookout, with a 600-foot elevation gain, gives supreme views. Look north for Mount Baker and east for Glacier Peak; you can almost reach out and touch Rainier. Plan the hike for a warm day in late summer when blueberries are ripe; the kids can cool off by wading or dunking in the lake.

 SPRAY PARK

BEFORE YOU GO
Maps Green Trails No. 269 Mount Rainier West; USGS Mowich Lake; Mount Rainier National Park Backcountry Trip Planner
Current conditions Mount Rainier National Park (360) 569-2211
National park annual or day-use pass required; backcountry permit required for camping

ABOUT THE HIKE
Day hike or backpack
Moderate for children
Mid-July–October
5½ miles
1100 feet elevation gain in, 300 feet out

At this time the extent of the 2006 flood damage is unknown. Call ahead to the managing agency for the current conditions before heading out.

GETTING THERE

- From Buckley, follow Highways 162 and 165 through Wilkeson and Carbonado, past the high, narrow bridge over the Carbon River, to the fork beyond.
- Keep right at the fork and follow the road to its end in 17 miles at Mowich Lake and a small parking lot, elevation 4929 feet.

ON THE TRAIL

Some of the most exquisite flower meadows on the north side of Mount Rainier National Park can be attained with a small expenditure of energy. Views of "The Mountain" above fields of avalanche lilies here are unforgettable. Although there is no camping in Spray Park, a few families can camp in the woods at nearby Eagle's Roost or the Mowich Lake walk-in campsite and then do the higher day trips above.

Start from the walk-in campsite south of the lake. The beginning is on the Wonderland Trail, which drops ½ mile to a junction. Go left, on the wide and gently graded Spray Park trail, through a forest of immense old-growth noble and silver fir. At 1½ miles, stop to peer over Eagle Cliff. Hold children's hands. They will be astonished to find themselves on top of a precipice with views across a deep valley to the snouts of the Mowich and Russell glaciers.

Just beyond are the campsites at Eagle's Roost. At 2 miles, a side trail goes off ¼ mile to Spray Falls—well worth the trip there to eat lunch with more views, in a cooling mist from the falls.

Back on the trail, switchback the last ¾ mile steeply upward to the meadows of Spray Park, elevation 5700 feet.

Here one can see avalanche lilies in June; lupine, anemones, and paintbrush in mid-July; and asters and deep blue gentian in August.

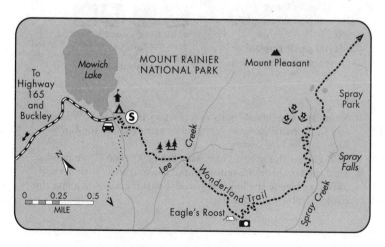

Blueberries continue into September. Some of the flower meadows are fringed with small subalpine firs that are encroaching, but nowadays the timberline is here, at the meadow edge, and as hikers continue upward, the views open wider and wider, until trees disappear altogether.

Resting on a log on the Spray Park trail (Photo by Ellie Ottey)

 GREEN LAKE

BEFORE YOU GO
Maps Green Trails No. 269 Mt. Rainier West; USGS Bearhead Mountain; National Park Service map; Mount Rainier National Park Backcountry Trip Planner
Current conditions Mount Rainier National Park (360) 569-2211
National park annual or day-use pass required

ABOUT THE HIKE
Day hike
Moderate for children
June to October
4 miles
1000 feet elevation gain

At this time the extent of the 2006 flood damage is unknown. Call ahead to the managing agency for the current conditions before heading out.

GETTING THERE
- From Buckley, follow Highways 162 and 165 through Wilkeson and Carbonado, past the high, narrow bridge over the Carbon River, to the fork beyond.
- At 8.4 miles the road divides; stay left on Carbon River Road.
- Find the trailhead 3.2 miles beyond the entrance, with a small parking place to the left and parallel parking allowed along the roadside, elevation 2020 feet.

ON THE TRAIL

A clear blue-green lake surrounded by forest and the steep cliffs of Arthur and Tolmie Peaks greet families at the end of this hike, but children may think the magnificent old-growth rain forest and Ranger Falls are reason enough to walk. The trail is easy to find, gets heavy use, and is eroded down to bony roots and rocks in some places, but it does gain its elevation gradually.

Begin in a grove of giant true firs and Douglas-firs that are centuries old. Their trunks are like tall pillars, and their size dwarfs small children. The forest floor is rich in oak fern, deer fern, and vanilla-leaf. One gnarled root system (called a root wad by foresters), on the edge beside the trail, could serve as a throne for a forest prince. Another root wad is 20 feet long and 12 feet high. Let the children stretch out their arms to get a sense of height and width.

Downed trees become nurse logs supporting rows of new hemlocks, their tops waving like small green feathers. Some logs have fallen above the path like bridges to be walked under. At 1 mile, listen for the sound of water falling. A short descent brings you to the tiered cascade of Ranger Falls. The lower portion of the 100-foot waterfall splits into two falls. Children will want to linger here to feel the mist on their faces, and again above while crossing Ranger Creek on a log provided with railings. At this point the creek is wide and smooth, with pools children will want to explore. Because the creek bed is more solid, wading is better here than in the lake, which is only ¼ mile or so farther.

Green Lake, elevation 3000 feet, is small and round, with columnar cliffs rising steeply on opposite sides. Gaze up on a clear day toward

Testing the water at Green Lake in Mount Rainier National Park

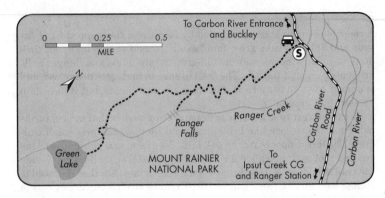

Tolmie Peak, where fire lookouts survey their territory. As we ate lunch by the lakeshore, a Canada jay swooped down to beg nuts and raisins from us.

Note: Camping is not permitted here.

CHINOOK PASS: STATE HIGHWAY 410 WEST OF CHINOOK PASS

 GREENWATER LAKES

BEFORE YOU GO
Maps Green Trails No. 238 Greenwater, No. 239 Lester
Current conditions
Snoqualmie Ranger District (425) 888-1421; summer only (360) 825-6585
Northwest Forest Pass required

ABOUT THE HIKE
Day hike or backpack
Easy for children
April–November
5½ miles
426 feet elevation gain

GETTING THERE

▪ From Enumclaw, drive east on State Highway 410 for 20.3 miles to Greenwater Road No. 70. Turn left (north) and drive 9.6 miles.

Opposite: Old growth trees on Greenwater Lakes trail

■ Turn right onto Road No. 7033. The trailhead is in 0.5 mile on the
right side of road, elevation 2600 feet

ON THE TRAIL

A magnificent old-growth forested trail leads families past waterfalls
along the Greenwater River up to two small lakes where children can
safely play. This hike has scenic attractions at any season. Children
will love crossing above the white water on at least three log and board
bridges with sturdy railings. At the lakes there are shallow pools and
islands to be reached on big logs. Shoreline campsites at both lakes are
excellent but likely to be taken on summer weekends.

Begin amid giant Douglas-fir and cedar trees growing out of a mossy
forest floor. In spring you may see trilliums, wild ginger, and yellow violets. The first waterfall is at ¼ mile and more white-water rapids and
falls continue the entire way. Knobby cliffs on either side of the trail
lined with moss and ferns are remnants of old volcanic activity millions
of years ago.

The first Greenwater Lake is at 1½ miles. The river runs through it,
keeping its water fresh and resident birds and ducks busy. Upper Greenwater Lake, at 2 miles, is larger and has a beaver lodge on one side for
kids to inspect. We saw goldeneye ducks dive and swim underwater, and

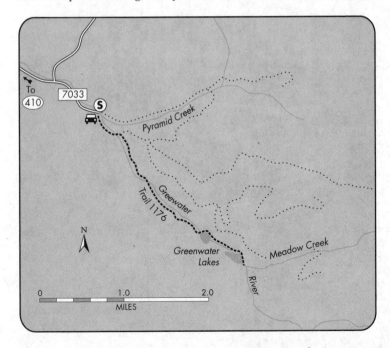

a water ouzel dipping along the shoreline. Deep pools alternate with shallow spots and are perfect for wading and swimming.

 CLEAR WEST PEAK

BEFORE YOU GO
Maps Green Trails No. 238 Greenwater; USGS Clear West Peak; USFS Mt. Baker–Snoqualmie
Current conditions Snoqualmie Ranger District (425) 888-1421; summer only (360) 825-6585
Wilderness Permit and Northwest Forest Pass required

ABOUT THE HIKE
Day hike or backpack
Moderate for children
July–October
3 miles
1000 feet elevation gain

GETTING THERE

■ From Enumclaw, drive east on State Highway 410 for 21.8 miles to West Fork Road No. 74. Turn right (south) and drive 7 miles to Road No. 7430.

■ Turn left (south) and drive 7.4 miles to the trailhead at the end of the road, elevation 4725 feet.

ON THE TRAIL

This is a child's chance to climb a short, steep mountain and exult that he is almost as high as Mount Rainier across the way. The trail is along a ridge in subalpine timber surrounded by clear-cuts. Compare the ridge to the backbone of a dinosaur. The reward is getting to the top.

Step out of the car and look left (south) over ridges clear-cut into a crazy quilt as far as the eye can see. Trail No. 1181 provides views back to the parking lot. Kids can watch the car get smaller. In July the fireweed, the first flower to return after fires and clear-cuts, is a brilliant magenta. Enter subalpine trees at ¼ mile, with only an occasional window north into the Clearwater Wilderness. There are no glimpses of Mount Rainier to warn children of what is to come. The trail levels for brief respites, long enough to reassure kids that it won't all be up, up, up. Small chips of shale cover the narrow path in some sections—tiresome walking for little feet. The first switchbacks begin at 1 mile, and shortly you will see the first heart-stopping view south to Mount Rainier.

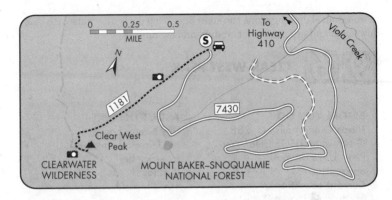

From this point on to the summit, expect to see penstemon, arnica, blueberries, lupine, and bear grass. Look down into the Clearwater Wilderness. Compare the amount of remaining old-growth forest with the clear-cut area, and decide whether we're doing a good job of caring for the Earth. There is so much to see in the last ½ mile that the top comes almost as a surprise. If you bring water, you could camp on the flat summit, the site of an old fire lookout. When early morning light shades the Emmons Glacier pink-gold, your children may think they are seeing the first-prize winner at the Puyallup Fair in the volcano division.

Look a long way to the north for a tiny microwave tower. To the south, the panorama of Mount Rainier is dominated by the sheer mile-high cliff of Willis Wall, where you might see—but not hear—an avalanche of crashing ice blocks. The ice blocks will be partly hidden by thrown up clouds of snow. To the left of the Emmons and Winthrop Glaciers is the sharp spire of Little Tahoma.

Coming back down, the children can watch the car get bigger again.

Hitchhikers

SKOOKUM FLATS

BEFORE YOU GO
Maps Green Trails No. 238
Greenwater; USGS Suntop
Current conditions
Snoqualmie Ranger District
(425) 888-1421; summer only
(360) 825-6585
**Northwest Forest Pass
required**

ABOUT THE HIKE
Day hike or backpack
Easy for children
Most of the year
**Skookum Creek Falls: 4
miles; suspension bridge:
8½ miles**
300 feet elevation gain

GETTING THERE

- From Enumclaw, drive east on State Highway 410 for 24.8 miles to Huckleberry Creek Road No. 73.
- Turn right (south) and drive 0.4 mile to the trailhead just past bridge, elevation 2460 feet.
- For the pickup point 4 miles upstream, follow State Highway 410 past the Dalles Campground at 1 mile and a Boy Scout Camp at 3½ miles and find the pickup point at 3.8 miles. A small parking spot is on the left side, and an unmarked trailhead is on the right.

ON THE TRAIL

A beautiful old-growth woodland walk leads along the White River to Skookum Creek Falls. If two cars are available, you may leave one at either end for a longer hike that includes a bouncy suspension bridge back to the highway. There are a number of river-level campsites and lunch stops where children can safely play in streams and pools.

Many people have worked to improve trail conditions since the river

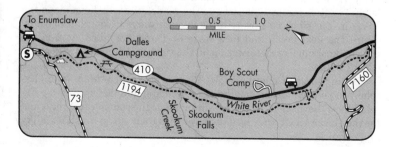

Chipmunk

has repeatedly changed its course. Families should know that this trail is popular with mountain bicyclists. The majority are friendly and courteous, but caution is advised.

Back at the trailhead, note the piles of cedar, fir, and hemlock trees on wide gravel bars that show the power of past winter floods. The trail immediately enters a forest of enormous old-growth firs and cedars that will cause you to strain your neck looking up. At your feet are prince's-pine, Indian pipes, vanilla-leaf, foamflower, twisted stalk, and devil's club. During the rainy season the mushroom display is impressive. The first campsite is close to the road, but floods have made the river inaccessible; be sure to bring enough water if you plan to camp. Until the next flood, find nice spots at 1 and 1½ miles. At 2 miles, reach Skookum Creek; upstream on the right are glimpses of Skookum Creek Falls.

During summer months, White River is best called "Mud River." Explain to your children that the mud is Mount Rainier flowing by. Explain how the glaciers on the mountain scour the soft volcanic rock, and as the glaciers melt, they load the river with their silt, giving it its milky appearance.

Indians gathered vanilla-leaf in bunches and hung them in their homes as an insect repellent, and even after the leaves have dried, they give off a sweet vanilla scent. Native Americans called this plant sweet-after-death and used it to wrap fish to preserve them as today we might wrap fish in foil or plastic wrap.

98 RAINIER VIEW TRAIL

BEFORE YOU GO
Maps USFS Suntop; USGS Noble Knob
Current conditions White River Ranger District (360) 825-6585
Northwest Forest Pass required

ABOUT THE HIKE
Day hike
Moderate for children
Mid-July–October
3 miles
350 feet elevation gain

GETTING THERE

- From Enumclaw, drive east on State Highway 410 for 31.6 miles to Corral Pass Road No. 7174.
- Turn left (east) and drive 6.7 miles to the developed parking area before the entrance to Corral Pass Campground, elevation 5650 feet

ON THE TRAIL

To my children, happiness was a mountain meadow with a trail leading past snowbanks for sliding, with flowers to enjoy, berries to pick, and marmots to whistle to. This is such a trail. In addition, on a clear

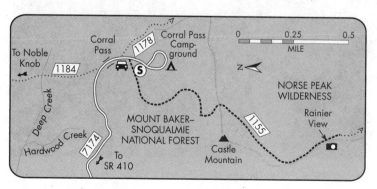

day, it comes with a guaranteed Your Socks Knocked Off View.

Begin in subalpine forest with a brief ½-mile steep section and, in early summer, some small snowbanks. Once they are surmounted, the trail levels out and travels the backside of Castle Ridge. Small creeks along the way appeal to kids to play in them. The trail is without views of Mount Rainier for a short time.

A Forest Service fire fighter who helped contain a fire on nearby Dalles Ridge says that some forest fire fighters are called Hot Shots. Children will be interested to know that the Hot Shots went in and cut underbrush for 6 feet all around the flames and then dug an 18-inch trench in the soil around the fire before they had any water to spray on the blaze. Once the hoses were brought up to them, in two long days they stopped the forest fire. Dalles Ridge is growing trees again.

At the trail's high point, children will feel they are on a rocky mountain summit and can look for mountain goats and elk on nearby peaks. The suddenly apparent view west toward Mount Rainier is breathtaking.

Mount Rainier from Rainier View Trail

NOBLE KNOB

GETTING THERE

- From Enumclaw, drive east on State Highway 410 for 31.6 miles to Corral Pass Road No. 7174.
- Turn left (east) and drive 6.7 miles to the trailhead, on left side of road just before the parking area, elevation 5650 feet.

ON THE TRAIL

A mostly level walk through lovely subalpine parkland offers children chances to see the site of an old fire lookout, to pick berries, and to look down on small alpine ponds just their size. The beginning of the trail

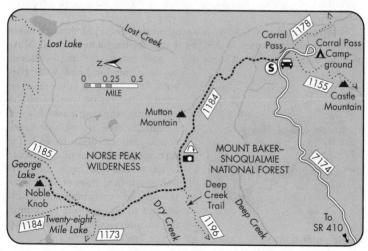

Mount Rainier from Noble Knob Trail

was once a road, so it is wide and comfortable walking for families. This trail has become a fashionable route for mountain bikers who like to pedal up the Corral Pass road and then make a loop trip out on another road. It has even been listed in a mountain biking book, so be prepared for them.

Begin on what was once an old road on trail No. 1184 through noble firs like Christmas trees. Is this the reason for the lookout name? Maybe. The old road/trail is at some points wide enough for small children

Hummingbird nest

to walk hand-in-hand with parents. At 1½ miles a large meadow extends out on both sides of the trail with stunning views toward Mount Rainier. If you stop for a snack, ask children to look for hummingbirds sampling nectar in the field of blue lupine and lavender self-heal flowers. Just over the edge are two small ponds calling out to be explored. Look next for an intersection with the Deep Creek Trail at 1¾ miles.

Continue on, entering the Norse Peak Wilderness at the 2¾-mile point, to a three-way junction where the trail drops 1800 feet to Lost Lake, with camping sites, or traverses around the mountain to the site of the old lookout, or leads on to Twenty-eight Mile Lake. Take the main trail to reach Noble Knob, the rocky site of the old lookout tower. From the summit children can pretend they are lookouts themselves and survey snags, stumps, snowfields, lakes, and, over them all, mighty Mount Rainier.

MOUNT RAINIER NATIONAL PARK: WHITE RIVER ENTRANCE

 **GLACIER BASIN**

BEFORE YOU GO
Maps Green Trails No. 270 Mount Rainier East; Mount Rainier National Park Backcountry Trip Planner
Current conditions Mount Rainier National Park (360) 569-2211
National park annual or day-use pass required; backcountry permit required for camping

ABOUT THE HIKE
Day hike or backpack
Difficult for children
Mid-July–October
7 miles
1700 feet elevation gain

At this time the extent of the 2006 flood damage is unknown. Call ahead to the managing agency for the current conditions before heading out.

GETTING THERE
- From Enumclaw, drive State Highway 410 east 38 miles toward Chinook Pass.
- Enter Mount Rainier National Park at 37 miles, turn right into the White River Entrance Station, and then go 5 miles more.
- Cross the White River and turn left on the White River Campground road. Go to the road's end for the trailhead and limited parking, elevation 4300 feet.

ON THE TRAIL
The meadow at Glacier Basin is a marmot metropolis. Elk graze in the lush grass; goats frequently amble on the ridge above, sometimes by the dozens. But perhaps the most exciting wildlife is the ubiquitous mountain climber, sure to be seen on summer weekends, usually in enormous

numbers, on the way to or from the summit of Mount Rainier. There also are the ghosts of the prospectors who began digging here at the turn of the century and now have vanished completely.

The trail begins at the upper end of the last campground loop on a miners' road, used until the 1950s, beside the glacier-silted Inter Fork White River. Much of the way, the old roadbed is wide enough for two to walk abreast. Children may see evidence of porcupine scratches low down on older tree trunks. The trail climbs alongside the Emmons Glacier moraine. At 1 mile, a side trail to the left crosses Inter Fork and climbs to a viewpoint of the snout of the Emmons Glacier and out over the immense expanse of ice, still strewn with enormous rocks from an avalanche that swept across the glacier from Little Tahoma in 1964.

After the intersection with the side trail, the path narrows to true trail, climbing through forest and rejoining the old road at about 2¼ miles. At 2½ miles is a switchback; look for some wheels and piles of rotten boards, the remains of the Starbo Mine's power generator. "Colonel" Starbo was the private miner who operated here until the National Park Service bought his claim. The steep final mile levels out at last in Glacier Basin at 3½ miles, elevation 6000 feet. Campsites are everywhere, if you choose to stay.

Marmot poses beside Glacier Basin Trail.

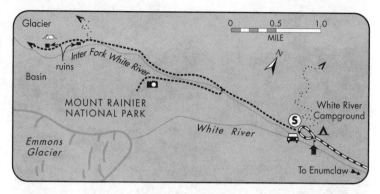

Watch for summit parties loaded with high-tech equipment for climbing glaciers. The route for summit climbers to Steamboat Prow starts right here, and children can watch them struggling above up Inter Glacier. On their way down, however, they may be glissading swiftly.

Continue into the meadowy basin and watch for hoary marmots. Children can whistle to them and think they are being answered by a network of marmot cousins; in fact, each "extended family" has a lookout marmot posted, usually on a big rock. They pick up and pass on other whistles whenever one spots an intruder who resembles a bear or coyote.

 **DEGE PEAK**

BEFORE YOU GO
Maps USGS Sunrise; National Park Service map; Mount Rainier National Park Backcountry Trip Planner
Current conditions Mount Rainier National Park (360) 569-2211
National park annual or day-use pass required

ABOUT THE HIKE
Day hike
Moderate for children
Late July–September
3 miles
900 feet elevation gain

At this time the extent of the 2006 flood damage is unknown. Call ahead to the managing agency for the current conditions before heading out.

GETTING THERE
■ From Enumclaw, drive 38 miles southeast on State Highway 410 to turn right into the Mount Rainier National Park White River entrance.

Yakima Park and Mount Rainier from Dege Peak trail

■ Continue past the White River Campground road toward Sunrise, to the large Sunrise Point parking area about 10 miles from the White River entrance. The Sourdough Ridge Trail, one of two trails that leave Sunrise Point, begins at the upper end of the parking lot, across the road, elevation 6000 feet.

ON THE TRAIL

This alpine ridge walk offers gorgeous views, widening on a clear day into sweeping panoramas, as you and your children climb upward to a little summit. Have them look for mountain goats on nearby ridges. The path along the ridge has borders of meadow flowers and glimpses of two alpine lakes below its north side, but the views of massive Mount Rainier directly south are overwhelming. Some of the switchbacks seem to lead directly toward it. Ask if your children can see a climber's track to the summit in the ice and snow. They will begin to dream of climbing the mountain, too.

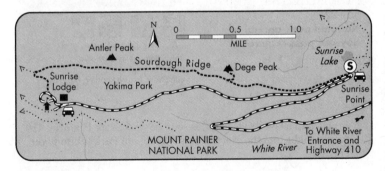

Begin upward to Dege Peak. The few alpine trees along the ridge are ancient old growth, which has never been cut. This is as big as they get at 6000 feet in elevation; they offer shade on a hot day. The other startlingly close volcano to the south is Mount Adams; the Cowlitz Chimneys lie close by. At the summit of Dege Peak, horizons to the north are unlimited. On a really clear day you may see Glacier Peak, certainly the Olympics to the west, and Mount Stuart to the east. It is also possible to hike this ridge from Sunrise Lodge and back, or to continue from the summit of Dege Peak down to Sunrise Lodge and an ice cream cone, if you have arranged to have a car at both points. The advantage of hiking the 3-mile Sourdough Ridge from Sunrise Point is that the view of Mount Rainier is always in front of you to entice you onward.

  BURROUGHS MOUNTAIN

BEFORE YOU GO
Maps Green Trails No. 270 Mount Rainier East; USGS Sunrise; Mount Rainier National Park Backcountry Trip Planner
Current conditions Mount Rainier National Park (360) 569-2211
National park annual or day-use pass required

ABOUT THE HIKE
Day hike
Moderate for children
Mid-July–September
First Burroughs: 2½ miles;
Second Burroughs: 4 miles
900 feet elevation gain

At this time the extent of the 2006 flood damage is unknown. Call ahead to the managing agency for the current conditions before heading out.

GETTING THERE

■ From Enumclaw, drive 38 miles southeast on State Highway 410 to turn right into the Mount Rainier National Park White River entrance.

■ From the entrance, drive about 20 miles to the end of the road at the Sunrise Visitor Center parking lot, elevation 6400 feet.

ON THE TRAIL

Burroughs Mountain is so close to Mount Rainier's gigantic north-side glaciers it seems to run right into them—in fact, it looks down on their lower paths to crevasses and around the corner to the base of Willis Wall. Some seasons, snow patches linger late on the trail and are very dangerous, so call ahead to ask the ranger if the snow is gone. Sometimes they are perilous even when the trail is legally "open." The trail is wide and, aside from the patches, smooth and well maintained. There may be an icy wind, so be sure to carry extra clothing for the summit.

Two trails from the parking lot go to First Burroughs Mountain. Each has a steep snow patch that seldom melts before August and some years doesn't melt at all. When the snow is gone, the upper trail past Frozen Lake is the easier, but the snow often stays longer on this north-facing slope. The lower route, past Sunrise Camp, loses 200 feet before climbing, but its snow faces south and thus melts earlier.

Sunrise Camp Route. From the southwest corner of the parking lot, take the service road or the trail to Sunrise Camp. Both ways are about 1½ miles and lose some 200 feet in elevation. At the campsites, find the trail, which climbs steeply upwards to Burroughs Mountain. In ¼ mile is a magnificent overlook of the White River and Emmons Glacier. Views get even better higher on the trail, which climbs 900 feet to First Burroughs and then joins the Frozen Lake trail.

Frozen Lake Route. From the picnic area behind the rest rooms at the Sunrise Visitor Center, the trail climbs steeply up Sourdough Ridge, gaining 400 feet. Stay left at the trail junction to reach Frozen Lake (actually a reservoir) and a junction of five trails. Take the trail on the left and follow it up along the rocky slopes of First Burroughs Mountain. Round a slope of andesite lava slabs and pass the late snowfield. This may be impassible if there is too much snow. In ¾ mile attain the plateau summit of First Burroughs Mountain, at 7300 feet, and the junction with the Sunrise Camp trail.

First Burroughs, a plateau as flat as a surveyor's table, overlooks the Emmons, Carbon, and Winthrop Glaciers. The reason it has so little plant life is that the moisture from rain and snowmelt drains underground, creating an arid condition here. The result is true tundra—a special alpine plant community like that found in northern Alaska. The scattered plants have a hard time surviving and must not be stepped on. Children (and parents) should stay on the marked paths to give the plants a fighting chance.

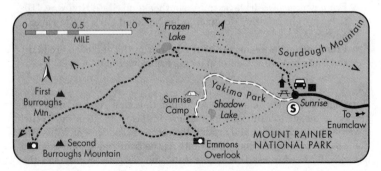

View of Steamboat Prow from Burroughs Mountain

The trail dips a little and then climbs again, and ½ mile from the First Burroughs junction it reaches the summit of Second Burroughs Mountain, elevation 7400 feet. Here the views expand outward to Grand Park, Moraine Park, Frozen Lake, and Glacier Basin, and upward to Inter Glacier, Steamboat Prow, and the chains of summit climbers moving slowly up or down. Tell the children a glacier is a great river of ice filled with crevasses caused both by the flow of ice moving more swiftly in the center than on the sides and by the resistance of boulders underneath. Tell the kids this living volcano is being sculpted by the enormous glaciers gouging at its sides.

 **FREMONT LOOKOUT**

BEFORE YOU GO
Maps Green Trails No. 270 Mount Rainier East; USGS Sunrise; National Park Service map; Mount Rainier National Park Backcountry Trip Planner
Current conditions Mount Rainier National Park (360) 569-2211
National park annual or day-use pass required

ABOUT THE HIKE
Day hike
Difficult for children
Late July–October
5½ miles
900 feet elevation gain

At this time the extent of the 2006 flood damage is unknown. Call ahead to the managing agency for the current conditions before heading out.

GETTING THERE
- From Enumclaw, drive 38 miles on State Highway 410 to turn right into the Mount Rainier National Park White River entrance.
- From the entrance, drive about 20 miles to the end of the road at the Sunrise Visitor Center parking lot, elevation 6400 feet.

ON THE TRAIL
Hike to one of the few remaining active high lookouts in the state, this one within Mount Rainier National Park. This hike offers children a glimpse of the life of a lookout and sweeping views of the north side of Mount Rainier. The trip is especially interesting to children when the lookout is staffed. Check at the park's White River entrance to find out before you start.

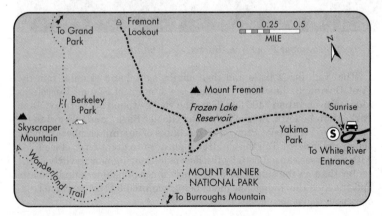

Natural cobblestones on trail near Fremont Lookout

From the visitor center, take the trail past the picnic area and climb very steeply up to Sourdough Ridge, keeping left at the fork near the top. Follow the ridge to Frozen Lake Reservoir and a junction of five trails. The Mount Fremont trail is the one on the far right, climbing a hillside to the north and gradually ascending through subalpine shrubs and flowers into the treeless true alpine zone.

For most of the way the trail is smooth but with sections of natural cobblestones that can be troublesome for children. Trees are pruned down to mats by prevailing winds and snow loads, until they disappear entirely. Foresters have a name for a tree that develops shrublike qualities and has lower branches that sweep out like skirts. They call it a krummholz, (pronounced "crumb holts"). Your children may enjoy looking for trees that have become krummholzen and calling them by that crazy name.

Climb through rock gardens of pink heather, rose and cream paint-brush, tiny lavender alpine lupine, golden cinquefoil, and mountain wallflowers. Listen for the thunder of avalanches off Willis Wall and the shrill whistle of marmots heralding your approach. A herd of mountain goats has occasionally been seen munching alpine flowers in meadows to the north. The trail reaches a 7300-foot high point and then descends to the lookout at 7181 feet.

Once at the lookout, gaze at the alpine meadows below in Berkeley and Grand Parks, and the glimmer of Puget Sound and the Olympics far to the west. Children will want to talk with the ranger about life on a lookout. If the little building is empty, explain to your children that the ranger's main responsibility is to watch for smoke rising from a new forest fire, then to locate it with a complicated device called an Osborne Fire Finder, and to radio in its exact location so that fire fighters could begin to put it out. Today, surveillance planes have taken over most of that job, so rangers have more time to meet hikers and their families.

CHINOOK PASS: STATE HIGHWAY 410 EAST OF CHINOOK PASS

 **NACHES PEAK LOOP**

BEFORE YOU GO
Maps Green Trails No. 270 Mount Rainier East, No. 271 Bumping Lake; USGS Chinook Pass; Mount Rainier National Park Backcountry Trip Planner
Current conditions Mount Rainier National Park (360) 569-2211

ABOUT THE HIKE
Day hike
Moderate for children
Mid-July–October
3½-mile loop
600 feet elevation gain

At this time the extent of the 2006 flood damage is unknown. Call ahead to the managing agency for the current conditions before heading out.

GETTING THERE
■ From Enumclaw, drive State Highway 410 east 44 miles through Mount Rainier National Park to 0.25 mile east of the Chinook Pass summit.

▪ Park in the parking lot; find the trailhead back at the old wooden overpass, elevation 5432 feet.

ON THE TRAIL

This is a dream hike for families. Children love picking berries along the easy trail and playing in the warm, shallow pond at its highest point. Parents will be inspired by the magnificence of the views. Small ponds and an early season waterfall invite children to a dunking of some kind or, on a hot day, a full shower. The trail is gently graded and, except for the early season snow patches, is a cinch for toddlers. Older kids may engage in snowball warfare. Note that there is not off-trail walking allowed in meadows here.

Walk across the overpass, then contour the east side of Naches Peak and enter the William O. Douglas Wilderness. Pass a small

First hike at Mount Rainier (Photo by Mark Fuller)

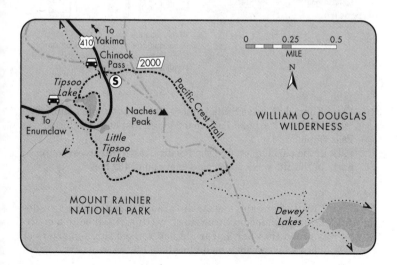

pond and climb over a 5800-foot spur ridge.

The way then drops a bit, enters Mount Rainier National Park, and at 1½ miles comes to a junction. The left fork drops to the Dewey Lakes. Go right, into a grand sprawl of alpine meadows. The stupefying views of Mount Rainier are framed by flowers, subalpine trees, and clumps of bear-grass. Look for pink Indian paintbrush, gray-bearded anemones (Old Man of the Mountain) gone to seed, lavender phlox, white valerian, and golden arnica. At 2 miles is a small, warm lake that cries out to be circled, tested, and waded in. You will have a hard time resisting the temptation yourself.

From here the continuation of the loop is all downhill to Tipsoo Lakes, then up a short trail, gaining 150 feet. Some road walking is required to reach the parked car.

 **SHEEP LAKE**

BEFORE YOU GO
Maps Green Trails No. 270 Mount Rainier East; USGS Chinook Pass; USFS Wenatchee
Current conditions Naches Ranger District (509) 653-1400
Northwest Forest Pass required

ABOUT THE HIKE
Day hike or backpack
Easy for children
Mid-July–October
6 miles
300 feet elevation gain in, 100 feet out

At this time the extent of the 2006 flood damage is unknown. Call ahead to the managing agency for the current conditions before heading out.

GETTING THERE

- From Enumclaw, drive State Highway 410 east 44 miles through Mount Rainier National Park to 0.25 mile east of the Chinook Pass summit.
- Park in the parking lot; find the Pacific Crest Trail access to the north of the old wooden overpass, elevation 5432 feet.

ON THE TRAIL

A side hill trail offers an easy stroll through meadowland to a delightful lake surrounded on three sides by cliffs. (I talked to a mother who was proud that her 3-year-old had walked three-quarters of the way and to a 5-year-old who had walked all the way, carrying his

own small pack. Was he proud!) Kids love looking for polliwogs along the lake's shallow shoreline.

The trail heads north, paralleling the highway and dropping slightly. The trail was blasted into the steep and rocky hillside, so sometimes it's a little rough. This is part of the Pacific Crest Trail, which is open to horses; while there are few horses, meeting one on a narrow trail on the steep hillside is very uncomfortable. There is no

Investigating the shallows at Sheep Lake

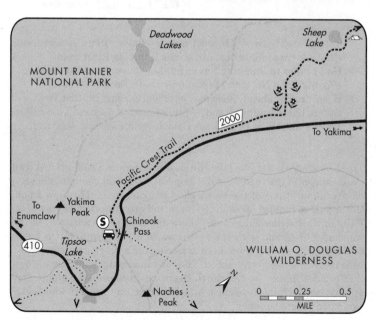

way the horse can turn around or back up, so the hiker must do so. Supreme Court Justice William O. Douglas took a bad fall from a horse near this trail once upon a time.

At 1¼ miles, the trail diverges from the highway, the tread becomes smooth, and a gentle ascent through a little meadow with trees leads to Sheep Lake, elevation 5700 feet. Campsites are scattered around the shore and above the outlet. For better views, although not of Mount Rainier, hike another mile up to Sourdough Gap.

 **TWIN SISTERS LAKES**

BEFORE YOU GO
Maps Green Trails No. 271 Bumping Lake, No. 303 White Pass; USFS Wenatchee
Current conditions Naches Ranger District (509) 653-1400
Wilderness Permit and Northwest Forest Pass required

ABOUT THE HIKE
Day hike or backpack
Easy for children
Mid-July–October
Little Twin: 3½ miles; Big Twin: 4½ miles
900 feet elevation gain

GETTING THERE
- Take State Highway 410 west from Yakima or 19 miles east from Chinook Pass and turn south on the Bumping River road.
- Go 11 miles to Bumping Lake and then follow Road No. 1800 (County Road No. 2008) to a junction with Road No. 1808.
- Keep straight ahead, following No. (1808)395 past the first Twin Sisters Lakes trailhead, and at 7 miles reach the second Twin Sisters Lakes trailhead at Deep Creek Campground, elevation 4300 feet.

ON THE TRAIL
These two large jewel-like lakes lie close together on a well-graded trail, close enough to the road for a day trip but delightful enough to deserve an overnight at one of the many excellent campsites. They are among the largest mountain lakes in the state and are protected as part of the William O. Douglas Wilderness. There are numerous campsites in this wonderful area, and with the assistance of a good trail map, a family could spend a week or more here exploring the area on day trips, once a base camp has been established. The road in is rough, but rest assured that the destination is well worth the drive. In season, the alpine flowers are wonderful; blueberries, huckleberries, and ground whortleberries ripen in late summer.

The trail is kept in good condition. The first half has a gentle grade; the last half steepens at 1¾ miles to Little Twin Sister Lake, with its sandy beaches and lovely inlets and coves. The best campsites are near the outlet, elevation 5200 feet. Go prepared for bugs, with good insect repellent.

The trail proceeds ½ mile, losing 50 feet, to Big Twin Sister Lake, elevation 5152 feet. Twice the size of the little sister, it too has great campsites at the outlet. Between the two lakes are numerous frog ponds and, of course, flowers by the thousands. Horses' hooves have trampled parts of the trail into mire.

Tell the children that William O. Douglas was best known as a Supreme Court Justice, and that he spent his summers near here enjoying this beautiful place until the end of his life. For a panoramic view of the William O. Douglas Wilderness, overnighters can climb to the old lookout site atop Tumac Mountain, an extinct volcano. Cross the outlet

Little Twin Sister Lake

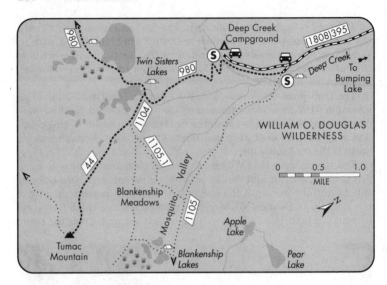

of Little Twin Sister Lake and follow trail No. 44. In ⅓ mile keep right at a junction and continue 2 miles on the Tumac Mountain trail. The trail starts on a gentle grade and then steepens as it spirals up to the 6340-foot summit, 1200 feet above the lake.

 **BOULDER CAVE**

BEFORE YOU GO
Maps Green Trails No. 272 Old Scab Mountain; USFS Wenatchee
Current conditions Naches Ranger District (509) 653-1400
Northwest Forest Pass required; parking fee

ABOUT THE HIKE
Day hike
Easy for children
June through October
1½ miles
300 feet elevation gain in, 100 feet out

GETTING THERE

- Drive State Highway 410 either east some 26 miles from Chinook Pass or west 25 miles from the town of Naches.
- Near the town of Cliffdell, between mileposts 95 and 96, turn south onto a road signed "Boulder Cave National Recreation Trail." Drive 1.25 miles to the trailhead, elevation 2450 feet.

ON THE TRAIL

Mother Nature sometimes provides unique treats for kids, and this is one of the best examples: a deep basalt gorge to explore, with a dark, 200-foot-long cave/tunnel, so cold that on a hot day it feels like you're stepping into a refrigerator. The day we were here children from two families, ages three to twelve, were having fun listening to their echoes, exploring the tunnel, and throwing rocks into the pool. The last we saw of them they were happily investigating other caves. Boulder Cave is the official name, but since you can walk through it, you could easily call it a tunnel. Be sure your family has a flashlight or, better yet, two or three, because the inside of the short cave/tunnel is dark.

Before starting out, read the interpretive sign, which will help you explain to your children how little Devils Creek formed the cave/tunnel. The trail starts directly behind the sign. (Don't confuse it with the paved nature trail loop leading to the river.) The way climbs gradually for ½ mile, levels off, and descends to a junction. Go either way, because this is the start of the loop trail through the cave, but the recommended direction is to the left, switchbacking 100 feet down to the level of Devils Creek, reduced to a mere trickle in summer. The trail enters the cave, where the tread is generally smooth, making an easy but dark passageway.

Bats hibernate and nest in this cave. Children probably won't see them, but the possibility that they may be sleeping nearby or could fly overhead adds to the cave's atmosphere. When this cave was discovered in the 1930s, it was thought to be home to more than a thousand Pacific long-eared bats, but by now, with tourists coming and going, there may be fewer than fifty. Boulder Cave is closed from November 1 through April 1 to help protect the bats. What do they eat, your kids may ask. Unlike vampire bats, which suck blood, these bats are happy to eat the insects constantly supplied to them by downdrafts in the gorge. Bats

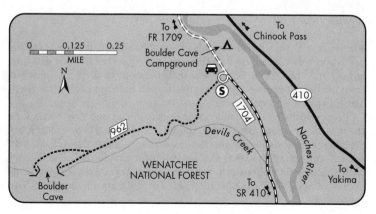

Boulder Cave trail

survive winter on a limited supply of stored fat and will come out of hibernation if disturbed. How do they see in the darkness? Their eyesight is poor, but they use a form of sonar. The echoes of their high-pitched cries bounce off ceilings and rocky walls, and bats are able to navigate according to the echoes.

Proper and safe cave behavior includes no running and being sure there is enough headroom before you venture inside. Have children experiment with the sound of their voices echoing against the walls. Words with vowels carry the best, and sometimes a simple "hello" will come back three or four times in quick succession. Try asking the question "Who are you?" But don't be too loud. The bats are listening to their echoes, too.

MOUNT RAINIER NATIONAL PARK: HIGHWAY 706 SOUTHWEST ENTRANCES

 **NISQUALLY NATIONAL WILDLIFE REFUGE**

BEFORE YOU GO
Map Nisqually National Wildlife Refuge brochure
Current conditions Nisqually National Wildlife Refuge (360) 753-9467
Entrance fee

ABOUT THE HIKE
Day hike
Moderate for children
Year round
Brown Farm Dike Trail:
5½-mile loop; Ring Loop Trail: ½ mile; Nisqually River Trail: ½-mile loop
No elevation gain

GETTING THERE

■ North of Olympia, leave I-5 at exit 114 and turn right (west) onto Brown Farm Road.

■ Drive 0.3 mile to the well-signed trailhead at the interpretive center, elevation 15 feet.

ON THE TRAIL

The Nisqually National Wildlife Refuge is a treasury of birds and wildlife at any time of the year, but children will especially love this hike in the spring, when ducklings, goslings, and baby rabbits are everywhere. The amazing colony of blue herons across McAllister Creek is on nests from mid-April through mid-June. The chance to watch the big birds swooping through the air to bring fish back to their babies is a special treat, even seen from ½ mile away. A boardwalk provides wheelchair and stroller access for parents of small children. The Nature Center at the entrance with a viewing platform over a small pond makes a good spot for a picnic. Note that pets are allowed only in the parking lot, and even there must be on a leash. Bikes, horses, and joggers are not allowed, and families are encouraged to walk and talk quietly so as not to disturb wildlife. The refuge is closed to the public past the interpretive center during parts of the winter to protect nesting sites and migratory feeding. Check with the refuge before heading out during this time of year.

The mouth of the Nisqually was an undiked delta—mostly marshes and wetland—before nineteenth-century settlers tried grazing cows here. The farmers wanted to hold back the saltwater, channel the creek, and provide road access around the farms, so, like the Dutch, they built

Coyote

dikes. The last of these farms—the Brown Farm—was sold to the U.S. government in the mid-1970s to form the refuge. Now the river and creek are part of a national refuge, with few reminders, such as old barns, of the earlier farms. Unfortunately, in the name of salmon restoration, many of the old dikes are being removed, and with them will go some access to habitat wetlands for birders and families.

The sounds of freeway traffic die away as you and the children hear only the sounds of birds' honks, quacks, and peeps, and peace. The Nisqually estuary is one of the few remaining undisturbed salt marshes in south Puget Sound. It is a nursery area for countless small plants and animals that, in turn, serve as food for birds and marine animals. The health of the salt marshes determines the survival of all the animals (fish, seals, birds) that depend on it.

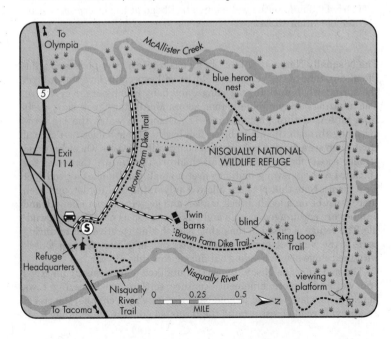

Children may not want to walk the entire flat 5½-mile loop. It is too long for toddlers. But any portion can provide a stunning glimpse of an eagle, coyote, goldfinch, or cormorant.

Start on the Brown Farm Dike Trail through an old orchard, which is in full bloom in early May. The apple tree trunks are encrusted with moss. Children will feel they have entered an enchanted place. Pass a moss-covered cistern that looks like an ancient tomb.

McAllister Creek was once called Medicine Creek and was the site of an important Indian treaty in the middle of the nineteenth century. Now a gray stump, the old tree under which the treaty was signed still stands near the freeway overpass. Children can find it if they look.

By turning left, or counterclockwise, you will reach McAllister Creek in only 1½ miles. Here the richness and diversity of ducks and shorebird species will suggest to children that Noah just landed his ark here. We saw gadwalls, goldeneyes, buffleheads, green-winged teals, shovelers feeding on surface plankton, American widgeons, mergansers, mallards, yellow legs, ruddy ducks, Canada geese, russet-colored horned grebes, and cormorants (the trained oriental fishing birds in the classic children's story, *The Five Chinese Brothers*).

We saw a slender American bittern in reeds, pointing its head and long beak up to the sky.

But the high point was watching the wonderful colony of blue herons soaring, feeding, and nesting. The herons' 7-foot wingspans appear almost prehistoric. Up and down the creek they flew, five and six at a time, now stopping to fish along the banks, now returning to their huge nests high in the Douglas-firs and perching to feed their young. Tell children this is the bird equivalent of feeding a baby in a high chair.

This entire trail is level and may seem tedious unless you see birds and animals. But if kids are quiet, they certainly will. Reach the first view of Puget Sound and the outside edge of the refuge at 2½ miles. Tidal salt marshlands beyond here are green hummocks above mud flats. Gaze out beyond the flats to the sound, back to Mount Rainier, and then over the

Great blue heron rookery seen from the refuge

dike for blinds where you can crouch to observe wildlife unnoticed. From the Centennial Platform at 3⅔ miles we saw two eagles perched on a driftwood stump, waiting for the tide to serve up their dinner.

Continue south along the swifter-flowing Nisqually River, pausing for two shorter trails. The Ring Loop Trail, at 4⅓ miles, leads ½ mile out into the delta and back to rejoin the main Brown Farm Dike Trail. This trail can also be taken as a separate trip by going clockwise at the start of the Brown Farm Dike Trail. The other short loop is the Nisqually River Trail—also ½ mile—which provides the closest short alternative trail in the refuge. Reach it by going counterclockwise from the parking lot. Children can't go wrong on any of them.

 **BERTHA MAY AND GRANITE LAKES**

BEFORE YOU GO
Maps Green Trails No. 301 Randle; USFS Gifford Pinchot
Current conditions Cowlitz Valley Ranger District (360) 497-1100
Northwest Forest Pass required

ABOUT THE HIKE
Day hike or backpack
Moderate to difficult for children
July–October
½ mile, 1½ miles, and 3 miles
600 feet elevation gain

GETTING THERE
- Drive Highway 706 east from Ashford 3.4 miles toward Mount Rainier.
- Turn right onto Highway No. 52, Kernahan Road, signed "Skate Creek Road." Cross the Nisqually River.

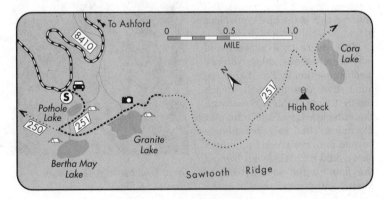

Foggy day in the Cascades

- At 6.5 miles from the highway, go right on Road No. 84. In 1.25 more miles, turn right on Road No. 8410, signed "Teeley Creek Trail."
- Drive 3.9 miles to trail No. 251, elevation 3600 feet. Watch carefully as the trailhead is poorly marked.

ON THE TRAIL

Three woodland lakes along a short forest trail are good choices for Boy Scout groups or families with young and inexperienced hikers. Children can swim in all three, but shorelines are soft and muddy in the first two.

An easy ¼ mile leads to Pothole Lake, a poor name for a lake large enough for several campsites and for a sizable outlet stream.

Climb steeply ½ mile through big old hemlocks to Bertha May Lake. Long and narrow, her shore lined with driftwood and blueberries, Bertha May has good campsites. Too bad that many hikers visiting this lake don't think to carry out their own garbage.

In ½ mile more, the trail climbs to the prettiest of the three, Granite Lake, elevation 4175 feet. Good campsites are near the outlet and scattered around the far side. Also near the outlet are picture-window views of Mount Rainier.

 **HIGH ROCK LOOKOUT**

BEFORE YOU GO
Maps Green Trails No. 301 Randle; USGS Sawtooth Ridge; USFS Gifford Pinchot
Current conditions Cowlitz Valley Ranger District (360) 497-1100
Northwest Forest Pass required

ABOUT THE HIKE
Day hike
Moderate for children
July–October
3 miles
1585 feet elevation gain

GETTING THERE

- From Elbe, head east on State Route 706 about 10 miles and turn right onto Kernahan Road (Road No. 52).
- Drive just over 4 miles, then turn right onto Road No. 84, signed for High Rock Trail.
- In 3 miles, at an unsigned road junction, go left on Road No. 8440.
- When you get to a junction for Road No. 8420, on the right, continue straight on Road No. 8440 for 2.8 miles to the High Rock/Greenwood Lake trailhead at Towhead Gap, elevation 4100 feet.

ON THE TRAIL

One of the few lookouts still operating in the state, High Rock offers children a rare opportunity to talk with the fire lookout operator if he is there, and see what his or her life is like. If the lookout is staffed, the kids can see the Osborne Fire Finder and radio in use during fire season. The kids can imagine finding smoke, then calling in the fire on the

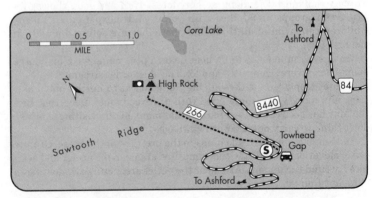

High Rock Lookout and Mount Rainier

radio. Lookout Martha Hardy wrote a book about her experiences, titled *Tatoosh*. The first fire she called in turned out to be a waterfall!

This tiny perch is no place for a sleepwalker. Despite the presence of a cable for gripping on the steepest portions of the rock and a railing at the top, you should watch children carefully here. The spectacular views of Mount Rainier and tiny Cora Lake, 2000 feet below, are like those from a small plane. Ask the lookout what it's like to be there in a storm—especially a lightning storm!

Trail No. 266, signed "High Rock," begins on the uphill side of the road and switchbacks steeply up through forest with occasional views of adjoining ridges. The last 200 yards are on steep, solid rock into which handrails, painted for high visibility, have been set. At their end is the lookout, elevation 5685 feet.

The building is perched on the corner of a precipice. In a burrow directly below it lives a family of marmots. They come out to bask in the sun on their airy ledge and ponder the view of Mount Rainier. In early summer, the young pups, much smaller than the adults, are extremely curious about hikers, especially the ones smaller than the adults.

 **LAKE CHRISTINE**

BEFORE YOU GO
Maps Green Trails No. 269
Mount Rainier West; USGS Mt.
Wow; USFS Gifford Pinchot
Current conditions Cowlitz
Valley Ranger District (360)
497-1100
**Wilderness Permit and
Northwest Forest Pass
required**

ABOUT THE HIKE
Day hike or backpack
Easy for children
July–October
1½ miles
400 feet elevation gain

GETTING THERE
- Drive Highway 706 east from Ashford toward the Nisqually Entrance of Mount Rainier National Park. In 3.8 miles turn left on Copper Creek Road No. 59. Drive 5 miles.
- Turn right on Road No. 5920 and go another 2.4 miles to the trailhead, elevation 4400 feet.

ON THE TRAIL
A lovely little alpine lake in the Glacier View Wilderness offers campsites less than a mile from the road. The lake is shallow, but children will enjoy wading from logs and from the little peninsula on one shore.

The first 100 feet of elevation gain on trail No. 249 are steep and badly eroded. Several portions of the trail have been sliced from a cliff; others are overhung by beetling cliffs. The ridges have been savagely clear-cut, and much of the remaining forest is by no means safe from the chainsaw, since only the last ⅛ mile is protected wilderness. At ¾ mile is Lake Christine, elevation 4802 feet.

Good camps, some with fireplace grills, are scattered on three sides of the lake. An interesting day trip is a 1-mile hike featuring a 700-foot ascent to the rounded, rocky dome of Mount Beljica, elevation 5475 feet. To do this, proceed along the same trail beyond the lake to a saddle and turn left on the Mount Beljica trail; a very steep ½ mile takes you to the summit. Enjoy the views of Mount Adams, the remains of Mount St. Helens, and the Puyallup Glacier of Mount Rainier. Notice the lookout building on far-off Gobblers Knob. Mount Beljica itself was once a lookout point but

Opposite: Lake Christine

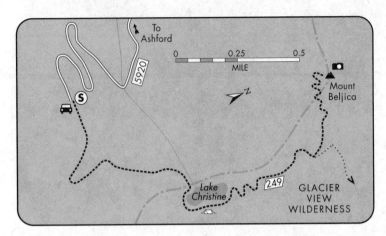

never had a building. Its unusual name is formed by the initials of the seven members of the La Wall family who made the first ascent in 1897: Burgon, Elizabeth, Lucy, Jessey, Isabel, Clara, and Alex.

 **GLACIER VIEW**

BEFORE YOU GO
Maps Green Trails No. 269 Mount Rainier West; USGS Mt. Wow; USFS Gifford Pinchot
Current conditions Cowlitz Valley Ranger District (360) 497-1100
Wilderness Permit and Northwest Forest Pass required

ABOUT THE HIKE
Day hike
Moderate for children
July–October
3 miles
730 feet elevation gain

GETTING THERE
- From Ashford, drive Highway 706 east for 3 miles and then turn left onto Copper Creek Road No. 59.
- Drive up the winding gravel road for 8.2 miles to the Glacier View trailhead, on the right side of the road, elevation 4720 feet.

ON THE TRAIL
The hike to the glorious views from this former lookout site offers a superb treat for children and families. Begin with a gradual ascent through

meadows, flower fields, and rock gardens ornamented with constantly changing flower species and the songs of birds. Follow a long path through trees before coming out into the open and the views. At the top, Mount Rainier is breathtaking. Glacier View indeed! Children will understand why Native Americans called it The Mountain That Was God.

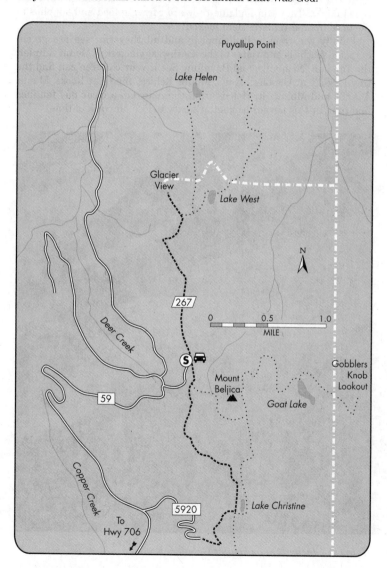

The first steep ¼-mile takes you to a signed path leading into the Glacier View Wilderness. Then catch your breath and take the left trail marked Glacier View, enter subalpine forest, and bypass a clear-cut through old firs and hemlocks. Follow the crest of a long ridge leading up to the old lookout site. Peek-a-boo views of the mountain will tease the children. They can imagine they are carrying food and supplies to the once-upon-a-time resident lookout.

Finally the trees will disappear and all they can see are green-carpeted foothills and vistas of the southwest glaciers of Mount Rainier: the Tahoma, Nisqually, and Puyallup. See if your children can find the tiny lookout at Gobblers Knob, Mount Beljica, the Goat Rocks, Mount Adams, and Mount St. Helens from the map. On a clear day families find that, at this former lookout, it's easy to lose all track of time.

Tahoma Glacier and lookout at Gobblers Knob

 **COMET FALLS AND VAN TRUMP PARK**

BEFORE YOU GO
Maps Green Trails No. 269 Mount Rainier West; USGS Mt. Rainier West; Mount Rainier National Park Backcountry Trip Planner
Current conditions Mount Rainier National Park (360) 569-2211
National park annual or day-use pass required

ABOUT THE HIKE
Day hike
Difficult for children
Mid-July–October
Comet Falls: 4 miles; Van Trump Park: 7 miles
1300 feet elevation gain

At this time the extent of the 2006 flood damage is unknown. Call ahead to the managing agency for the current conditions before heading out.

GETTING THERE

- From I-5 in Tacoma, take State Highway 7 south to State Highway 706.
- Turn east and drive to Mount Rainier National Park's Nisqually Entrance.
- Just over 10 miles from the entrance station is the signed trailhead and limited parking for Van Trump Park, elevation 3600 feet.

ON THE TRAIL

There are four good reasons to take this steep and rocky hike: (1) a spectacular waterfall, 320 frothing feet from brink to plunge basin; (2)

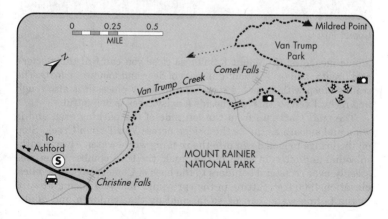

Comet Falls

alpine meadows; (3) Mount Rainier so close you can feel the glacier's cold breath; and (4) frequent glimpses of deer and mountain goats. The trail is steep with some big steps, and in many places it is also rough and rocky. Even so, this hike beside a noisy creek is delightful.

The trail starts up from the left side of the parking area and is wide and smooth as far as the bridge across Van Trump Creek. Stop on the bridge to look down into the rushing white water. Always within sound and often in sight of the creek, the trail climbs, sometimes steeply, over roots and boulders to the base of Comet Falls, at 2 miles, elevation 4900 feet. Sitting in the spray and mist and gazing upward at the falling water can be so fascinating that children and adults lose track of time. A favorite pastime is to pick out a spot of water as it runs over the brink and follow it until it blurs into the spray at the bottom.

If you have enough energy (and older children who like a challenge), continue another steeply switchbacking mile (but on better trail) to Van Trump Park, where flower meadows extend into the very moraines of the Kautz Glacier, which tumbles from the summit ice cap. At 3 miles is a junction. Go right, climbing an exhausting staircase to a 5700-foot viewpoint amid flowers and subalpine trees.

Once my son invited friends from the East Coast to hike to Van Trump Park. They left home on a cloudy day and reached the trailhead in fog. They had climbed the entire distance before Mount Rainier revealed itself. As the clouds blew away, the easterners were completely overwhelmed by its size and majesty. "Wow!" was all they could say.

ALTA VISTA AND PANORAMA POINT

BEFORE YOU GO
Map USGS Mt. Rainier West; Mount Rainier National Park Backcountry Trip Planner
Current conditions Mount Rainier National Park (360) 569-2211
National park annual or day-use pass required

ABOUT THE HIKE
Day hike
Moderate to difficult for children
July–October
Alta Vista: 1½ miles;
Panorama Point: 3 miles
Alta Vista: 500 elevation gain;
Panorama Point: 1500 feet gain

At this time the extent of the 2006 flood damage is unknown. Call ahead to the managing agency for the current conditions before heading out.

GETTING THERE

- From I-5 in Tacoma, take State Highway 7 south to State Highway 706.
- Turn east and drive to the Nisqually entrance, on the southwest side of Mount Rainier National Park.
- Follow signs to Paradise. Go past the Paradise Visitor Center to the large parking lot in front of the ranger station near Paradise Inn, 5420 feet. Plan to arrive early; traffic is stopped at Nisqually when the parking lot is full.

ON THE TRAIL

Take your pick. Walk a short but steep paved trail to Alta Vista, the green knoll above the inn, overlooking Paradise valley. Or continue on a steep, rugged trail to Panorama Point and a magnificent view of Mount Rainier.

A network of paved trails leaves from the visitors center. Climb the cement steps and follow the trail through the meadows. Children can look back at the Tatoosh Range from this perspective to compare it with later views. Pass the first trail for Alta Vista at about ½ mile; it is extremely steep. The meadows are a flower lover's paradise. The number of varieties of flowers that bloom here during the season runs into the hundreds.

In ¼ mile, find a better trail contouring west of Alta Vista and then dropping to a two-way junction. The Glacier Vista route is a bit longer, but it's easier. Take the trail on the right, climbing to a saddle overlooking Edith Creek Basin, and then go right again, climbing to the top of Alta Vista, elevation 5940 feet, and the views overlooking Paradise valley, the Tatoosh Range, and Mount Adams.

For Panorama Point, continue toward Mount Rainier as the pavement ends. Along the ridge, watch for marmots and ptarmigans. In places, the trail climbs awkward stone steps where young children will need help. So will grandparents with creaky knees.

Last winter's snow patches are often encountered even in early August. At about ¾ mile, just below the switchback, is an ideal place to see the Nisqually Glacier. Scan it from its gleaming white snowfield near the summit down to the blue ice cliffs that often break off with a thundering bang. From here you can look into the crevasses and below to the rock-covered snout of the glacier. This is a good turnaround point

Marmot in a Paradise Valley flower field

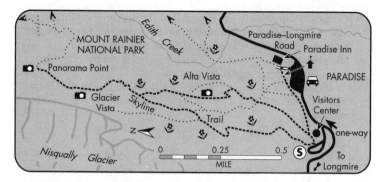

if you can go no farther. But beyond the switchback, the trail is blasted from cliffs, with ever-increasing views. After a few more switchbacks it reaches Panorama Point, elevation 6900 feet.

From the point, you see over the top of all but the highest reaches of the Tatoosh Range to Mount Adams and Mount St. Helens. On a clear day, Mount Hood, 96 miles south in Oregon, can be seen. If kids sit quietly, they will hear the groans of massive Nisqually Glacier moving inexorably down the mountain. Have them watch for avalanches and for climbers moving up the snowfield toward Camp Muir on the most popular route. The immense rock tower on the skyline is Little Tahoma, and the block-shaped profile is Gibraltar Rock.

 **PINNACLE SADDLE**

BEFORE YOU GO
Maps Green Trails No. 270 Mount Rainier East; USGS Mt. Rainier East; Mount Rainier National Park Backcountry Trip Planner
Current conditions Mount Rainier National Park (360) 569-2211
National park annual or day-use pass required

ABOUT THE HIKE
Day hike
Moderate for children
Mid-July–October
3 miles
1200 feet elevation gain

At this time the extent of the 2006 flood damage is unknown. Call ahead to the managing agency for the current conditions before heading out.

GETTING THERE

■ From I-5 in Tacoma, take State Highway 7 south to State Highway 706.

- Turn east and drive to the Nisqually entrance, on the southwest side of Mount Rainier National Park. Pass through Longmire and continue uphill on the Longmire–Paradise Road.
- After two switchbacks above Narada Falls, turn right onto Stevens Canyon Road, signed "Ohanepecosh."
- Go about 2 miles and park at the first Reflection Lake. The Pinnacle Saddle trail starts on the opposite side of the road, elevation 4854 feet.

ON THE TRAIL

A short but steep walk above Reflection Lakes reaches a breathtakingly lovely view across valleys to the southern majesty of Mount Rainier. Wide and safe enough for small children, the trail switchbacks upward 1000 feet in 1¼ miles. Remember to stay on established trails. Feast on the fat blueberries that line the trail in August and September.

Stop at the first Reflection Lake to admire the mountain's reflection, a good reason for the lake's name. A quick search here for tadpoles is mandatory, but do not touch or disturb them. The smooth, well-maintained path crosses some snow patches, which in early summer may stop the trip short. Mount Rainier stays behind your back, so you may want to turn around for frequent rest-stop views. At the saddle, the trail is a shelf blasted out of Pinnacle's rocky shoulder. Hold children's hands here; the drop-off is abrupt. Turn around and gape. Above the lakes and Paradise are the moraines of Nisqually Glacier; follow the ice stream upward to the jutting buttress of Gibraltar Rock and, beyond that, the massive summit ice cap. At 1¼ miles and 6000 feet, go through the saddle between Pinnacle and Plummer Peaks for a whole new view of the South Cascades. This was one of Ira Spring's favorite photo spots.

Mount Rainier from Pinnacle Saddle Trail

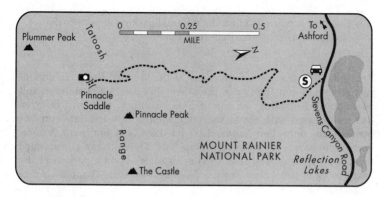

Climbers (and some in slippery shoes) often scramble up the hazardous cliffs to the top of Pinnacle Peak. This is not recommended for hikers and certainly not for children. Families will find plenty of satisfaction snacking amid the flowers.

116 FARAWAY ROCK

BEFORE YOU GO
Maps USGS Mt. Rainier West; Mount Rainier National Park Backcountry Trip Planner
Current conditions Mount Rainier National Park (360) 569-2211
National park annual or day-use pass required

ABOUT THE HIKE
Day hike
Easy (but steep) for children
July–October
1½ miles; loop: 2½ miles
350 feet elevation gain

At this time the extent of the 2006 flood damage is unknown. Call ahead to the managing agency for the current conditions before heading out.

GETTING THERE
- From I-5 in Tacoma, take State Highway 7 south to State Highway 706.
- Turn east and drive to the Nisqually entrance, on the southwest side of Mount Rainier National Park. Pass through Longmire and continue uphill on the Longmire–Paradise Road.
- After two switchbacks above Narada Falls, turn right onto Stevens Canyon Road, signed "Ohanepecosh."

■ Go about 2 miles and find the minimal parking area near the eastern end of the first Reflection Lake.

ON THE TRAIL

This hike offers a magnificent view of the Tatoosh Range in one direction and Mount Rainier in the other. However, while children will be impressed standing on top of Faraway Rock, they will be even more impressed with the chances for wading in warm late-summer ponds. Hang onto their hands; don't let them beat you there. A near-vertical 200-foot cliff drops off on one side. The hike can be extended for a 2½-mile loop. The hike to Faraway Rock is on a portion of the eastern leg of the Lakes Trail, a 5½-mile loop from Paradise Inn to Reflection Lakes and back.

Walk the road east past Little Reflection Lake and go left on the Wonderland Trail. In a couple of hundred feet, the Wonderland Trail goes right. Stay left, on the Lakes Trail. The way steepens. In a short ½ mile, cross a stream and continue climbing steeply to Faraway Rock, ¾ mile from the road, and stunning Artist's Pool, with Mount Rainier reflected one way and the Tatoosh Range the other, elevation 5200 feet. Photographers love this beauty spot, so you may meet tripod carriers seeking an undisturbed reflection who wish children would not make a ripple. Compromise may be in order.

Look down on beautiful Louise Lake and across the highway to Bench Lake, sitting on the edge of a cliff. Have kids guess by the telltale horn which of the Tatoosh Peaks is named Unicorn. The kids won't want to waste much time looking at the view because the shallow lake will call to them to wade. If photographers are glaring, move up the trail several hundred feet to the beginning of High Lakes Trail and find two more

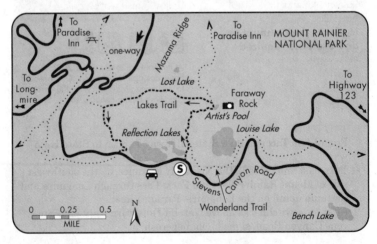

pools where kids can join the frogs and polliwogs.

High Lakes Trail connects the east and west legs of the Lakes Trail. You can retrace your steps. For the long way home, leave the ponds behind and walk the meadows on the side of Mazama Ridge. Mount Rainier is mostly out of sight, but views south to the Tatoosh Range are impressive. In a short mile, the way drops steeply to join the western leg of the Lakes Trail and then even more steeply for the ⅓ mile back to Reflection Lakes.

Artist's Pool and Tatoosh Range

 **SNOW LAKE**

BEFORE YOU GO
Maps Green Trails No. 270 Mount Rainier East; Mount Rainier National Park Backcountry Trip Planner
Current conditions Mount Rainier National Park (360) 569-2211
National park annual or day-use pass required; backcountry permit required for camping

ABOUT THE HIKE
Day hike or backpack
Easy for children
July to October
Snow Lake: 2⅔ miles;
Bench Lake: 1⅓ mile
340 feet elevation gain in, 280 feet out

At this time the extent of the 2006 flood damage is unknown. Call ahead to the managing agency for the current conditions before heading out.

GETTING THERE
- From I-5 in Tacoma, take State Highway 7 south to State Highway 706.
- Turn east and drive to the Nisqually entrance, on the southwest side of Mount Rainier National Park. Pass through Longmire and continue on uphill on the Longmire–Paradise Road.

■ After two switchbacks above Narada Falls, turn right onto Stevens Canyon Road. At 1.2 miles past Reflection Lakes find the trailhead on the right, elevation 4520 feet.

ON THE TRAIL

Another Snow Lake? A permanent snow patch may give this one the best right to the name. This child-delighting lake in Mount Rainier National Park is at the end of a short trail through subalpine meadowland. The lake has two campsites, a wading beach, and a permanent snow patch at one end where kids can slide and throw snowballs.

The trail starts in a jungle of vine maple and willows, gaining 300 feet in the first ¼ mile. Children will need help on some of the giant steps the park service has built into the trail. The path levels off and enters flower fields punctuated with silver snags from a forest fire that swept through here seventy years ago.

A short side trail on a hold-your-child's-hand bluff gives an airy view of Bench Lake. The trail loses most of the elevation gain, passing a side path to Bench Lake at 4542 feet. This is a possible turnaround point, but the lake is surrounded by heavy brush and has little to offer a child. From Bench Lake the trail continues its up-and-down ways, climbing again past a field of bear-grass and great patches of heather, paintbrush, lupine, and little alpine trees, some small enough to be Christmas trees for mice.

The sound of Unicorn Creek flowing from the lake alerts you to the last climb, to the lip of Snow Lake. If you were lucky enough to get one of the two backcountry camping permits per day for this lake, take the trail across the creek to your campsite, located on a little finger of land. If you are day hiking, continue on the trail along the shore of the deep

Snow Lake vista

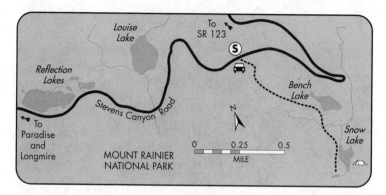

blue lake to its shallow end, for wading. Since this is melted snow water, the wading is chilly, but most kids don't mind the temperature for short dips. Use caution when crossing the logjam over the outlet stream that leads to the camps.

On an August afternoon while we ate lunch on logs, we found a frog, heard a marmot whistle, and saw a pika. We looked up at the horn of Unicorn Peak and the fortresslike walls around the cirque. Waterfalls coursed down them to enter the lake. We continued the hike to the end of the lake and an avalanche snow slope. We found a gently tilted snowbank that made safe sliding for three little children with us. Then we turned around to discover the only view from the lake of Mount Rainier. The mountain had been watching over us all the time.

 **GROVE OF THE PATRIARCHS**

BEFORE YOU GO
Maps Green Trails No. 270 Mount Rainier East; USGS Chinook Pass; Mount Rainier National Park Backcountry Trip Planner
Current conditions Mount Rainier National Park (360) 569-2211
National park annual or day-use pass required

ABOUT THE HIKE
Day hike
Easy for children
May–November
½ mile
No elevation gain

At this time the extent of the 2006 flood damage is unknown. Call ahead to the managing agency for the current conditions before heading out.

Hemlock root system in Grove of the Patriarchs

GETTING THERE

- From Enumclaw, drive Highway 410 south to Highway 123.
- Turn right (south) and drive 11 miles to the Stevens Canyon Road entrance of Mount Rainier National Park.
- Turn right; the trailhead is just beyond the entrance station, on the right across the Ohanapecosh River Bridge beside the comfort station, elevation 2200 feet.

ON THE TRAIL

The tremendous trees are bound to impress children—and grandparents, too—with their size, age, and venerable beauty. There are interpretive signs for parents, hollow trees for imaginative children to crawl into, and a shallow creek for everyone to soak or splash in. This is a great spot to cool off on a hot day, featuring a big, wide trail.

The trail is mostly level. Look for the "squirrel overpass," a log suspended 10 feet over the trail like a freeway overpass. At a trail junction, turn right and descend a short switchback to a suspension bridge that spans a shallow branch of the river to a loop trail. Go either way, winding through the Grove of the Patriarchs.

There are thirty-five trees over 25 feet in diameter, some over 300 feet high, and all estimated to be between 800 and 1000 years old. Long ago forest fires missed these patriarchs partly because they were protected by surrounding creeks, but you can find burn scars in their bark to show how close the fires came. Notice that some of the hemlocks are standing in midair on giant roots. These trees were germinated and grown on nurse logs that long ago decayed and disappeared. Tell the children they provide homes for elves and other friendly woodland creatures.

Hemlock

 **SILVER FALLS**

BEFORE YOU GO
Maps Green Trails No. 270 Mount Rainier East; USGS Chinook Pass
Current conditions Mount Rainier National Park (360) 569-2211
National park annual or day-use pass required

ABOUT THE HIKE
Day hike
Easy for children
May–November
3 miles
200 feet elevation gain and loss, in and out

At this time the extent of the 2006 flood damage is unknown. Call ahead to the managing agency for the current conditions before heading out.

GETTING THERE
- From Enumclaw, drive Highway 410 south to Highway 123.
- Turn right (south) and drive 13 miles to Ohanapecosh Campground, 2 miles past the Stevens Canyon Road entrance of Mount Rainier National Park, elevation 1850 feet.

ON THE TRAIL
Many rivers in Mount Rainier National Park come from its glaciers. Children can learn that most rivers are milky because, as the glaciers move down the mountain, the ice plucks dirt from its bed and deposits it in the rivers. Ohanepecosh River, however, is clear. Tell children that the river is clear because it starts not from melting ice but from little creeks as it gathers size to become a river.

Silver Falls

From the road we see the river as peaceful with lazy ripples, but the lazy river turns into a plunging, thundering torrent called Silver Falls as it passes through a narrow gorge, losing 200 feet in a series of rapids, with waterfalls intermingled with deep pools. Early in the summer as the snow melts, the volume and velocity of the falls is spectacular. There is no safe place to get near the water, but even from a safe distance the sight of the torrent will be fascinating to children as they feel the spray and mist on their faces. The best way to enjoy the forest and falls is on the 3-mile loop starting at Ohanepecosh Campground.

Begin in old forest filled with mossy boulders, Canadian dogwood, vanilla-leaf, twinflower, and old snags riddled by woodpeckers. With minor ups and downs the wide trail continues to descend. In about ⅓ mile the easy trail turns steep as it loses 200 feet beside the wide torrent. Children can look down the rocky ravine while clinging to parents' hands and a rail fence. Some of the rock seems to have been carved by water into pools, bathtubs, and white-water whirlpools.

Pass up several viewpoints in favor of the Silver Falls viewpoint, which offers viewers spray from one of the largest falls, ½ mile from the rest area. Better yet, go a few hundred feet farther where the trail crosses the river on a high bridge with an excellent postcard view back to Silver Falls.

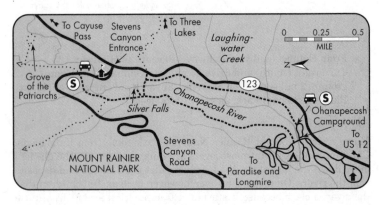

Opposite page: Fun on the trail (Photo by Veer)

amilies hiking in the South Cascades can see that they are less deeply carved than the North Cascades. But they have just as much volcanic sculpturing, as can be seen dramatically from Norway Pass, where children can gaze at the vast ruined crater of Mount St. Helens and see the start of the new volcano. Other volcanically formed places are Tongue Mountain, Badger Ridge, and Hamilton Buttes. Many beautiful waterfalls in the Gifford Pinchot National Forest make for short hikes: Middle Falls, Langfield Falls, and Falls Creek Falls are a few. Children will love dropping into the caves of Ape Cave, Layser Cave, Ice Caves, and the Trail of Two Forests. The Indian Heaven Wilderness; Bird Creek Meadows, near Mount Adams; and Snowgrass Flats, in the Goat Rocks, are trails that reach particularly lovely alpine meadow parklands. The Dark Divide proposed wilderness includes hikes to high points without roads, such as Juniper Shoulder and Sunrise Peak. Children will love the short hikes to Steamboat Mountain and Sleeping Beauty and seeing the reasons for their names in their shapes.

WHITE PASS: HIGHWAY 12

 **PACKWOOD LAKE**

BEFORE YOU GO
Maps Green Trails No. 302 Packwood; USFS Gifford Pinchot
Current conditions Cowlitz Valley Ranger District (360) 497-1100
Wilderness Permit and Northwest Forest Pass required

ABOUT THE HIKE
Day hike or backpack
Moderate for children
June–November
9 miles
200 feet elevation gain

GETTING THERE

- From US 12 at the east end of Packwood, near the former U.S. Forest Service ranger station, go right on Snyder Road/Road No. 1260, signed "Packwood Lake."
- Enter the Gifford Pinchot National Forest at 0.9 mile, and drive 6.2 miles more to a large parking lot and the start of trail No. 78, elevation 2700 feet.

ON THE TRAIL

One of the largest woodland lakes in the South Cascades is an easy stroll on a smooth, wide, and gentle trail. Camping, boating, and fishing continue undisturbed on a shore beloved by families since early in the twentieth century.

All is not well, however. The outlet stream was dammed in 1963 for a power project. Although the permit states that the lake level is to be maintained, it is often lowered. But worst of all, the dam was built 5 feet higher than it needed to be, so there is always the possibility that the power-hungry utility will flood the lakeshore. To add insult to injury, motorcycles, three-wheelers, and four-wheelers are allowed on the power company's service road to the lakeshore. But there they stop. The lakeshore itself is off-limits to them.

The trail starts in second-growth forest, entering the Goat Rocks Wilderness at ¾ mile. Watch for spectacular views of Mount Rainier. At 1½ miles, the old-growth forest begins. Children will be awed by these real-life giants, some at least 500 years old. Look, too, for groves of yew trees, whose bark is used to create Taxol, a cancer treatment drug. Just before dropping to the lake, pass through an ancient rock slide that may have had a part in the creation of the lake by damming Lake Creek. At 4½ miles reach Packwood Lake, elevation 2857 feet.

This is a very popular destination. At the lake are two guard stations, one of them a log structure built in 1910 and preserved as a historic

Packwood Lake

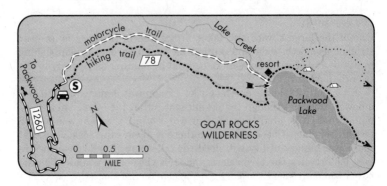

landmark. A resort rents rowboats, rafts, and cabins in fishing season. The campground is just beyond the store. To escape the motorcyclists and their portable radios, lanterns, and beer, continue on to quieter campsites up the lake.

The partly glacier-fed lake, turquoise from suspended rock flour, has a large wooded island in the center. Above rises 7487-foot Johnson Peak, where a band of mountain goats is headquartered. Originally named Ackushnesh by the Taidnapam Indians, who used it as a fishing and camping site, the lake was renamed for Billy Packwood, who found it while prospecting with his son in the early 1900s. It was established as a recreation area in 1934 and then as a limited area in 1946, but that status was removed in 1962 so the dam could be built.

 BLUFF LAKE

BEFORE YOU GO
Maps Green Trails No. 302 Packwood; USFS Goat Rocks Wilderness
Current conditions Cowlitz Valley Ranger District (360) 497-1100
Wilderness Permit and Northwest Forest Pass required

ABOUT THE HIKE
Day hike or backpack
Moderate for children
July to October
3 miles
800 feet elevation gain

GETTING THERE
■ From Packwood, drive north on US 12 for 4.4 miles and turn right on Road No. 46.

- Drive 1.6 miles and go right on Road No. 4610. In another 1.5 miles the road makes a sharp right turn and becomes Road No. 4612.
- At 5.6 miles from the highway, reach the trailhead, elevation 3000 feet.

ON THE TRAIL

Swim or fish in a forest lake high in the Goat Rocks Wilderness. Since the bottom is muddy, there is no chance for wading, and small children should be careful. While we were here on a hot July morning, older children who were good swimmers were jumping from a large rock on the east shoreline into the deepest part of the lake. Bleached drift logs line one end of the lake, and little children could sit on them and kick safely for water fun and games. This trail was used by the Cowlitz Indians to reach a mountain ridge where they hunted mountain goats.

Head east along Purcell Creek and climb steeply up through hemlock and fir forest to reach the lake. Along the trail we came upon two tiny grouse chicks, only hours old, looking for their mother. The trail passes two rounded, rocky balds, covered with moss but obviously of volcanic origin—perhaps the remains of an old lava flow. The lake is unmarked,

Bluff Lake

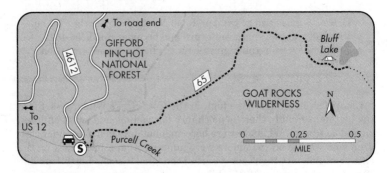

and it is possible to walk by and miss it unless you are alerted by the sounds of splashing kids.

To get to the large rock campsite, continue another ¼ mile east past the first lake access. Small native trout can be caught here, we were told. Curling smoke from a campfire atop the rock looked like the signal from an Indian's camp.

122 DEER LAKE AND SAND LAKE

BEFORE YOU GO
Maps Green Trails No. 303 White Pass; USFS Wenatchee
Current conditions Cowlitz Valley Ranger District (360) 497-1100
Northwest Forest Pass required
Wilderness Permit required

ABOUT THE HIKE
Day hike or backpack
Easy for children
July–October
Deer Lake: 5 miles; Sand Lake: 7 miles
800 feet elevation gain

GETTING THERE
- From Packwood, drive US 12 east 20 miles to the summit of White Pass.
- Find a Pacific Crest Trail crossing at 0.8 mile east of the pass. Just north, turn left on Road No. 1284 and go 0.2 mile to the hikers' parking area, elevation 4400 feet.

ON THE TRAIL
These two neat and tidy lakes lie along the Pacific Crest Trail in the William O. Douglas Wilderness. Deer Lake is deep and surrounded by forest. Sand Lake, the farther one, is bordered by meadows and tall

Pacific Crest Trail near Sand Lake

trees but is so shallow that, by midsummer, finding usable water can be a problem.

This trail was once part of the Yakama–Cowlitz trail. Start out heading north in forest on the Pacific Crest Trail; in summer, this stretch is very dusty from horse traffic. At 1 mile enter the William O. Douglas Wilderness. At 2½ miles, a short side trail leads to Deer Lake, elevation, 6206 feet, offering good campsites and a sandy swimming beach.

Another scant 1 mile brings hikers to Sand Lake, elevation 5245

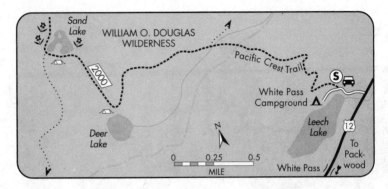

feet, and an interesting shoreline of alpine trees and flowers. A long-time hiker of these parts mused, after the most recent Mount St. Helens blast, "I always wondered where all this sand came from." Mount St. Helens has been blowing "sand"—actually, pumice and lava dust—for centuries. Where the trail is cut into side hills, exposing soil layers, you can see streaks of "sand" just like that now on the surface. Camping is just beyond the lake.

SOUTH CASCADES AND MOUNT ST. HELENS NATIONAL MONUMENT

 **NORWAY PASS**

BEFORE YOU GO
Maps Green Trails No. 332 Spirit Lake; USGS Spirit Lake East; USFS Gifford Pinchot
Current conditions Mount St. Helens National Volcanic Monument (360) 247-3900
Northwest Forest Pass required

ABOUT THE HIKE
Day hike
Moderate for children
Mid-June–October
4 miles
900 feet elevation gain

GETTING THERE
- From I-5 take exit 68 and follow Highway 12 east for 50.4 miles to Randle.

- In Randle, turn south on Road No. 25 and drive 22 miles.
- Turn uphill on Road No. 99, signed "Mount St. Helens—Windy Ridge Viewpoint." At 8.9 miles from the junction, turn right on Ryan Lake Road No. 26.
- In 1 mile reach the Norway Pass trailhead, elevation 3600 feet.

ON THE TRAIL

A hot, dry trail through a desolation of timber downed by the 1980 blast of Mount St. Helens leads to one of the most spectacular viewpoints of the disaster area. You can look across Spirit Lake to the crater and its smoldering dome. One-third of the lake is still covered by trees knocked over by the 1980 eruption and washed into the lake in the ensuing tidal wave. On the lakeshore below Norway Pass, the giant wave swept everything bare for 500 feet up the hillside. Notice how the trees facing the mountain lie flat in a straight line from the crater, while behind the ridge the trees are crisscrossed, an indication of how the turbulent wave of supersonic air eddied behind the ridge tops. Be sure to carry plenty of drinking water, which is available from a metal pump near the parking lot and at the trailhead rest rooms; all shade trees have been flattened. Note that this area is used by mountain bikers; keep an eye out.

The trail starts at the far end of the parking lot, first meandering a bit through fallen timber and silvery snags and then starting a long series of switchbacks above Meta Lake. At about 1¼ miles, the trail rounds a shoulder, drops a bit, and levels off. At 2 miles come to Norway Pass, elevation 4508 feet, and the view.

Children will be excited to see that in the crater the new volcano dome is growing upward. Also, a new horseshoe-shaped glacier has begun to extend itself around the volcano dome. Unless molten lava melts it or the spasms of uplift crack it apart, the glacier will continue to grow, the first new glacier in the Cascades for many years.

The trail continues up Mount Margaret, but the views of the lake are no better higher up.

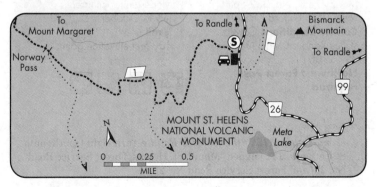

Log-covered Spirit Lake after Mount St. Helens eruption

Everywhere new beginnings of life are springing up: fireweed, berries, and little alpine firs. For some reason, the avalanche lilies on this hill often flower with six or seven blossoms to a stem, unlike the usual pattern of two or three.

1 2 4 BADGER RIDGE

BEFORE YOU GO
Maps Green Trails No. 333 McCoy Peak, No. 332 Spirit Lake; USFS Gifford Pinchot
Current conditions Cowlitz Valley Ranger District (360) 497-1100
Northwest Forest Pass required

ABOUT THE HIKE
Day hike
Moderate for children
July to October
2 miles
400 feet elevation gain

GETTING THERE

■ *From Highway 12 at the center of Randle,* turn right (south) onto State Route 131 (signed "Mount St. Helens, Forest Service Road No. 23, and Forest Service Road No. 25").

- In 1 mile, at the sign for Mount St. Helens, turn right.
- Pass Iron Creek Campground on the left in 9 miles. In 10 more miles, at the fork of Road No. 25 and Road No. 99, bear left, staying on Road No. 25.
- In 1 mile turn left onto Road No. 28.
- In 2.7 miles turn right onto primitive Road No. 2816, signed "Badger Ridge Trail." Drive 4.5 miles to the trailhead, elevation 4900 feet.
- *Or from Woodland,* drive County Road No. 503 to Yale—a service station. The road becomes Road No. 90. Follow it past the Yale and Swift Reservoirs and the Pine Creek Visitors Center, and continue on Elk Pass Road No. 25. Drive 2 miles to Road No. 28; see directions above.

ON THE TRAIL

Why Badger Ridge? Badgers are typically an eastern Washington animal and are not usually seen in this area. Did a badger wander west of its normal range to give this ridge its name? More likely, the name-giver mistook a marmot for a badger. Ask children which one they would rather meet on a trail: an ornery predator like the badger, or a placid, meadow-dwelling, grass-eating marmot?

Whatever the name, this point is a high and lovely spot, well worth the drive and short walk. It is so remote that more elk than people use this trail. (Have the kids look for elk tracks.) At the saddle, youngsters can scan green parkland meadows and two volcanoes, and then continue on to a rewarding destination. Older kids might also want to drop down to little spring-fed Badger Lake and to climb to the old lookout site, but there is a dangerous snow slope on the trail until late July and so much soft pumice that the trail is not recommended for little children.

Begin walking in subalpine meadow on a sandy trail that drops and regains 100 feet in the first ¼ mile. The cliff above and to the left almost seems to lean out over the soft sandy trail. Look over your shoulder to

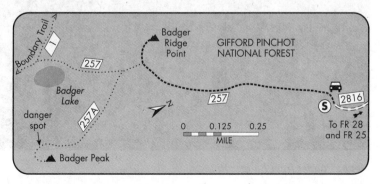

see whether Mount Rainier is still there. This is a good place to teach children to use a map and the landmark of Mount Rainier to orient themselves. Can they find the four compass directions? Where will the sun come up tomorrow? Notice the numerous game trails that crisscross the path, and the huge footprints.

In a short mile the trail reaches a ridge top. Turn right on a fainter trail to Badger Ridge Point at the end of the ridge, elevation 5100 feet. Join the kids as they survey their kingdom. Plateaus and rocky tables clothed in bright green meadows spread between you and Mount Rainier and Mount St. Helens.

Where did all the pumice come from? Off and on for a thousand years, Mount St. Helens has spewed pumice, but soft hailstone-size pumice showered down especially thickly in the 1980 eruption, covering everything inches deep. Although much has since washed away, the layer can still be seen on top of old stumps. Badger Peak was directly downwind from the mountain that day and got more than its share.

Late in July, when the snowbank has melted enough so that the trail is safe, if older children are determined to climb to the former lookout site,

Mount Rainier from Badger Ridge

try it. Return to the main trail, go over the ridge top, and descend steeply 500 feet to a junction. The right fork goes 1 mile more to Badger Lake; go up to the left for the 5664-foot summit, where views are even grander because Mount Adams is unobscured. Early one morning we found a mountain goat there curled up like a dog, sleeping on the summit.

 **LAYSER CAVE**

BEFORE YOU GO
Map Green Trails No. 333 McCoy Peak; USFS Gifford Pinchot
Current conditions Cowlitz Valley Ranger District (360) 497-1100
Northwest Forest Pass required

ABOUT THE HIKE
Day hike
Easy for children
Year round
¼ mile
100 feet elevation loss

GETTING THERE

- On Highway 12 at the center of Randle, turn right (south) onto State Route 131 (signed "Mount St. Helens, Forest Service Road 23, and Forest Service Road 25").
- In 1 mile, at the sign for Cispus Center, turn left.
- In 7 miles turn left onto Spur Road No. 2300-083/4, marked to Layser Cave.
- The 1½-mile spur road is narrow and steep, but the parking area is large enough to accommodate buses. Elevation at the trailhead is 1700 feet.

ON THE TRAIL

This ancient Indian cave, used by long-ago Indian families for shelter and as a place to skin animal hides for clothing, will intrigue children.

The trail drops to the right. Pause after 100 yards for a view of the Cispus valley before going on to the cave. According to the Indians, one of their gods, Coyote (who also had a reputation as a trickster), named everything on the horizon. Look up to see Mount Adams, look over the Cispus valley to Tongue Mountain, and look across Juniper Ridge. Indians once drove deer and elk into a nearby steep box canyon, where they killed them with an *atlatl,* a dart shaft.

Continue on to Layser Cave, a natural 32-foot declining cave. Even on a hot day, when you enter the cave's mouth, it will feel cool and damp. Once inside, your eyes will adjust to the darkness. Picture Indian families

sheltering here, making necklaces with shells traded from coastal Indians, and preparing hides for clothing. What would it have been like if fathers had not been able to find food for their families, you might ask children. They couldn't just go to the store, the freezer, or the cupboard for supplies. Would the families have gone hungry? Or would they have moved on to another area? Stone tools and bones of 108 deer that were found here tell experts that this cave was used for more than 7000 years.

Looking out from Layser Cave

 **TONGUE MOUNTAIN**

BEFORE YOU GO
Maps Green Trails No. 333 McCoy Peak; USGS Tower Rock
Current conditions Cowlitz Valley Ranger District (360) 497-1100
Northwest Forest Pass required

ABOUT THE HIKE
Day hike
Difficult for children
July–October
2 miles
1200 feet elevation gain

GETTING THERE

- From Highway 12 at the center of Randle, turn right (south) onto State Route 131 (signed "Mount St. Helens, Forest Service Road No. 23, and Forest Service Road No. 25").
- In 1 mile, at the sign for Cispus Center, turn left.
- In 8 more miles, turn right on Road No. 28. The pavement ends in 1 mile. Continue straight, onto Road No. 29.
- In 4 more miles, turn left onto Road No. 2904. Go another 4 miles to the trailhead for Tongue Mountain Trail No. 294, on the left; elevation is 3600 feet.

ON THE TRAIL

A short, steep hike up Tongue Mountain, a small extinct volcano on the edge of the Dark Divide, leads to breathtaking views. Mount Rainier, Mount Adams and Mount St. Helens look close enough to touch. The Cispus River winds through the valley of the Dark Divide directly below. A forest fire devastated Juniper Ridge in 1918, leaving silver snags along its length. This mountaintop held a lookout from 1934 to 1948,

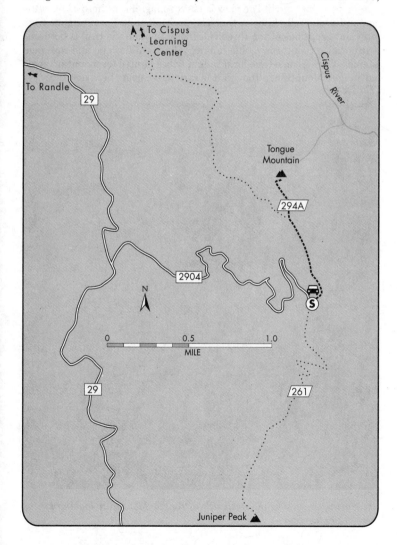

built in response to that fire. The rock in this area is unstable, and children should not go beyond the trail. Mountain bikers also use the area. But views and the satisfaction of reaching the top where the building once stood are compensation enough.

This short trail, No. 294A, is steep for children and ends about 100 feet from the summit of the old lookout site. The foot trail to the site has long since worn away and only experienced rock climbers should attempt the last pitch. The view is just as magnificent here as from the summit rock. Tell children that the path is made up of pumice from previous eruptions of the three volcanoes. In June the trail is bordered with orange paintbrush, blue lupine, yellow wallflowers, and rose penstemon. Once upon a time local Indian tribes hunted for mountain goats on Tongue Mountain, although it is rare to see goats here now.

Ira Spring traversing the steep side of Tongue Mountain, looking for the perfect photograph

 **JUNIPER SHOULDER**

BEFORE YOU GO
Maps Green Trails No. 333
McCoy Peak; USGS McCoy
Peak
Current conditions Cowlitz
Valley Ranger District (360)
497-1100

ABOUT THE HIKE
Day hike
Moderate for children
Late June to October
4 miles
1200 feet elevation gain

GETTING THERE

- From Highway 12 at the center of Randle, turn right (south) onto State Route 131 (signed "Mount St. Helens, Forest Service Road No. 23, and Forest Service Road No. 25").
- In 1 mile, at the sign for Cispus Center, turn left.
- In 8 miles turn right onto Road No. 28.
- In 1 mile the pavement ends; continue straight onto Road No. 29.
- In 4 more miles turn left onto Road No. 2904. Drive 4 more miles to the trailhead for Juniper Ridge Trail No. 261, elevation 3600 feet.

ON THE TRAIL

A grand panorama spreads out in all directions for children to enjoy on top of this subalpine meadowy ridge. Woodland switchbacks sometimes offer the sounds of ruffed grouse, tracks of elk, and sights of deer along the way. Mountain goats and bears have been seen here. Hummingbirds, juncos, and butterflies may buzz families as they continue wandering upward. Most of the way the tread is wide, but it does narrow for 100 feet on a steep slope below the shoulder. Keep the kids in sight. A 4500-foot saddle makes a great turnaround point, with views of three giant

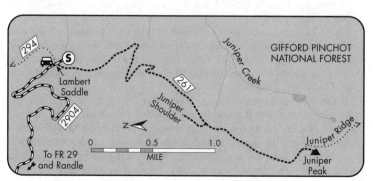

Mount Adams from Juniper Shoulder

gleaming volcanoes—Mounts Adams, Rainier, and what is left of crumbling St. Helens—and the odd-shaped core of an old volcano, Tongue Mountain. Children can feel they are masters of all they survey.

Unfortunately, Gifford Pinchot National Forest management has allowed motorcycles on this fragile meadow trail. Families will hear them long before they see them, but they should be prepared to get out of their way.

Begin upward in cool old forest on moderately steep switchbacks. Children will love knowing that elk herds and cougars have been sighted from this trail. At 2 miles and 4500 feet, look out at the first sweeping views. For Juniper Shoulder, follow the ridge crest northward to the 4800-foot high point.

These summit meadows have a history. The area burned in 1902 and again in 1918, clearing the alpine forests. Sheepherders used burned-over Juniper Ridge as a stock drive through the 1930s. No wonder the flowery meadows are so open! The whole area has been proposed for a Dark Divide wilderness.

If the kids (and their parents) have more energy to burn, follow the trail upward another 2 miles to the rounded top of 5611-foot Juniper Peak. In season, huckleberries and blueberries are thick on either side of the trail from this point on and are delicious. At 4 miles find timberline and the highest point on the ridge. Flowery meadows offer children a sense of nature's fragility, abundance, renewal, and majesty.

Berries in late summer and early autumn include blueberries and purple and red huckleberries, which like to grow in decaying cedar logs, and low Oregon grape and salal, which provide dark purple berries Native Americans once made into a form of pemmican cakes.

 **HAMILTON BUTTES**

BEFORE YOU GO
Maps Green Trails No. 334 Blue Lake; USFS Gifford Pinchot
Current conditions Cowlitz Valley Ranger District (360) 497-1100

ABOUT THE HIKE
Day hike or backpack
Moderate for children
July to October
2 miles
800 feet elevation gain

GETTING THERE

- From Highway 12 at the center of Randle, turn right (south) onto State Route 131 (signed "Mount St. Helens, Forest Service Road No. 23, and Forest Service Road No. 25").
- In 1 mile, at the sign for Cispus Center, turn left.
- In 3.5 miles turn left on Road No. 22.
- Drive 5.7 miles to Road No. 78 and turn right.
- Go 6.8 miles to the intersection with Road No. 7807; turn left.
- Drive 1.8 miles to Road No. 7807-029 and turn right. Pass Mud Lake and find the trailhead at the road end, elevation 5000 feet.

ON THE TRAIL

A stunning panorama of South Cascades peaks will reward families for this short, steep hike. If you wish for a high campsite on a windless summer night, you could not improve on Hamilton Buttes. Picture moonlight and starlight on three icy volcanoes. A lookout once presided over this majestic scenery, watching for forest fires. Today, airplane surveillance has replaced the lookout, but families who hike to this spot can pause, marvel, and enjoy the glorious view for as long as they wish. Carry water because there is none here.

Your family may be unpleasantly surprised by the sudden appearance of a motorcycle on this high trail, since it remains open to off-road vehicle traffic. Steep basalt cliffs on one side mean you should hold on to little children and watch older ones carefully. Despite these risks, this is one of the best hikes in the area and will give a child a sense of beauty and accomplishment.

Begin walking upward through alpine trees on an old roadbed, the path sandy with Mount St. Helens ash. At a fork at ½ mile, keep left; a bit farther on the old road becomes trail. Switchback upward on tread deeply rutted by motorcycle tires, through basalt outcrops and alpine flower gardens to the summit. Children will feel suspended between heaven and earth. Is this the highest point? A rock a bit farther looks higher. Tell the children that despite appearances, the other rock is not higher because you can see over its top.

Look south to Mount Adams, looming close enough for you to inspect its snowfields and glaciers in detail. Beyond and farther south is the faint silhouette of Mount Hood; westward is the gray, steaming crater of Mount St. Helens. Look north to the enormous mass and sweep of

Hamilton Butte trail and Mount Rainier

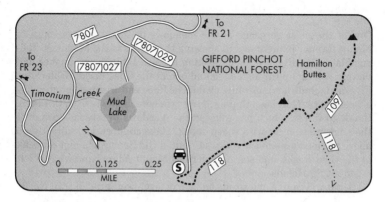

Mount Rainier, and east to the Goat Rocks, the oldest volcanic formation in the 360-degree panorama. Listen to the sighing, whispering, singing winds coming from every direction, and feel the peace of this place.

1 2 9 SNOWGRASS FLATS

BEFORE YOU GO
Maps Green Trails No. 303 White Pass, No. 335 Walupt Lake, No. 302 Packwood Lake; USGS Walupt Lake, Old Snowy Mountain; USFS Goat Rocks Wilderness
Current conditions Cowlitz Valley Ranger District (360) 497-1100
Northwest Forest Pass and Wilderness Permit required

ABOUT THE HIKE
Day hike or backpack
Difficult day hike, easy backpack for children
July–November
8 miles
1100 feet elevation gain

GETTING THERE

- From Highway 12, about 3 miles southwest of Packwood and just after the rest area, turn right onto Road No. 21, also known as Johnson Creek Road.
- At just under 12 miles from Highway 12, turn left onto Road No. 2150, signed to Chambers Lake.
- Drive 1.5 miles to Road No. 2150-040; turn right.
- Then turn right again in 2.5 miles onto No. 2150-405, and arrive at the parking area for the Snowgrass trailhead, elevation 4600 feet.

ON THE TRAIL

One of the most gorgeous alpine meadows in the state lies south of Mount Rainier in an area still showing the effects of the Mount St. Helens blast. Children will enjoy looking for 4-inch blueberry bushes and flowers poking up through sand and ash in the Goat Rocks Wilderness. Flowers include fields of white avalanche lilies and cream-colored spikes of bear-grass. The sheep that used to graze here are gone from this area, thank goodness, which has allowed the meadows to return—including the snowgrass, a favorite sheep snack. Have children look directly up above the meadows to the rocky summit of Old Snowy, the highest peak in the Goat Rocks, and south to glorious Mount Adams and what is left of Mount St. Helens.

Begin walking in the woods on nearly level, well-graded trail No. 96

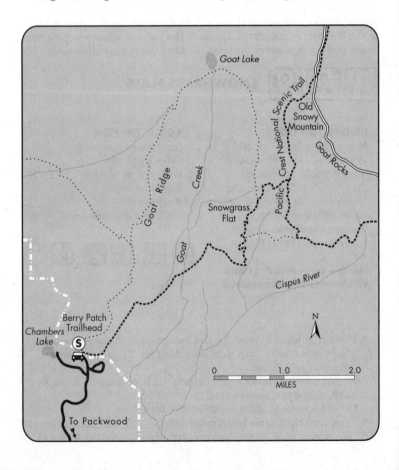

Pacific Crest Trail through Snowgrass Flats

along Goat Creek. At 2 miles come to a bridge over Goat Creek and begin climbing on switchbacks into subalpine trees and heather. Optional campsites are at Bypass Trail and Camp, about ¾ of the way in. But you will want to continue on to the loveliness of open meadows. Alaska yellow cedars, alpine firs, and hemlocks frame the wide expanses of flower-studded Snowgrass Flats. To allow for regrowth after overuse, camping is not allowed right in the ten-acre meadow bowl, but there are many wonderful camps a few hundred feet above it. Fresh water issues from springs, snowmelt, and little streams and waterfalls all around you. This trail connects with the Pacific Crest Trail at 6400 feet, so children can watch for through-hikers on their way to Canada or Mexico.

Children will enjoy watching playful marmots, who flick their tails just before they start to run and will often stand on their hind legs to peer at them, and Canada jays, the bold, begging camp robbers, who will take nuts from their hands. Perhaps the biggest thrill of all is the possibility of seeing mountain goats grazing in meadows high above. The day we were here we saw eighteen goats, six of which were young kids.

If you camp, consider a day hike to Cispus Basin and taking the Lily Basin trail to Goat Lake.

 **SUNRISE PEAK**

BEFORE YOU GO
Maps Green Trails No. 333 McCoy Peak, No. 334 Blue Lake; USGS McCoy Peak, Tower Rock
Current conditions Cowlitz Valley Ranger District (360) 497-1100
Northwest Forest Pass required

ABOUT THE HIKE
Day hike
Difficult for children
July–October
1.6 miles
1480 feet elevation gain

GETTING THERE
- High clearance vehicle recommended
- From Highway 12 at the center of Randle, turn right (south) onto State Route 131 (signed "Mount St. Helens, Forest Service Road No. 23, and Forest Service Road No. 25").

Summit view from Sunrise Peak

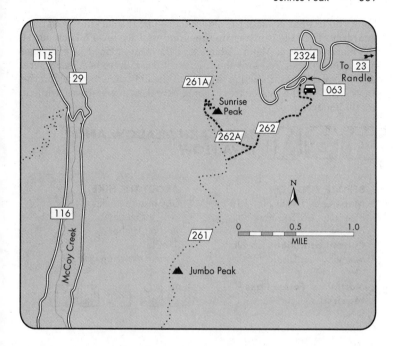

- In 1 mile, at the sign for Cispus Center, turn left.
- In 19 miles turn right onto Road No. 23. Drive 4.6 miles.
- Turn right onto Road No. 2324. In 4.2 miles go sharply right at an unmarked intersection.
- In 1 mile turn left onto Road No. 2324-063 and drive a short distance to the trailhead, elevation 4292 feet.

ON THE TRAIL

This is considered one of the best short hikes in the Dark Divide, a proposed wilderness area called after an early settler whose name was Dark. A winding, rough trail to a former lookout leads children up and through one of the Gifford Pinchot's most magnificent old-growth forests, and out into the meadows of Juniper Ridge. Alpine parkland and berry bushes lie all around. Tell children to look outward to find, set in a triangle, the three white-capped volcanoes—Rainier, Adams, and what's left of St. Helens, its gaping crater. In late summer here, kids can pick all the berries they can eat.

Trail No. 262 begins high on the edge of Juniper Ridge. It winds through giant trees that are 12, 18, and even 25 feet around. Motorcycles also occasionally use this trail, but you will hear them before you see them. A long, steep meadow ascent through berry bushes brings hikers up to what is left of the old lookout—just the old stairs and their guardrail. The kids can step up them and wait for lift-off. Look out at the massive bulk of Mount Adams and the white-topped jagged ridge of the Goat Rocks. Tell kids that mountain goats have been seen here. A long pause for lunch will give you and the kids time to reflect on the Dark Divide and why Congress should save it as a wilderness, while it is still undeveloped.

 ## TAKH TAKH MEADOW AND LAVA FLOW

BEFORE YOU GO
Maps Green Trails No. 334 Blue Lake; USFS Gifford Pinchot
Current conditions Cowlitz Valley Ranger District (360) 497-1100
Northwest Forest Pass required

ABOUT THE HIKE
Day hike or backpack
Easy for children
July to October
1 mile
80 feet elevation gain

GETTING THERE

- From Highway 12 at the center of Randle, turn right (south) onto State Route 131 (signed "Mount St. Helens, Forest Service Road No. 23, and Forest Service Road No. 25").
- In 1 mile, at the sign for Cispus Center, turn left.
- In 19 miles turn right onto Road No. 23.
- In 12.8 miles, at Baby Shoe Pass, turn left onto Road No. 2329, and drive 1.6 miles to the Takhlakh Lake campground turnoff and trailhead, elevation 4570 feet.
- To cut 0.5 mile from the hike, drive 1 mile beyond the campground to where the signed trail crosses the road for the second time.

ON THE TRAIL

Takhlakh Lake is the loveliest place in the Gifford Pinchot National Forest, with its famous calendar-picture setting of Mount Adams reflected in the lake. The lake and popular campground are readily accessible by car. However, there also are two great trails here for kids. One, an easy 1-mile trail, circles the beautiful lake. The other, to Takh Takh Meadow, will fascinate five- and six-year-old children, as it climbs onto a 2000-year-old rough lava flow and weaves its way through lava solidified into chunks. Older kids will love exploring the rock crevasses and battlements like those on top of an ancient fort. Watch children carefully. The trail is excellent, but if you are exploring rock crevasses and battlements, parents should lead the way. Be sure to bring plenty of mosquito repellent with you. The meadows are fine breeding grounds for these pests up until the beginning of August.

From the road crossing, the signed, well-defined trail crosses the edge of Takh Takh Meadow. *Takh Takh* means small prairie in the Taidnapam language. In mid-July have the kids look for "elephant's heads," with their tiny trunks; shooting stars, with curved petals shaped like a rocket blasting off; and cotton-grass, with tufts like white cotton. Next, the trail switchbacks steeply up what appears to be a rock slide but is actually the old lava flow. This lava may be 10,000 years old, or less. Tell the kids it probably came from a vent on the side of Mount Adams.

The Hawaiians have names for two forms of lava: the kind that cools slowly and is very rough *(a'a)*, and the kind that cools quickly, solidifies like a river in motion, and is smoother *(pahoehoe)*. Ask the children which kind they think this is. It flowed downhill slowly, carrying huge chunks of solid lava that formed the great pile of rock that the trail

Takhlakh Lake reflecting Mount Adams

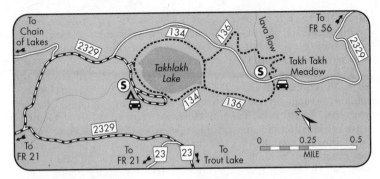

climbs. Although the lava looks very recent, the trees growing on it show it is much, much older.

On top, the trail follows the lava flow downhill, passing the battlements and rock crevasses, finally descending into forest and at ½ mile reaching the road again. Either return the way you came or walk the road ½ mile back to the car. On a clear day magnificent Mount Adams will watch over you like a sentinel for the entire distance.

TRAIL OF TWO FORESTS

BEFORE YOU GO
Maps Green Trails No. 364 Mount St. Helens; USGS Mt. St. Helens; USFS Mount St. Helens National Volcanic Monument handout
Current conditions Mount St. Helens National Volcanic Monument (360) 247-3900
Northwest Forest Pass required

ABOUT THE HIKE
Day hike
Easy for children
April to November
½ mile
80 feet elevation gain

GETTING THERE
- Leave I-5 at exit 21 and head east on State Highway 503. Drive 35 miles, passing the town of Cougar, where the highway becomes Road No. 90.
- At 7 miles past Cougar, turn left onto Road No. 83 and drive 2 miles to Road No. 8303. Turn left.
- Drive 0.2 mile to the signed trailhead on the right, elevation 1820 feet.

ON THE TRAIL

Nature trails are usually a bore for young children. But someone, 1900 years ago, must have had kids in mind when a lava flow from Mount St. Helens covered a forest and created an 80-foot tunnel just big enough for kids between the ages of five and fifty to crawl through. Other holes, both horizontal and vertical, show where trees once stood and have become a network of tunnels. The Trail of Two Forests winds through an existing forest to lava casts of one that stood here 1900 years ago, so children can easily see the reason for the name of this trail.

The Trail of Two Forests starts at the parking lot, close to the rest room. The trail is a boardwalk level enough for strollers and wheelchairs. Interpretive signs explain that a "recent" lava flow covered a living forest. The intense heat from the molten lava consumed the wood, and the lava took the shape of the living trees. In some cases the trees were standing when the lava hardened, leaving deep, vertical wells. When the lava covered trees lying on the ground, they burned, leaving horizontal, pipe-like tunnels. Many of the tree wells and partially formed tunnels are visible from the trail to intrigue and tantalize children into exploring them.

Barrier-free trail around tree casts

By a lucky chance, one of the tree wells leads to a tree tunnel, which leads to an opening 55 feet away, which leads to a bunch of happy kids crawling through it. Rangers say they pop in and out of the holes like chipmunks.

A word of caution. Crawling through the lava tunnel is hard on knees and guaranteed to get hands and pants dirty. Warn your kids that shorts will leave their knees exposed, so be sure they wear long pants. It is dark—very dark—in the tunnel, with only a tiny light a long distance ahead. I recommend that a parent crawl through first to determine whether it is suitable for his or her children and perhaps to lead the way. (If you can manage a tiny flashlight while crawling, all the better.) You might as well see it for yourself, because your children will talk about their adventure for a long time.

 **APE CAVE**

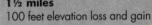

BEFORE YOU GO
Maps Green Trails No. 364 Mount St. Helens; Mount St. Helens National Volcanic Monument handout
Current conditions Mount St. Helens National Volcanic Monument (360) 247-3900
Northwest Forest Pass required

ABOUT THE HIKE
Day hike
Easy for children
March–November
1½ miles
100 feet elevation loss and gain

GETTING THERE
- Leave I-5 at exit 21 and head east on State Highway 503 for 35 miles, passing the town of Cougar, where the highway becomes Road No. 90.
- At 7 miles past Cougar, turn left onto Road No. 83 and drive 2 miles to Road No. 8303. Turn left.
- Drive 1.5 miles to the signed trailhead and very large parking lot on the right, elevation 1900 feet.

ON THE TRAIL
"Hey Mom! It's the secret hiding place of a slime mold!" said the delighted little boy as he descended the steps into the cave. Another child said with a gleeful smile, "Now we're inside the volcano!" Of course she wasn't, but these are the longest intact lava tubes in the United States, visited by 96,000 visitors each year, and representing volcanic activity

Descending into Ape Cave

of Mount St. Helens perhaps 2000 years before the 1980 eruption.

Children will be disappointed when they hear how the Ape Cave got its name: It was discovered in 1951 by members of a mountaineering club called the Mount St. Helens Apes. No, there are no Bigfoot apes found here.

But the kids will be intrigued by the adventure of exploring the caves with a flashlight and learning how they were formed. Explain that lava tubes form in flows of ropy, molten basalt when the cooling lava forms an outer crust. At the end of the eruption, the warm, inner lava drained from the tube, leaving an open tunnel. For a simplified geological explanation of the formation of the caves, look at the interpretive sign at the tunnel opening. Rent a lantern if you don't have one, and carry jackets for the temperature change. The kids will be surprised at how cool the bottom of the cave becomes.

The cave is divided into two parts. The upper section is extremely rough and recommended for older children only, but the lower section, described here, has a fairly smooth sand floor, and children find it exciting, safe, and easy going. The cave wind is caused by differences in air temperature inside and outside the cave.

Walk the paved trail 500 feet to the entrance of the lower cave. Descend a flight of stairs into the cave, enter, and descend another flight to the main chamber. One can choose to walk ¼ mile, ½ mile, or all the way to the cave's end (¾ mile). Any distance will be interesting to the kids.

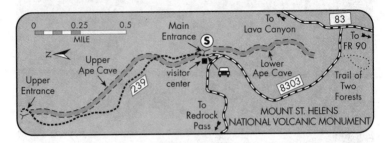

Note the shapes that the molten lava took when it solidified, and feel the texture of the walls. Ledges along the walls mark stages as the lava declined in the tube. Look upward for a "meatball" wedged into the ceiling in a groove. This was a block of solidified lava that was carried along in the lava stream, then became wedged in a narrow portion of the passage 12 feet above the floor as the flow receded. Children who have read the book or seen the movie *The Fellowship of the Ring* will expect to hear Gollum's voice saying, "Not here, my precious!" To experiment with total darkness, turn off your lights when you are alone underground. Children may be surprised at how much darker the blackness of underground can be. Even starlight is missing.

 **LEWIS RIVER TRAIL**

BEFORE YOU GO
Maps Green Trails No. 365 Lone Butte; USFS Gifford Pinchot
Current conditions Mount Adams Ranger District (509) 395-3400
Northwest Forest Pass required

ABOUT THE HIKE
Day hike or backpack
Easy for children
Year round
4 miles
200 feet elevation gain

GETTING THERE

- Leave I-5 at the Woodland exit 21 and head east on State Highway 503 for 35 miles, passing the town of Cougar where the highway becomes Road No. 90.
- Stay on Road No. 90 after its intersection with Road No. 25 from Randall for another 5.2 miles.
- Turn left on Road No. 9039 and drive 1 mile. Cross the Lewis River bridge and find the large parking area shortly beyond on your left.

ON THE TRAIL

The pride of the Gifford Pinchot National Forest is a gorgeous riverside walk among old-growth firs and cedars, past pools and rapids of the blue-green, glacier-fed Lewis River. Swimming, fishing, and camping are other good options. And the elevation is so low that the trail is open all year.

Start your walk with a stroll through the parking lot to view the lovely Curly Creek Falls as it pours through a sculptured arch. Walk left, upriver, to the intersection of Road No. 9039 near the bridge. Cross the road to find Lewis River trail No. 31. It begins in beautiful old-growth forest—fated to be just about the last preserved example of low-

Lewis River near Bolt Camp

elevation big trees in this area. The way drops slightly and then levels to follow the riverbank for ¾ mile. Nurse trees—downed logs sprouting new growth—give parents the chance to explain the birth–death–rebirth cycle of a forest left to nature's management. The trail moves from deep woods into second-growth deciduous trees and is bordered by oxalis, vanilla-leaf, and heart-shape leafed vancouveria, named for Captain George Vancouver, whose botanist, Archibald Menzies, found it in 1792. Briefly follow part of an old logging road; look for giant stumps from the really old growth, now gone. Visualize the logger of

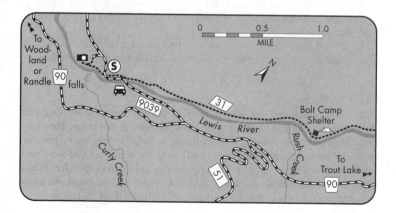

yesteryear balancing on narrow springboards inserted in the slots chopped in the sides.

At about 1½ miles is a high point where you can see the crystal-clear waters of Rush Creek entering the opaque green Lewis River. From here the trail follows the river closely, passing moss-festooned maples and, at 1¾ miles, a good campsite near a deep pool. Bolt Camp, at 2 miles, has a three-sided shelter built in the 1930s, still habitable and a lucky find in a rainstorm.

If time and energy permit, on returning to the car, you can drive a scant 1 mile farther on Road No. 9039 and walk the ½-mile trail to the Curly Creek viewpoint. On the opposite side of the river, Curly Creek flows under a natural bridge and drops over a 60-foot waterfall directly into the Lewis River.

 **MIDDLE FALLS**

BEFORE YOU GO
Maps Green Trails No. 365 Lone Butte; USFS Gifford Pinchot
Current conditions Mount Adams Ranger District (509) 395-3400
Northwest Forest Pass required

ABOUT THE HIKE
Day hike
Easy for children
Year round
1-mile loop
250 feet elevation loss and gain

GETTING THERE
- Leave I-5 at exit 21 and head east on State Highway 503 for 35 miles, passing the town of Cougar where the highway becomes Road No. 90.
- At 18.3 miles beyond Cougar, and just past Lower Falls Campground, look for parking on the right for Middle Falls, elevation 1800 feet.

ON THE TRAIL
The South Cascades are second only to the Columbia River Gorge in boasting some of the most impressive waterfalls in the state. This easy loop trail includes views of two of these waterfalls from every possible vantage point. Families can gaze together at the beauty of Copper Creek and the Lewis River as they break loose into falls and plunge freely and then regain their fluid composure. Kids love walking downward alongside the waterfall, being sprayed and deafened as they follow its course.

At the far end of the parking area find the trail that goes to Copper Creek. Because of the opportunity for a side trip, go clockwise on Trail No. 31. Start by dropping steeply through old-growth trees to cross a bridge over the top of the first waterfall, Copper Creek. The trail contours around, still dropping, to a viewpoint across the ravine and back up beside the stream of white water coursing over a ledge from below the bridge just crossed. At ½ mile turn toward Middle Falls at a fork and continue the descent to the level of the Lewis River.

The Middle Falls wrap around a projecting rock like a white curtain around the prow of a ship. Children stand immobilized and hypnotized by the waterfall. Benches allow a family to sit and enjoy the view and the cool spray. The trail along the river provides more rapids and pools before climbing back to the parking area. Children can throw sticks and branches or launch leaf boats, then watch them swirl and be swept away in the current.

Middle Falls of the Lewis River

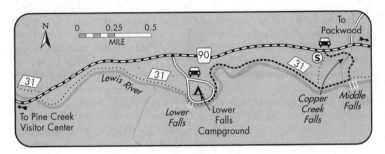

If your family would like to continue to the Lower Falls along the Lewis River, you have the option of letting some of your party continue on the trail 1¼ miles, while others climb back to the parking lot to drive the 1.2 miles to the Lower Falls Campground and trail access for a pickup point.

SIOUXON CREEK

BEFORE YOU GO
Maps Green Trails No. 396 Lookout Mountain; USFS Gifford Pinchot
Current conditions Mount St. Helens National Volcanic Monument (360) 247-3900
Northwest Forest Pass required

ABOUT THE HIKE
Day hike or backpack
Easy for children
March to November
West Creek Falls: ½ mile;
Horseshoe Falls: 3 miles
300 feet elevation loss and gain

GETTING THERE

■ From I-5 take exit 21 at Woodland. Drive east on Highway 503, following it south across the Lewis River to the town of Chelatchie, and the headquarters of the Mount St. Helens National Volcanic Monument.

■ From here go left, or east, on a signed county road that becomes Forest Road No. 54.

■ Just beyond the entrance to Gifford Pinchot National Forest turn left, uphill, onto Road No. 57, then go left again in 1 mile onto Road No. 5701.

■ Find the trailhead of Trail No. 130 in a short distance at the road end, elevation 1550 feet.

ON THE TRAIL

This low-level river hike, accessible when snow buries higher trails, will appeal to children for several reasons. Close enough to the creek in a number of places to dip in toes and sample the current, the trail is relatively wide and level after an initial drop. Mountain bikers have discovered it, though, so families should be prepared occasionally to jump out of their way.

The moss-covered forest alongside the trail has a magical Emerald City feeling, with trilliums, ferns, and oxalis. A number of waterfalls call out to be examined from above, beside, and below. One even has a possible campsite next to its plunge pool. This roadless forest with its pockets of ancient trees is rare natural regrowth from a historic 1902 fire that burned about 40,000 acres, the Yacolt Burn. The forest is now in what is called Late Successional Reserve, so no logging is presently scheduled. Siouxon Creek has been proposed for Wild and Scenic River status, but no action has occurred.

Find a trail to Siouxon Creek to the right. The trail closely follows the creek's uphill bank. Paths lead down to the creek and nice pools. Old cedar stumps and logs are visible on both sides—some have hollow cores. What kinds of animals make cozy homes in those hollow logs? Logs that have recently fallen across the trail have been cut away by trail builders, and their cut ends display their age. Explain to children that the rings that form in the tree represent each season's growth—fat rings for wet years, thin rings for dry years. The dark line allowing us to distinguish one ring from its neighbor is called latewood, formed at the very end of each growing season.

At ¼ mile cross a bridge and watch as the waterfall on West Creek plunges below, channelling into a narrow funnel of gray-green rock. Children like crossing over the top of the waterfall and pausing midway to lean out and look down its face. Hang onto hands here. A bench on the other side of the bridge offers a safer vantage point, and an entirely different perspective can be reached by taking the ⅛-mile Falls Viewpoint path to the base of the falls. The trail ends at a possible single campsite or picnic area alongside the pool at the base of the

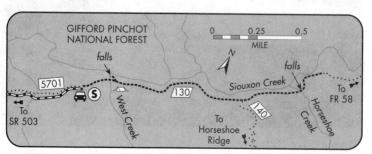

fan-shaped falls. If you are tired, this is a good turnaround point.

Follow the Siouxon upward. Rapids and white water increase as the trail leads on. Pass the trail to Horseshoe Ridge at 1 mile and watch for an overhanging cliff dappled with ferns and dripping seeping moss. On a wet day every surface is saturated. Children love the squishing noises they can make as they pass by.

Regain lost elevation by returning to the main trail, stepping over several tiny creeklets. Siouxon Creek seems to gain in volume and turbulence, and children can look down on white-water rapids and fern-encrusted walls. At 1.5 miles come to another impressive waterfall viewpoint: Horseshoe Falls. Above Horseshoe Falls, if children want to go on, they can see five major waterfalls and a plunge pool. Again, benches have been provided. Children can rest for a moment and ponder the enormous U-shaped bowl the river has created and the power of the waterfall. Far enough for a day. Pause and enjoy the beauty of the Siouxon.

Siouxon Creek Falls

 **MURPHY GRADE TRAIL**

BEFORE YOU GO
Map Clark County map
Current conditions
Vancouver-Clark Parks and
Recreation Department (360)
619-1111

ABOUT THE HIKE
Day hike
Easy for children
Year round
5 miles
33 feet elevation gain

GETTING THERE

- From I-5 take exit 14 and follow signs to SR 502 and Battle Ground.
- Turn north on Road No. 503 and continue east about 6 miles on Rock Creek Road, which becomes NE Lucia Falls Road. Turn right on Lucia Falls Road and drive 5 miles to Lucia Falls Park.
- Continue beyond on NE Lucia Falls Road, now Hantwick Road. Turn right, cross old railroad tracks, and continue for ¼ mile to the road end, trailhead, and new parking lot of Lucia Falls County Park, elevation 2480 feet.

ON THE TRAIL

A new segment of the Chinook Trail on the site of a former logging railroad follows the East Fork of the Lewis River between two county parks with swimming opportunities for the kids. Paved part of the way for barrier-free access, it makes an easy walk with a stroller for parents of little children, offering outlooks over the river and benches to enjoy the forest views. At Moulton Falls Park there are opportunities for older children to swim and wade.

Start on pavement along the old railway grade following the river

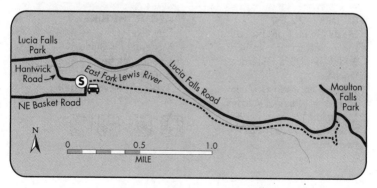

Mother and baby on Murphy Grade (Photo by Joan Burton)

between the two county parks. Children will be delighted to see beaver ponds and an old beaver dam. Ancient cedar stumps testify to the history of logging in Clark County, when mills were built following the Yacolt Burn in 1902 to salvage partly burnt logs. Lucia and Moulton were builders of the mills. This railroad grade was a spur of the Lewis and Clark Railway. Children may think the canopy of second-growth fir, alder, and maple leaning inward over the trail looks like tent poles. The trail leads past rocky pools and rapids, with small tributary brooks entering beside the trail.

About one mile from the parking lot, the trail nears the south side of the East Fork of the Lewis River, here only a few feet deep. The water rushes over rocks and slows down in pools, but there's no way to get down to it for most of the remaining 1½ miles of the trail. However, at the trail's end at Moulton Falls Park, a wooden bridge arches three stories above the river. On a hot day I saw kids floating on rafts and jumping into the cool pools under the arched bridge. The park offers a network of trails for hiking.

 **STAIRWAY TO THE STARS**

BEFORE YOU GO
Maps Green Trails No. 396 Lookout Mountain, No. 428 Bridal Veil; USFS Gifford Pinchot
Current conditions Mount St. Helens National Volcanic Monument (360) 247-3900
Northwest Forest Pass required

ABOUT THE HIKE
Day hike
Moderate for children
June to October
5 miles
1200 feet elevation gain

GETTING THERE

- From I-5 take exit 14 and follow signs to State Route 502. Take 502 east for about 5 miles.
- At the town of Battle Ground, turn north on Road No. 503, then turn east on Rock Creek Road, which turns into Northeast Lucia Falls Road.
- Drive to the intersection with Sunset Falls Road, just east of Moulton Falls County Park, and go east for 7.6 miles to Sunset Campground.
- Cross the East Fork Lewis River, and follow Road No. 41 for 3.4 miles to the junction with Road No. 4109. The junction is poorly marked, but find it at a wide spot on Road No. 41.
- Turn right and go 4.2 miles to the Silver Star trailhead, elevation 3200 feet.

ON THE TRAIL

We named this trail the Stairway to the Stars because it includes a small staircase to nowhere, left over from the old lookout, which suggests that children can climb to the stars. Silver Star Mountain was named for the star-shaped five ridges that radiate from its summit. Such a beautiful mountain deserves protection, some of which it has received, and more is promised. It is now called a Special Interest Area, partly because of its unique botanical status.

The Forest Service has designated it the Silver Star Scenic Area and has converted many of the old roads to trails. Now barriers are being added to keep the jeeps and quads away from the hiking families who long to walk in the ridge-top meadows and enjoy the views of the Columbia Gorge, the south Cascades and Mount Hood, the wheat fields of Eastern Oregon, distant Portland, and closer Vancouver. Parkland extends in every direction, with the white torches of bear-grass dominant in May and June. Note that this area is heavily used by mountain bikers; be alert.

Children will want to know what happened to the forest that used to stand here. A few ancient gray snags hint at a long-ago disaster. The truth is that this is what remains of the famous Yacolt Burn of 1902, the largest

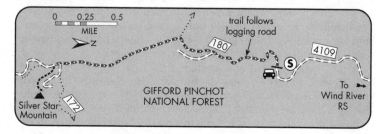

Future hiker

the largest and most destructive forest fire in state history. Rains finally contained the fire but not before it had destroyed 238,000 acres of forest. "Why haven't the trees come back?" the kids ask. The soil still isn't ready for them, according to foresters who make studies of these beautiful meadows. But a century after the fire holocaust, kids can fly kites and run and play in the flowery meadows that are the legacy of the Yacolt Burn.

The hiking route follows the old service road, which is wide enough to let you hold a child's hand, and climbs upward in lush flower and grass fields to ever-expanding views of Mounts Adams, Rainier, and St. Helens, and west beyond to forests and cities. In about 1¾ miles the road reaches a 4000-foot high point. Children will want to begin looking ahead for the site of the old lookout and its stairway to nowhere, but they can't see it from here. The way then dips a bit into a forested saddle. (Ask them why they think trees can grow here.)

At 2¼ miles, keep left at a junction and ascend more steeply on the badly eroded old road to reach the summit ridge. Suddenly the lookout site appears amid the alpine meadows, and children can also see Mount Hood and the Columbia River. The lookout building is gone, but the three stairs leading up from the old foundation make a great jumping-off place. Children can climb up, close their eyes, and wait for lift-off.

 **BEACON ROCK STATE PARK**

BEFORE YOU GO
Maps Green Trails No. 428
Bridal Veil, Oregon; USFS
Gifford Pinchot
Current conditions
Washington State Parks (360)
902-8844
**State park annual or
day-use pass required**

ABOUT THE HIKE
Day hike
Easy for children
Year round
2 miles
600 feet elevation gain

GETTING THERE

■ From I-5 at Vancouver, take Highway 14 east 34.5 miles, along the Columbia River, to the base of the towering rock and a large parking lot and rest room, elevation 250 feet.

ON THE TRAIL

The most famous rock in the Columbia Gorge makes a short and exciting hike for children, safe enough if they understand the hazards of stepping off the railed pathways. The Lewis and Clark Corps of Discovery saw and named this distinctive rock in 1805. In 1915, Henry Biddle, Beacon Rock's original owner, began building the trail, some of which still bears the marks of his blasting. The rock was not set aside as a Washington State Park until Biddle, who had offered it to Washington and been refused, offered it to Oregon, which was eager to get it. At that point, Washington also became eager and accepted it. The views

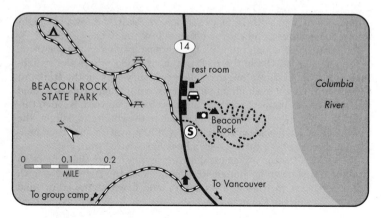

Hikers climb a few of the 52 switchbacks on the way to the top of Beacon Rock.

extend east to Bonneville Dam, west to Crown Point, and down to freight trains, boats, barges, and cars on either side of the river.

The trail, wide enough to walk two abreast, begins on the west side of the parking lot. Circle the rock to the riverside, where the switchbacks start up. Children are in no danger if they stay on the trail, but if the handrails are too high for short arms, parents may choose to hold children's hands instead. The way zigzags steeply upward. Wooden catwalks bridge cracks in the rock and, much to the children's delight, the trail itself, which lies a switchback below. A new overlook has been added, and there is also a Little Beacon Rock barrier-free trail.

Views from the top are as exhilarating as those from the wing of an airplane. Gaze down on Bonneville Dam, across the river to Nesmith Point, northeast to Hamilton Mountain, and down at the trains and ships traversing the Columbia River below.

GRASSY KNOLL

BEFORE YOU GO
Maps Green Trails No. 388
Willard; USFS Gifford Pinchot
Current conditions Wind
River Information Center (509)
427-3200
**Northwest Forest Pass
required**

ABOUT THE HIKE
Day hike
The Knoll: moderate for
children; Grassy Knoll: difficult
for children
March to November
**The Knoll: 3 miles; Grassy
Knoll: 6 miles**
The Knoll: 800 feet elevation
gain; Grassy Knoll: 1000 feet
in, 200 feet out

GETTING THERE

■ From Carson, follow the
Wind River Highway 4.2
miles across High Bridge
over the Wind River, and
turn right in less than a mile onto Bear Creek Road.

■ Drive this paved county road for 3.5 miles, and continue as it
turns to gravel and becomes Road No. 6808. Go 7.2 miles to Triangle Pass. Take the left fork, turning onto Road No. 68, and drive
2 miles to the first road on the right, Road No. 6800-511. The road
number sign may be missing.

■ Go 50 feet up this side road and park at the road's end, in a rock
quarry. Look on the north side of the road for the Grassy Knoll
trail sign and the path climbing through a meadow, elevation
2800 feet.

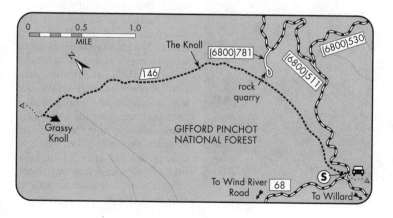

ON THE TRAIL

This large, rounded, meadowy knoll offers supreme views of the Columbia River and Mount Hood to the south, and of Mount Adams, with its enormous old lava flow, to the east. Children feel happy and excited about reaching the site of an old lookout on what used to be part of the Pacific Crest Trail. Their summit exhilaration is tempered with awe, however, by the majesty of the view.

From the main trailhead, begin with a short walk in grassy meadow, and then enter steep, wooded switchbacks. The forest is filled with tigers, princes, and bears, and—tiger lilies, prince's-pines, and bear grass. This trail is steep for kids; lures and inducements such as candy and fruit are appropriate here. At 2900 feet and 1 mile, pass the old rock quarry. Next, pass the burned remains of a clear-cut, and at 1½ miles reach a basalt summit. Called simply The Knoll, it is dominated by a fine view of Mount Adams and makes a good turnaround point.

But of course, this is not the Grassy Knoll. From The Knoll, the trail descends into forest with a carpet of moss, bear grass, lupine, and a few more tigers. It dips and rises for another ½ mile until a distinct barren rock appears on the horizon. As you approach it, the knoll shows its grassy rug. Climb for ¼ mile to the site of the old lookout, distinguishable by a bit of broken glass and foundation posts. The views south are down the Columbia River and over Dog Mountain to Mount Hood, and east to Mount Adams, which often wears a cap of clouds. Most of the rolling foothills are forested, with only a few clear-cuts. Have the kids listen for the sound of distant boat horns on the river. Tiny plants blowing in the wind on the summit include phlox, yarrow, wild onion, and gray lichen. Like all "belly-flowers," they bear close examination. Time stands still in this lovely place.

Tiger Lily

 **FALLS CREEK FALLS**

BEFORE YOU GO
Map Green Trails No. 397
Wind River
Current conditions Mount
Adams Ranger District (509)
395-3400

ABOUT THE HIKE
Day hike
Moderate for children
Year round
3 miles
300 feet elevation gain

GETTING THERE

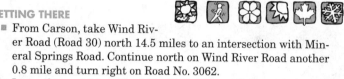

- From Carson, take Wind River Road (Road 30) north 14.5 miles to an intersection with Mineral Springs Road. Continue north on Wind River Road another 0.8 mile and turn right on Road No. 3062.
- In 1 mile, go right on Road No. 3062-057 and drive to the end of the road, elevation 1300 feet.

ON THE TRAIL

A superb three-tiered waterfall lures the hiker at the end of a riverside trail. Listen. The sound of the creek from below the trail, beside it, and above it, will cue your family to the nearness of the rapids and the waterfall. Have the kids listen carefully and guess how close they are to the cataract.

Begin alongside the creek on a narrow, winding trail, and then watch the creek disappear into a ravine that deepens and then rises to trail level once more. Cross the creek at ¾ mile among huge old trees and begin to climb up and away from the water. Point out to the kids that you must gain some elevation in order to reach the level of the waterfall. At 1¼ miles in spring and early summer pass under a trail-side waterfall.

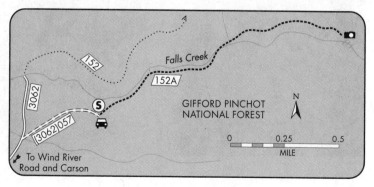

Children love being splashed as they run under it, and some feel the waterfall is like a giant sprinkler. A cable suspension bridge crosses the rock canyon and gives kids a great view of the upcoming falls. Some kids will love a suspension bridge, and some will not.

By continuing on for less than a mile you will come to the base of the waterfall. Be prepared for all to stop in their tracks when they first see Falls Creek Falls. Only the upper two falls are visible through the trees at first, but the trail ends in ¼ mile more, directly in front of the plunge pool and lower falls. Aficionados of waterfalls rate this one with five stars. But Falls Creek is such a poor name for it. Maybe your children can think of a better name. Magnificent Falls would be more like it, don't you think?

The magnificent falls at Falls Creek

 **THOMAS LAKE**

BEFORE YOU GO
Maps Green Trails No. 365 Lone Butte, No. 366 Mount Adams West; USFS Gifford Pinchot
Current conditions Mount Adams Ranger District (509) 395-3400
Wilderness Permit and Northwest Forest Pass required

ABOUT THE HIKE
Day hike or backpack
Easy for children
July–October
1½ miles
200 feet elevation gain

GETTING THERE
- From Carson on Columbia River Highway 14, drive north on Wind River Road.
- Go right on Road No. 65, signed "Panther Creek Campground." (*Note:* A bridge is out on Road 65 north of the Thomas Lake trailhead; you can no longer approach the trailhead from the north.) At 6 miles from the junction find the trailhead, elevation 4100 feet.

ON THE TRAIL
Take a short, easy trail to a cluster of five lakes, the most accessible in the Indian Heaven Wilderness. It's a great place to swim and catch fish, and offers any number of good campsites. This would be an ideal hike to start a week-long vacation with small children, exploring the Indian Heaven Wilderness. You can walk across the entire wilderness in a day: It is only 7½ miles from Thomas Lake to the farthest lake, Tombstone Lake. The trail is fine up to Thomas Lake, but beyond that, the horse

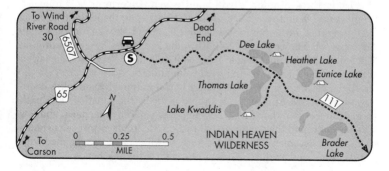

Fun of kids fishing in a high alpine lake

riders, traveling while the ground is still soft from melting snow, have turned the tread into quagmire. Once turned to mud, the trail isn't passable again for hikers until after a month of dry weather.

Thomas Lake trail No. 111 starts out in a clear-cut dotted in season with Indian paintbrush and lighted by the white torches of bear grass. At ½ mile, the way enters the Indian Heaven Wilderness. At ¾ mile is a campsite between three lakes: Dee and Heather on the left and Thomas on the right. A few hundred feet beyond Thomas Lake is a junction; keep left to reach Eunice Lake. Lake Kwaddis is reached by a trail around Thomas Lake. All the lakes are at about 4300 feet. Very little elevation change makes for easy hiking with young hikers.

If you decide to explore the center of the Indian Heaven lakes country, head toward Eunice Lake and go right at the junction. The path gains 150 feet and then levels off and passes marshy meadows, shallow Brader Lake, and the quagmire left by horses. Children will be enchanted as forest becomes intermingled with parklike meadows dappled with ponds, pools, and shallow lakelets, one right after another.

 **PLACID LAKE AND CHENAMUS LAKE**

BEFORE YOU GO
Maps Green Trails No. 365
Lone Butte; USFS Indian
Heaven Wilderness
Current conditions Mount
Adams Ranger District (509)
395-3400
**Wilderness Permit (register
at trailhead) and Northwest
Forest Pass required**

ABOUT THE HIKE
Day hike or backpack
Easy for children
Late June–November
**Placid Lake: 1 mile;
Chenamus Lake: 3 miles**
Placid Lake: 60 feet elevation
loss; Chenamus Lake: 160
feet gain

GETTING THERE

■ You can reach this trail from Indian Berry Fields, near Mount
Adams to the west, by Road No. 24 and Road No. 30. To reach this
trail from Carson, drive north some 30 miles to the end of Wind
River Road.

■ Turn right on Road No. 30, signed "Lone Pine"; drive 2.3 miles;
then turn right again, on Road No. (3000) 420.

■ Go another 1.2 miles to a large parking lot—usually crowded—
and Trail No. 29, elevation 4100 feet.

ON THE TRAIL

Two warm, shallow woodland lakes await at the end of a short, level
trail on the northwest side of Indian Heaven Wilderness. Good wading
beaches will appeal to children, and camps are available in the meadows surrounding both lakes. But because they are so close to the road,

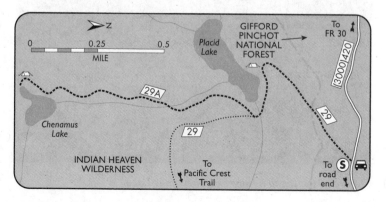

they get heavy use; best not to count on finding a campsite but rather enjoy either or both lakes as day hikes with your children.

Begin on a wide, level trail under shady, old-growth trees, among such plants as bear grass, vanilla-leaf, and tiny wild strawberries. Placid Lake comes up quickly, and you will find kids taking off their shoes before you can say a word. Wading is a little muddy in the shallow lake, but children love it anyway. The morning we were here, two rangers were having an earnest talk with a group of older kids about the "limits of acceptable change" in terms of campers' abuse of campsites. Campers with hatchets had been hacking living trees, damaging them severely, for no apparent reason. The young people looked abashed, though not one held a hatchet. Maybe people who like to chop need to be provided with chopping posts, like cats that need scratching posts.

Take a sharp left at an unsigned fork at the Placid lakeshore to continue on the trail to Chenamus Lake. At another fork, marked for Trail No.

Children listening to a ranger at Chenamus Lake

29A, go right. Cross three small creeks on stones, the last of which can be a difficult crossing during snowmelt. For this reason the Chenamus trail is recommended for midsummer. In another ¼ mile the trail levels off and the lake comes into view. The best wading and best campsites are here. Follow a trail around the lake to a small inlet for a pretty view. Chenamus is filling in with reeds, which attract dragonflies and hummingbirds. We saw a salamander swimming underwater (the kids would have envied his technique) and a mother duck followed by a convoy of five fat balls of fluff.

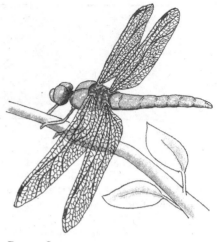

Dragonfly

  JUNCTION LAKE

BEFORE YOU GO
Maps Green Trails No. 365 Lone Butte, No. 397 Wind River; USFS Indian Heaven Wilderness
Current conditions Mount Adams Ranger District (509) 395-3400
Wilderness Permit (register at trailhead) and Northwest Forest Pass required

ABOUT THE HIKE
Day hike or backpack
Moderate for children
July to October
5 miles
700 feet elevation gain

GETTING THERE
- From Trout Lake, drive west on County Road No. 141 and pass the Mount Adams Ranger Station. At the Skamania County line the road becomes No. 24. Follow signs for Carson and Berry Fields.
- At the first major junction go straight ahead, following pavement onto Road No. 60.
- Eleven miles from Trout Lake, go straight ahead onto Road No. 6035. Find Trail No. 48 at 4 miles from Road No. 60, elevation 4070 feet.

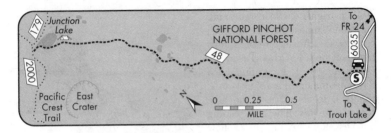

ON THE TRAIL

A warm, shallow wilderness lake surrounded by subalpine meadows, Junction will please families because there are a number of small ponds to lure kids with along the way. What is the junction? Its name evidently comes from the connection of this trail with the Pacific Crest Trail at the far end of the lake.

In ¼ mile step into the Indian Heaven Wilderness and feel and smell the difference. Nothing has been cut down, graded, or gouged with motorcycle tracks. Children will like searching the lichen-encrusted tree trunks to see old men's beards, mustaches, and eyebrows in their shapes. The trail is wide and gains elevation gradually. There is some evidence of volcanic activity. To the left the tree-covered hill is a small dead crater, without a trail, and the little ponds along the ridge top between miles 1 and 2 are volcanic potholes. The potholes have mud bottoms, and some are filling in with grass and reeds, but they provide wading-pool-size places where children can stop and play or turn around.

Continue, and at 2½ miles drop slightly to find Junction's shore. The lake is probably too shallow for fish, but in midsummer it is just the right temperature for kids to play in. (Some like to stretch out prone, resting on the bottom, to pretend they are beached whales.) Camps around the edge of the lake have meadow and tree settings. If you stay, you may see the animals who come to drink in the evening or early morning.

*Camping at Junction Lake
(Photo by Ellen Burton)*

 INDIAN HEAVEN WILDERNESS VACATION

BEFORE YOU GO
Maps Green Trails No. 365 Lone Butte, No. 366 Mount Adams West; USFS Gifford Pinchot
Current conditions Mount Adams Ranger Station (509) 395-3400
Wilderness Permit and Northwest Forest Pass required

ABOUT THE HIKE
Day hike or backpack
Moderate for children
July–October
Cultus Lake: 4 miles; loop: 15 miles
1800 feet elevation gain

GETTING THERE

- Take State Route 14 east about 60 miles from Vancouver to near White Salmon, along the Columbia River.
- Just before town locate State Route 141, signed to Trout Lake, and head north.
- Pass through Trout Lake. State Route 141 becomes Road No. 24, also called Carson Guler Road, and then eventually becomes Twin Butte Road.
- At about 36 miles from White Salmon, look for Cultus Creek Campground on the left. Parking for the trailhead is near the entrance, elevation 3958 feet.

ON THE TRAIL

Surrounded by a giant tree farm, Indian Heaven Wilderness is a wild oasis, with 38 miles of trail through forest intermingled with parklike meadows, over 30 named lakes, and 100 or more nameless tarns. Indian Heaven is one of the three best places in the state to take young children on a weeklong backpack. There are nine trails leading into the long, narrow wilderness.

Cultus Creek Campground features a life-size carving of Smokey the Bear, which children will love. Before starting out, be sure to take a look at the large, hand-carved wooden Smokey, wearing his signature hat and grin.

Trail No. 33 starts at the west border of the campground and climbs steeply through forest (it gains 700 feet in the first mile) to a good view of Mount Adams. Thereafter, the trail is more moderate, climbing 400 feet in the second mile to Cultus Lake and campsites near the outlet, at 5150 feet.

Among the day trips from Cultus Lake is Deep Lake, a short distance away; the trail is near the outlet stream. For another side trip, continue on trail No. 33 for ¼ mile and then turn up and southeast onto trail No. 34 to climb to a 5600-foot viewpoint on the side of Lemei Rock.

The most fun is a lazy two- to four-way loop from Cultus Lake. Stay on trail No. 33, climbing over a 5300-foot pass. In a scant mile, go left on trail No. 179 and camp near Lemei Lake, elevation 4800 feet. Then move on for 1 mile to campsites at Junction Lake, elevation 4700 feet, at the junction of trail No. 48 and the Pacific Crest Trail. From there take a 2½-mile side trip (each way) on the Pacific Crest Trail to Blue Lake.

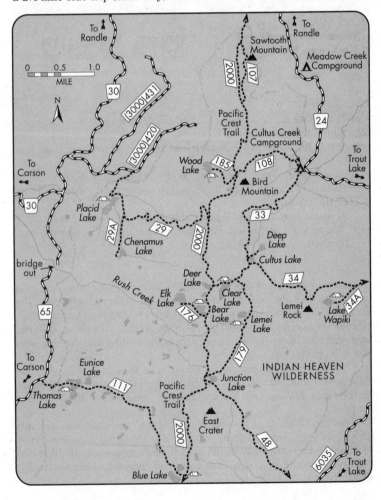

From Junction Lake you can also join the Pacific Crest Trail and hike north 1 mile to Bear Lake, at 4700 feet. Camp here and, with the help of a map, find Elk, Deer, and Clear Lakes. Then return to Cultus Creek Campground.

The entire loop can be hiked in a long day. But don't try. Take time to do all the important things—wading and swimming in the lakes and searching for tadpoles in ponds and frogs in the meadows. Because snow patches linger into August at this altitude, on a hot day snowball fights are inevitable. Just one precaution: All those lakes and ponds mean hordes of mosquitoes, so be prepared. But once in Indian Heaven, no child will ever want to leave.

Eating huckleberries in Indian Heaven

 LANGFIELD FALLS

BEFORE YOU GO
Maps Green Trails No. 366 Mt. Adams West; USFS Gifford Pinchot
Current conditions Mount Adams Ranger District (509) 395-3400
Northwest Forest Pass required

ABOUT THE HIKE
Day hike
Easy for children
Year round
½ mile
100 feet elevation loss and gain

GETTING THERE

■ From Trout Lake, go west on SR 141 past the Mount Adams Ranger Station. Turn right on Road No. 88 (also signed "Trout Creek Road") and drive 14 miles to Tire Junction, a local landmark with a huge tire in the center of the road.

■ Keep right on Road No. 88 for 0.1 mile and find the Langfield Falls Trail on the right, elevation 3505 feet.

ON THE TRAIL

The trail to this exquisite fan-shaped waterfall is an easy walk for young children. The trail begins above the falls and switchbacks down to its plunge pool, which is shallow enough for children to play in. On the way back up, take a side trail out to a stunning overlook of the top of the cascade.

Begin on a gentle descending trail, bypassing the first trail leading to the right (leave it for the return). At the midway point, find a bench and sign that explains that the falls were discovered by and named for K. C. Langfield, a Mount Adams ranger from 1933 to 1956, who loved this beautiful spot. Next, kids can look for a hollow log with a porthole or foxhole on one side. Ask them who might use the hole.

Mosquito Creek tumbles 110 feet over a wide conglomerate wall. Small round rocks are embedded in the basalt; the pool basin is also rocky. Except at melt-water flood stage, the current is gentle, and children can soak their feet, wade, or throw pebbles and sticks into the stream. On the way back up, be sure to take the short side trip to look

Langfield Falls

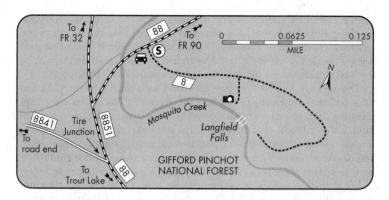

over the top of Langfield Falls. Ask the children to imagine how you might feel if you were paddling your canoe along this stream and came without warning upon the falls just ahead!

 **ICE CAVE AND NATURAL BRIDGES**

BEFORE YOU GO
Maps Green Trails No. 388 Willard; USFS Gifford Pinchot
Current conditions Mount Adams Ranger District (509) 395-3400
Northwest Forest Pass required

ABOUT THE HIKE
Day hike
Easy for children
Year round
Ice cave: ¼ mile; bridges: ¼ mile
No elevation gain

GETTING THERE
- From Trout Lake, go west on SR 141. Pass the Mount Adams Ranger Station. At the Skamania County line the road becomes No. 24.
- At 6 miles from Trout Lake, turn left on a dirt road (2400)301 and go 0.2 mile to the ice caves.
- To reach the bridges, back on Road No. 24 continue another 0.8 mile, turn left on (2400)041, and go 0.5 mile, then turn right to the Natural Bridges (Big Trench) parking area, elevation 2900 feet.

ON THE TRAIL
Two lava tubes formed by long-ago Mount Adams lava flows resulted in fascinating play areas for kids. The first, an ice cave within a collapsed lava

tube, contains ice stalactites and dripping ice masses that last all summer long. Kids climb around on the ice in semidarkness, calling out to one another, "This place is awesome." The second is a pair of nearby natural bridges the family can walk over. The arched bridges are all that remain of more lava caves, whose tops have collapsed inward into a basalt basin.

The ice cave has been known and used for almost a century. At one time, before freezers, the towns of Hood River and The Dalles were supplied ice from the caves, transported on barges up and across the Columbia River. One end of the cave traps and holds moist, cold air, which settles during winter, forming into ice columns, stalactites, and pools. Temperatures have warmed up since the turn of the century, and it is hard to picture the cave's present ice supplying two towns' needs today.

What it does supply is excitement for kids. On a hot day they descend a flight of stairs with flashlights in hand and their eyes grow wide in disbelief. "I'm gonna get me some ice to keep," they say. The cave recesses extend beyond the main room to a wind vent and a narrow tunnel exit on the other side of the parking lot. Be sure the children have sturdy footwear and warm clothes, and plan to carry at least two flashlights for a family. The cave floor is covered with slippery loose ice chips, so be wary.

From the trailhead to the Natural Bridges, walk 300 yards to a dry rocky basin spanned by two arches of bubble-filled basalt. Trails cross both of them, to the joy of children. If you doubt the bridges can support your weight, take note of the size of the tree trunk growing on top of one of them.

One can speculate about the river of lava that came through eons ago. Did its surface freeze on the top before the rest had cooled and solidified? When did it collapse inward? At both ends of the basin, find caves with roofs that the trail crosses over. In another thousand years will more natural bridges develop here? Kids don't spend much time wondering. They like to run across, and then turn and walk slowly to the middle, kneel, and peer under the bridge to see what they can see beneath. Some like to play at being trolls to scare others crossing over.

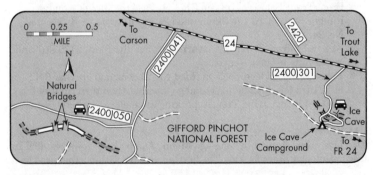

Ice cave in early summer

 **STEAMBOAT MOUNTAIN**

BEFORE YOU GO
Maps Green Trails No. 366
Mount Adams West; USFS
Gifford Pinchot
Current conditions Mount
Adams Ranger District (509)
395-3400
**Northwest Forest Pass
required**

ABOUT THE HIKE
Day hike
Moderate for children
June–October
2 miles
800 feet elevation gain

GETTING THERE

- From Trout Lake, take SR 141 west for 1 mile, then turn left (northwest) on Road No. 88, and in 14 miles reach Tire Junction. Turn left on Road No. 8851.
- In 3.2 miles head right on Road No. 8854 and at a Y-junction in another 0.8 mile continue left, or east, on Road No. (8854)021.
- The road ends in 1.6 miles at the trailhead of Trail No. 14 and a parking lot in a gravel quarry, elevation 4700 feet.

ON THE TRAIL

The stunning view of four volcanoes—Adams, St. Helens, Rainier, and Hood—makes clear why this was a lookout site from 1927 to 1971. Today,

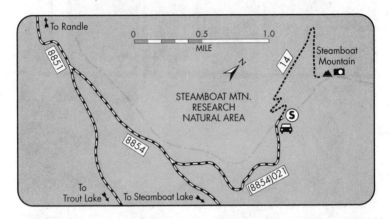

it is part of a Research Natural Area set aside for scientific studies by forest ecologists. Children can enjoy the spooky character of the old subalpine trees as the trail winds up to a summit cliff. Once there, they can imagine being on the prow of a ship. Hang onto hands as you gaze down at three lakes and miles of forest, and out to four massive ice mountains.

Steamboat Mountain trail No. 14 is on the left side of the quarry. Before starting, look up at the awesome cliffs where the lookout once stood and where you will soon stand. Fortunately, the trail goes around the wooded backside.

The well-graded path is only a little over 1 mile long, but it's a very steep mile. Old subalpine firs with moss hanging from their branches create an especially spooky "guardians of the mountain" atmosphere. Just short of 1 mile, the trail reaches the crest of the ridge. Go right, along the ridge to the summit, elevation 5424 feet.

The east side of the broad summit is the edge of the cliff you saw from below. Look down to parked cars 800 feet below and out to spectacular views. We watched a raven that was level with us, only 50 feet away, riding an updraft. Keep a tight grip on small children here, lest they forget they don't have wings.

Mosquito Lake from cloud-shrouded Steamboat Mountain

 **SLEEPING BEAUTY**

BEFORE YOU GO
Maps Green Trails No. 366
Mount Adams West; USFS
Gifford Pinchot
Current conditions Mount
Adams Ranger District (509)
395-3400
**Northwest Forest Pass
required**

ABOUT THE HIKE
Day hike
Moderate for children
June–November
3½ miles
1400 feet elevation gain

GETTING THERE
- In Trout Lake, drive west from the Mount Adams Ranger Station for 0.9 mile to Road No. 8810. Turn right and proceed north.
- At 5 miles, turn right on Road No. 8810-040, a spur road, to the trailhead, elevation 3500 feet.

ON THE TRAIL
The rocky profile of a lady, best seen from the town of Trout Lake, provides hikers with a trail that ascends to exciting views of Mount Adams, Mount Hood, and the many little extinct volcanoes of Indian Heaven. Children love looking for the beauty stretched out against the skyline and then scrambling upward on switchbacks to the summit. The trail has steep exposures. Watch children carefully.

Sleeping Beauty trail No. 37 begins on the south side of the peak. The way climbs steeply in an old forest of Douglas-firs and grand firs. The wildflowers and undergrowth—buckbrush, pyrola, dogbane, wild rose, pipsissewa, and vancouveria—are typical of the dry side of the Cascades. The trail follows the base of the peak for about 1¼ miles to

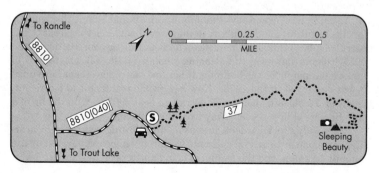

Sleeping Beauty

the north side, leaving the woods to emerge onto exposed rock. From here, the trail switchbacks up ½ mile to the summit on tread blasted from the cliff. A man-made rock wall banks up the steep side. Kids can marvel at the hand labor it took to wedge tiny chips of stone vertically between larger rocks.

An old Indian legend says that Mount Adams and Mount Hood fought for this beautiful maiden. Because they would not stop, the Great Spirit petrified her, so that she would sleep forever. During construction of the 1931 lookout, however, the sleeping woman's nose was blasted off to make a flat perch for the building. It became her replacement nose until it was destroyed in the 1970s. Now her profile is difficult to figure out. Is she still a sleeping beauty? The trail ends at 4907 feet, on the lip of a cliff. Be sure children keep away from the cliff edge.

In the lady's rock gardens, in season, find glowing lavender and scarlet penstemon, arnica, and valerian. Children will be exhilarated by the summit scramble and the feeling of being masters of all they survey.

 **BIRD CREEK MEADOWS**

BEFORE YOU GO
Map USFS Mount Adams
Current conditions Mount
Adams Ranger District (509)
395-3400
**Northwest Forest Pass
required; day-use fee**

ABOUT THE HIKE
Day hike
Easy for children
July through September
3 miles
500 feet elevation gain

GETTING THERE

- From Trout Lake, about 60 miles south of Randle, follow Road No. 23 east about 1 mile and turn right (straight ahead) on Road No. 80.
- In 0.5 mile go right on Road No. 8290. (Check first at the Mount Adams Ranger Station at Trout Lake to be sure the road is open.) Enter the Yakama Indian Nation, which charges a modest day-use fee to help with tribal expenses. This access road can be very rough.
- Continue past Mirror Lake and turn left on Road No. 184 to Bird Lake and the Bird Creek Meadows trailhead, elevation 5585 feet.

ON THE TRAIL

A gorgeous flower-filled meadow with wide panoramas of the south side of Mount Adams and the golden Klickitat valley has been a family delight

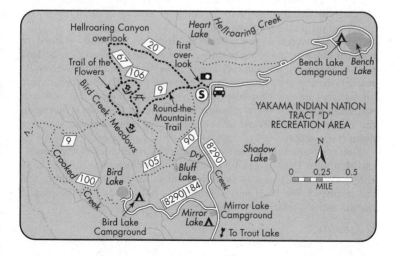

Crooked Creek Falls

for generations. The day hike to this superb subalpine park is filled with child-friendly features, such as shallow little lakes for wading. Plan to walk to the Hellroaring Canyon overlook, 6550 feet, and once there, explain the icefall, glacial moraines, and volcanic evidences to the kids. The name Hellroaring was given at the turn of the twentieth century to this dramatic canyon, and new names were given to other parts of the mountain by C. E. Rusk, an early explorer and lover of Mount Adams.

Begin on a wide, gradual trail, passing the first overlook to Hellroaring Canyon and continuing on to the Round-the-Mountain Trail at 1½ miles. Children will find little creeks and waterfalls to play in, and they will enjoy the camp robbers and Steller's jays that zoom in at the sight of families to beg for handouts. Have sunflower seeds ready, and they may eat from your children's hands. At the Trail of the Flowers turn right. Be ready with a flower guide to identify all those in bloom throughout the summer, ending in September with clumps of deep blue gentians.

Since Mount Adams is a volcano, children may spy yellow-stained ice near the summit, the result of the volcanic sulfur. Children can also look up to a 300-foot icefall and rock headwall below the Mazama Glacier. Be ready to explain that when a glacier flows over a cliff, the ice breaks into blocks and tumbles down like children's blocks in a kind of slow, frozen waterfall. Along the green meadow below, look for the glacial moraines, the ridges of earth pushed by the glacier like a bulldozer as it moves down the mountain.

Return to the family car by following the ridge back to the Round-the-Mountain Trail on Trail 9 and continuing down past Bluff Lake to Bird Lake, or backtrack to take the trail to Bird Creek Meadows and the trailhead. The Washington Trails Association has been helping to maintain these trails in recent years.

Olympic Peninsula hikes include some walks along the Strait of Juan de Fuca, such as those found at Point Wilson, Dungeness Spit, and Freshwater Bay, and some in the Olympic National Forest mountains and Olympic National Park. From the Hood Canal side find hikes to Mount Zion, along the Dungeness and Duckabush Rivers, and up to Lower Lena Lake. Within the park there are trails to Blue Mountain and Hurricane Hill, along the north side of Lake Crescent on the historic lake-level Spruce Railroad, and to pretty Marymere Falls. Rain forests are distinguished from other surrounding forests by the tremendous amount of annual rainfall—up to 270 inches a year. The scenery is green, lush, and soggy. The hike in the famous Hoh Rain Forest and the lovely Bogachiel rain forest trail are beautiful explorations of this environment. A hike on the east side, Ranger Hole, leads to the oldest ranger's cabin in the park, which is available for rent. A signed walk tells children what it was like to keep house here in the early 1900s, when Mrs. Maybelle Finch made her own soap and butter, canned salmon and berries, and washed clothes on a washboard.

STRAIT OF JUAN DE FUCA

 **POINT WILSON**

BEFORE YOU GO
Map Jefferson County road map
Current conditions Washington State Parks (360) 902-8844
State park annual or day-use pass required

ABOUT THE HIKE
Day hike
Easy for children
Year round
2½ miles
No elevation gain

GETTING THERE
- Cars may be left at either end of the walk. *To begin at the west end,* drive to Port Townsend and find the city courthouse. From there, follow signs to Fort Worden State Park.
- At the entrance to the park, turn left on W Street, angle right on Spruce Street, left on Admiralty Street, curve right on San Juan Avenue, then left on 49th Street, and right on Kuhn Street to

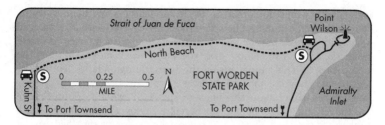

reach the road end at the North Beach of Fort Worden State Park, elevation sea level.

■ *To get to the east end of the walk,* enter the park following signs to Point Wilson.

ON THE TRAIL

A fine sandy beach extends beneath high bluffs and between two access points on the way to the Point Wilson lighthouse. The hike can be made in either direction: Children won't care. Of all the hikes along the strait, this may be the one they will love the best. Water and sand play possibilities are infinite. On a clear day, Mount Baker stands as guardian over them as they wade, dig, build sand castles, and throw sticks to dogs to fetch from out in the waves. A trail-less lagoon along the way is called Chinese Gardens because at one time Chinese immigrants grew truck-farm produce around it.

Begin walking east beside low banks covered with beach grass. Children can watch for giant oil tankers and container cargo ships passing close enough to make waves lap the beach beside them. Take binoculars and look at the ships' flags. Ask kids to figure out which countries the ships come from.

At low tide the wide, sandy shore is easy walking and offers kids the chance to write their names or leave messages in the sand. The bank quickly becomes a high, sandy cliff, sloughing off with winter rains to add to the beach sand. Children may be surprised to see long-necked, black cormorants perched on rocks in deeper

Point Wilson Lighthouse

water, with wings outspread to dry their feathers. Without warning, they will dive deep to find fish. The rocks are covered with sharp-edged barnacles, interesting for kids to inspect closely. Each acorn barnacle looks like a miniature empty gray volcano, which comes alive when the tide covers it. The animal inside the barnacle extends its featherlike legs to catch microscopic food drifting by.

Children can imagine this place in May 1792, when Captain George Vancouver and a party of men, anchored in Discovery Bay, started out to explore the coastline. The fog was heavy when Vancouver pushed around this small headland, which he named Point Wilson for a friend, so he was not aware of the size of this body of water until the sun broke through the fog. Vancouver was so impressed with the beauty of this setting and the extent and character of the bay that he named it Port Townsend for a famous English marquis of the time. Your kids may think it strange that these places were named for men who never saw them.

Views are wonderful across to Vancouver Island, the San Juan Islands, the high bluffs of Whidbey Island, and the snow-covered Cascades beyond them. Round a small cove and continue the walk to the red-roofed Coast Guard lighthouse at Point Wilson, built in 1913. Unfortunately, the building is off-limits to visitors now, but there are picnic tables nearby, recessed out of the wind, should you want to stop for lunch. A functioning radar tower and an old searchlight tower are standing nearby.

 DUNGENESS RIVER

BEFORE YOU GO
Maps Green Trails No. 136 Tyler Peak; Custom Correct Buckhorn Wilderness
Current conditions Hood Canal Ranger District, Hoodsport Office (360) 765-2200
Wilderness Permit and Northwest Forest Pass required

ABOUT THE HIKE
Day hike or backpack
Moderate for children
April–November
Camp Handy: 7 miles
700 feet elevation gain

GETTING THERE
- On US 101 about 5 miles east of Sequim and 0.1 mile from the entrance to Sequim Bay State Park, turn south onto Louella Road.
- In 1 mile turn left at the stop sign onto Palo Alto Road.

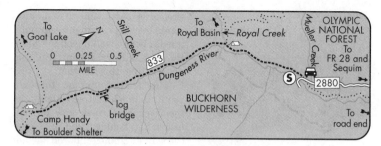

- Palo Alto Road eventually becomes Road No. 28. At the intersection with Road No. 2880, turn right and pass the Dungeness Forks Campground.
- In 8.7 miles the road drops slightly just before crossing the Dungeness River Bridge; the trailhead is on the right, signed "Upper Dungeness River Trail (833) and Royal Basin," elevation 2500 feet.

ON THE TRAIL

Children should experience this beautiful river valley, with its awe-inspiring, enormous old trees next to white-water rapids. The Dungeness River has been proposed for Wild and Scenic River status. An easy and fairly level trail follows the Dungeness for many miles in both unprotected national forest and the Buckhorn Wilderness. The trail also offers an interesting contrast in climates: The first 2½ miles are in lush rain forest; then the trail climbs into the rain shadow of the Olympics, and the environment becomes as dry as an Eastern Washington forest. The ultimate reward is in seeing the meadows high above the Dungeness River.

Begin up two short switchbacks to a level shelf alongside the river. In early spring the trail can be muddy. I met three little boys with dirty tennis shoes who were clearly enjoying stamping their feet into the mire at every step. Wind up and down through moss-lined cedar stumps, with woodland plants such as oak fern, vanilla-leaf, sweet-after-death, occasional rhododendrons, and yew trees.

At 1 mile find an excellent riverside camp at the confluence of the Dungeness and Royal Creek. The camps next to the bridge would make a fine turnaround or picnic

Camp Handy

Porcupine

site, or a base camp if a family wants to carry overnight gear only this far before walking on to Camp Handy. The Royal Basin Trail also departs from this junction.

The trail continues through beautiful ancient trees alongside the river. Fishermen love to cast from mossy boulders and logs along the way. At 2 miles children should look for a salt lick frequently used by deer, porcupines, and other animals. If you are lucky you will see deer here. If not, your children will have to be contented with examining the animal tracks around it. Cross Royal Creek on a log at 2½ miles, and climb a hillside. Look out to the beginning of the first alpine meadows, dry because they are in the rain shadow of the range. Children can look for shrubs such as Rocky Mountain juniper. At 3 miles cross the Dungeness River on a sturdy log. The water looks threatening, and the handrail is too high for a little child, so be ready to help.

Camp Handy, at 3½ miles, is a three-sided shelter so popular that a family should not count on being able to stay inside it. But the open meadow contains a campsite by the river and one more lies in the grove south of the shelter. Enjoy the view over the meadows of the Upper Dungeness valley. This area was never covered by the continental ice-age glaciers and was isolated for thousands of years, so some of its plants are unique or rare. Even the marmots are different. Some plants have close relatives many hundreds of miles away. Kids can imagine this meadow long ago as an island rising above the glacial ice fields.

 **TUBAL CAIN MINE**

BEFORE YOU GO
Maps Green Trails No. 136 Tyler Peak; Custom Correct Buckhorn Wilderness
Current conditions Hood Canal Ranger District, Quilcene office (360) 765-2200
Wilderness Permit and Northwest Forest Pass required

ABOUT THE HIKE
Day hike or backpack
Difficult for children
May–November
7½ miles
1000 feet elevation gain

GETTING THERE

- On US 101 about 5 miles east of Sequim and 0.1 mile from the entrance to Sequim Bay State Park, turn south onto Louella Road.
- In 1 mile turn left at the stop sign onto Palo Alto Road.
- Palo Alto Road eventually becomes Road No. 28. At the intersection with Road No. 2880, turn right and pass the Dungeness Forks Campground.
- In 6 miles, just before the road ends, find the trailhead on the right, elevation 2500 feet. Parking is limited.

ON THE TRAIL

An historic mining area dating from the turn of the century offers children a chance to walk into an old tunnel that still smells of sulfur and to explore mining relics in what is left of the mining camp. Older children will want to try to find the broken sluice box and 2-inch iron pipe beside a ruined shaft ventilator, and to search for the old power plant below camp.

Tell them Tubal Cain was the Biblical smith who forged bronze and iron tools—a fitting name for the mine, since iron and copper were being sought here. Thirty years before the mining claim, an exploring party must have met a bear here, because early hikers found a tiny grave, with a cross dated August 5, 1865, beside an old tree, paying tribute to a dog killed by a bear in the explorers' defense. This trail is a rhododendron garden of unsurpassed beauty from mid- to late June.

Begin the trail alongside Silver Creek. Cross the creek and begin a gradual ascent through a garden of rhododendrons, moss, and forest flowers. Enter the Buckhorn Wilderness at ¼ mile and look up the valley through the trees for the snow and rocks of Mount Buckhorn.

Along the way, steep creeks cascade directly down the mountain beside the trail, over it, and straight down below. None is too wide to step over, and children will enjoy walking over these waterfalls. Picture pack trains of mules a century ago, burdened with dynamite on the same trail. At 3 miles come to a small mine tunnel just above the trail. As a mining venture, Tubal Cain was a failure. Not a penny's profit was

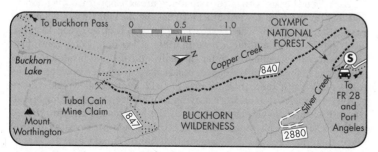

Old mining equipment was originally carried in on the backs of horses, mules, and men.

ever recorded, despite an estimated $200,000 investment over a twenty-five–year period.

Reach the old townsite at 3¼ miles. Cross Copper Creek at 3¾ miles and look left, at the base of Iron Mountain, for a 100-foot slope of mine tailings. Tubal Cain's drilling took the miners 2800 feet into the mountain, with 1500 feet of side tunnels. Climb the soft dirt trail to the rock tunnel, and be prepared for a whiff of old sulfur. Families with boots and flashlights will want to at least step inside, but go no farther. In 1972 the shaft was still passable for 600 feet, but no mine tunnel can ever be considered safe, so don't go in. The water running underfoot may come from melting snow or from springs deep inside Iron Mountain.

Explore either or both of the two living areas. Copper City is another 500 feet up the trail toward Marmot Pass, while Tull City is below the tunnel. These "cities" were inaccessible for much of the year. Because electricity was not available here in 1904, a log dam (long gone) provided water-power generation for the drills and sawmill needed to build a bunkhouse for thirty-five men, a cookhouse, an office, a powder house, and a blacksmith shop. In the winter of 1912, avalanches wrecked some of the buildings the men were staying in. Children can look for bits of rusty iron and broken glass to suggest the locations of the bunkhouse and cookhouse. A lot of dreams and hard work were invested in this place: Listen for echoes of the ghosts that haunt Tubal Cain.

 **DUNGENESS SPIT**

BEFORE YOU GO
Map Delorme Mapping: Washington Atlas
Current conditions U.S. Fish and Wildlife Service (360) 457-8415
Entrance fee, payable at trailhead

ABOUT THE HIKE
Day hike
Easy for children
Year round
Beach: 1 mile; end of spit: 10 miles
100 feet elevation loss

GETTING THERE

- On US 101, 5 miles west of the second Sequim exit, turn north on Kitchen-Dick Road and go 3 miles to the Dungeness Recreation Area.
- Drive through the recreation area to the refuge parking lot. The trailhead is behind the key house, where the entrance fee is collected; elevation is 100 feet.

ON THE TRAIL

One of the longest natural sand spits in the United States, Dungeness Spit thrusts out into the Strait of Juan de Fuca. A short descent through forest to the beach leads to its base. The spit reaches far out in the strait and then curves inward like a gigantic arm, with a lighthouse in its "hand." The spit is accessible to families at any time of the year; it also attracts harbor seals, orcas, and bald eagles. Reaching the lighthouse requires a 5-mile walk, but there's plenty of fun along the way and no need to go more than 1 or 2 miles.

The graveled trail wanders ½ mile through forest to a bluff above the Strait of Juan de Fuca and the first big view of the spit. Drop to the beach and begin the walk on the hard sand of the surf side. Tidal

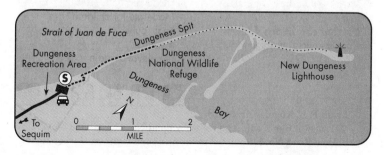

Driftwood with Olympic Mountains in background

fluctuations will make a difference in the amount of beach exposed for walking.

The beach is as pretty at the start as at the end. The views north are across the water to Vancouver Island, with Mount Baker floating above to the northeast, and views southwest are to the Olympic Mountains. Even a day in total fog, with no view at all, is a mystical experience. Only the sound of foghorns will penetrate the velvet enveloping the spit.

To get away from crowds and for the best chances to see seals, marine birds, and migrating shorebirds, hike some distance. Killer whales, the famous orcas, are unpredictable visitors, but they often swim on the open side of the spit. Harbor seals supplement their fish diet with the eelgrass on the bay side. Older children may want to go the whole 5 miles and climb the steps of the Coast Guard's lighthouse tower, built in 1857. Because in 1792 Captain Vancouver saw a resemblance to the Dungeness in England, the site of a lighthouse since 1746, he called this place New Dungeness. Today's hikers to the old lighthouse can see the irony.

 **FRESHWATER BAY**

BEFORE YOU GO
Maps Green Trails No. 102 Joyce
Current conditions Clallam County Parks Department (360) 417-2291

ABOUT THE HIKE
Day hike
Moderate for children
Year round
5 miles
No elevation gain

GETTING THERE

■ From Port Angeles drive US 101 west 4.6 miles and go right on Road No. 112, signed "Joyce."
■ Follow Road No. 112 for 4.2 miles and turn right on Gerber Road.

■ Go 2.5 miles to Lawrence Road and follow it 1 mile west to Freshwater Bay County Park, where the road ends and there is a boat launch, elevation sea level.

ON THE TRAIL

Walk a rocky beach cove along the Strait of Juan de Fuca on Freshwater Bay; the scenery is varied and interesting. If the kids watch the horizon for marine traffic, they will see an assortment of powerboats, sailboats, occasional kayaks, barges, freighters, and container cargo ships headed for Port Angeles and Puget Sound. Children who are fortunate or very observant may even spot marine traffic of the natural variety: whales and seals. They might also encounter scuba divers, who collect Pacific abalone and kelp greenling from deep below the surface, and Indians and local folks who collect clams, crab, and oysters at low tides. Kids can watch and enjoy the sea harvest, or simply throw rocks and wade into the gentle waves of this protected cove. But children should take no marine life and disturb nothing they see.

Plan on taking at least half a day to walk to a turnaround point at Coville Creek. At high tide there is no beach, so check the tide table

Boaters at Freshwater Bay

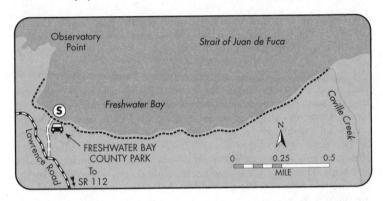

before starting out and make sure you turn around before the tide comes back in. Children will need sturdy boots to walk through wet sand and rocks.

Look west to Observatory Point, where there once was a World War II installation. Walk east (right) under a tall bank. The marine life along the way—the crabs, seals, fish, birds, and kelp beds—are remnants of the beach life once relied upon by Native American cultures and visible in only a few places today.

HOOD CANAL: US 101

 **SOUTH FORK SKOKOMISH RIVER**

BEFORE YOU GO
Maps Green Trails No. 199 Mount Tebo; Custom Correct Mount Skokomish–Lake Cushman
Current conditions Hood Canal Ranger District (360) 765-2200
Northwest Forest Pass required

ABOUT THE HIKE
Day hike or backpack
Moderate for children
April–November
Sandbar: 2½ miles; campsites: 12 miles
400 feet elevation loss and gain

GETTING THERE

- From Shelton, drive north on US 101 for 6.5 miles and turn up-river on the South Fork Skokomish River Recreation Area Road.
- In 5.7 miles go right on a road signed "Brown Creek Camp-ground." The road becomes Road No. 23. Fifteen miles from US 101 reach a major junction.
- Straight ahead is a road that is gated in winter. Go right on Road No. 2353 toward Brown Creek Campground, first crossing the South Fork Skokomish River, then go left, staying on Road No. 2353 and crossing LeBar Creek. Go 0.5 mile to the trailhead, elevation 650 feet.

ON THE TRAIL

Here is a short hike to a riverbank through old-growth forest, with several attractions for children. In 1¼ miles they can reach a river with wide sand and gravel bars. On the way (if there is solitude) they can look for elk and deer; in the spring they may even see elk calves and deer fawns. Mother elk and deer shelter their babies in secret, nestlike hideaways. If you should approach a hidden fawn, the mother deer will act nonchalant, to fool you into thinking she has no fawn nearby. In contrast, a mother elk is likely to charge you to protect her calf. If you find any baby wild animal, the best policy is to leave it alone. Most likely the mother is nearby.

The old trees have mossy carpets beneath them, ornamented with ferns, trilliums, and three-lobed sweet-after-death. But the drop to the river level is steep, and the climb back up will be a pull for little children. Floods had severely damaged this trail until volunteers from the Washington Trails Association began to restore it to its former beauty. Be prepared to encounter mountain bikers who love this trail, too.

The South Fork Skokomish River Trail No. 873 begins on long switchbacks for ¼ mile, leading into luxuriant old-growth forest. Fallen cedar logs will raise questions in the minds of kids. How old were these trees? How long since they fell? Huge 300-year-old firs dominate the forest, but moss-wrapped roots rise from the ground like green octopus arms writhing beneath the sea. Bigleaf maples are also dressed

South Fork Skokomish River trail

in green velvet and are studded with ferns up and down their branches and trunks. Children might feel they are in a special place and begin to whisper. If they don't, encourage them to whisper anyway. Elk and deer move through the forest silently and may appear unannounced if not alarmed by the sound of voices.

At ¼ mile look left, down a steep bank to the South Fork. Go straight ahead. Drop steeply on switchbacks for another ½ mile, passing over two creeks, to the river level. At the bottom, step into an open glade with more mossy old maples. Parallel the river for another ¼ mile, then look for an off-trail route on the left, to the riverbank. The Skokomish has often changed its channel or been affected by winter floods, and where it has abandoned its course there remains a wide, sandy bar. Children will enjoy the feeling of being on a beach, throwing sticks into the river, and watching them be swept away. For children this is a great turnaround point.

The trail continues to follow the river for many miles, with more big trees and another sandbar along the way. Campsites at 3 and 4 miles are small and primitive.

 **LOWER LENA LAKE**

BEFORE YOU GO
Maps Green Trails No. 168 The Brothers; USFS Olympic National Forest/Olympic National Park
Current conditions Hood Canal Ranger District (360) 765-2200
Northwest Forest Pass required

ABOUT THE HIKE
Day hike or backpack
Moderate for children
May–November
7 miles
1200 feet elevation gain

GETTING THERE
■ Drive US 101 along Hood Canal to 1 mile north of the Hamma Hamma River bridge. Go uphill on Hamma Hamma River Road No. 25.
■ At 9.5 miles from the highway, reach the Lena Lake trailhead, elevation 685 feet.

ON THE TRAIL
Dominated by a shoulder of The Brothers, this forest lake was formed thousands of years ago by a massive rock slide that dammed the valley. The "dam" leaks, and the lake resembles a reservoir in that the water rises and falls with the season. Wading and swimming are possible, but

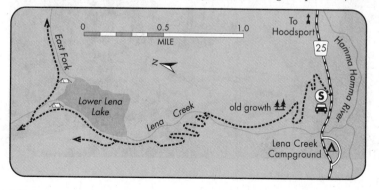

even in summer the water is so cold that only a child will enjoy it. This is one of the most popular hikes on the eastern slope of the Olympic Mountains. Expect many roots and rocks for little feet to tumble over.

Lower Lena Lake has no protection. While Upper Lena Lake is in Olympic National Park and The Brothers is in The Brothers Wilderness, a hydroelectric proposal has Lower Lena Lake facing a possible road construction and logging.

The trail switchbacks through an area that was first logged by railroad in 1931. The half-century-old trees look pretty big until, at approximately ¾ mile, the trail enters old-growth forest, where you find the really big trees. At 1½ miles, the way crosses a dry streambed of Lena Creek, which runs underground most of the year. If time permits, explore the caves made by giant boulders lying on top of nature's dam and marvel at the size of the trees growing on it. That rock slide was a long time ago! At 3 miles, reach the shore and outlet of Lower Lena Lake, at 1800 feet.

Camping at Lena Lake

For camping, follow the trail around the lakeshore. When the lake is full, there will be a 150-foot climb over a rock buttress. At 3½ miles, at the inlet, are the best campsites, some of which have substantial fireplaces and even barbecue grills. Point out to children the scar on the hillside across the lake where the landslide came from.

 **RANGER HOLE**

BEFORE YOU GO
Maps Green Trails No. 168 The Brothers; Custom Correct Mt. Anderson; USGS The Brothers
Current conditions Hood Canal Ranger Station (360) 765-2200
Northwest Forest Pass required

ABOUT THE HIKE
Day hike
Easy for children
Year round
1⅗ mile
119 feet elevation loss and gain

GETTING THERE

- On US 101, 15 miles south of Quilcene and 22 miles north of Hoodsport, turn west onto Duckabush River Road, which also is Road No. 2510.

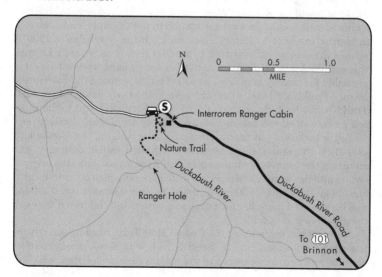

Second growth forest around first ranger station in Olympics

■ Go 4 miles to the end of pavement to find parking at the Interrorem Ranger Cabin, elevation 319 feet.

ON THE TRAIL

Two trails here will appeal to children—one with a historic ranger's cabin and signs telling about life in the early 1900s, and another leading to an overlook of a loud white-water rapid of the Duckabush River. Children will see the first ranger station in the Olympic Forest, housed in a structure built by Emory Finch for his bride, Maybelle, in 1906. A square three-room cabin with a pyramidal roof, it later was a Depression-era WPA and CCC station, and then a fire guard station; today it is available for rent by families. The interpretive signs on the Interrorem Nature Trail No. 804 tell about life here in the early days. Ranger Hole Trail No. 824 leads down through old second-growth forest to the ranger's private steelhead fishing hole and the beautiful Duckabush River.

Begin by looking at the Interrorem Cabin; walking the ½-mile loop east through giant stumps, some as much as 8 feet in diameter; and admiring the tunnels of vine maples that have grown since the original cedars and firs were cut. Mrs. Finch's life here is spelled out graphically; she did laundry on a washboard, cooked on a wood stove, canned salmon and berries, and made her own soap and butter. Ask children if they can imagine living such a life.

Now you can begin along the Ranger Hole Trail, heading directly for the river. The second-growth forest is lush with ferns, mossy maples, stumps, and boulders covered in green. Have children listen; who will be first to hear the sound of the river? The first stretch is level, then it drops gently, then abruptly becomes quite steep. The roar of the river as it cuts through a narrow rock channel is almost deafening.

Hang onto children's hands here. The rock promontory overlook has no rails, and this river cannot be floated. White water rushes by, then turns into a broad pool. Ranger Finch and others after him have cast their fishing lines into this pool to catch their trout and steelhead dinners.

 **DUCKABUSH RIVER**

BEFORE YOU GO
Maps Green Trails No. 168 The Brothers; USGS The Brothers
Current conditions Hood Canal Ranger District (360) 765-2200
Wilderness Permit and Northwest Forest Pass required

ABOUT THE HIKE
Day hike
Moderate for children
Year round
5 miles
430 feet elevation gain

GETTING THERE
■ On US 101, 15 miles south of Quilcene and 22 miles north of Hoodsport, turn west onto Duckabush River Road, which also is Road No. 2510.
■ Drive 6 miles. The trailhead is on your right, elevation 270 feet.

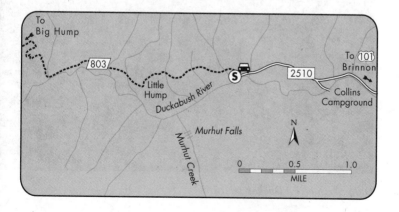

ON THE TRAIL

Two previous users of Duckabush valley have left us evidence of their passing. Ask children to look for glacially deposited moss-covered boulders left by the Duckabush Glacier during the last Ice Age. Thousands of years later, an old logging railroad early in the twentieth century was used here to drag out huge cut-down trees. Rusty logging cables and a few old rails lie beside the trail to tell their tale. Children can still find and touch them. The first 2½ miles of this trail are gentle enough for children, and are lush with forest ferns, moss, flowers, and berries. Rainfall here is 140 inches a year, so you can see why the understory is so much like that of the rainforest.

Begin on a former logging road, climbing gradually to surmount Little Hump, a rocky glacial step left by the glacier. Several small creeks cross the path on their way to the Duckabush River, but you will not see it yet. Enter The Brothers Wilderness at 1 mile, drop down the other side of the Hump, and notice that the old road has disappeared. You will be walking along a straight raised railroad bed, with vine maple branches making tunnels above you. At 2¼ miles find more glacial erratic boulders; listen for sounds of the river, and at 2½ miles come to a wide spot at the river's

Old growth along Duckabush trail

edge, suitable for a picnic lunch. Children will love looking at the water, throwing stones, dipping feet, and playing by the river's edge.

 **MURHUT FALLS**

BEFORE YOU GO
Maps Green Trails No. 168 The Brothers; USGS The Brothers
Current conditions Hood Canal Ranger District (360) 765-2200
Northwest Forest Pass required

ABOUT THE HIKE
Day hike
Easy for children
Year round
1²⁄₅ miles
200 feet elevation gain

GETTING THERE
- On US 101, 15 miles south of Quilcene and 22 miles north of Hoodsport, turn west onto Duckabush River Road, which also is Road No. 2510.
- Drive 6.2 miles to Road No. 2530. Turn right and drive 1.3 miles to the Murhut Falls trailhead, elevation 800 feet. The sign is small and there is limited parking.

ON THE TRAIL
A new trail to a lovely, narrow, woodland waterfall rewards photographers and families with exquisite beauty. In spring native rhododendrons bloom along the trail, which apparently was once a logging road.

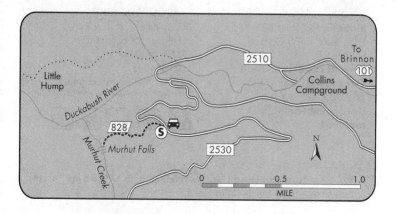

Curled-up frond of sword fern

At the waterfall children will love watching the water spill over the top of the highest ledge, drop, then level off in a plunge pool, and then hurtle down again. On a hot day the cool breeze, shade, and spray will cool you. Hold onto children's hands here.

Begin upward through old cedar stumps on a moss-lined path. The trail levels off and widens out at ½ mile. Listen for the sound of the falls, and when you hear it, begin a short drop to the shady falls viewpoint. The trail ends here, and children should not try to descend farther but should stay on the path overlook. Tell them to look and listen to the 100-foot horsetail-shaped falls.

The blossoms of the dainty pink-and-white twinflower *(Linnaea borealis)* rise in pairs and have a delicate fragrance. Tell children that Linnaeus was the eighteenth-century Swedish botanist who classified the plant kingdom into genera and species. The twinflower was his favorite flower, and it was named for him because he loved it so.

161 MOUNT ZION

BEFORE YOU GO
Maps Green Trails No. 136 Tyler Peak; USFS Olympic National Forest
Current conditions Hood Canal Ranger District (360) 765-2200
Northwest Forest Pass required

ABOUT THE HIKE
Day hike
Difficult for children
May to October
3¼ miles
1300 feet elevation gain

GETTING THERE
■ From Quilcene, on Hood Canal, drive north on US 101 for 2 miles, and turn left on Lords Lake Road.

■ Pass the Little Quilcene River Dam, after which the road becomes No. 28. Seven miles from US 101 keep right at an intersection with Road No. 27.

■ At 8.5 miles reach Bon Jon Pass, turn right on Road No. 2810, and drive another 2 miles to the trailhead for the Mount Zion Trail No. 836, elevation 2950 feet.

ON THE TRAIL

This short but steep trail climbs 900 feet per mile through tree-size rhododendrons to a summit with a big view. Children will like the challenge of climbing a little mountain, and they can be proud of the view they have earned: north to the Strait of Juan de Fuca, Mount Baker, and Discovery Bay; south to the skyscrapers of Seattle; and west to Port Townsend, the Dungeness valley, and into the heart of the Olympic Mountains. The site of a former lookout, Mount Zion has a trail that varies from steep to very steep. Large steps are like waterbars. This trail has been discovered by mountain bikers, who like to zoom silently downward, so be on the lookout. Plan your trip for mid-June, when walking through and under the pink native rhododendron blossoms will remind you of walking through a tropical forest.

View from Mount Zion trail

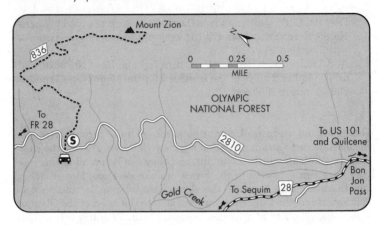

The trail starts up steeply, but the reward is a beautiful canopy of rhododendrons overhead and an understory of ferns, twinflowers, Oregon grape, violets, and ocean spray. Because the trail is so steep, children may need to be coaxed with frequent energy stops and the promise of treats on top, elevation 4273 feet. Interesting rock formations suggesting marine origins provide seats for families who want to enjoy the views. Ask your children how they think rocks with seashell fossils on a mountaintop could once have been sandy tide flats under the ocean.

OLYMPIC NATIONAL PARK

 **BLUE MOUNTAIN**

BEFORE YOU GO
Maps Green Trails No. 135 Port Angeles
Current conditions Olympic National Park (360) 956-2400
National park annual or day-use pass required

ABOUT THE HIKE
Day hike
Easy for children
July to October
½ mile
250 feet elevation gain

GETTING THERE
- From Sequim, drive west on US 101 some 11 miles.
- About 4 miles short of downtown Port Angeles, near milepost 253,

turn south and go uphill 17 miles on Deer Park Road, paved only the first 5 miles.

■ At 16 miles pass Deer Park Campground and continue upward another mile to the road end, elevation 5750 feet.

ON THE TRAIL

An easy ¼-mile walk on an abandoned road seems to lead to the top of the world. Young children will enjoy the challenge of reaching the site of a fire lookout built in 1931 on the top of the mountain, where the family will find a breathtaking view of the Olympic Mountains and the waterways of the Strait of Juan de Fuca, Victoria, Vancouver Island, Bellingham, and Mount Baker. They will also be intrigued by the tiny ocean-going ships, like toy boats in a bathtub, and the plume of smoke rising from a pulp mill in distant Port Angeles, and by a solar-powered radio structure near the top of Blue Mountain.

Hike the abandoned road upward in subalpine forest and meadows as it traverses the west side of the mountain. Children can walk holding hands with parents on the wide old roadbed to reach the broad summit that once housed a lookout, at an elevation of 6007 feet. The lookout building was removed in the 1950s, but children can imagine what it might have been like to spend a heroic summer up here, spotting and telegraphing in to headquarters the location of the first wisp of smoke before it could grow into a dangerous forest fire. Expect them to be overwhelmed with the vastness and the beauty of the Olympic Mountains.

Elk Mountain from Blue Mountain

 **HURRICANE HILL**

BEFORE YOU GO
Maps Green Trails No. 134 Mount Olympus
Current conditions Olympic National Park (360) 956-2800; Hurricane Ridge Visitor Center (360) 565-3131
National park annual or day-use pass required

ABOUT THE HIKE
Day hike
Easy for children
Late July–October
2½ miles
700 feet elevation gain

GETTING THERE
- From Port Angeles, follow signs south to the Hurricane Ridge road, pass the Olympic National Park Visitors Center, and enter the park.
- Pass the Hurricane Ridge Visitors Center at 18 miles and continue a short distance to the road end, elevation 5000 feet.

ON THE TRAIL
A stroll through flower fields on a gently graded asphalt path to the site of a former National Park Service lookout enables families with very little children to gaze at 360 degrees of glorious views. You can even push a stroller up this hill, if you feel strong. To the south lie the great chasm of the Elwha River and the peaks of the Central Olympics. Below lie Port Angeles and the Strait of Juan de Fuca. Beyond the strait is Vancouver Island. If the day is cloudless, look east for the San Juans and Mount Baker. This is a popular trail in the summer months, but there is plenty of parking available. The weather can turn stormy rapidly at this location, and it is not uncommon that the whole trail is blanketed in a mist

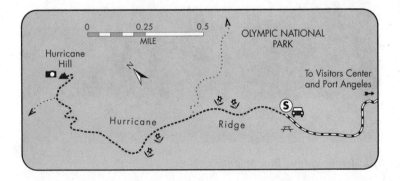

Old Hurricane Hill Visitor Center and supervisor

of swirling clouds as the colder ocean air mixes with warmer air out of the Puget Sound basin. Children and adults alike should be prepared for changing weather on this very scenic walk.

Follow the asphalt path 1½ miles, gaining 700 feet, to the top of the hill. The meadows are dappled with clumps of subalpine fir and carpeted with lupine, valerian, penstemon, and paintbrush. In fall, the blueberry bushes flame red and orange.

164 SPRUCE RAILROAD

BEFORE YOU GO
Maps Green Trails No. 101
Lake Crescent; Custom Correct
Lake Crescent–Happy Lake
Ridge
Current conditions Olympic
National Park (360) 956-2400

ABOUT THE HIKE
Day hike
Moderate for children
Year round
**First tunnel: 2 miles;
second tunnel: 6½ miles;
west trailhead: 9 miles**
50 feet elevation gain

GETTING THERE

- Drive west from Port Angeles on US 101. Between Lake Sutherland and Lake Crescent, near milepost 232, turn right at East Beach Road, signed "East Beach–Piedmont."

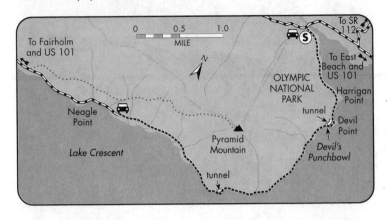

- In 3.3 miles go left, crossing the Lyre River at the outlet of the lake. At 4 miles reach the trailhead parking lot and walk 200 feet to the trailhead, elevation 600 feet.

ON THE TRAIL

This historic railroad grade with ruined tunnels offers children a level lakeshore walk, a swim, a chance to examine the entrances to two tunnels, and the opportunity to look down from a bridge into the Devil's Punchbowl. On a hot day, whole families have been known to jump into chilly Lake Crescent to cool off. The apple trees at the trailhead are remnants from the orchard of an old homestead.

Parents should tell kids that the Spruce Railroad was built by the U.S. government to carry out spruce logs for World War I airplane wings. The war ended before any spruce was carried, but the tracks did carry carloads of logs and workers on the Port Angeles Western Railroad along the lake's north shore until the 1950s. Old-timers tell of crossties made of alder and maple, which quickly rotted (explaining the nickname "The P. A. Wobbly"), and of the sunken locomotive resting in one of the coves. Another legend has it that train employees ate fruit as they traveled, and where they tossed apple cores and cherry pits out the windows, fruit trees stand today. This trail is open to mountain bikes, the only such trail in Olympic National Park.

For a 4½-mile, one-way hike, leave one car here and go back to US 101. Drive around the lake to Fairholm, at the west end. Turn right on a road signed "Campground—Camp David Junior." Pass the campground, at 1.5 miles pass Camp David Junior, and at 5 miles reach the road end and the Spruce Railroad Trail.

For a round trip with children, I recommend beginning at the eastern end of the trail. Start on a wide, muddy path with a sign warning of poison oak ahead. Don't expect to see it until the rocky cliff section of the trail, but prepare children not to touch any low-growing plants. At ½ mile drop 50 feet to the lakeshore. Powerboats zoom close to the bank, creating wake that laps beside you, a delightful sound to hear on a hot day. At about ¾ mile there is a small meadow with a picnic area and the best place for beginners to swim.

Just before 1 mile, children should look for the first collapsed railroad tunnel, to the right of the trail. They will be excited about exploring it, but tell them that the tunnel is extremely unsafe to enter now. Contour around the ridge the tunnel penetrates, and gaze down at the wonderful Devil's Punchbowl, a small, deep-blue cove crossed by an arching bridge. Many families never get beyond this magical point.

Ask children to imagine that if the lake were drained, this trail would be high on the edge of a cliff.

Spruce Railroad trail over Devil's Punchbowl

Fishermen love to cast for the lake's unique trout, the Beardsley, from this bridge. Beyond here the trail has some patches of poison oak. Around the corner, children can inspect the other side of the tunnel by climbing a short way above the trail. If your family has the energy to continue, the trail stretches along a cliff-side ledge to a second tunnel at 3¼ miles. Take a flashlight to the mouth. This tunnel may be inspected more closely than the first one, although fallen rocks and collapsed beams cover the floor.

Now have the children turn and look across the deep-blue lake to Lake Crescent Lodge, then up to Storm King Mountain. If you were on a Scottish loch in the Highlands, the scene would look very much like this. The trail continues the length of the lake, and if you wish to walk the entire trail, you will need to leave a car at the west end of the lake.

 **MARYMERE FALLS**

BEFORE YOU GO
Maps Green Trails No. 101 Lake Crescent; Custom Correct Lake Crescent–Happy Lake Ridge
Current conditions Olympic National Park (360) 956-2400

ABOUT THE HIKE
Day hike
Easy for children
Year round
2 miles
400 feet elevation gain

GETTING THERE
- Drive US 101 to Lake Crescent, 21.5 miles west of Port Angeles.
- Turn right on the road signed "Lake Crescent Lodge—Marymere." In a few feet go right again to a large parking lot, elevation 600 feet.

ON THE TRAIL
Much like movies and restaurants, waterfalls can be evaluated and rated with stars for their scenic qualities. This four-star waterfall with a short and easy access trail has been a favorite with families for generations. The trail, through old-growth forest, is wide and level for ¾ mile before crossing Barnes Creek and starting up the ridge alongside the falls. Children love walking its log bridge and climbing up alongside the waterfall. They run ahead to scout what comes next, then run back to report to parents.

Start on a level trail that passes the old ranger station and then crosses under US 101. Kids will enjoy running through the underpass beside the creek and listening to the echoes of vehicles overhead.

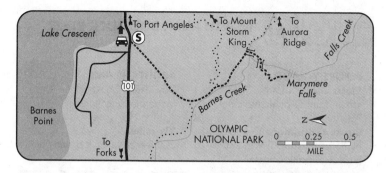

The trail follows the highway for a long ¼ mile, then turns inland beside Barnes Creek. A junction with the Storm King Mountain Trail is marked with an enormous boulder at ¾ mile. (Don't take children up that trail—it's steep!) Continue through vine maples reaching for the sun, beneath ancient cedars. The log bridge with railings across Barnes Creek has only one lane, so this busy trail sometimes has lines of people waiting to cross the bridge, but the setting is so beautiful that not even children become impatient. Some kids love stepping out over the water and being the center of attention for all those waiting their turn.

Another log bridge over Falls Creek is the preamble to the climb up the falls. The trail has ninety-one wooden steps with railings for the safety of old and very young hikers. There is even a loop, with one trail section for the upward bound and another for the downward bound. Go right and don't fight the crowd—the downward flow is overwhelming.

A bench opposite the 98-foot falls allows a close-up view of the catch basin and a breath of spray. Kids will sit transfixed watching the water drop. Take a camera to try to capture the tiered column of water framed by moss-covered cliffs and maidenhair fern. It is enough to stand here and gaze at beautiful Marymere Falls, and then, of course, have the children pose for pictures in front of it.

Marymere Falls

 **NORTH FORK SOLEDUCK RIVER**

BEFORE YOU GO
Maps Green Trails No. 133
Mount Tom; Olympic National
Park map
Current conditions Olympic
National Park (360) 956-2400
**National park annual
or day-use pass and
Wilderness Permit required**

ABOUT THE HIKE
Day hike or backpack
Moderate for children
April to November
2½ miles
300 feet elevation loss and gain

GETTING THERE

- From Port Angeles drive 30 miles west on US 101 to the Sol Duc
  Hot Springs road.
- Turn left and at 8.3 miles look for the trailhead on the right side
  of the road, elevation 1500 feet.

Note: Footlog at first crossing has been washed away. Check with
park before starting out.

ON THE TRAIL

This lightly used woodland trail follows the north fork of the Soleduck River into a meadow that can be either a base camp for further explorations up the river, or a turnaround point. In August and September children can expect to see spawning salmon from the bridge or from natural rock benches along the riverbank. Elk and deer are frequent visitors all year round, and if children miss seeing them, they may find their tracks instead. The elk act as lawnmowers and grounds-keepers for the forest, grooming and trimming plants such as devil's club and salmonberries so that the trail looks neat and tidy. A family's best chance to see the big animals is in the fall and winter months, either early in the morning or late in the evening. This river has been proposed for Wild and Scenic River designation.

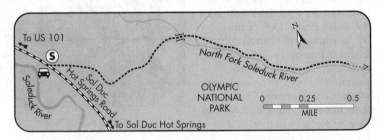

Bridge across North Fork Soleduck River

Begin by climbing up and over a 300-foot ridge separating the two forks of the river. If children huff and puff, tell them that in ½ mile it will be all downhill. (Don't mention the return.) As the sounds of the Soleduck die away, the trail levels out and begins to drop. Old cedar stumps and prone nurse logs are part of a fairyland of moss, oak fern, and twinflowers. One giant log has a 5-foot cut facing the trail. Have the kids count as many of the rings as they can in order to get a sense of its age. Or stand them against the log to get another kind of feel for its size. Children can watch for spotted "appaloosa" slugs (actually banana slugs) that are spotted like the horses, chewing their way along through forest greenery.

At 1 mile look down on the North Fork Soleduck. At 1¼ miles cross it on a log bridge, and hang on to children if they aren't tall enough to reach the railing. In late summer this is a great place to watch spawning salmon swimming upstream. Tell children that spawning females actually dig a small nest, or redd, with their tails in which to lay their eggs. The narrow, elk-groomed glade begins on the other side of the bridge, the turnaround.

For those who choose to continue, many good campsites present themselves in the next ½ mile. Narrow river chutes where the water is channeled through a

Slug

414 ■ Olympic Peninsula

funnel occur at 2⅓ and 2½ miles, with wonderful expanses of bedrock right at river level, and where children can also watch for fish or at least admire the white-water rapids. The river trail extends for 9 miles; you might choose to camp along the way and continue your explorations.

 **SOLEDUCK FALLS AND DEER LAKE**

BEFORE YOU GO
Maps Green Trails No. 133 Mount Tom; Olympic National Park map
Current conditions Olympic National Park (360) 956-2400
Northwest Forest Pass and national park annual or day-use fee required; backcountry permit required for camping

ABOUT THE HIKE
Day hike or backpack
Easy for children
June–October
Soleduck Falls: 2 miles;
Deer Lake: 8 miles
Soleduck Falls: no elevation gain; Deer Lake: 1500 feet gain

GETTING THERE
- Drive US 101 west 30 miles from Port Angeles and turn left on the Soleduck River road.
- Drive 14.2 miles, passing Sol Duc Hot Springs Resort, and continue to the road-end parking lot, elevation 2000 feet.

ON THE TRAIL
This hike takes you through an old-growth forest with a green shag-rug covering of moss and flowers to a thundering waterfall in a deep gorge. If

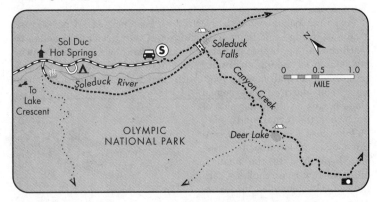

Soleduck Falls

the children are willing, climb to campsites near subalpine Deer Lake.

With minor ups and downs, the broad, smooth trail travels through a magnificent stand of old-growth fir, hemlock, and occasional Sitka spruce. In 1 mile, reach a junction and shelter. Descend to a good view of the falls from the trail bridge, elevation 2000 feet. Children should be carefully supervised here, because the falls lie below in a deep canyon. Campsites are located above the falls.

To continue on to Deer Lake, cross the Soleduck River on the bridge, wet with the spray from Soleduck Falls. The Soleduck River is named after the Sol Duc Hotsprings near its headwaters. The Indian spelling, Sol Duc, means "sparkling water." Children will enjoy standing here in the spray, watching the water drop. Beyond this point, the trail steepens in earnest. At 2 miles cross Canyon Creek, and at 4 miles reach Deer Lake and the campsites, elevation 3500 feet. Spend a day here and wander up through heather and flower fields to High Divide, with its dramatic views across the Hoh valley to the glaciers on Mount Olympus.

 BOGACHIEL RIVER STATE PARK

BEFORE YOU GO
Maps Green Trails No. 132 Spruce Mountain; Olympic National Park map
Current conditions Olympic National Park (360) 956-2400, Washington State Parks (360) 902-8844
Wilderness permit required for camping

ABOUT THE HIKE
Day hike or backpack
Moderate for children
June to November
Bogachiel River: 4 miles;
Mosquito Creek: 6 miles
No elevation gain

GETTING THERE
- Drive west 56 miles on US 101 from Port Angeles, passing through the town of Forks and continuing south 5 more miles to Bogachiel State Park.
- Across from the state park entrance, turn left on Undi Road, which becomes Road No. 2932, and drive 5.5 miles to reach a gate and the trailhead, elevation 350 feet.

ON THE TRAIL
An elk-groomed rain-forest river valley offers families all of the primitive magic of the Hoh areas, without the crowds. Huge, moss-shrouded,

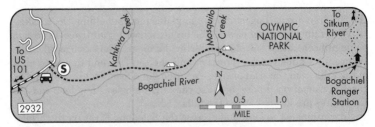

Bogachiel River trailhead sign

second-growth maples and alders lean over the trail, then give way to even more beautiful old-growth forest pruned by resident herds of elk. As the elk lose more of their habitat to logging, they clip ever more diligently any wayward buttercup, salmonberry, sword fern, thimbleberry, and devil's club. The groomed, park-like result would make a British garden club gasp. There may be more elk tracks on the trail than people tracks. Have kids guess the size of the animals from the tracks. This trail is muddy most of the year, because it is located in a rain-forest setting. Wearing waterproof shoes or boots is highly recommended to keep little feet happy—big feet, too.

The trail drops to an abandoned roadbed, which crosses several creeks that may be impassable during the rainy season. The first 2 miles lie mostly away from the river. At 1 mile look across Kahkwa Creek, to the right, to see the remnants of early day homesteads—old pastures and the ruins of barns and fences.

Enter the park at 1⅔ miles in woodland meadow lighted by filtered sunlight, and hear the screeing sound of chickarees (Douglas squirrels) warning of your approach. Children can watch for elk all the way, but don't expect to hear them move. Despite their 1000-pound bulk, elk can move through brush almost silently. Children may want to know that elk feed in upland flats by day, then move slowly back down by night on established paths to the river, to bed down on grassy river bars.

Continue on through old cedar stumps, cut early in the century, into second-growth hemlock forest, and reach the Bogachiel River at about two miles. A good camp here would make a possible turnaround point.

Grassy meadows between you and the river are also elk-cropped, representing old flood plains, called benches, of the Bogachiel. The rain forest becomes increasingly wild and luxuriant as you move upriver.

Climb a few feet for the first time, and from a bench viewpoint look down on the wide riverbed, draining Bogachiel and Misery Peaks. You can see some distance up and down the meandering channel and wide flood plain. At Mosquito Creek, at 3 miles, choose from grass-covered gravel bars for a campsite. If your children are willing, you might leave gear here and continue on another 2½ miles to the old Bogachiel ranger station and horse-barn shelter.

But beware! The farther you go, the greater are your chances of falling under the enchantment of the Bogachiel.

Along the way, have kids look for wedge-shaped fungus called conks, growing on the trunks of spruce, fir, and hemlock. They are a sign of the health and diversity of the rain forest. Children may also see bright-orange chicken-of-the-woods mushrooms growing like coral on tree trunks along the trail. Whether you want to try tasting them is up to you, but mushroom fanciers say they are safe and delicious.

 **HOH RIVER RAIN FOREST**

BEFORE YOU GO
Maps Green Trails No. 133 Mount Tom; Olympic National Park map
Current conditions Olympic National Park (360) 956-2400
Backcountry permit required for camping; entrance fee

ABOUT THE HIKE
Day hike or backpack
Easy for children
Year round
6 miles
120 feet elevation gain

GETTING THERE
- Drive US 101 north 93 miles from Aberdeen or south 14 miles from Forks and turn east on the Hoh River road.
- Drive 19 miles to the Hoh Visitors Center, elevation 578 feet.

ON THE TRAIL
This world-famous rain forest is accessible most of the year. Olympic rain forests are extraordinarily lush in vegetation because they receive

approximately 12 feet—144 inches—of rainfall a year. Show the kids on a tree just how much that is. Children will love seeing the huge Roosevelt elk, which by means of their browsing and grazing keep the forest floor cropped of undergrowth. The chances of seeing them are best in late fall and winter, when herds are down in the valley and most tourists are gone, but one resident band can be seen even in busy summer months. The Hoh River trail extends 17 miles, all the way to the edge of the Blue Glacier on Mount Olympus. However, families can amply savor the beauty of the rain forest in the 3 miles to the Mount Tom Creek trail junction.

Begin at the visitors center on a paved trail that turns to gravel and then to soil. Hikers pass through old-growth Sitka spruce and Douglas-fir interspersed with bigleaf maple, festooned with club moss and feathered with licorice fern. Elk have cropped the forest floor

Beneath moss-hung trees in the Hoh Rain Forest

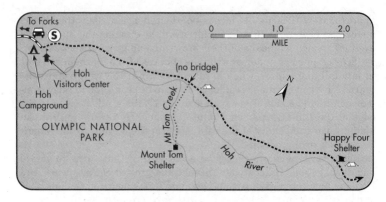

plants they find tasty, leaving a tidy green carpet of ferns, moss, and oxalis. The most likely times and places to see the big animals, silently moving together, are early in the morning on the grassy terraces and gravel bars.

One October morning when I was here, a large bull was moving his twenty cows across the terrace and through the river. A long strand of moss was draped rakishly across one horn. He bugled a challenge at me to make it clear they were his cows and I couldn't have them. I didn't try to answer but wondered if he wanted me to join them!

At 3 miles, reach the Mount Tom Creek trail and follow it to the bank of the Hoh River, elevation 700 feet. The river's grassy terrace offers excellent tent sites, but you should plan to build campfires on the gravel bar, not in the meadow. Children can play in the backwater pools.

Happy Four, at 6 miles from the visitors center, is an excellent destination for a second day.

PACIFIC OCEAN

Pacific Ocean beaches are a source of wonder to children. From the overlook trail at Cape Flattery, the northwesternmost point in the United States, to the Lighthouse Traverse and Benson Beach hikes along the Columbia River, ocean beach hikes are a delight. Enormous waves, huge driftwood logs, and the sense that there is nothing but ocean until one reaches Japan give children the joyful experience of discovery. Shi Shi has been called the most beautiful wilderness ocean beach in Washington. Others that have shorter access trails, such as Hole-in-the-Wall, Third Beach, and Ruby Beach, may not be wilderness but are surely among the most beautiful ocean beaches in our state.

 **CAPE FLATTERY**

BEFORE YOU GO
Map Green Trails No. 98S
Cape Flattery
Current conditions Makah
Tribe (360) 645-2711
**Makah Recreational Use
permit required**

ABOUT THE HIKE
Day hike
Easy for children
Year round
1 mile
200 feet elevation loss and gain

GETTING THERE

- From Port Angeles, take Highway 112 west 60 miles to Neah Bay.
- Pass the Makah Museum and travel west 1.5 miles through town (follow the sharp corner as it goes left).
- Take a right at the Presbyterian Church (on the left). Go one block, turn left, and follow signs to the Tribal Center (do not go up the hill), about 2.5 miles on a paved road.
- Go past the Makah Tribal Center for 0.25 mile to a gravel road. Continue on the gravel road for about 4 miles. At a sign for Cape Trail, stay left and travel a short distance to the trailhead and parking area, elevation 100 feet.

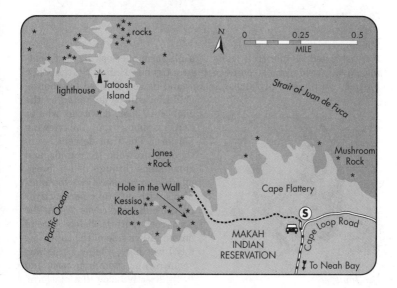

Cape Flattery cove

ON THE TRAIL

A constructed ½-mile trail leads to a platform overlooking surf beating on the westernmost point of the contiguous United States, Cape Flattery, with views to Tatoosh Island and its red-towered lighthouse.

Children will be delighted by the chance to look down on whales and sea lions from the viewing platform. The trail descends gently on boardwalk, log rounds, and stone steps through dense forest, offering three more viewing platforms with different perspectives on the cliffs and coves. Along the way, rock portals below extend out on either side of the cape. The day I was here, a baby whale was spouting and swimming back and forth directly below the platform.

Sea lions

Perhaps its mother was off fishing and had told it to stay right there until she returned.

The Makah recreational permit required for this area may be purchased at the Makah Tribal Council, Makah Marina, Big Salmon Fishing Resort, Washburn's General Store, Makah Museum, Neah Bay Charter and Tackle, Makah Fuel Company, and the Makah Smoke Shop. Permits are valid for the calendar year in which they are purchased.

The sounds of the Tatoosh Island foghorn will call out to children, who will want to run ahead to find it. Because the trail is popular and crowded, and the boardwalk is only wide enough for one at a time, they should not run. Tell them to walk slowly and to let the anticipation grow as they hear the horn. Unless it is foggy, they will be able to glimpse the ocean from various windows through trees.

The rock coves and inlets have been carved and eroded over time by millions of waves. They represent the Juan de Fuca Plate and the North American Plate in collision at the edge of the continent. Children may not care about tectonic plate geology, but they will love searching for spouting, breaching whales and giant sea lions lounging on offshore rocks below.

 **SHI SHI BEACH**

BEFORE YOU GO
Map Green Trails No. 98S Cape Flattery
Current conditions Makah Nation (360) 645-2711; Olympic National Park (360) 956-2400
Makah Recreational Use and backcountry permits required; camping fee; bring a current tide table

ABOUT THE HIKE
Day hike or backpack
Moderate for children
Year round
5 miles
50 feet elevation loss and gain

GETTING THERE
- From Port Angeles, take Highway 112 west about 60 miles to Neah Bay.
- At the west end of town, follow signs to Cape Flattery in about 2½ miles and then turn left, following signs marked "To Beaches." The road is paved all the way. It ends at a gate, which, according to the signs, is closed at night.
- Before the gate find a large gravel parking lot, elevation 50 feet.

ON THE TRAIL

Children love this secluded and scenic ocean beach, with its rugged reefs and headlands curving out to Point of Arches. Campers find wooded campsites that provide shelter during storms and high tides. Beach camping is available at Petroleum and Willoughby Creeks, but campers should be sure not to leave garbage behind and will need to pay for a per-party backcountry permit and a per-person camping fee. Hard-sided food containers, such as bear canisters, are required to store all food, garbage, and scented items. Beachcombing here is superb for those with sharp eyes. Fishing net floats and all manner of flotsam and jetsam can be collected. At low tide, the kids can look for tide pools and gaze at the rock arches. Be sure not to start out toward them without a tide table.

The Makah recreational permit required for this area may be purchased at the Makah Tribal Council, Makah Marina, Big Salmon Fishing Resort, Washburn's General Store, Makah Museum, Neah Bay Charter and Tackle, Makah Fuel Company, and the Makah Smoke Shop. Permits are valid for the calendar year in which they are purchased.

The trail starts at the parking lot. The first mile of the trail is new and in excellent condition, because it was recently rebuilt as a cooperative effort, like the Cape Flattery trail. This part of the trail is partly gravel and partly wooden planks, with good bridges and signs. But it ends after about a mile and joins the old trail, which is very muddy for about 2 miles, and which may give children some trouble.

Shi Shi Beach and Point of Arches

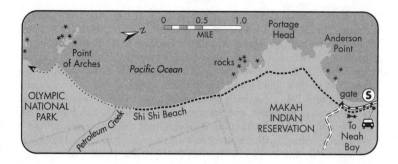

At the ocean-access trailhead, drop steeply down the cliff on rock steps and switchbacks. A bull's-eye nailed to a tree trunk will help you remember the trail location on your return from the beach. Walk as far as you wish, but remember to check the tide. Waves can quickly cover your footprints and can even come as high as the forest rimming the shore in some places. Campfires are allowed on the beach here.

 **SAND POINT**

BEFORE YOU GO
Maps Green Trails No. 130S Ozette
Current conditions Olympic National Park (360) 2400
National park annual or day-use fee required; reservations for camping required; bring a current tide table

ABOUT THE HIKE
Day hike or backpack
Moderate for children
Year round
Sand Point: 6 miles;
Wedding Rocks: 9 miles
120 feet elevation gain

GETTING THERE
- From Port Angeles, drive west 4.6 miles on US 101.
- Turn right on Road No. 112, which takes you along the Strait of Juan de Fuca some 2 miles past Sekiu.
- Turn left on Ozette Lake Road and drive 21 miles to a ranger station, Ozette Lake Campground, and a parking lot, elevation 36 feet.

ON THE TRAIL
This ocean campground, reached after a short 3-mile walk, promises crashing breakers, sandy beach, and further along the beach, old Makah

petroglyphs on rock. Two trails depart from the Ozette Lake Campground. The preferred trail is the one to Sand Point, which is shorter than the one to Cape Alava, and easier because it is all on boardwalk. The sandy beach is more attractive to kids than the cannonball-shaped rocks at Cape Alava. Possible campsites are protected from wind by trees that shelter, shade, and frame beach views. If you wish, you can camp at Sand Point, continue up the beach past Indian petroglyphs to Cape Alava, camp again, and return to the trailhead—but Sand Point alone is a fine beach destination. Be aware that campsites are limited.

Begin by crossing the Ozette River on an arching concrete bridge. In 100 yards the trail forks; take the left fork, to Sand Point. Children will delight in climbing up onto the springy boardwalk, sometimes almost 2 feet above the forest floor. They feel they are "following the yellow brick road" to the ocean. However, it can be slippery when wet or frosty. The dense, lush underbrush, the result of almost constant precipitation nine months of the year, has a magical quality when surveyed from a board sidewalk. Evergreen huckleberry, salal, young cedars, and hemlocks tangle together on either side. Several huge old-growth cedars occur together at about 1 mile, having escaped the fires that took out their neighbors. Immense, upended fir root wads face the trail in several places. Kids will want to stop and examine the underside of a tree trunk. There is no taproot. "Whatever held it in place?" they may ask. It makes you wonder how other such giants remain upright.

After 3 miles the trail descends to a campsite and a short way farther to wide sandy beaches, scenic sea stacks, and inaccessible rock islands

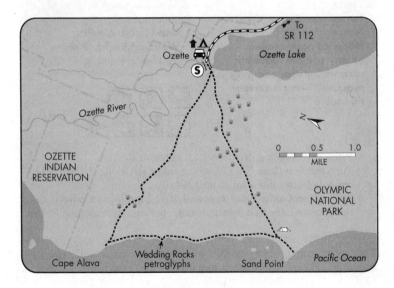

Petroglyphs at Sand Point

receding in the distance. We saw an eagle and a pair of raccoons here. Children should be warned against trying to feed the raccoons, which have become so tame they beg from hikers and tear open packsacks. Be careful: They will bite the hand that feeds them.

Rangers tell us bears can be a problem here. Hard-sided food containers such as bear canisters are required to store all food, garbage, and scented items. When my children and I went backpacking at Sand Point many years ago we had a bear experience. We walked out to the ocean intending to hike for a week. We had a lovely sunset and slept well in a tent and driftwood shelter. The next morning Mama Bear and her cub smelled my homemade maple syrup and came close for a helping. We threw rocks and banged on pots and pans, but she was undeterred. In fact, she was getting cross about our lack of hospitality. What could we do? Our backs were to the sea. Finally, we retreated, and that was the end of our beach hike. It made an exciting story for the kids to tell their friends about, but I wished we had gone north the extra 1½ miles on the beach to see the Indian petroglyphs.

The petroglyphs may just be early graffiti and are located at the high-tide mark on the only rock outcropping. Look carefully, because you can easily walk past them.

 **HOLE-IN-THE-WALL**

BEFORE YOU GO
Map Green Trails No. 130S
Ozette
Current conditions Olympic
National Park (360) 956-2400
Bring a current tide table

ABOUT THE HIKE
Day hike or backpack
Easy for children when tide is
out, difficult when tide is in
Year round
2½ miles
No elevation gain

GETTING THERE
- From Port Angeles on US
  101, drive west approximately 50 miles.
- Just 2 miles north of Forks,
  turn west on La Push–Mora Road, then go right on the Mora
  Campground road.
- Drive 5 miles to the trailhead at the Rialto Beach parking lot, elevation 10 feet.

ON THE TRAIL
The power and majesty of the ocean waves here will awe kids. These
waves are not to be trifled with. They throw enormous stumps and logs
far up the beach and reduce headlands to gravel and sand. Explain to
children how the block-shaped rock 2 miles out to sea, Cake Rock, was
once attached to the mainland, but that wave action has made it into
an island.

The walk down the beach to Hole-in-the-Wall, also carved by wave
action, is a thrilling adventure for children. The Ellen Creek crossing
at 1 mile can be somewhat difficult and hazardous if tides are high. Be
 prepared: Hiking above the high-tide mark is possible but more difficult
than when the tide is low.

Start by walking right, or north, along a few forested yards of trail,
then cross the piles of driftwood to reach the sloping shoreline.

Children are fascinated by the surf. When a skidding wave puts on
its brakes, it kicks up pebbles and rocks in its path, then recedes in
tongues of foam like a bubble bath. With a clatter, it drags the same
pebbles back down the beach.

Kids may find the walking slow going in the sand and rocks if the
tide is high, but they will be rewarded by the beach-combing possibilities. Have them look for polished pebbles of white quartz or scraps of

Opposite page: Hole-in-the-Wall

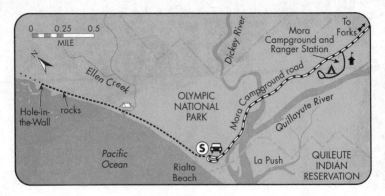

wood shaped like animals or ray guns. They may wish to play in the piles of spent foam called spindrift.

Cross Ellen Creek at 1 mile on a combination of logs and stumps. The brown water is stained harmlessly by cedar roots and can be treated with iodine or filtered for drinking. There are campsites here for families interested in backpacking to this first ocean beach camp. This is also a possible turnaround point if you don't care to cross the creek.

Hole-in-the-Wall is guarded by three sentinels. Sea stacks once connected to the mainland have been carved and isolated as monolithic rocks. Around the cove beyond the last one, children can see sky through the hole in Hole-in-the-Wall. If the tide is low, they may even be able to walk through it. To continue up the beach, when the tide is in, you will have to climb up the steep trail over the headland. However, you may want to linger in this cove and enjoy the superb beachcombing and tide pools containing starfish, swaying seaweeds, and anemones.

174 THIRD BEACH

BEFORE YOU GO
Map Green Trails No. 163S La Push
Current conditions Olympic National Park (360) 956-2400
Bring a current tide table; backcountry permit required for camping

ABOUT THE HIKE
Day hike or backpack
Easy for children
Year round
3 miles
300 feet elevation loss

GETTING THERE

- Drive US 101 to exactly 1 mile north of Forks and turn west on La Push–Mora Road.
- At 7.9 miles the road to Mora Campground and Rialto Beach branches off to the right.
- At 3.9 miles from the junction is the Third Beach trailhead, elevation 300 feet.

ON THE TRAIL

This is a more secluded "wilderness ocean" beach that also offers a wide sand beach along a crescent-shaped shore and tree-studded offshore islands. Even in mid-winter this hike is enjoyable. Try it during a storm, when your children can lean their full weight against the wind without falling and watch waves that have come all the way from Japan.

The mostly level 1½-mile trail to Third Beach travels through old

Climbing in a driftwood stump

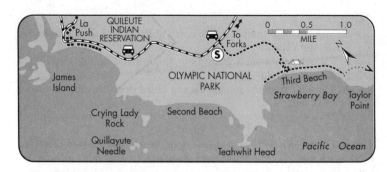

forest and then abruptly plunges off the plateau in a series of switch-backs before arriving at the long, curving beach of Strawberry Bay.

Campsites in the creek ravine at the trail end are protected from the wind unless it comes from the west (which it usually does.) Getting across the wide belt of slippery driftwood onto open beach can be difficult and somewhat dangerous.

Walk the beach ½ mile south for a closer view of the waterfall plummeting down the sea cliffs of Taylor Point into the surf. Backpackers take the trail over Taylor Point to begin a 20-mile wilderness beach walk to the mouth of the Hoh River.

This beach offers wonderful play possibilities: exploring tide pools, climbing giant driftwood logs, and running in the surf. Gray whales are often observed here from February to May, and, throughout the year, eagles perch on snags. Camping near the ocean can be memorable on a windless night—or a stormy one.

 **RUBY BEACH**

BEFORE YOU GO
Map Green Trails No. 163S LaPush
Current conditions Olympic National Park (360) 956-2400
National park annual or day-use pass required; bring a current tide table

ABOUT THE HIKE
Day hike
Easy for children
Year round
Cedar Creek mouth: 1⅗ miles
50 feet elevation gain and loss

GETTING THERE
- From the town of Forks on US 101, drive south about 27.5 miles to the Ruby Beach trailhead at milepost 164.7, elevation 50 feet.

ON THE TRAIL

A short, easy walk leads families to another popular ocean beach with unbroken sands, which are supposed to be tinted slightly pink by the presence of tiny grains of garnet, the color of rubies. Don't be disappointed if you can't see the color; it's very subtle. Huge rocks stand like stone pillars against the sea. Logs and broken trees are ground to pieces by the surge of breakers. The sea stacks and islands visible from the beach have led to some historic shipwrecks. Destruction Island is one of the islands, historically named by a British ship captain because Indians attacked crewmembers there while they were collecting water. The closest one is Abbey Island, which the kids can enjoy looking at, particularly at low tide.

Follow the short, easy, 300-yard trail alongside Cedar Creek to the surf. The creek's outlet is filled with brackish water and piles of silver

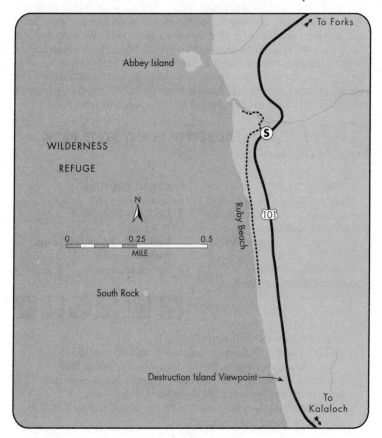

Short walk to a Pacific Ocean beach

driftwood floating in a kind of tidal lagoon. Offshore sea stacks and huge rocks host starfish, anemones, and occasional seals and sea lions. In ½ mile look for a small cave eroded by waves in the cliffs. Walking south is easier than walking north, but north of Abbey Island lie the Hoh Indian Reservation and the Hoh River. In late winter and early spring you may see migrating gray whales spouting as they pass. The islands are the nesting grounds of horn-billed auklets, which look a little like penguins and make a shrieking sound. No pets and no camping are allowed.

 **LEADBETTER POINT STATE PARK**

BEFORE YOU GO
Map Washington State road map; USGS Oysterville
Current conditions Washington State Parks (360) 902-8844
State park annual or day-use pass required

ABOUT THE HIKE
Day hike
Moderate for children
Year round
Bay Trail: 2½ miles; Loop Trail: 2¼ miles
No elevation gain

GETTING THERE
- From Aberdeen, travel south on Highway 101 to Seaview and the intersection with SR 103.
- Turn north on SR 103 and drive 11.5 miles to Ocean Park.
- Turn east on Bay Avenue and drive nearly 1 mile before turning left (north) on Peninsula Highway/Sand Ridge Road.
- Go 4 miles and then turn west on Oysterville Road. In 0.25 mile, turn right (north) on Stackpole Road.

- Continue to the end of the road (about 4.5 miles) and park at Leadbetter Point State Park, elevation 20 feet.

ON THE TRAIL

Blue herons and geese winter here; in the spring, hundreds of thousands of shorebirds migrate through with a great rushing of wings; and in the summer, endangered snowy plovers nest, protected, in the Willapa National Wildlife Refuge. You can follow state park trails leading across Willapa Bay mud flats, pine forest, bogs, and sand dunes—all with their diverse plant and animal species. Unlike Chesapeake Bay, Willapa Bay remains much as it was when first discovered. Because part of Leadbetter Point is a National Wildlife Refuge, children will find tracks of deer, elk, cottontail rabbits, raccoons, and birds in the wet sand. At low tide one can walk for miles on the sandy beach of Willapa Bay, exploring the vegetation-covered sand dunes. Salt-tolerant eelgrass, pickleweed, and glasswort on the bay side seem to attract deer and elk, judging from tracks and munched plants. Could these plants taste like pickles to them?

From the parking lot, choose one of three directions to go: Right leads directly to Willapa Bay, left leads to the forest loop described later and to the ocean beaches, and straight ahead are miles of tree-covered sand dunes. For children, our suggestion is to walk north, through the sand dunes, to look for animal tracks. Once we actually saw a small bear on this walk, which later, as the children repeated the story, grew so large that it must have been a grizzly. Return to the starting point by the beach.

Bay Trail. For this route, go left ⅓ mile; this area is subject to flooding from October through May. Then make your way northward ½ mile on a maze of trails. Watch for coyote droppings and tracks. The best place for tracks is on the inland trails that go north through the old dunes. Cottontail rabbits land on their hind legs with the two front ones together

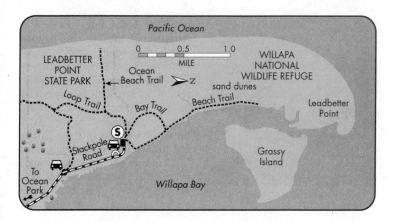

almost as one, so kids can look for their telltale three-footed tracks.

Eventually the way leads to Willapa Bay and a sandy beach. Listen for the honks of Canada geese and the "preep-preep" notes of sandpipers. Leadbetter Point is famous for its thousands of migrating shorebirds and its populations of brant (a migratory black goose resembling a small Canada goose) and snowy plover, which are rare and protected, and are most likely to be found farther north, at the tip of the point. The north half of the wildlife area is closed from April 1 to August 31 to protect the snowy plover.

One can either follow the beach back to the starting point or walk northward about a mile to the closed boundary of the wildlife refuge. Back on the bay side of the trail, the vista of Willapa Bay, on your right, will call to your children. The tide flats here contain enough mud to grow hummocks of eelgrass. No matter the season or tide, children will find enough room to run and countless gulls, ducks, and sandpipers to watch. How many different kinds of sandpipers can your children pick out? Other birds to look for include loons, Western grebes, scaups, widgeons, gulls, and scoters. These brackish mud flats have some of the qualities of saltwater life and some of fresh. A few of the birds and plants here are unlike those found elsewhere and give a kind of moonscape feeling to the area. The eelgrass stabilizes the mud and creates a nursery for fish.

When you have run out of room to explore, double back and retrace your steps rather than trying to enter the woods and intercept a trail. You may succeed, but it's easy to become confused and lose your way in the pine forest without obvious landmarks.

Loop Trail. Of less interest to children but popular with adults is a

A pair of brant

3¼-mile forest trail with a ¾-mile road walk back to the starting point. The 2¼-mile loop begins at the end of Stackpole Road. First apply insect repellent—remember, bogs breed bugs! From the road end, go left. The trail is wide and made of sand, so children can watch for tracks early in the morning. Angle south, listening to the roar of the breakers, but do not be tempted to try to get to the ocean. It is a long way out through sand dunes; many people have gotten lost in the never-never land.

Continue on the loop through shore pine forest on the soft, level trail. Tell children that ocean waves once washed over this place, and that these are old dunes where plants have established themselves and held the sand in place long enough for larger plants to take root. In ¼ mile the trail turns southward. In October and November kids may see red-and-white-spotted mushrooms, but don't let kids pick them. They are poisonous.

A less attractive form of wildlife is the insect world. If you pause very long, mosquitoes and gnats will attack with a vengeance. A good insect repellent, long-sleeved shirts, and long pants will help protect your family. Vegetation becomes denser, older, and more established the farther south you go. At 1¾ miles reach the road and follow it back to the starting point, or cross it and check out the tide and trail along the bay.

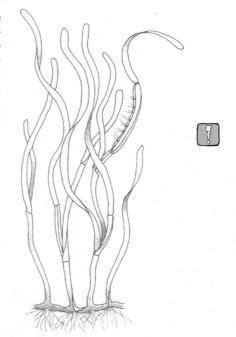

Eelgrass

 **BENSON BEACH**

BEFORE YOU GO
Map Cape Disappointment State Park brochure
Current conditions Washington State Parks (360) 902-8844
State park annual or day-use pass required

ABOUT THE HIKE
Day hike
Easy for children
Year round
4 miles
No elevation gain

GETTING THERE
■ From the Ilwaco stoplight at First and Spruce Streets, follow signs west 3.4 miles along a winding road to the entrance of Cape Disappointment State Park, elevation sea level.

ON THE TRAIL

This 2-mile-long, wide, sandy ocean beach invites children to run and chase waves. Unlike the other beaches of the Long Beach Peninsula, where vehicles are free to speed along next to waves, this motorfree beach allows families to dig safely in the sand, fly a kite, or just let the children run, unthreatened by cars and off-road vehicles. As tempting bonuses, it has a spectacular headland cave and rock jetty to explore.

Explain to them that jetties on either side of the Columbia River channel the outflow and make it easier for mariners to know where they must cross the bar. The bar is the wall of fresh water from the Columbia colliding with the surf of the Pacific. Since it was built in 1917, the rock jetty has captured and held the sand that makes up the campground. Sand has become soil and trees and grass now grow where once waves washed. At one time there may have been a roadbed along the jetty, but it has collapsed into the big rocks with the force of seasons of waves.

You can reach Benson Beach from some of the park campsites or from the end of the North Jetty parking lot. Wherever you start, walk the beach north to the impressive rock cliffs below the North Head Lighthouse. Backtrack a few hundred feet and take the first trail inland to find

Benson Beach cave

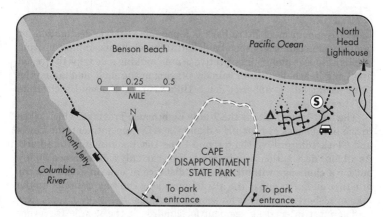

a maze of informal paths that weave amongst giant boulders. Look for a cave that surely must have housed Indian families long ago. Children will want to explore the cave. Ask them what they think it was like to live here in the winter when storms blew waves high into driftwood. These informal trails can also be reached between campsites 104 and 105.

When my children were small we walked out to the end of the north jetty along the rolling boulders. We scrambled out as far toward the end as we dared, surrounded by crashing breakers on either side. The kids were thrilled by the spray of those waves and watched as ships and fishing boats disappeared over the horizon. It was a moment to remember forever.

 **LIGHTHOUSE TRAVERSE**

BEFORE YOU GO
Map Cape Disappointment State Park brochure
Current conditions Washington State Parks (360) 902-8844
State park annual or day-use pass required

ABOUT THE HIKE
Day hike
Moderate for children
Year round
7 miles
250 feet elevation loss, 200 feet gain

GETTING THERE

■ From the Ilwaco stoplight at First and Spruce Streets, follow signs west 3.4 miles along a winding road to the entrance of Cape Disappointment State Park, elevation sea level.

ON THE TRAIL

Cape Disappointment State Park is a popular vacation destination for families. One can easily spend a delightful week here camping, visiting two lighthouses and an interpretive center, making side trips to Oregon and Long Beach, fishing for salmon, playing in the sand, and hiking the three park trails. Leadbetter Point (Hike 176) and Benson Beach (Hike 177) are nearby.

The best-known trail is the 7-mile Lighthouse Traverse, which takes in the lighthouses at North Head and Cape Disappointment, the Lewis and Clark Interpretive Center, and Cape Disappointment State Park. As all four destinations can be reached by car, only a determined family out for a challenge will hike the full distance at one time. Leave a car at either end or at one of the attractions along the way, or break up the hike into shorter segments for separate outings.

The most interesting segment for children is the ½-mile Discovery Trail from the entrance station of Cape Disappointment State Park to the Lewis and Clark Interpretive Center. The rewards are thrilling surveys over the Columbia bar, the North Jetty, and remnants of old Fort Canby, with magnificent groves of old-growth Sitka spruce along the way. Children can learn how Captains Vancouver and Meares missed discovering the Columbia River (Meares named it Cape Disappointment because he was so disappointed not to have found the river's mouth), and how Captain Gray discovered the river, named it for his ship, the Columbia, and claimed it for America. Captain Vancouver at first did not believe him. You can share in Captain Gray's thrill at the first view of the river.

A sign will direct you to the road to the North Head Lighthouse. Children will find it easy to walk a level ¼ mile to the old lighthouse. Opened originally in 1898, the red-roofed North Head Lighthouse now hosts tour groups. As you climb the steep, winding staircase, a guide will tell you and your children about 160-mile-per-hour winds that blew out windows, and about the tending of the light by night and day for over

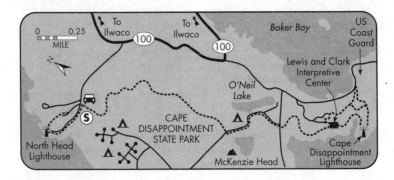

Cape Disappointment Lighthouse

seventy-five years. The tour takes about half an hour, and the view from the top of the lighthouse is worth the fee alone.

Once there, find a smaller trail marked "McKenzie Head, 2 Miles," leading down steeply through lush meadow plants. You are actually going to descend only 1¾ miles to the campground road, instead of to McKenzie Head. (Someone will need to drive the car to the park entrance.) The trail drops through groves of enormous old-growth, barrel-trunked Sitka spruce, some many hundreds of years old. Have children look at the crooks of the trees' bent elbows, which hold clumps of fern. Benches along the muddy descent provide resting points and views out over the Cape Disappointment campground.

The Columbia's north jetty was completed in 1917, and old pictures show that all the land paralleling it, where the campground stands today, was once under water and has filled in since that time. The building of the jetty has changed the shape of the beach. If you are camped in the campground, tell the kids that their campsite was once under ocean waves, and that the jetty changed the ocean currents. Continue the descent, passing nearby marshy, lily-pad-covered O'Neil Lake just before exiting onto a roadbed. Follow it until you reach the paved campground road, turn left, and walk the road for ¼ mile to the gatehouse. This makes a good stopping point or turnaround point.

On the other side of the two-lane road, look for a trail starting upward.

This is the Discovery Trail, leading to the Lewis and Clark Interpretive Center. Climb and wind through old second-growth trees on a moss-lined path until the first view at ½ mile. Climb still higher on concrete steps to an old military observation overlook point, a relic from Fort Canby.

Swallow and catch your breath as you gaze out at freighters from across the Pacific Ocean crossing the bar to enter the Columbia River. Before the jetty was built, crossing the bar was a much more hazardous affair, as the captains of hundreds of lost ships could attest. Listen for ships' bells and the low grumble of their engines. Imagine this view 100 years ago with tall-masted sailing ships, and 200 years ago when it was first discovered by Europeans and claim was being disputed by the British and the Americans. Climb higher on the headland into fields of grass and wild roses sculpted by the wind.

At the interpretive center, at ¾ mile, have children look for turn-of-the-century gun emplacements, a Lewis and Clark Trail exhibit told in pictures and dioramas. Directly below the cyclone fence along the cliff, children can see a rookery of nesting black cormorants. Take field glasses so you can look down into their nests. The parking lot below the center is another place you can leave a car for a stopping or turn-around point.

The last mile of trail leads to the Cape Disappointment Lighthouse, through more enormous old-growth Sitka spruce trees, down a muddy trail, around a fjordlike finger of ocean beach, and above the Coast Guard station. You can also drive to the lighthouse parking area and walk up an old two-track paved road to the black-roofed Cape Disappointment Lighthouse, built in 1916. From the lighthouse you can look south across the river to the Oregon side and the river's south jetty.

In memory of all the sailors and ships lost here, a sign is printed with the poem "Crossing the Bar," by Alfred Lord Tennyson. If you read it aloud, children can appreciate the poignant significance of the words.

KITSAP PENINSULA

ovely Kitsap Peninsula marine trails take families to Point No Point, with its historic lighthouse and surf fishermen, and to Foulweather Bluff Preserve, with a bird-filled lagoon and low beach walk. Many of these shoreline hikes have only recently been preserved. The Theler Wetlands Preserve leads out on boardwalks to the entrance of the Union River into Hood Canal. Two trails on Bainbridge Island, Grand Forest and Gazzam Lake, introduce children to natural old second-growth forest, a glacially carved lake, a way across to the west side of the island, and a drop to Port Orchard Bay beach.

 **POINT NO POINT**

GETTING THERE

- From the Kingston ferry terminal, drive west on State Highway 104 to George's Corner (or Kingston Crossing). Turn right onto Hansville Road NE and drive 7.4 miles.
- Before reaching Hansville, turn right onto NE Point No Point Road and drive 1 mile to the old lighthouse. Parking is limited; elevation is sea level.

ON THE TRAIL

A lighthouse tour can be combined with a beach walk around Point No Point and a short forest hike through a county park to make a loop walk. Children will love the old lighthouse, the sugar-sand beach, the big rock from which sea creatures can be inspected, and the short woodland loop hike. During salmon runs, fishermen stand in the waves at the point

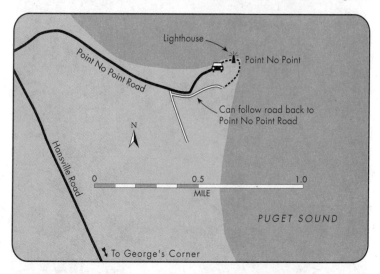

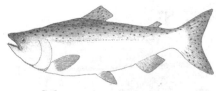

Salmon

to cast their lines from the shore. The kids can see the fish hooked, netted, and brought ashore.

Begin by touring the old lighthouse, open on weekend afternoons. Continue beyond it on a brief trail lined with wild roses between a wetland and the driftwood-studded, sandy beach. An elevated memorial blind invites children to a surveillance stop for ships, pleasure boats, and birds. Two public beaches are on DNR land.

The waterway is a major shipping lane for tankers and freighters, so the kids can always see some kind of craft. Kayakers and fishermen like Point No Point, too. Continue north on the beach for a check of the tides from the big glacial erratic rock and for a view of gleaming Mount Baker floating above on a clear day. A flight of stairs leads up into the ½-mile forest trail into Point No Point County Park's woodland shaded by

Lighthouse at Point No Point

old second-growth trees, refreshing on a hot day. The trail emerges onto Hillview Lane Northeast. Follow it back down to the lighthouse.

A nearby alternative hiking trail network is at the Hansville Greenway near Buck Lake, a large, warm freshwater lake.

 **FOULWEATHER BLUFF PRESERVE**

BEFORE YOU GO
Map The Nature Conservancy map for Foulweather Bluff Preserve
Current conditions The Nature Conservancy (206) 343-4344

ABOUT THE HIKE
Day hike
Easy for children
Year round
1 mile
No elevation gain

GETTING THERE

▪ From the Kingston ferry terminal, drive west on State Highway 104 to George's Corner (or Kingston Crossing). Turn right at Hansville Road Northeast and drive 8 miles to Hansville.

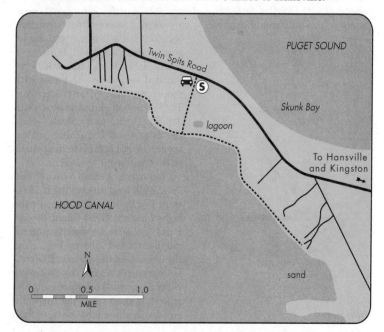

View of Foulweather lagoon from low beach

■ In Hansville, turn left onto Twin Spits Road and go 2.8 miles. If you reach Skunk Bay Road, you've gone too far. The Nature Conservancy sign on the left side is small, so be alert. The marked trailhead has parking on the road's shoulder, elevation sea level.

ON THE TRAIL

The Nature Conservancy has saved 100 acres and maintains a delightful short forest walk to a low beach on the north end of the Kitsap Peninsula across from the Hood Canal Bridge. Once called the Secret Beach by local residents, it's no secret anymore. The level trail winds through old second-growth Douglas-fir, cedar, and madronas. A driftwood-covered beach fronts a half-mile sandy expanse, with sweeping views of the Olympics; behind it lies a pristine wetland lagoon, usually filled with birds.

Begin walking through fern-studded second-growth forest with some roots for children to step over. The low gravel and sand beach will delight them, particularly when the tide is out. Returning saltwater can be at bathtub temperature, so they will want to wade.

You may not camp here or build fires. Walk west around the bluff toward The Brothers or south past the lagoon toward Hood Canal Bridge, Port Gamble, and a waterfront community named Shorewoods. Find the lagoon and the surrounding wetland preserve behind the driftwood. No trails or road offer access to the lagoon, so don't try to get there. Instead look above into the trees for a

Blue heron

heron rookery directly over the lake. The day I was here we saw five blue herons sitting in one Douglas-fir and a proud mother duck with eight tiny ducklings paddling behind her.

 **GRAND FOREST PARK**

BEFORE YOU GO
Map Bainbridge Island Park and Recreation District map; Bainbridge Island map
Current conditions Bainbridge Parks and Recreation (206) 842-2306

ABOUT THE HIKE
Day hike
Easy for children
Year round
2 miles
100 feet elevation gain

GETTING THERE
- From the Bainbridge Island ferry dock, go uphill. At the second stoplight from the ferry dock turn left onto High School Road NE.
- At the road's end at 2 miles, turn right onto Fletcher Bay Road. Continue for 1.6 miles.
- Pass Tolo Road and look for a Grand Forest sign on the right.
- At 0.2 mile beyond the sign, find an off-road area for parking.

ON THE TRAIL
A large forest park on Bainbridge Island will delight children at any season with its wide trails, green wetland, and many birds. The Grand Forest was purchased from the DNR by the citizens of Bainbridge Island in 1991. A contest was held among the grade schools to name the property. Over 100 entries were submitted to the Park District committee, which made the final decision. Ben Belieu, a fourth-grader at Ordway Elementary School, won with the name, "The Grand Forest."

Grand Forest trailhead map

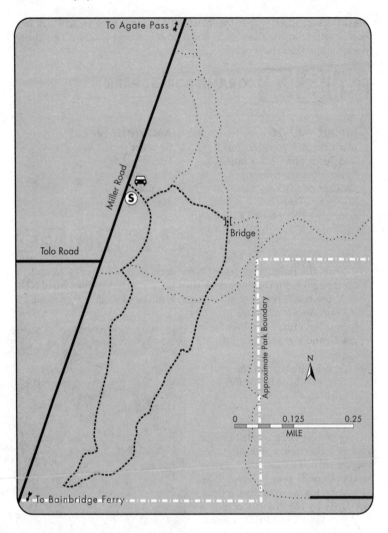

Separated into three sections by private homes, the Grand Forest West trails off Miller Road are particularly recommended. Issei Creek runs through Grand Forest, and farther downstream it supports a salmon run. Tell children that *Issei* is the Japanese word for first-generation Japanese immigrants and that, before the Second World War, Bainbridge had a large Japanese population. This creek name is one of the reminders of that legacy.

A short loop hike is recommended. Turn left at the first fork, finding a picnic table within the first hundred yards. A handout for the self-guided interpretive nature trail identifies various trees and shrubs in Grand Forest. Tall samples of lush evergreen huckleberry line the trail. Children may not care about the names but will love the old second-growth feeling of the woods.

A bridge over Issei Creek leads up and into a wetland, the home of herons, woodpeckers, and flickers. Tell the kids if they are quiet they may hear the woodpeckers or see a winged flash of colors. This trail ends at the preserve boundary in about ½ mile, so you will need to backtrack to the trail before the bridge, follow it south to a junction at 1 mile, and then take a trail north paralleling the highway back to the parking lot.

 **GAZZAM LAKE PARK**

BEFORE YOU GO
Map Bainbridge Island Park and Recreation District; Bainbridge Island map
Current conditions Bainbridge Island Parks and Recreation District (206) 842-2306

ABOUT THE HIKE
Day hike
Easy for children
Year round
Lakeshore: 2 miles;
waterfront: 2 miles
200 feet elevation gain and loss

GETTING THERE

- From the Bainbridge Island ferry dock at Winslow, drive straight on State Highway 305 for 1 mile.
- At the signal light, turn left onto High School Road and drive 2 miles.
- Turn left onto Fletcher Bay Road and go 0.3 miles.
- Turn right onto Island Center Road and go 0.6 mile.
- Turn right onto Marshall Road and drive 0.4 mile to the Gazzam Lake Wildlife Preserve trailhead. Park in the small parking area at the trailhead, elevation 100 feet.

ON THE TRAIL

A large glacial tarn on south Bainbridge, filling in with reeds, water lilies, and ducks, will charm and attract children. It is part of an island park that offers a network of trails in island second-growth and open space. The best trail in the park links to a recent 64-acre addition, the Close Property, on Port Orchard Bay on the island's west side. This means children can walk both the 550 feet of beach waterfront and/

or the peaceful forested trail to the lake. The park was named for W. L. Gazzam, an influential landowner in 1916. Tell the kids that at one time, the Puget Sound Glacier covered all of Bainbridge and scoured out this lakebed, leaving large boulders in other places as reminders that it had passed this way. The same glacier set the shape of the sound itself.

Begin by walking west on an old logging road. At a signed intersection in a few hundred yards, turn left onto a wide trail for Gazzam Lake.

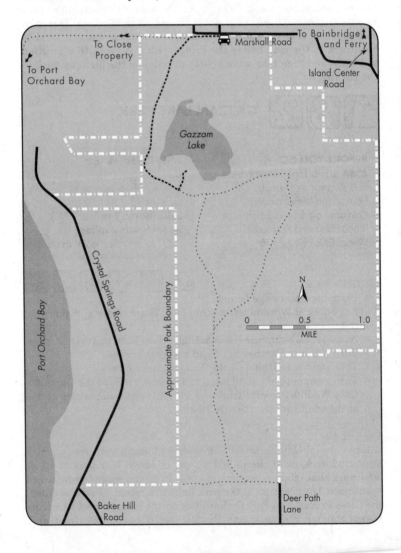

Walking on trail near Gazzam Lake

It winds past the outfall stream of the lake and then provides two short optional trails to the water's edge. The first one has a viewpoint with a bench, where families can watch for ducks, coots, and kingfishers. Although the lake bottom is muddy, the water is not cold, and children will agree that wading is a good choice on a hot day.

But if you choose to see Port Orchard Bay first, continue west along the former logging road past the sign marked "Close Property." You will hear the sounds of Douglas squirrels and woodpeckers in the old trees. We heard and then saw a pileated woodpecker on a winter's day. The road becomes a trail following a sword fern-studded ravine and drops steeply downward on small switchbacks and winding wooden steps, with a bench placed at a viewpoint. Children will enjoy the low-bank rocky beach with its overhanging trees. At low tide they can play on the 500-foot beach and gaze across the Port Orchard Narrows to the Kitsap Peninsula.

 **THELER WETLANDS TRAILS**

BEFORE YOU GO
Maps Available at trailhead;
USGS Belfair; Kitsap County
map
Current conditions Theler
Wetlands Information (360)
275-0721

ABOUT THE HIKE
Day hike
Easy for children
Year round
7 miles
Minimal elevation gain and loss

GETTING THERE

- *From Bremerton,* go west about 2 miles on Highway 304 to State
  Highway 3. Follow it 8 miles to Belfair.
- The park is about 1.5 miles farther on Highway 3, on the right
  side behind the Mary Theler Community Center and the Belfair
  Elementary School, at 22871 East Highway 3, elevation sea level.

ON THE TRAIL

A large tidal wetland and educational center have been set aside and
are privately maintained near Belfair, on the Kitsap Peninsula. Children can walk out on old dikes past salt marshes on a floating boardwalk to see the freshwater Union River as it reaches the headwaters
of Hood Canal. The estuary trail leads out to stunning views of water,
woodlands, and Olympics. Birds, native plants, and Native American art
are displayed in the educational center.

The trail network is a part of the 135-acre preserve given by the Theler family to the community and school district. For those with children
in strollers, there are four miles of barrier-free scenic trails. The Mary
E. Theler Watershed Project Center at the trailhead offers interactive
educational exhibits about migratory birds and resident wildlife.

Walk through a large wishbone-shaped entrance gate past rock walls
to the Project buildings. Begin by touring the educational center to see
Indian sculptures, a hand-carved dugout canoe, salmon replicas, and a
gray whale skeleton. Viewing platforms and a floating boardwalk extend
out over the salt- and freshwater marshes. The South Tidal Marsh Trail
loop, 1⅛ mile long, leads along boardwalk and gravel trail toward the
estuary of Union River. Children can look left, or southwest, from the
viewing platform to the wide expanse of Hood Canal and the Olympic
peaks above. Swooping swallows and red-winged blackbirds soar above
the saltwater marsh. Six species of salmon return to spawn here, though
there are water quality problems because of poor water circulation. The
salty prairie is made up of exposed sedges, rushes and grass at low tide,

Aerial view of Union River entering Hood Canal at Theler Wetlands

and shallow water when the tide is in. Children will love standing on viewing platforms above it.

A shorter loop is the Alder Cedar Swamp Trail, a ⅛-mile boardwalk that leads over backwater pools of the Union River and into old forest. Once a dairy farm with dikes to keep out the water, and a logging area, this reclaimed land is a treasured heritage now.

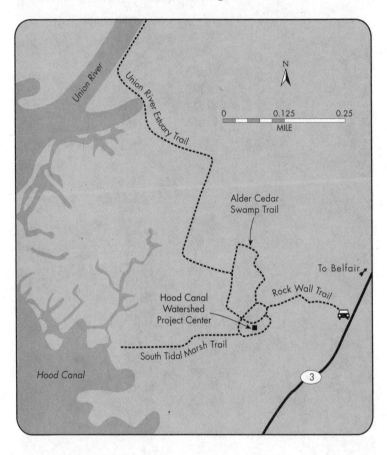

CAMPGROUNDS NEAR THE HIKES

So that you might take full advantage of all the hikes suggested in this book, we've included here a listing of campgrounds that are found near the hiking trails. The type of campsite varies with the land management agency. Forest Service camps can be very simple and primitive, while campsite quality in state parks tends to be better, generally speaking. Fees will vary with the land management agency and your camping plans. Trailers and RVs will be more expensive than tents. Call the phone numbers provided for information about reservations, space availability, and fees.

Type	Name	Number of sites	Directions	Phone number
Hikes 1–6				
Forest Service	Douglas Fir	30	Drive Hwy 542 to 2 miles E of Glacier, near milepost 36	(360) 856-5700
Forest Service	Silver Fir	21	Drive Hwy 542 for 14 miles E of Glacier	(360) 856-5700
Hikes 7–15				
Puget Sound Energy	Kulshan	79	W of Upper Baker Lake Dam	(360) 853-8341
State Park	Rockport State Park	62	1 mile W of Rockport	(360) 853-8461
North Cascades National Park	Newhalem Creek	107	S of Hwy 20 and across Skagit River	(360) 856-5700
North Cascades National Park	Colonial Creek	62	Near shore of Thunder Arm on Diablo Lake on Hwy 20	(360) 856-5700
Hikes 16–18				
Forest Service	Lone Fir	27	From Winthrop drive 27 miles NW on Hwy 20 to campground	(509) 996-4000
Hikes 16–18				
Forest Service	Klipchuck	46	19 miles NW of Winthrop, turn N on Forest Road 300 and go 1 mile to campground	(509) 996-4000
Forest Service	Early Winters	13	Go to milepost 177 just N of Mazama turnoff	(509) 996-4000

Hikes 19–31				
County Park	Squire Creek	32	Drive Hwy 530 to 3 miles W of Darrington	(360) 436-1283
Forest Service	Bedal	20	Drive 18 miles S from Darrington on Mountain Loop Hwy to Barlow Pass, then 6.5 miles N to campground	(360) 436-1155
Forest Service	Turlo	19	From Granite Falls drive 11 miles E to campground	(360) 436-1155
Forest Service	Verlot	25	Across the Hwy from Verlot Public Service Ctr	(360) 436-1155
Forest Service	Gold Basin	92	From Verlot Public Service Ctr, go 2.4 miles E	(360) 436-1155
Hikes 32–38				
State Park	Larrabee State Park	85	Take Chuckanut Drive (Hwy 11) 7 miles S from Bellingham or 14 miles N from Mount Vernon	(360) 676-2093
State Park	Bay View State Park	76	From I-5 in Mount Vernon, take Hwy 20 exit, turn W, go 7 miles to Bay View Edison Road; turn right and drive 4 miles to park	(360) 757-0227
State Park	Camano Island State Park	88	From Everett, take I-5 N for 18 miles to exit 212, turn W on Hwy 532 and go 14 miles to park	(360) 387-3031
State Park	South Whidbey State Park	54	From Clinton follow Hwy 525 for 9 miles N, turn W, and follow signs to park on Smuggler's Cove Road	(360) 321-4559

Type	Name	Number of sites	Directions	Phone number
State Park	Fort Casey State Park	35	From the Mukilteo Ferry terminal at Clinton, take Hwy 525, following signs to the Keystone Ferry terminal; pass the ferry parking lot and take first entrance to the left	(360) 678-4519
City Park	Washington Park	75	From Commercial Ave. in Anacortes, turn west on 12th Street and go 2 miles, staying left past ferry terminal, and continue to park	(360) 293-1918
Hikes 39–46				
State Park	Spencer Spit State Park	37	From Lopez Island ferry dock, follow signs 5 miles S; go left at Center Rd, left at Cross Rd, right at Port Stanley Rd, and left at Bakerview Rd	(360) 378-2044
County Park	Odlin County Park	30	From Lopez Island ferry dock, follow Ferry Road for 1.3 miles	(360) 378-8420
County Park	San Juan County Park	20	Drive W of Friday Harbor on Beaverton Valley, Mitchell Bay, and West Side Roads	(360) 378-8420
State Park	Moran State Park	166	From Orcas Island ferry dock, turn left and drive 14 miles NE to park	(360) 376-2326
Hikes 47–49				
State Park	Deception Pass State Park	261	From I-5 at Mount Vernon, take Hwy 20 E to Whidbey Island and Deception Pass	(360) 675-2417

State Park	Fort Ebey State Park	50	From Hwy 20 about 8 miles S of Oak Harbor and 2 miles N of Coupeville, turn W on Libbey Road, go 1.5 miles to Hill Valley Drive, turn left, and follow signs to park	(360) 678-4636
Hikes 50 and 51				
State Park	Wenberg State Park	75	From I-5 about 12 miles N of Everett, take exit 206 & follow signs for 6.7 miles W on Hwy 531	(360) 902-8844
County Park	Kayak Point County Park	34	From I-5 at Marysville, take exit 199, cross under freeway on Tulalip Way, and follow signs 13 miles W to park on Marine Drive	(360) 652-7992
Hikes 52–61				
State Park	Wallace Falls State Park	6 walk-in	From Everett, drive 28 miles to Gold Bar; turn left at First St, go 0.5 mile to May Creek Rd, and follow signs 1.5 miles to park	(360) 793-0420
Forest Service	Troublesome Creek	30	From US 2 at Index, turn N on Galena Road and drive 12 miles NE to campground	(360) 677-2414
Forest Service	Money Creek	24	Drive US 2 to milepost 46, 4 miles W of Skykomish	(360) 677-2414
Forest Service	Beckler River	27	From US 2 just E of Skykomish, turn N on Road No. 65 and drive 1.5 miles to campground	(360) 677-2414

Type	Name	Number of sites	Directions	Phone number
Hikes 62–66				
Forest Service	Nason Creek	73	From US 2 at Cole's Corner (19 miles NE of Leavenworth), turn N on Hwy 207; in 3.5 miles turn left on Cedar Brae Road to campground	(509) 763-3103
State Park	Lake Wenatchee State Park	197	From US 2 at Cole's Corner (19 miles NE of Leavenworth), turn N on Hwy 207 and drive 3.5 miles to campground	(509) 763-3101
Forest Service	Glacier View	20	From US 2 at Cole's Corner (19 miles NE of Leavenworth), turn N on Hwy 207; in 3.5 miles turn left on Cedar Brae Road; turn left at Lake Wenatchee Park entrance, pass it, and continue 5 miles to campground	(509) 763-3103
Hikes 67–69				
Forest Service	Tumwater	84	From Leavenworth, drive NW 10 miles on US 2	(509) 548-6977
Forest Service	Eightmile	45	From US 2 at W end of Leavenworth, drive 7 miles SW on Icicle Road	(509) 548-6977
Forest Service	Johnny Creek	65	From US 2 at W end of Leavenworth, drive 12.4 miles SW on Icicle Road	(509) 548-6977
Forest Service	Rock Island	22	From US 2 at W end of Leavenworth, drive 17.7 miles SW on Icicle Road	(509) 548-6977

Hikes 70–71

Forest Service	Beverly	16	From Cle Elum, follow Road No. 970 about 8 miles NE to Teanaway River Road; drive 13 miles to Road No. 9737, turn and go 4 more miles to campground	(509) 674-4411
Forest Service	Swauk	22	From I-90 near Cle Elum, follow Road No. 970 for 12 miles NE to US 97; follow US 97 for 9.8 miles to campground	(509) 674-4411

Hikes 72–84

Forest Service	Tinkham	47	From 8 miles E of North Bend on I-90, take exit 42, turn right under the freeway, and follow signs for 1.5 miles E on Tinkham Road No. 55	(425) 888-1421
Forest Service	Denny Creek	33	From 13 miles E of North Bend on I-90, take exit 47, drive N under the freeway, and turn right at a T; drive 0.25 mile, turn left on Denny Creek Road No. 58, and drive 2 miles to campground	(425) 888-1421

Hikes 85–91

Forest Service	Kachess	120	From I-90 take exit 62 (Crystal Springs), cross over the freeway, and follow signs 5 miles N to campground	(509) 674-4411
State Park	Lake Easton State Park	135	From 15 miles E of Snoqualmie Pass on I-90, take exit 70 and follow signs to park	(509) 656-2586

Type	Name	Number of sites	Directions	Phone number
Forest Service	Wish Poosh	39	From I-90 E of the pass, take exit 80, follow signs to Roslyn, then follow Hwy 903 for 6.5 miles to campground	(509) 674-4411
Forest Service	Cle Elum River	23	From I-90 E of the pass, take exit 80, follow signs to Roslyn, then follow Hwy 903 for 11.5 miles to campground	(509) 674-4411
Forest Service	Salmon La Sac	99	From I-90 E of the pass, take exit 80, follow signs to Roslyn, then follow Hwy 903 for 15.5 miles to campground	(509) 674-4411
Forest Service	Owhi	22	From I-90 E of the pass, take exit 80, follow signs to Roslyn, then follow Hwy 903 for 21 miles to campground via Road No. 46	(509) 674-4411
Hikes 92–94				
Mount Rainier National Park	Mowich Lake	30	From Puyallup drive State Hwy 410 to Buckley, turn right onto Hwy 165, and enter Carbon River entrance; just beyond Carbon River Gorge bridge, turn right on Mowich Lake Road; drive 17 miles to campground at road end	(360) 569-2211

Hikes 95–99

Forest Service	The Dalles	44	Drive 26 miles SE of Enumclaw on State Hwy 410	(360) 825-6585
Forest Service	Silver Springs	55	Drive 32 miles SE of Enumclaw on State Hwy 410	(360) 825-6585
Forest Service	Corral Pass	20	From State Hwy 410, 31 miles southeast of Enumclaw, turn E on Road No. 7174 and drive 6 miles to campground	(360) 825-6585

Hikes 100–103

Mount Rainier National Park	White River	112	From Enumclaw drive 43 miles E to the park's White River entrance; continue 5 miles to campground	(360) 569-2211

Hikes 104–107

Forest Service	Lodge Pole	33	Find campground near milepost 76 on State Hwy 410, 8 miles E of MRNP boundary	(509) 653-2205
Forest Service	Hell's Crossing	18	Find campground near milepost 83.4 on State Hwy 410, 38 miles NE of Naches	(509) 653-2205
Forest Service	Cedar Springs	15	From Enumclaw, drive 47 miles E on State Hwy 410 to Chinook Pass, then 19 miles E to Bumping Lake Road (Road No. 18) at milepost 88.4; turn right and drive 0.5 mile to campground	(509) 653-2205

Type	Name	Number of sites	Directions	Phone number
Hikes 108–119				
Mount Rainier National Park	Cougar Rock	188	From Tacoma go S on Hwy 7 to Elbe, then 12 miles E on Hwy 706 to Nisqually entrance; drive to Longmire, then go 2.3 miles to campground	(360) 569-2211
Mount Rainier National Park	Ohanepecosh	205	Summer only: Reach the campground from Hwy 706 (Stevens Canyon Road) from W, or State Hwy 410 (Chinook Pass Hwy) from N	(360) 569-2211
Hikes 120–122				
Forest Service	La Wis Wis	90	From Packwood, drive about 6.5 miles E on US 12; turn N on Road No. 1272 and drive 0.5 mile to campground	(360) 497-1172
Forest Service	Walupt Lake	51	From US 12, about 2.5 miles W of Packwood, turn S on Road No. 21; go about 16.5 miles and turn E on Road No. 2160 to campground	(360) 497-1172
Forest Service	Big Creek	29	Drive 4 miles S from Ashford or about 23 miles N from Packwood on Hwy 706 and Road No. 52	(360) 497-1172

Hike 129 [Snowgrass Flats]

State Park	Millersylvania State Park	168	From I-5 S of Olympia, take exit 95 and follow signs, driving E on Maytown Road, then N on Tilley Road, to campground	(360) 753-1519
Hikes 123–138				
State Park	Lewis and Clark State Park	25	From I-5 S of Chehalis, go about 2.5 miles E on US 12 to Jackson Hwy; turn right and drive 1.5 miles to park	(360) 864-2643
Tacoma Power	Mayfield Lake Park	54	From I-5 S of Chehalis, take exit 68 (US 12) and drive 17 miles E to Beach Road; turn left (N) and drive 0.25 mile to park	(360) 985-2364
State Park	Ike Kinswa State Park	103	From I-5 S of Chehalis, take US 12 for 14 miles E to Silver Creek Road; turn N and follow signs 3.5 miles to the park	(360) 983-3402
Tacoma Power	Mossyrock Park	203	From I-5 S of Chehalis, take US 12 and drive 21 miles to William Street; turn right and continue to a T; turn left on State Street and go 3.5 miles to the park	(360) 983-3900
Tacoma Power	Taidnapam Park	68	From I-5 S of Chehalis, take US 12 and drive 37 miles E to Kosmos Road; turn right, then left onto Road No. 100; go 4 miles to the park	(360) 497-7707
Forest Service	North Fork	33	From US 12 at Randle, follow Hwy 131 for 1 mile S, turn left at Road No. 23, and go about 11 miles S to campground	(360) 497-1100

Type	Name	Number of sites	Directions	Phone number
Forest Service	Iron Creek	98	From US 12 at Randle, follow Hwy 131 about 10 miles S to camp, a short distance beyond Cispus River bridge	(360) 497-1100
Forest Service	Takhlakh Lake	62	From US 12 at Randle, follow Hwy 131 for 1 mile, then turn left on Road No. 23; drive 29 miles to a junction with Road No. 2329, turn left, and go 1.5 miles to campground	(360) 497-1100
State Park	Seaquest State Park	88	From I-5 at Castle Rock, turn E on Hwy 504 and go 6.5 miles to park	(360) 274-8633
Mount St. Helens Monument	Lower Falls Recreation Area	43	From I-5 at Woodland, turn E on Hwy 503 and go about 23 miles; at a junction go straight on Hwy 503 Spur (Lewis River Road) for 7 miles, which becomes Road No. 90; continue for 21 miles to campground	(360) 449-7800
Hike 139 [Beacon Rock State Park]				
State Park	Beacon Rock State Park	29	Beacon Rock is 35 miles E of Vancouver on Hwy 14	(509) 427-8265
Hikes 140–150				
Forest Service	Peterson Prairie	30	From Hwy 14, 66 miles E of Vancouver, turn N on Hwy 141 and go 25 miles to Road No. 24, then 2.5 miles to campground	(509) 395-3400

Forest Service	Cultus Creek	51	From Hwy 14, 66 miles E of Vancouver, turn N on Hwy 141 and go 25.5 miles to Road No. 24 (5.5 miles beyond Trout Lake); follow Road No. 24 about 13.5 miles NW to campground	(509) 395-3400
Hikes 151–155				
State Park	Fort Flagler State Park	115	Follow signs from Hwy 20 and drive to the park at the N end of Marrowstone Island, 8 miles NE of Port Hadlock on Fort Flagler Road	(360) 385-1259
State Park	Old Fort Townsend State Park	40	Follow signs 4 miles S of Port Townsend on Hwy 20	(360) 385-3595
State Park	Fort Worden State Park	80	From Hwy 20 at Port Townsend, follow signs to park, about 1 mile N of town	(360) 344-4400
State Park	Sequim Bay State Park	76	Drive 4 miles SE of Sequim on US 101	(360) 683-4235
Clallam County	Dungeness Recreation Area	67	From US 101 at Sequim, go 4.5 miles to Kitchen-Dick Road; turn right and follow signs 3 miles to park	(360) 683-5847
Hikes 156–161				
Forest Service	Seal Rock	41	Drive US 101 to 2 miles N of Brinnon on shores of Hood Canal	(360) 765-2200
State Park	Dosewallips State Park	140	Drive US 101 for 1 mile S of Brinnon	(360) 796-4415

Type	Name	Number of sites	Directions	Phone number
Forest Service	Collins	16	From US 101, 2 miles S of Brinnon, turn W on Road No. 2510 (Duckabush Road) and go 4.8 miles to campground	(360) 877-5254
Forest Service	Lena Creek	16	From US 101, 14 miles N of Hoodsport, turn W on Hamma Hamma River Road (Road No. 25) and drive 8 miles to campground	(360) 877-5254
Hikes 162–169				
Olympic National Park	Deer Park	18	From US 101 about 6 miles E of Port Angeles, follow Deer Park 18 miles up steep gravel road to campground	(360) 565-3130
Olympic National Park	Heart o' the Hills	105	From US 101 at Port Angeles, follow signs 5 miles S on Hurricane Ridge Rd	(360) 565-3130
Olympic National Park	Fairholm	87	From Port Angeles, follow US 101 SW 25 miles past E shore of Lake Crescent to North Shore Rd; turn right and go 0.5 mile to campground	(360) 565-3130
Olympic National Park	Soleduck	82	From Port Angeles, go W on US 101 to Lake Crescent; at lake's end turn left (S) on Soleduck River Rd and go 13 miles to campground	(360) 327-3534
State Park	Bogachiel State Park	42	Find the park on US 101 at 6 miles S of Forks	(360) 374-6356

Olympic National Park	Hoh	89	From US 101 at 14 miles S of Forks, turn E on Hoh Rain Forest Road and go 18 miles to campground	(360) 374-6925

Hikes 170–175

Olympic National Park	Ozette	14	From Port Angeles, follow US 101 W to Hwy 112; go W to Ozette Road; turn left (S) and drive 22 miles to campground	(360) 963-2725
Olympic National Park	Mora	94	From US 101 at 2 miles N of Forks, go W on La Push Hwy and follow signs for 12 miles, staying right at the Y, where La Push Road goes left	(360) 374-5460
Olympic National Park	Kalaloch	177	Drive US 101 for 35 miles S of Forks to find campground on the ocean	(360) 962-2283

Hikes 176–178

State Park	Cape Disappointment State Park	250	From downtown Ilwaco, take Robert Gray Drive 3.5 miles S to park	(360) 642-3078

Hikes 179–183

State Park	Belfair State Park	184	From Hwy 3 at Belfair, follow signs 3 miles W on Hwy 300 to campground	(360) 275-0668
State Park	Fay Bainbridge State Park	36	From ferry dock, drive 5 miles on Hwy 305 to Day Road turnoff; turn right (N) and go 2 miles to a T; turn left on Sunrise Drive NE and continue 2 miles to park	(206) 842-3931

RANGER DISTRICT AND VISITOR CENTER PHONE NUMBERS

Massive floods in the fall of 2003 have made for trail, road, and bridge changes. Dates for repairing them are uncertain. For current conditions, please check with the appropriate ranger district or land agency before setting out for a hike.

GIFFORD PINCHOT NATIONAL FOREST
Coldwater Ridge Visitor Center (360) 274-2114
Cowlitz Valley Ranger District (consolidation of Packwood and Randle Ranger Districts) (360) 497-1100
Johnston Ridge Observatory (360) 274-2140
Mount Adams Ranger District (509) 395-3400
Mount St. Helens National Volcanic Monument (360) 449-7800
Mount St. Helens Visitor Center (360) 274-0962

MOUNT BAKER–SNOQUALMIE NATIONAL FOREST
Darrington Ranger District (360) 436-1155
Glacier Public Service Center (360) 599-2714
Marblemount Ranger District (360) 873-4500
Mount Baker Ranger District (360) 856-5700
North Bend Ranger District (425) 888-1421
Skykomish Ranger District (360) 677-2414
Snoqualmie Pass Visitor Center (425) 434-6111
Snoqualmie Ranger District (425) 888-1421 or (360) 825-6585 (summer only)

OKANOGAN/WENATCHEE NATIONAL FOREST
Methow Valley Ranger District (509) 997-2131
Methow Valley Visitor Center (509) 996-4000
Tonasket Ranger District (509) 486-2186
Chelan Ranger District (509) 682-2576
Cle Elum Ranger District (509) 852-1100
Entiat Ranger District (509) 784-1511
Lake Wenatchee Ranger District (509) 763-3103
Leavenworth Ranger District (509) 548-6977
Naches Ranger District (509) 653-2205

OLYMPIC NATIONAL FOREST

Hood Canal Ranger District, Quilcene Office (360) 765-2200
Quinault Ranger District (360) 288-2525
Sol Duc Ranger District (360) 374-6522

MOUNT RAINIER NATIONAL PARK

Henry M. Jackson Visitor Center (360) 569-211 x 2328
Longmire and White River Hiker Information Center (360) 569-2211 x 3317
Ohanapecosh Visitor Center (360) 494-2229
Sunrise Visitor Center (360) 663-2425

NORTH CASCADES NATIONAL PARK

Golden West Visitor Center (360) 856-5700 x 340 then x 14
North Cascades Visitor Center (206) 386-4495
North Cascades National Park (360) 856-5700

OLYMPIC NATIONAL PARK

Hoh Rain Forest Visitor Center (360) 374-6925
Hoodsport Ranger Station (360) 877-5254
Olympic Park Visitor Center (360) 565-3130

OTHER HELPFUL BOOKS

Arno, Stephen and Hammerly, Ramona. *Northwest Trees: Identifying and Understanding the Region's Native Trees.* Seattle: The Mountaineers Books, 1977.

Alt, David and Hyndman, Donald. *Roadside Geology of Washington.* Missoula: Mountain Press, 1994.

Carline, Jan; Lentz, Martha; and Macdonald, Steven. *Mountaineering First Aid: A Guide to Accident Response and First Aid Care, 4th ed.* Seattle: The Mountaineers Books, 1996.

Cissel, John and Diane. *Best Old Growth Forest Hikes: Washington and Oregon Cascades.* Seattle: The Mountaineers Books, 2003.

Dittmar Family. *Visitors' Guide to Ancient Forests of Western Washington.* Washington, DC: The Wilderness Society, 1989.

Judd, Ron C. *Camping! Washington.* Seattle: Sasquatch Books, 2003.

Kozloff, Eugene. *Plants and Animals of the Pacific Northwest.* Seattle: University of Washington Press, 1976.

Kruckeberg, Art; Spring, Ira; Sykes, Karen; Romano, Craig. *Best Wildflower Hikes in Washington.* Seattle: The Mountaineers Books, 2004.

Lyon, C. P. *Wildflowers of Washington,* 2d ed. Vancouver, British Columbia: Lone Pine Publishing, 1999.

——*Trees and Shrubs of Washington.* Vancouver, British Columbia: Lone Pine Publishing, 1999.

Manning, Harvey. *Backpacking One Step at a Time,* 7th ed. New York: Vintage Books, 2003.

Morse, Bob; Aversa, Tom; and Opperman, Hal. *Birds of the Puget Sound Region.* Olympia: Morse Company, 2003.

Mueller, Marge and Ted. *Washington State Parks: A Complete Recreation Guide, 3d ed.* Seattle: The Mountaineers Books, 2004.

Petrides, George A. *Tracks of the Pacific Northwest.* Mechanicsburg, PA: Stackpole Books, 2005.

Plumb, Gregory. *Waterfall Lover's Guide to the Pacific Northwest,* 4th ed. Seattle: The Mountaineers Books, 1989.

Pocket Naturalist Series: *Washington Birds, Northwestern Seashore Life, Washington Wildlife, Washington Trees and Wildflowers.* Phoenix: Waterford Press.

Pojar and McKinnon. *Plants of the Pacific Northwest Coast: Washington, Oregon, British Columbia, and Alaska.* Vancouver, British Columbia: Lone Pine Publishing, 1994.

Pyle, Jeanne Louise. *The Best in Tent Camping: Washington.* Birmingham, Alabama: Menasha Ridge Press, 2005.

Spring, Ira and Fish, Byron. *Lookouts: Firewatchers of the Cascades and Olympics.* Seattle: The Mountaineers Books, 1981.

Spring, Ira and Manning, Harvey. *Mountain Flowers of the Cascades and Olympics,* 2d ed. Seattle: The Mountaineers Books, 2002.

Spring, Vicky and Kirkendall, Tom. *An Outdoor Family Guide to Washington's National Parks and Monuments.* Seattle: The Mountaineers Books, 2004.

Stall, Chris. *Animal Tracks of the Pacific Northwest.* Seattle: The Mountaineers Books, 1981.

Whitney, Stephen and Sandelin, Rob. *Field Guide to the Cascades and Olympics,* 2d ed. Seattle: The Mountaineers Books, 2003.

INDEX

ABOUT THE AUTHOR

Seattle resident Joan Burton was introduced to hiking as a child, and by the time she was a teenager, she had climbed the six highest mountains of Washington. Later, as a parent with growing children, she introduced not only her own family to the joys of outdoor exploring but also members of the Girl Scout and Cub Scout groups of which she was leader. Burton is a long-time member of The Mountaineers and a graduate of both the basic and intermediate climbing courses taught by that club. After a number of years teaching high school English, Burton became program coordinator to the University of Washington Retirement Center, from which she has since retired. She has published magazine articles on outdoor subjects; *Best Hikes with Children* was her first book. Since then she has coauthored *Urban Walks: 23 Walks Through Seattle's Parks and Neighborhoods* with Duse McLean, published by Thistle Press, and has become a grandmother.

THE MOUNTAINEERS, founded in 1906, is a nonprofit outdoor activity and conservation club, whose mission is "to explore, study, preserve, and enjoy the natural beauty of the outdoors . . . . " Based in Seattle, Washington, the club is now the third-largest such organization in the United States, with seven branches throughout Washington State.

The Mountaineers sponsors both classes and year-round outdoor activities in the Pacific Northwest, which include hiking, mountain climbing, ski-touring, snowshoeing, bicycling, camping, kayaking, nature study, sailing, and adventure travel. The club's conservation division supports environmental causes through educational activities, sponsoring legislation, and presenting informational programs.

All club activities are led by skilled, experienced instructors, who are dedicated to promoting safe and responsible enjoyment and preservation of the outdoors.

If you would like to participate in these organized outdoor activities or the club's programs, consider a membership in The Mountaineers. For information and an application, write or call The Mountaineers, Club Headquarters, 300 Third Avenue West, Seattle, WA 98119; 206-284-6310. You can also visit the club's website at www.mountaineers.org or contact The Mountaineers via email at clubmail@mountaineers.org.

The Mountaineers Books, an active, nonprofit publishing program of the club, produces guidebooks, instructional texts, historical works, natural history guides, and works on environmental conservation. All books produced by The Mountaineers Books fulfill the club's mission.

Send or call for our catalog of more than 500 outdoor titles:

The Mountaineers Books
1001 SW Klickitat Way, Suite 201
Seattle, WA 98134
800-553-4453
mbooks@mountaineersbooks.org
www.mountaineersbooks.org

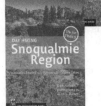
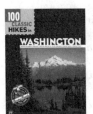

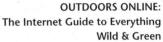